T0026530

Praise for
Ed Slott and *The Retirement Savings Time Bomb*

"Unless you consider cat food a viable dinner option, it's wise to take action now to bulletproof your retirement assets. Sooner or later, we pay taxes. But why allow your retirement savings to become a windfall for Uncle Sam when the money should go to you and your heirs? [Slott] will show you how to keep your cash all in the family."

—*USA Today*

"Ed Slott's advice could save your retirement plan from something worse than a bear market—the tax collector!"
—Terry Savage, author of *The Savage Truth on Money* and nationally syndicated personal finance columnist

"Ed Slott is my go-to resource on the nuances of tax and retirement planning. His no-nonsense style makes the dizzying changes in the rules and laws surrounding these often-confusing topics understandable and, more importantly, actionable."
—Jill Schlesinger, CFP®, CBS News Business Analyst

"Ed Slott is my go-to person for smart, tax-saving advice on retirement plans. Right now, people planning for retirement especially need his help. Congress has passed a slew of new laws affecting your personal tax-favored plans, some of which make them *less* secure. This book shows you how to wring all the tax benefits possible from your plans, including smart ways of passing any remaining money to your heirs. Highly recommended!"
—Jane Bryant Quinn, author of *How to Make Your Money Last: The Indispensable Retirement Guide*

"Ed Slott's mastery of IRA dos and don'ts makes this book must-reading for any IRA owner who wants to know how to save for retirement."
—Paul Katzeff, senior reporter/writer, *Investor's Business Daily*

"If you have questions about IRAs or other retirement plans, you'll find every last answer in this easy-to-understand and hugely informative book. Ed Slott is truly Mr. IRA."
—Lynn O'Shaughnessy, author of *The Retirement Bible*

"If you're planning for or living in retirement, this book is required reading. Ed Slott is among the most trusted and knowledgeable retirement experts in the United States and the insights you will gain from reading this book will be invaluable. You'll learn how to create tax-efficient retirement income and take advantage of the most recent tax laws, as well as pass on more of your hard-earned wealth to your loved ones. The world is filled with those who proclaim to be retirement experts, but Ed Slott is truly that—an expert who deserves your time and attention."
—Robert Powell, editor of Retirement Daily and TheStreet, *USA Today* columnist, editor of *Retirement Management Journal*, and host of *The Exceptional Advisor* podcast

"Retirement planning is more complicated than it ought to be, but that's where Ed Slott comes in. He has a knack for providing tax- and retirement-planning guidance that's easy to understand, up-to-the-minute current, and—dare I say it?—fun. This book will be an indispensable part of many retirees' tool kits."
—Christine Benz, director of personal finance, Morningstar

"If you need to understand the ins and outs of retirement, look no further than this book by Ed Slott. He is the go-to expert for reporters and media folks like myself. When I have a question, I call Ed!"
—Erin Arvedlund, author of *Too Good to Be True: The Rise and Fall of Bernie Madoff* and financial writer, *Philadelphia Inquirer*

"Congress has turned retirement savings into a quagmire of laws, regulations, and acronyms that can serve as tax traps or opportunities. Ed Slott can explain them with care and flair."
—Kathleen Pender, financial writer

"If you have assets in a retirement plan *The NEW Retirement Savings Time Bomb* will save you money."
—Natalie B. Choate, author of *Life and Death Planning for Retirement Benefits: The Essential Handbook for Estate Planners*

"Ed Slott is the go-to expert on IRAs in an era when legislative and regulatory changes are popping up as fast and furious as a whac-a-mole game. Arm yourself with the latest insights on how to protect future retirement savings by making tax-savvy moves today."
—Mary Beth Franklin, CFP, contributing editor, *Investment News*

PENGUIN BOOKS

THE RETIREMENT SAVINGS TIME BOMB TICKS LOUDER

Ed Slott, CPA, America's IRA Expert, is a nationally recognized speaker, television personality, and bestselling author known for his unparalleled ability to turn advanced tax strategies into understandable, actionable, and entertaining advice. Named "The Best Source for IRA Advice" by *The Wall Street Journal,* he is the go-to resource for media, regularly providing insight on breaking news affecting retirement and tax-planning laws and strategies. Slott is a professor of practice at the American College of Financial Services and has been recognized by leading industry organizations for his significant thought leadership and contributions. He is one of the top pledge drivers of all time with his public television specials, and his popular website includes *The Slott Report* blog, which is followed by tens of thousands of readers. In 2022, he launched a podcast, *The Great Retirement Debate,* that provides lively commentary on opposing sides of retirement planning strategies. Ultimately, through all these efforts combined, Slott has taught millions of Americans (and their financial professionals) how to get the most out of their retirement savings. For more information, visit his website: www.irahelp.com.

Whether your retirement dreams are five years away or fifty, the single greatest threat standing in your way is taxes. Unlike losses experienced in the stock market, money lost to taxes never recovers. With untaxed retirement accounts likely to become your largest asset, you face an explosive landscape of costly tax traps, penalties, and a complex maze of rules when the time comes to tap into those savings.

THE RETIREMENT SAVINGS TIME BOMB TICKS LOUDER

How to Avoid Unnecessary Tax Landmines,
Defuse the Latest Threats to Your Retirement
Savings, and Ignite Your Financial Freedom

ED SLOTT

PENGUIN BOOKS

PENGUIN BOOKS

An imprint of Penguin Random House LLC
penguinrandomhouse.com

First published as *The New Retirement Savings Time Bomb* in Penguin Books 2021.
This revised edition published in Penguin Books 2024.

Copyright © 2021, 2024 by Ed Slott
Penguin Random House supports copyright. Copyright fuels creativity, encourages diverse voices, promotes free speech,
and creates a vibrant culture. Thank you for buying an authorized edition of this book and for complying
with copyright laws by not reproducing, scanning, or distributing any part of it in any form without permission.
You are supporting writers and allowing Penguin Random House to continue to publish books for every reader.

LIBRARY OF CONGRESS CATALOGING-IN-PUBLICATION DATA
Names: Slott, Ed, author.
Title: The retirement savings time bomb ticks louder :
how to avoid unnecessary tax landmines,
defuse the latest threats to your retirement savings,
and ignite your financial freedom / Ed Slott.
Other titles: New retirement savings time bomb
Description: Revised edition. | New York : Penguin Books, [2024] |
"First published as The New Retirement Savings Time Bomb in Penguin Books 2021"—Verso |
Includes bibliographical references and index.
Identifiers: LCCN 2024007456 (print) | LCCN 2024007457 (ebook) |
ISBN 9780143138501 (paperback) | ISBN 9780593512579 (ebook)
Subjects: LCSH: Pension trusts—United States. |
Pension trusts—Taxation—United States. |
Retirement income—United States—Planning. |
Finance, Personal—United States.
Classification: LCC HD7105.45.U6 S485 2024 (print) |
LCC HD7105.45.U6 (ebook) | DDC 332.024/0140973—dc23
LC record available at https://lccn.loc.gov/2024007456
LC ebook record available at https://lccn.loc.gov/2024007457

Printed in the United States of America
2nd Printing

Set in Yoga Pro
Designed by Sabrina Bowers

This publication is designed to provide accurate and authoritative information in regard
to the subject matter covered. It is sold with the understanding that the publisher is not engaged
in rendering legal, accounting, or other professional services. If you require legal advice
or other expert assistance, you should seek the services of a competent professional.

While the author has made every effort to provide telephone numbers, internet addresses, and other contact
information that are accurate at the time of publication, neither the publisher nor the author assumes any
responsibility for errors or for changes that occur after publication. Further, the publisher does not have any
control over and does not assume any responsibility for author or third-party websites or their content.

To my mom and dad. They truly lived a wonderful life.
To my wife, Linda, our children, Ilana, Andrew, Rachel, and Jennifer,
and our grandchildren, Simon, Victoria, Kaitlyn, and Alexandria (Lexie).

CONTENTS

PART THREE:
When Things Don't Go as Planned

AUTHOR'S NOTE

This book is about the jeopardy that you—and everyone you know—will face when the taxman shows up at distribution time, regardless of the type of tax-deferred retirement savings plan you have. Now, your retirement savings are at even greater risk with new tax laws like the massive SECURE Act (which actually makes your retirement savings *less* secure—thanks, Congress!). Every type of plan is affected, be it an Individual Retirement Account (IRA), a Roth IRA, a 401(k), a Roth 401(k), a 403(b), a Roth 403(b), a 457(b), a Roth 457(b), a Keogh plan, a SEP-IRA, a SIMPLE IRA, or a mixture of accounts. I'll be using the term *IRA* throughout the book as an umbrella term for all these retirement savings plans because the tax rules governing IRAs are generally the same as those for every type of retirement account. However, I will clearly point out those areas where the rules for a particular plan differ from those of IRAs. Likewise, I'll be using the term *company plans* throughout this book as an umbrella term for all types of employer plans, not just qualified plans. (See "Talking the Talk" for the difference.)

I want to give a special nod up front to Sarah A. Brenner, J.D., our director of retirement education at Ed Slott and Company; and Andy Ives, CFP®, AIF®, and Ian Berger, J.D., our IRA analysts, who gave tremendous help with checking and double-checking this manuscript for technical accuracy. They went above and beyond, generously contributing their time and energy to make this book as reliable and error-free as possible. Thank you, Sarah, Andy, and

Ian for helping me defuse the retirement savings time bomb, and especially for your insights on the many recent tax law changes included in this edition. I can assure my readers that any inaccuracies that may still lurk herein are mine, and I take full responsibility for them.

—ED SLOTT

INTRODUCTION

Playing the "Back 9"

Taxes will be the single biggest factor that separates people from their retirement dreams.

—Ed Slott

In the not-so-distant past, the issue of protecting retirement savings rather than investing for retirement might have been considered putting the cart before the horse.

Not any longer.

Today, Americans have invested trillions of dollars in retirement plans, turning them into the biggest, most valuable assets they own—often worth more than even their homes. As a result, *savings protection* has become the name of the retirement plan game.

Most, if not all, retirement planning strategists, however, focus on why you should save for retirement and how to grow your money through a variety of investment vehicles.

That's valuable information, but it's not enough.

Look at it this way. What good is making even a 50 percent return on an investment if, at the time of withdrawal, taxes will step in to claim 70, 80, or maybe even 90 percent of your nest egg?

Even though income and estate tax rates have come down significantly, the great unknown is what future tax rates will be, and what new plan money-hungry Congress may devise to separate you from your retirement savings. If history is any lesson, tax rates on retirement savings will likely increase substantially just when you need the money the most—upon withdrawal in retirement. In addition, given the financial mess our country is currently in (hope springs eternal), taxes *will have to increase*. Look at the bulging deficits, including the trillions we added by providing relief during the COVID-19 pandemic. This bill will soon come due, hitting hardest those who have saved the most. So, you need to be prepared for future tax increases when it comes time to reach into your retirement funds. At this point, any politician who tells you they can cut your taxes is really just saying "I'm bad at math!" Remember that much of the money in Americans' retirement funds is tax-deferred, meaning it has not yet been taxed, so it is a sitting duck for future tax hikes.

Think of it like coming down the stretch of the U.S. Open Golf Championship. The "Front 9" is where you position your lead by building up your assets; holding on to your lead—i.e., protecting your assets from excessive taxation—is the "Back 9" where, ultimately, you win or lose.

Crucial Component

This book addresses the critical issue that every other retirement- and tax-related book on the market ignores: *protecting from excessive taxation the assets you've spent a lifetime building.* No single factor is more significant to your ability to live the lifestyle you've been saving for all your life, or to pass on your hard-earned savings to those you love.

Why is this component so crucial?

Due to a complex combination of distribution and estate taxes that kick in at retirement or death, millions of you are at risk of losing much—perhaps even most—of your retirement savings.

This dire turn of events, already happening now, will put a huge financial burden on you, your children, and society as the ranks of the retiring and already retired swell to historic proportions in the coming years when the retirement savings time bomb explodes (see Chapter 1).

And so, the overriding purpose of this book is to give savers like you the knowledge and the tools to defuse that bomb on your own—or with the help of your professional financial advisor—before detonation occurs.

Complex Web

I'll expose the complex web of dark secrets and traps in the tax code governing retirement savings using layman's terms, and I'll present an easy-to-use plan for helping the millions of you at risk to save a fortune in retirement income—income that might otherwise be lost to you and your families forever.

I'll deal with all aspects of IRA (and Roth IRA) distribution planning, which encompasses virtually any type of retirement account you might have—401(k), Roth 401(k), 403(b), Roth 403(b), 457(b), Roth 457(b), a Keogh plan, SEP-IRA, SIMPLE IRA, corporate pension plan—since virtually all retirement money is distributed according to what is commonly referred to as the "IRA distribution rules." These are among the most complicated rules in the entire U.S. tax code.

I'll go beyond the tax rules to provide easily understandable explanations of the planning opportunities available (including many new ones created by the recent massive tax reforms), and clear answers to some of the most perplexing and frequently asked questions, like: "I know the rule says X, but how can I accomplish Y without problem Z?"

I'll cut through the complexities of these rules and make them easy to grasp so that you can prevent your retirement nest egg from being decimated by taxes and keep your savings in the hands of your family, not the IRS.

In addition, if you're already a knowledgeable professional financial advisor, I will give you the tools to better guide and communicate with your clients, thereby attracting and retaining more assets under management, the key to growing your business.

A Total Solution

This book will help you devise and implement a simple, workable strategy to protect your retirement assets and keep your hard-earned money in the family—and growing—for generations.

My strategy grew out of my more than 40 years of experience "in the trenches" as a CPA preparing tax returns and has evolved while on the circuit as a keynote speaker, teacher, and coach to consumers and professional financial advisors. I have conducted more than a thousand seminars and workshops during the past 20 years, honing my action plan into one that works for *anybody* with an IRA, 401(k), or other retirement account—from hardworking folks such as teachers, doctors, and CPAs who have accumulated modest but still substantial retirement assets, to high-net-worth corporate executives and entertainers.

The new economy has also sprouted many self-employed people, including small-business owners and independent contractors, like writers, consultants, Uber drivers, home health aides, home improvement pros, and all those professionals helping us set up our homes and offices to broadcast over Zoom! The action plan in this book is particularly critical to any of you in business for yourselves, because you don't have a company taking care of any of this for you. You are the company! So, it's up to you to create your own retirement, health, and other company benefits that many employees already access through their employers. Read on so you too can retire safely and securely.

Everyone wants to pay less, to keep more of their earnings, and to make their savings last. What I've put together for you is a **total solution**—one that you can achieve, and benefit from, without tax expertise and regardless of how the stock market and economy are faring. It is a solution that will show you how to:

- Move your retirement savings from accounts that are forever taxed to never taxed
- Protect company stock owned in a 401(k)

- Make the most of retirement savings

- Save a fortune by avoiding excessive, often needless taxation

- Pass on more assets to loved ones and other beneficiaries

- Keep retirement assets in the family for decades, even generations, with minimal or no taxes

- Get more from your financial advisor

- Expand your knowledge of retirement distribution planning

- Tap retirement funds for emergency cash—without big penalties

- Take advantage of the latest tax law and IRA rule changes

- Learn how the SECURE Act and the SECURE 2.0 Act impact your retirement savings

- Discover alternatives to the stretch IRA

- Create larger inheritances, with more control and less tax

- Get *your* plan . . . NOT the government plan!

- Integrate a retirement account with an overall estate plan to create the *perfect* estate plan

- Avoid falling into tax traps with inherited IRAs or other retirement accounts

- Protect retirement accounts from creditors, divorce, bankruptcy, lawsuits, or other problems that could expose them to confiscation

As you read each chapter, keep in mind what I mentioned at the outset of this introduction: Retirement planning is like a golf tournament. Building assets is only part of the game—just the "Front 9."

There are nine more holes left to go in the equally, and perhaps even more, tortuous "Back 9"—the final holes where holding on to the assets you've built up becomes the biggest challenge of all.

Remember, where taxes are concerned, it's what you keep that counts!

WHAT'S NEW IN THIS EDITION— AT A GLANCE

Saving and investing for retirement is tough enough, but it's only one part of the retirement game. Since you can spend only what you keep, *after* taxes, you'll have to take steps now to protect your savings. I want you to have more, keep more, and make it last. That is my focus in this newly revised edition.

Our tax laws are constantly changing, and you need to know how the most current rules can affect your planning. This special 2024 edition has been revised to include the most up-to-date information on all retirement, income tax, and estate law changes and provisions enacted and now in effect since we last went to press. It includes the latest changes made to the SECURE Act and SECURE 2.0 Act—including the elimination of the stretch IRA, which will likely upend many of your existing retirement strategies. This devious provision inserted into the SECURE Act will be a big blow to even the best-laid plans.

The major overhaul of our tax system affects virtually everyone in some way, and many of the provisions have time limits. I will guide you through all of this, so you'll know how to best take advantage of the changes and avoid some of the traps.

For up-to-the-minute information you can rely on regarding any potential changes in the tax rules for retirement accounts that our legislators spring on us, stay tuned to my website: www.irahelp.com.

Here are some of the major changes explained in this new edition:

The Setting Every Community Up for Retirement Enhancement or "SECURE Act" (enacted December 20, 2019):

- Repeal of age 70½ restriction for making contributions to traditional IRAs

- Penalty-free withdrawals from company plans and IRAs for births or adoptions

- Required Minimum Distribution (RMD) age raised to 72 from 70½ (later raised to age 73 in SECURE 2.0 Act—see below)

- Elimination of the stretch IRA for many beneficiaries

IRS–Proposed SECURE Act Regulations (issued February 23, 2022):

- A surprising rule requiring annual RMDs (required minimum distributions) for some IRA or plan beneficiaries subject to the 10-year rule

- Adjustments to who can qualify as an eligible designated beneficiary and still stretch payments from an inherited IRA

- Clarifications to the rules that apply when a trust is a beneficiary

- A new automatic waiver of the penalty for a missed year-of-death RMD is available if the RMD is taken before the beneficiary's tax-filing deadline, including extensions.

SECURE 2.0 Act (enacted December 29, 2022):

- The age for required minimum distributions (RMDs) increased to 73 as of January 2023. This age will increase to 75, but not until January 1, 2033. Anyone currently subject to RMDs under the old 70½ or 72 RMD age rules is not impacted and must continue to follow their existing RMD schedule.

- As of 2023, a one-time only, $50,000 qualified charitable distribution (QCD) to a charitable gift annuity, charitable remainder unitrust, or a charitable remainder annuity trust is allowed. Also, the QCD limit of $100,000 is now indexed for inflation as of January 2024.

- Individuals age 50 or over can make an additional IRA catch-up contribution of $1,000. This amount is indexed for inflation, as of January 2024.

- Effective in 2027, the underutilized Saver's Credit, which had been intended to help lower-income savers by providing a tax credit for retirement account contributions, has been overhauled into a government match paid directly to retirement accounts.

- Effective in 2024, beneficiaries of 529 college savings accounts are permitted to roll over up to $35,000 aggregate over the course of their lifetime from a 529 account in their name to a Roth IRA. These rollovers are subject to Roth IRA annual contribution limits, and the 529 account must have been open for more than 15 years. This new rule will allow any "leftover" 529 funds to avoid tax or penalty if rolled over.

- The 25 percent of assets limit for purchasing a qualified longevity annuity contract (QLAC) is repealed. Now, up to $200,000 can be used from an account balance for such a purchase.

- A slew of new 10 percent penalty exceptions have been added, with different effective dates. These include distributions for terminal illness (effective immediately); federally declared natural disasters: $22,000 limit (effective retroactively to January 26, 2021); pension-linked emergency savings accounts: $2,500 limit (effective 2024); domestic abuse: $10,000 limit (effective 2024); financial emergencies: $1,000 limit (effective 2024); and long-term care (LTC): $2,500 limit (effective 2025).

- The age-50 exception to the 10 percent early distribution penalty is extended to include public safety workers with at least 25 years of service. Corrections officers and private-sector firefighters are added to the list of public safety workers who can take advantage of this exception.

- The SECURE Act included a provision that allows individuals to receive penalty-free distributions from their retirement account in the case of birth or adoption. There was no time limit on repaying these distributions. SECURE 2.0 Act imposes a three-year time limit.

- The hefty 50 percent penalty for missed RMDs is reduced to 25 percent. If the missed RMDs are corrected in a timely manner, the penalty is further reduced to 10 percent. A three-year statute of limitations for the RMD penalty is also added.

- When an IRA excess contribution is removed before the applicable deadline, the net income attributable (NIA) is no longer subject to the 10 percent early distribution penalty if the individual is under age 59½. For contributions removed after the deadline, a six-year statute of limitations now applies to the 6 percent excess IRA contributions penalty, even if Form 5329 was never filed. However, this statute of limitations will not apply if the 6 percent penalty involved a bargain sale to the IRA.

- New legislation allows a special needs trust with a charity as a remainder beneficiary to still qualify as an applicable multibeneficiary trust. This preserves the stretch payout option for these trusts.

- As of 2024, higher salary deferrals and additional nonelective contributions to SIMPLE IRAs are allowed.

- Unlike Roth IRAs, Roth accounts in workplace plans have been subject to RMDs during the owner's lifetime. As of 2024, this is no longer the case.

- Starting in 2025, individuals ages 60, 61, 62, and 63 will be eligible to make larger catch-up contributions to their plans.

- The trend toward "Rothification" continues as Congress seeks immediate tax revenue. SEP and SIMPLE plans can allow Roth contributions beginning in 2023.

- Further, all plan catch-up contributions for higher-income employees (more than $145,000 in wages in the prior year) age 50 or over must be Roth contributions, originally scheduled to start in 2024, but delayed by the IRS until 2026. Finally, beginning immediately, plans can allow employer matching contributions to be made on a Roth (after-tax) basis.

- The IRS self-correction program, called the Employee Plans Compliance Resolution System (EPCRS), will be expanded to include inadvertent IRA errors.

The Tax Cuts and Jobs Act (enacted December 22, 2017), most of which became effective in 2018 and much of which will expire after 2025:

- Repeal of Roth recharacterizations (for Roth conversions done after 2017)

- Lowered tax-bracket rates

- Increase in standard deductions (many more people are using these now)

- Estate, gift, and generation-skipping transfer (GST) tax exemption increases

- Repeal of many popular itemized deductions such as tax preparation, advisor and investment fees, and IRA losses

- Back-door Roth IRAs OK'd by Congress and IRS

THE
RETIREMENT SAVINGS
TIME BOMB
TICKS LOUDER

TALKING THE TALK

A Foolproof Primer of Essential but Often Confusing Tax Terms and Definitions

The hardest thing in the world to understand is the income tax.
—ALBERT EINSTEIN (1879-1955)

You don't have to become a CPA to understand tax lingo. (I'm a re-covering CPA myself.) But you will need to grasp a few key techni-cal terms to get the most out of this book as well as benefit from any other information you may come across on the topic of retire-ment distribution planning and savings protection.

Rather than give you the standard boring glossary that is usually stuck at the rear of a book, requiring you to constantly flip back and forth between pages, accumulating a lot of paper cuts, I've cre-ated a primer right here at the beginning, where it'll be more useful and convenient for you (no Band-Aids required).

Also, instead of going the typically sleepy A-to-Z route, I've liv-ened up the format with a fresher presentation called "What's the Difference Between . . . ?"

My rationale (apart from wanting to educate in an entertaining manner) is this: As you read through this book, there will be times when you will need to know not only what a specific tax term means but also how it differs from another tax term that may ap-pear on the surface to have a similar meaning.

How could such conflicts occur?

The writers of our tax rules—Congress and the IRS—have at times conspired to create a broad panoply of easily recognizable words, which, in tax talk, have completely different meanings than in their common usages.

At other times, these writers just make up words out of convenience, words that cannot possibly be defined with any known form of logic—in our lexicon, anyway. (I know they're made up because they don't appear in any spell-check software I've ever seen.)

Likewise, there are terms that some of you may *think* you know because they seem familiar—but if you guess wrong, the mistake could cost you a bundle at tax time.

Reading through this section to familiarize yourself with these terms before moving on will not only help you to avoid such potentially expensive misinterpretations but will take much of the mystery out of all that follows in the coming chapters. At first this terminology may feel dense, but you'll get used to it in no time, and going through this section now will make the rest of the book much easier to read.

WHAT'S THE DIFFERENCE BETWEEN . . . ?

Adjusted Gross Income (AGI) vs. Taxable Income

AGI is your gross income before any standard or itemized deductions or tax credits. It's an important term to know because many provisions in the tax code are based on AGI, not *taxable income*, the income on which you are actually taxed. The best tax-planning moves are strategies that lower AGI and in turn lower your tax bill. One great example is qualified charitable distributions (QCDs), which are charitable donations that get transferred directly from your IRA to the charity, reducing your AGI. Learn more about this tax-saving move in Chapter 4.

After-Tax vs. Pre-Tax Money

Either of these can be a good option, depending on your preference. For example, if you scarf up your vegetables fast to get them out of the way so you can get on with dessert, you're a "pay-me-later" (after-tax money) person. But if you like to put the veggies off until last and start with dessert, you're the "pay-me-now" (pre-tax money) type. For example, money that goes into a Roth IRA or a Roth 401(k) is *after-tax money* because you had to earn it as ordinary income first and pay tax on it before you could contribute it to the Roth. By contrast, 401(k) contributions are *pre-tax money* because you received a tax deduction on the portion your salary you contributed and will pay tax later when the funds are withdrawn. Most money accumulating in tax-deferred retirement accounts is pre-tax funds.

It comes down to this: After-tax money is taxable now; pre-tax money is taxable later. It's important to know the distinction so that you don't get into a situation where you're inadvertently shelling out money for taxes on distributions of what should be tax-free funds. Also, the IRS requires that you and your plan keep track of after-tax and pre-tax funds so that it knows how much is taxable when you begin withdrawals.

Beneficiary vs. Designated Beneficiary vs. Eligible Designated Beneficiary

In everyday English, these terms are interchangeable, but in tax language *designated beneficiary* has special meaning under the retirement distribution rules. And the SECURE Act gave us yet another category of beneficiary that Congress named *eligible designated beneficiary* or EDB, which is a special type of designated beneficiary that enjoys first-class status, so to speak. While Congress eliminated the stretch IRA for most designated beneficiaries, EDBs still continue to enjoy stretch IRA perks. But to gain EDB status, your beneficiary must first qualify as a designated beneficiary. So, let's first describe what the difference is between a beneficiary and a designated beneficiary.

A designated beneficiary is the beneficiary named on an IRA or company plan beneficiary form, and must be a person—in other words, someone with a pulse and a birthday. If you cannot prove that you have both, you fall into the nonhuman beneficiary category (a beneficiary, but a non-designated beneficiary). One example of an entity that can *never* become a designated beneficiary is an estate. Another is a trust, but the *beneficiaries* of trusts can be considered designated beneficiaries if the trust meets certain requirements (see Chapter 10). Here are other entities that can never be designated beneficiaries: charities or any other nonperson in your life, including pets or imaginary friends such as Mr. Snuffleupagus; Calvin's tiger friend, Hobbes; or the Overlook Hotel's ghostly bartender in *The Shining*; not to mention the characters on the TV show *Friends*. (My daughter used to think they were real people.) Deceased relatives also fall into the nonperson category because, even though they have birthdays, they're lacking in the pulse department.

Good, that's out of the way. Now, here's something else you must know. A beneficiary can be a person who is *not* a designated beneficiary. Shall I repeat that? Yes, a beneficiary can be a person who is *not* a designated beneficiary. For example, say you neglect to name a beneficiary on your IRA's beneficiary designation form before you die. After your will goes through probate and your loving but greedy family finally finishes scrounging around beneath the split piñata that was once your estate, your son (whom you would have named as beneficiary had you gotten around to filling out the form) winds up inheriting your IRA.

So, what's the difference? Even though your son is a person, he is *not* a designated beneficiary because he inherited through your estate (the nonperson beneficiary of your account, according to the IRS). Yes, he is deemed a beneficiary and will inherit the IRA funds, but he's a "non-designated beneficiary." On the surface, this may seem like a lot of tortuous nuancing since the outcome in our example is the same either way, right? Not exactly. The distribution rules for a "non-designated beneficiary" and a "designated beneficiary" can result in payout period differences that come with significant tax consequences.

Reaching EDB Status

If your beneficiary is a human (with a pulse) and is named on the beneficiary form, he or she qualifies as a designated beneficiary. Designated beneficiaries fall under two categories: noneligible designated beneficiaries (NEDBs) or eligible designated beneficiaries (EDBs). As explained in detail Step #2: SECURE It (Chapter 6), NEDBs are subject to the 10-year post-death payout rule and therefore cannot use the stretch IRA. EDBs are eligible for the stretch. But first they must (in addition to being named) qualify for this special status through inclusion in one of the five classes established in the SECURE Act. Here is the select club of EDB members who still get the stretch IRA:

FIVE CLASSES OF ELIGIBLE DESIGNATED BENEFICIARIES (EDBs)

1. Surviving spouses
2. Minor children, until age 21—but *not* grandchildren
3. Disabled individuals—under strict IRS rules
4. Chronically ill individuals—also under strict IRS rules
5. Individuals not more than 10 years younger than the IRA owner (for example, a sibling, partner, or friend)

The final class of designated beneficiaries considered EDBs includes any designated beneficiaries (including qualifying trusts) who inherited *before* 2020. These beneficiaries are grandfathered under the pre-2020 stretch IRA rules. In addition, trusts for the sole benefit of these EDBs should qualify as an EDB. EDB status is determined at the date of the owner's (or plan participant's) death and cannot be changed. The only exception is when there is a change in qualifying status, such as when a minor child loses EDB status once he or she reaches majority.

Capital Gains vs. Ordinary Income

Capital gains are what everybody wants, and *ordinary income* is what most people get. A capital gain results from the sale of what is called a "capital asset," which is generally defined as something you own: stocks, bonds, mutual fund shares, your home. Income from your trade or business, or IRA distributions on the other hand, is defined as "ordinary," which means it gets taxed at a higher rate for many taxpayers. For example, if you are in a 32 percent tax bracket, you would pay 32 percent on ordinary income, whereas a capital gain would be taxed at 15 percent if the property was held more than one year before it was sold. The maximum long-term capital gains rate is currently only 20 percent, and the lowest rate is 0 percent. (That's right, nada.)

3.8 Percent Additional Tax on
Net Investment Income

For many higher-income taxpayers, the maximum long-term capital gains rate may actually be 23.8 percent once you add the extra 3.8 percent tax onto net investment income (investment income minus certain expenses). This extra tax applies when your income (your AGI plus any foreign income excluded from AGI) exceeds $250,000 (married, filing jointly), $200,000 (single), or $125,000 (married, filing separately).

Conversion vs. Recharacterization

What language are we speaking here? This is an example of the IRS stumping spell-check once again by using two words to describe the same thing: the transfer of assets between a traditional IRA and a Roth IRA. *Conversions* can be accomplished through a rollover or a trustee-to-trustee transfer (see "direct transfer" later in this section). A *recharacterization* (find that one in any dictionary!) of a Roth conversion is when you transfer converted funds back to an IRA, thereby annulling the conversion (and thus any liability, if the conversion was taxable). But the tax law did away with recharacterizations of Roth conversions completed after 2017. Now Roth conversions are permanent and cannot be undone, but recharacterizations are still available for Roth IRA or traditional IRA *contributions*. This would occur when an account owner makes a traditional IRA contribution and later wants to change it to a Roth IRA contribution or vice versa.

Cost vs. Basis

Cost is what you paid for a property, whether a stock, a bond, a mutual fund, or a home. *Basis* is the amount used for figuring any gain or loss when property is sold. To calculate basis, certain adjustments are added to or subtracted from your cost. Here are some examples:

■ For a home, the amount you pay for improvements will be added to the home's original purchase price to arrive at an *increased* basis.

■ For a stock, any reinvested dividends on which you paid tax in the year they were earned will be added to the purchase price of the stock to arrive at an *increased* basis.

■ For, say, equipment used in business, such as a tractor on a farm, any depreciation taken will be subtracted from the purchase price of the tractor to arrive at a *decreased* basis.

Increasing basis results in a decrease in capital (or ordinary) gains and the tax you'll pay, while decreasing basis results in an increase in capital (or ordinary) gains and the tax you'll pay. You must earn basis. It is earned by spending after-tax dollars. When you invest money on which you have already paid taxes, you create basis.

Basis is reduced by any tax deductions you receive. For example, if you contribute $5,000 to a tax-deductible IRA, you do not have basis, because the tax deduction reduced your basis to zero. If, on the other hand, you contribute to a nondeductible IRA or Roth IRA (which is nondeductible by definition), you have created basis.

The basis concept is needed to figure out how much of your IRA distribution will be taxable under the pro-rata rule (see Chapter 3) when you withdraw from an IRA and you have made nondeductible contributions to your IRA, or if your IRA includes after-tax funds rolled over to your IRA from your company plan. After-tax funds and nondeductible IRA contributions are basis in an IRA because they represent funds that have already been taxed. They should not be taxed again upon withdrawal, but to make sure that doesn't happen you must keep track of your IRA basis.

Deductible IRA vs. Nondeductible IRA Contributions

A *deductible* contribution to an IRA is taken as a current tax deduction and becomes taxable only when withdrawn. A *nondeductible* contribution to an IRA receives no current tax deduction, but also is not taxable when withdrawn. The traditional IRA is an example of an IRA that can be *deductible* (if you don't make too much money while you're active in your company's plan), whereas a Roth IRA is an example of a nondeductible IRA. You never receive a tax deduction for money contributed to a Roth IRA.

Direct Transfer vs. Rollover

A *direct transfer* (aka direct rollover) is the process of moving funds from one retirement account to another. It is also referred to as a *trustee-to-trustee transfer*, which means that the funds go directly from one bank or brokerage firm to another without you ever touching the money en route. This is my preferred method of moving money because it's not only safe but also tax-free. The IRS prefers you to use it too but for a different reason—they tremble at the thought of your taking the money, failing to redeposit it, and not telling them. With a trustee-to-trustee transfer, the IRS is assured (as are you) that your funds arrived safely at their new destination.

A *rollover* is when you withdraw money from your IRA or qualified plan, such as a company 401(k), and redeposit it in an IRA or into your new company's qualified plan. If you choose to have the funds paid directly to you, the IRS allows you 60 days to redeposit the money into an IRA or your new company's plan. Some people refer to this as a *60-day IRA loan* because you get to use these funds for the 60 days, but I would be very, very careful here and *not* take this approach without serious thought and an understanding of the tax consequences if the funds cannot be repaid in time. If you miss the deadline, the withdrawal becomes taxable, which spells *the end of your retirement account*! If you still prefer the rollover method as opposed to the trustee-to-trustee transfer after reading that, be advised that you can do a 60-day IRA-to-IRA or Roth IRA-to-Roth IRA rollover only once a year (every 365 days—not calendar year), so I would again strongly advise against this. The rules have tightened in this area and a mistake here could end your IRA. The IRS has no authority to provide relief in this area, even for honest errors (see Chapter 4). On the other hand, you can do as many direct transfers as you like in a year, if the funds go from trustee to trustee.

Estate Tax vs. Income Tax

Income tax is the one you're still alive to complain about.

Final Tax Return vs. Estate Tax Return

The *final tax return* refers to your last income tax return (Form 1040) for the year of death. The *estate tax return* (Form 706) is used to calculate how much estate tax the estate owes now that you're no longer here to say differently.

Gift vs. Bequest and Gift Tax vs. Estate Tax

A *gift* is something that you present while you are alive, whereas a *bequest* is presented after your death through a will or trust. *Gift tax* is assessed on taxable gifts such as property that are made by the giver during his or her lifetime. The giver is responsible for paying the tax, if there is one. *Estate tax* is levied on assets in an inherited estate after death and is paid out of the estate. The tax system in place for gift and estate taxes is supposed to establish that whether you give something away while you are alive or it gets taxed in your estate after you're gone, the tax will be the same. But this doesn't always happen; paying a gift tax will cost less than paying an estate tax on the same amount of property.

IRA vs. Inherited IRA

A reader recently asked a *New York Times* advice columnist, "Would it be OK to ask my parents for an advance on the money they will be leaving me, since I'd like to enjoy it now?" The *Times* writer responded: "Here's the thing about your parents' money: It's theirs!" The IRS also likes to say it's THEIRS, as in (spell it out): TheIRS (aka not yours).

I think you get the point. That explains the difference between your own IRA (which is yours) and an inherited IRA (which was not yours, even though you may now have inherited it). The IRS too draws a significant and strict distinction between the two. They are separate accounts, not to be commingled.

First, under the tax law, an inherited IRA is an IRA inherited from anyone except a spouse, because as you'll see throughout this book, spouses enjoy numerous inheritance tax benefits that other inheritors, like children and grandchildren, do not. For example, when a husband inherits an IRA from his wife, he can do a spousal rollover, transferring his deceased wife's IRA funds to his own IRA, and treat the funds as if they were always his. A nonspouse beneficiary cannot do that. In addition, the SECURE Act eliminated the stretch IRA for most nonspouse beneficiaries, but spouses are exempt. You'll learn a lot more about this in the new chapters on the SECURE Act (Chapters 5 and 6).

You can contribute to your own IRA, but you can never contribute to an inherited IRA. An IRA is made up of only your own funds that you contributed, or from funds that you rolled over from your workplace 401(k) plan, for example. In either case, aside from the spousal benefits mentioned above, your own IRA is funded only with money that you contributed to it.

WARNING: You cannot mix your own IRA with your inherited funds (except from a spouse), otherwise the entire inherited IRA will be taxable and gone! That's a warning and the reason I have included this section here. I've seen too many horror stories of lost inherited IRAs. Inherited IRAs also follow different required distribution rules than your own IRA, which you'll see in Chapter 6.

IRC vs. TRA86

The *Internal Revenue Code (IRC)* is the tax law as written by Congress. For example, if you see a reference to "IRC Section 408," this means Section 408 of the Internal Revenue Code, and it's the law. *TRA86 (The Tax Reform Act of 1986)* is part of the tax code and is the notorious legislation that gave birth to most of the arcane rules on retirement plan distributions that are putting our savings in jeopardy of IRS confiscation today. Some of these laws were revised again as part of the massive tax reform known as the *Tax Cuts and Jobs Act* (enacted December 22, 2017), the *SECURE Act* (enacted December 20, 2019), the *CARES Act* (enacted March 27, 2020), and the *SECURE 2.0 Act* (enacted December 29, 2022). Like all tax laws, these are now part of the IRC.

Life Expectancy (for Taxes) vs. Life Expectancy (Actual)

Making the most out of your IRA means keeping it growing tax-deferred over your life expectancy and that of your beneficiary. For tax purposes, *life expectancy* is based on the IRS life expectancy tables. These tables are based on actuarial assumptions of how long people of a given age will live. They have nothing to do with predicting *actual* life expectancy (that's left to crystal balls). If you work out, eat right, and have genes suggesting a longer potential life span than the IRS estimate, that's all well and good, but from the point of view of extending your retirement plan's growth, it's the IRS estimate that counts—and that estimate will be the same for you as for someone else your age who has given up that gym membership and eats hamburgers and French fries for breakfast every morning (with a side of bacon, of course). In fact, it will be the same for a 50-year-old who is healthy and one who is terminally ill. However, the SECURE Act limits the life expectancy of the inherited accounts of most nonspouse beneficiaries, regardless of how long they might live.

Probate Estate vs. Non-probate Estate vs. Taxable Estate

The *probate estate* consists of assets that are wholly in your name and pass to your heirs through your will. The *non-probate estate* consists of assets that are jointly owned, in trust, or that pass to your heirs by beneficiary form. The *taxable estate* is the amount of your estate that is subject to tax and may include both probate and non-probate estate assets. For example, a house you leave in your will to an heir is considered probate property and thus is included in the taxable estate. A Roth IRA with a designated beneficiary is an example of non-probate property and is also included in the taxable estate. However, there is no estate tax on any of your assets when your total taxable estate is valued at less than the current estate exemption amount (either federal or state).

Qualified Plan vs. Nonqualified Plan

For an employee retirement plan to be *qualified,* the benefits generally must be offered to all eligible employees, not just a chosen few. *Qualified plans* provide tax advantages generally unavailable to *nonqualified plans.* The major advantages are these: Employers receive current tax deductions for contributions to the plan made for the employees, and employees pay no tax on these contributions (or their own, for which they also get a deduction), which grow tax-deferred until distributed, usually in retirement. Examples of qualified plans are a company 401(k) and other profit-sharing plans, defined benefit plans, defined contribution plans, and Keogh plans. Section 403(b) tax-deferred annuity plans and 457(b) deferred compensation plans are technically not qualified plans but, because of the Economic Growth and Tax Relief Reconciliation Act of 2001 (better known as EGTRRA 2001), they generally follow the same distribution rules. Similarly, individual retirement accounts (IRAs), simplified employee pension plans (SEP-IRAs), and savings incentive match plans for employees (SIMPLE IRAs) are not company plans or qualified plans. They are personal retirement savings accounts, but they too follow similar distribution rules.

Nonqualified plans do not have to meet the same stiff legal requirements (under federal retirement law) as qualified plans, such as being offered to all employees. Nor are they subject to spousal consent and discrimination rules. But they also do not enjoy the same tax benefits as qualified plans. So, why would anyone want a nonqualified plan? Employers use them to provide special benefits to certain employees and executives, such as special tax-deferred compensation packages, pension arrangements, insurance, or annuities. In other words, they're a vehicle for attracting and taking care of the "really important people" in a company—the brilliant, big-shot executives who often run it into the ground, as Sears, Enron, General Electric, and many others have demonstrated so magnificently.

Regs vs. PLRs vs. Revenue Rulings

Regs is short for *regulations*; it is interchangeable with *rules*. I'll be using both words throughout the book not only for variety but to be very clear when something isn't "optional." Once a tax bill is passed by Congress and signed by the president, it becomes law. As Congress and the president typically have no idea what they have passed and signed, the IRS is charged with interpreting the bill as "Proposed Regulations," which are then released for public comment. At some point thereafter, the IRS makes any changes deemed appropriate and necessary from the public's inspection, and issues "Final Regulations." These represent the IRS's official interpretation of the bill's measures, and thus they become, as Regis once liked to say, the "final answer." Until Final Regs are issued (which can take years and years), we're stuck with following the Proposed Regs, even though they're still under review.

I can hear you now: "But how can they be 'rules' if they're only 'proposed'?" Good question, to which I have no good answer, except to say, that's how the system works. For 15 years, the TRA86 provisions on retirement accounts were Proposed Regs. They were reproposed with a major overhaul in January 2001, but it wasn't until April 2002 that they became final. Now, we have a similar situation with the SECURE Act. In 2022, the IRS issued new proposed SECURE Act regulations, but it could be awhile until we have final regulations. In the meantime, we must follow the proposed ones.

A *PLR (private letter ruling)* is the IRS's official written response to a request from a taxpayer like you or me to clarify a regulation impacting our situation specifically, which falls into a particular gray area. (I know, the whole tax code seems like a gray area.) Used here, the word *private* is a bit misleading, though, because the IRS makes its pronouncements on these cases available to the public. Also, many professional financial advisors then use them as a tool for gauging how the IRS might rule on their clients who find themselves in a similar regulatory predicament. For example, the tax law never considered the possibility that some folks might miss the 60-day rollover deadline, so over the years IRS has stepped in to provide relief for many who have requested their own PLRs. Then the IRS went even further by creating something called "self-certification," where you can get a free pass without requesting your own PLR (find out more about this in Chapter 3).

Requesting a PLR from the IRS is both time-consuming and expensive. You can't simply dial up the IRS and ask, "Hey, can I do this?" The process involves filling out pages and pages of application forms and questionnaires and being familiar enough with the tax code to form a sound legal argument favoring your side of the regulatory issue you want resolved. Professional fees (lawyers, CPAs, etc.) for researching, preparing, writing, and submitting a PLR request can cost from $5,000 to $10,000 or more, depending on the complexity of the issue. Then you're hit with the IRS's own fees, which can run from a few thousand dollars all the way up to $12,500 (or way more in some cases, depending on your income and the type of ruling you are requesting). It's not unusual for the IRS to take upward of nine months to get back to you. And, after all that investment of time and money, you may wind up not getting a favorable ruling! So, unless there are big bucks at stake, it's not often worth requesting a PLR. I've described what it is because I'll be referring to some PLRs along the way to show how the IRS ruled on a specific provision that was unclear in the law or the Regs.

When the IRS feels a clarification applies broadly to all taxpayers and not just an individual case, it issues a *revenue ruling.* This is an authoritative position taken by the IRS that every taxpayer or financial advisor can rely on with respect to how the IRS will rule in their own or a respective client's case. The IRS also uses revenue rulings as vehicles for closing any perceived loopholes in the tax code.

In addition to PLRs and revenue rulings, the IRS also issues several other kinds of guidance that have the effect of law (without having been enacted by Congress). These have various names such as revenue procedures, Technical Advice Memos, and IRS Notices and Announcements, and you'll see me referring to many of these throughout the book where an important rule that you must follow when you are moving your retirement funds has been changed or newly created. For example, the new more restrictive "once-per-year" IRA rollover rule (see Chapter 3) was a result of an IRS Announcement, not an actual tax law, but the rule still applies, and harshly too! In fairness, the IRS has also harnessed this power to help taxpayers facing hardships. Following several natural disasters, the IRS has provided rapid relief assistance through issuing pronouncements, rather than waiting for Congress to act.

So, in this book, when I say, "these are the tax rules," they may come from a variety of sources, not just the actual tax code.

Rollover IRA vs. Conduit IRA

Here's another example of two terms for the same thing: money that goes from a company plan to an IRA. In the past, it was important to keep this money separate from other IRA money so that it could be rolled over to a new company plan if you change jobs. The so-called *conduit IRA* account would contain just the funds that were rolled over from the company plan plus the earnings on those funds. If you mixed any other IRA contributions with those funds, you would "taint" the conduit IRA, and it would no longer be considered, or enjoy the benefits of, "pure rollover" money. Now, all taxable IRA funds can be rolled over to company plans, not just *conduit* (aka *rollover*) *IRA* funds, and so it is no longer important to worry about "tainting."

Rollover vs. Distribution vs. Lump-Sum Distribution

All cats are animals, but not all animals are cats. Similarly, all rollovers are distributions, but not all distributions are rollovers.

Funds withdrawn from a retirement account payable to you at any time are considered a *distribution*. But if these funds then get deposited into another retirement account, you've got a *rollover* situation. If funds are withdrawn but never redeposited, you have a distribution, but no rollover. Rollover money is tax-free because it goes into another tax-sheltered account. Throughout this book, when I refer to a rollover as "tax-free" I mean that there is no current income tax on the transfer of funds from one retirement account to another. But that money is not free of tax forever. It will be taxed later when it is withdrawn (and not rolled over to another tax-deferred account). Distribution money is taxable (unless after-tax funds are being distributed) and, therefore, not sheltered anymore.

The term *lump-sum distribution* refers to money received from a company plan, not an IRA. It may sound like it applies only to folks with big bucks. After all, why would it be called a "lump" if it were just peanuts? But a lump-sum distribution doesn't always equal a boatload of cash. It just refers to emptying that plan by withdrawing the entire balance, regardless of its size.

For example, if you left your old job, which you hadn't had very long, to take a new job with another company, you might have accumulated only, say, $612 in your old company's 401(k). If you withdraw the whole $612, it's a lump-sum distribution, even though it's a pretty small lump. Taking a lump-sum distribution doesn't always mean that you must take the money and run. Those funds can be, and often are, rolled over to an IRA tax-free. Taking a lump-sum distribution may also qualify you for favorable tax breaks under special circumstances. (See Chapter 3.)

Roth Contribution vs. Roth Conversion

These are two different ways to add money to Roth IRAs. The tax rules that apply here are often confused, so allow me to explain. A Roth *contribution* refers to the limited annual amount you are permitted to deposit into your Roth IRA. A Roth *conversion* occurs when you transfer funds into your Roth IRA from an account such as a 401(k) or your IRA. While the government doesn't limit how much you can put in through a conversion, bear in mind that any pre-tax funds you convert will be taxable. Thus, your pain threshold for how big a tax bill you can withstand determines the only limit.

Roth IRA vs.
Roth 401(k), Roth 403(b), and Roth 457(b)

The *Roth 401(k)* is a component of a company-sponsored retirement plan that became available in 2006. To contribute to a Roth 401(k), employers must offer the plan as part of their traditional 401(k) plan. They do not have to offer the Roth 401(k), but most companies do, especially since the Pension Protection Act of 2006 made Roth 401(k)s permanent. The *Roth 403(b)* is similar in concept except that, like traditional 403(b) plans, it is offered by schools, universities, hospitals, and other public institutions, not companies. The *Roth 457(b)* is a component of a 457(b) plan, a deferred-compensation plan available for certain state and local government employees, such as firefighters or police, but not for nongovernmental tax-exempt organizations, such as hospitals, unions, or charities. You do not receive tax deductions when you contribute to any of these Roth accounts (contributions are from after-tax funds), but the funds grow tax-free within the account. Once the funds are held for at least five years and you've reached age 59½, you can withdraw them tax-free, a windfall that can also carry over to your beneficiaries. And once you reach age 73, there are no required distributions from Roth IRAs or Roth 401(k)s.

People can put more money in Roth 401(k)s than Roth IRAs because Roth 401(k)s have higher contribution limits. But a company plan's rules can be more restrictive than what the IRS allows. Generally, when you leave a company, you can access your 401(k) funds or roll them over to a traditional IRA. Roth 401(k) funds can be rolled over to either another Roth 401(k) or a Roth IRA, but Roth IRA funds cannot be rolled over to Roth 401(k)s.

Simplify vs. Complicate

These words are used frequently in connection with taxes—in fact, I use them often throughout this book. So, I think I should explain what they mean. In English, they are opposites—like *fat* vs. *thin* or *rich* vs. *poor*. But when it comes to tax law they mean the same thing—"to render incomprehensible." Therefore, whenever you read or hear of Congress or your state and local legislators *simplifying* the tax laws, you've got a heads-up that "something complicated this way comes."

Tax Audit vs. Tax Examination

There is no difference. They both stink.

Tax Avoidance vs. Tax Evasion

Tax avoidance is legal; *tax evasion* isn't. For example, this book will help you to *avoid* taxes, not evade them.

Tax Bill vs. Tax Law

A *tax bill* spells out what prognosticators tell you coming tax law changes will be. A *tax law* spells out what they actually turn out to be.

Tax-Free vs. Tax-Deferred Money

Tax-free means you never have to pay the piper. *Tax-deferred* means you don't have to pay the piper now, but you will in the future. For example, retirement accounts are tax-deferred because you pay no tax on the income earned until the funds are withdrawn.

Traditional IRAs vs. Roth IRAs vs. Coverdell Savings Accounts (Formerly Known as Education IRAs)

Legend has it that the *traditional IRA* is named after an IRS pension specialist named *Ira* Cohen (no, I'm not making this up). It's also an acronym—for "Individual Retirement Account," right? Wrong! IRA stands for "Individual Retirement *Arrangement.*" I'm tossing this in so that when your friends want to go double or nothing in a game of Trivial Pursuit after falling victim to the Ira Cohen answer, you can stump them again and clean up. The traditional IRA is what might be called the "plain vanilla" IRA, which has been around since 1975, when it supposedly got its name from Mr. Cohen. The contributions you make to an IRA can be tax-deductible or not, depending upon your level of income and whether you are active in a company plan. One of the big changes in the SECURE Act is the elimination of age restrictions for making contributions to your traditional IRA, if you still have the earnings to qualify. In the past (before 2020), you could not contribute to a traditional IRA after age 70½, but that limitation has been removed. You cannot withdraw from a traditional IRA before you reach age 59½ without a penalty (but there are exceptions). And you must begin taking the money out of your traditional IRA when you reach age 73 (see Chapter 4).

Named after former Senate Finance Committee chairman William Roth from Delaware, who championed their creation, the *Roth IRA* was born in 1998. Contributions to a Roth IRA are not tax-deductible but, unlike a traditional IRA, distributions are tax-free—if you play by the rules (see Chapter 7). Contributions to a Roth IRA can be made annually or by converting a traditional IRA to a Roth IRA. When you convert, you pay tax on the funds that are converted. Unlike with a traditional IRA, you never have to withdraw from a Roth; if you qualify, you can keep contributing after you reach age 70½ or beyond.

Coverdell education savings accounts (named after the late Georgia senator Paul Coverdell) are not retirement accounts; they are education-funding vehicles.

Withholding vs. Penalty

These seem the same since they both involve the IRS taking your money, but when it comes to *withholding* tax you get that money back as a credit when you file your taxes, the same as income tax that's been withheld from your pay. A *penalty* is very different. It is a fine you pay for breaking the rules. A *penalty* is not withheld; once you pay it, it's never coming back. Retirement penalties can be an expensive drain on your savings, so be watchful to avoid them.

When you take a distribution from your company plan or IRA, it may be subject to mandatory or even voluntary *withholding*. Some people choose to have funds withheld from their distributions so that they don't have to come up with the tax money when they file their taxes or to avoid paying quarterly estimated taxes. That can lessen your paperwork and worry.

PART ONE

WHAT TO DO WITH
THE BIGGEST CHECK
OF YOUR LIFE

ONE

THE BROKEN PROMISE

The difference between death and taxes is death doesn't get worse every time Congress meets.

—WILL ROGERS (1879-1935), ACTOR

We all had a deal with the taxman, and Congress just reneged. Why? Because, as usual, the government needed money. When Congress passed the SECURE Act on December 20, 2019, we lost out on the three-part deal that many retirees and their beneficiaries had been banking on, literally. These were the terms many savers counted on when they planned their retirement strategies:

1. We would save for our retirement and, along the way, receive tax deductions for our contributions.

2. Then, in retirement, we would pay back that tax but in small increments over our lifetimes.

3. Any funds we didn't use could continue being withdrawn by our beneficiaries over their lifetimes. In some cases that could be decades or generations.

This deal, commonly known as the *stretch IRA* since distributions and tax deferral could extend over lifetimes, was all perfectly legal under the tax code. It required no loopholes or abusive tax tactics. Many of us hinged our financial planning around that arrangement because we not only wanted to save for ourselves but also for our children and grandchildren. Then Congress went ahead and changed the rules that had been in place when we plotted out our strategy maybe 20, 30, or more years ago. This was a classic bait and switch. We fell into their trap.

The SECURE Act stepped up Congress's never-ending raid on our retirement accounts and punished diligent savers by breaking the stretch IRA promise made decades earlier. The new tax laws derailed the plans of people like you who have worked, sacrificed, and saved, making careful, disciplined investments, and setting up calculated plans for yourselves and your beneficiaries. Then, at the last minute, Congress went looking for money to fill government coffers, and of course the low-hanging fruit was our retirement savings. Because most retirement savings are tax-deferred (meaning the funds haven't yet been taxed), this money often looks to Congress like the perfect remedy for revenue shortfalls—a big, juicy steak.

After constantly encouraging us to save for our retirement years (so that they won't have to come in and bail us out like they do for the banks, CEOs, and Wall Street), Congress turned the tables on us. Whenever we do a good job saving, it seems Congress wants *us* to bail *them* out! Once again, our tax system has penalized savers, and that should be a crime.

> "Favorable tax treatment isn't a holy writ.
> But before saving money over decades in a
> special account, people need to have faith that
> future politicians won't rewrite the rules. . . .
> Congress has shown how carelessly
> it is willing to break its end of the bargain."
>
> —*The Wall Street Journal*, December 23, 2019

These days, the number one question people ask me is: Can I trust the government to keep its word that these will be the rules? My answer: Of course not! Fact is, Congress can change the rules again anytime. There's an old saying in accounting: "The tax code is written in pencil."

Given that uncertainty, it's important to keep in mind which direction tax rates are headed so you can plan accordingly. (Hint: Not down.)

> **"I'm putting all my money into taxes—**
> **the only thing sure to go up."**
>
> **—Henny Youngman (1906–1987), comedian**

A History of U.S. Tax Rates

Many people don't realize how low tax rates are right now. A look at the history offers a little perspective. U.S. income tax began in 1913, with the passage of the Sixteenth Amendment, at a starting rate of just 7 percent. Those were the days. At the time, opponents argued for a provision to cap the tax rate at 10 percent, but tax proponents pooh-poohed such a cap as unnecessary. They couldn't imagine rates would ever exceed 10 percent. Just five years later, when the government sought funds to fight World War I, the top rate spiked to 70 percent.

TOP FEDERAL INCOME TAX RATE BY YEAR

Year	Rate	Year	Rate	Year	Rate	Year	Rate	Year	Rate
1913	7%	1936	79%	1959	91%	1982	50%	2005	35%
1914	7%	1937	79%	1960	91%	1983	50%	2006	35%
1915	7%	1938	79%	1961	91%	1984	50%	2007	35%
1916	15%	1939	79%	1962	91%	1985	50%	2008	35%
1917	67%	1940	79%	1963	91%	1986	50%	2009	35%
1918	77%	1941	81%	1964	77%	1987	38.5%	2010	35%
1919	73%	1942	88%	1965	70%	1988	28%	2011	35%
1920	73%	1943	88%	1966	70%	1989	28%	2012	35%
1921	73%	1944	94%	1967	70%	1990	28%	2013	39.6%
1922	58%	1945	94%	1968	70%	1991	31%	2014	39.6%
1923	58%	1946	91%	1969	70%	1992	31%	2015	39.6%
1924	46%	1947	91%	1970	70%	1993	39.6%	2016	39.6%
1925	25%	1948	91%	1971	70%	1994	39.6%	2017	39.6%
1926	25%	1949	91%	1972	70%	1995	39.6%	2018	37%
1927	25%	1950	91%	1973	70%	1996	39.6%	2019	37%
1928	25%	1951	91%	1974	70%	1997	39.6%	2020	37%
1929	25%	1952	92%	1975	70%	1998	39.6%	2021	37%
1930	25%	1953	92%	1976	70%	1999	39.6%	2022	37%
1931	25%	1954	91%	1977	70%	2000	39.6%	2023	37%
1932	63%	1955	91%	1978	70%	2001	39.1%	2024	37%
1933	63%	1956	91%	1979	70%	2002	38.6%		
1934	63%	1957	91%	1980	70%	2003	35%		
1935	63%	1958	91%	1981	70%	2004	35%		

Flash forward three decades and the rate topped 90 percent. Notice that the tax rate exceeded 90 percent for every "baby boom" year (1946–1964) until 1964 (when the Beatles arrived) when rates plummeted to a mere 77 percent!

Not until 1982 did the top tax rate finally drop from 70+ percent down to 50. The whole country did a happy dance. Finally, taxpayers were equal partners with the government on our own money, and we thought that was fantastic. Today, of course, the rates are much lower. Today's top tax rate reaches just 37 percent, although many of us pay rates as low as 22, 12, or even 10 percent. In other words, bargain-basement prices!

But these rates can't remain this low. It's simple math. Congress needs money, they're going to have to raise the rates, and the last thing you want is to have your money subjected to the uncertainty of what future higher rates can do to your retirement savings. Today, baby boomers just reaching, or already in, retirement will have to withdraw their funds. What tax rate will they pay when they pull out their hard-earned cash? How high will rates have to climb to pay for all that the U.S. government has promised?

Just look at the deficit that the federal government has amassed. Even before the COVID-19 pandemic that led Congress to issue checks for trillions of dollars, the U.S. had a huge national debt problem. If you or I wrote a $50 check on an empty account, that check would bounce, and we'd be in trouble. But that's not how our government works. The government just keeps printing money and writing checks. At some point, however, the bill collectors will come calling. And the people paying will be those who've accumulated the most money that hasn't yet been taxed. What's the take-home here? Your retirement savings are at higher risk than ever before.

Remember, retirement planning is a long-term process. That's why we tell young people to start squirreling away funds in their twenties and thirties for when they are sixty or seventy. Many of you reading this book did just that—you planned for your future, relying on the rules in effect at the time. So, how can you prepare for the inevitable moment when Congress once again pulls the rug out from under savers like you?

"History does not repeat itself, but it rhymes."
—Mark Twain (1835–1910)

To predict the future, it helps to examine the past. Before 1974, there were no personal retirement accounts. Back then, people relied on company pensions—many of which got swallowed up by bankruptcies or companies not keeping their pension promises. Worried that retirees would wind up with nothing, Congress created the Individual Retirement Arrangement (IRA). At that time, personal retirement plans were designed to provide for an *individual* during retirement. They were never intended as a vehicle to transfer wealth to heirs. But when some people fortunate enough to save over a long while had built up more than they would ever need, they wanted to leave that money to their children and grandchildren. Many people arranged their affairs to leave more to their progeny. Maybe they sacrificed spending, making less lavish choices because they knew there was a greater purpose for this money: passing a legacy on to their heirs.

That's not a bad thing of course, but it wasn't what the law intended. Four decades later, when Congress swooped in to eliminate the stretch IRA, they argued that these funds were intended for *your* retirement, not for your beneficiaries.

So how do you protect yourself from a revenue-hungry Congress, growing hungrier by the day as the deficit mounts, when every time they come to eat, it's your retirement savings on the menu? Today, we're in a new economy—a yo-yo economy. YOYO stands for You're On Your Own.

That is why it pays to follow the steps I outline in this book. I will help you build a plan that is more stable and certain over the long haul. This book offers solutions that will hold up over time despite growing threats to your savings. The chapters on Roth conversions, life insurance, and estate planning, for example, all focus on new tactics designed to withstand future assaults by Congress. This is probably the better planning you should have been doing all along, but we all got a little complacent thinking that our current plans would hold up. Here's the reality: Every time Congress thinks they've eliminated a key strategy for your legal wealth accumulation plans, they've actually just incentivized people to find alternative solutions—*better* solutions. Fact is, there are solutions that are *even better* than the stretch IRA. By following my guidelines, you will build a larger inheritance for your family with more control and less tax.

Time Bomb

Like everything in life, this won't happen by itself. You must take action and get this process started before even those tax breaks still left get yanked away. It's crucial to keep our eyes on the long-term big picture. The problem is most people don't—or, worse, won't—see the forest for the trees when it comes to things financial. Far too often, people devote more time going over their supermarket receipts to make sure they haven't been overcharged than they'll spend keeping their life savings from becoming a windfall for Uncle Sam. As a matter of fact, I've had clients cancel their estate-planning appointments with me to hit a sale at their local Costco. Believe me, they'll have to score some mighty big bargains there, plus rob several banks, to make up the percentage of their life savings they'll lose to taxes if they don't get smart.

That's what seeing the big picture is all about, and I've spent the better part of the past 30 years pointing this out. In all that time, I've seen as many horror stories as there are run-on sentences in the tax code. Now retiring in record numbers, the baby boomers (including me—except that I'm not retiring, especially when so many people need all this tax stuff explained!) are starting to take distributions from their retirement accounts. That means more and more costly and avoidable mistakes are being made.

Many new retirees are running up against some hard economic times and need to protect their funds from future taxes. Some are leaving their jobs with the biggest check they've ever had (and biggest asset they own)—their retirement savings—and thus potentially opening themselves up to big financial problems. Having been so busy chasing investment returns all their working lives, they've often neglected the distribution part of the equation, and thus risk losing to the taxman a whopping amount of what they've saved.

In the coming years, I have no doubt that there will be an explosion of excessive taxation reaching epic proportions—an explosion that will give millions of ill-prepared and underprotected American savers like yourself the financial shock of their lives. The fallout from this "new retirement savings time bomb" will continue to affect you, your children, the economy, and society for years and years to come. Now is the time to step up and follow my 5-Step Action Plan, which will save big money for you and your family.

How much at risk are YOU personally? Read on and see.

TWO

WHAT'S YOUR RISK IQ?

A good scare is worth more to a [person] than good advice.
—ED HOWE (1853-1937), AMERICAN EDITOR AND NOVELIST

The Roach That Came to Dinner

Let me tell you a story—a parable, really—about a man and his wife who eat regularly at a favorite local restaurant because the food there is absolutely scrumptious. They are unaware that the kitchen has a roach problem. Yet even if they did know, while obviously not cottoning to the idea, they'd probably keep coming back for the food just as long as the roaches stayed unseen.

Once the creatures started crawling onto their plates, however, the man and his wife would probably get so upset that they'd call the Board of Health. By then, of course, it would be too late. The place would have to be shut down because the problem had grown into an epidemic.

It's the same with your IRAs and other plan savings.

Most of you haven't yet experienced the shock of losing the bulk of a retirement account to taxes. But when this happens, you'll wish something could be done to reverse the damage. By then, however, it'll be too late. Unfortunately, it's human nature not to call in the exterminator until the roaches are on our plates.

When it comes to our retirement savings, the roaches aren't out of the kitchen yet, but they are on the way.

If you don't address the issue of protecting your 401(k), IRA, or other retirement plan distributions from excess taxation now, while you're still breathing, your family will pay the price. Worse, they'll spend the rest of their lives wondering how you could have worked so hard and been so smart and so disciplined as to have accumulated such an impressive nest egg only to have been careless or ignorant enough to have left it to the IRS.

"Everybody Should Know About This!"

When the distribution rules for IRAs and all other retirement plans were first issued by the IRS in July 1987, they received virtually no attention. The country was still reeling from the savings-and-loan debacle, better known as the greatest bank robbery in American history, and that story was a whole lot sexier (and easier to untangle) than a bunch of complicated tax rules on retirement accounts. And yet these rules had set in motion a plan that would effectively rob America's savers of their nest eggs down the road—a road that is now a minefield of tax traps.

Today, most company plan money ultimately ends up in an IRA, through either rollovers or inheritances. This means that more money is now going into IRAs than into any other type of retirement plan. Rollovers from 401(k)s and other plans into IRAs now total trillions of dollars. As the baby boomers retire and inherit from their parents, IRAs are fast becoming the largest single asset people own! This constitutes a major economic change in the distribution of wealth. So, the big deal about those complex IRA distribution rules issued back in 1987 is their impact today on all our tax-deferred savings, regardless of what type of retirement plan we're in.

For example, an executive from a major television network came to me for help in evaluating the tax ramifications of his 401(k) plan. As we focused on tax planning for his retirement account, I walked him through the same five steps for keeping the taxman at bay that I'll present to you in this book. They're applicable to anyone, rich or poor, with any type of retirement plan. (In fact, the less you have, the more important it is to protect it.)

At the conclusion of our session, the network exec expressed amazement at how little of his retirement money would now be going to the government and how much of it would be going to his family as a result of following my five simple steps. He could not believe what a difference they had made in the financial legacy he would now be able to leave to his family and was absolutely thrilled. On his way out, feeling as if he'd just slain the tax dragon, he said, "Ed, this is unbelievable. *Everybody* should know about this!"

I agreed. "Think how people would feel if *their* retirement account simply vanished. How they would feel if it disappeared legally, confiscated by their own government—and if they had only themselves to blame!"

Within three days, at his urging, I appeared on his network's nightly news talking about this very subject. And yet tens of millions of Americans remain largely in the dark about how their retirement savings are at risk.

This means that if you don't know there is a problem, it doesn't bother you. Or, to put it another way, "Out of sight, out of mind."

Until the bug bites.

How Safe Is *Your* Retirement Account?

Now that I've put a good scare into you with my prognostication of things to come, here's where seeing is believing.

Take this simple self-evaluation of your personal retirement plan risk. It is designed to flush out the biggest mistakes people make with retirement distribution planning. Each question highlights a situation that could lead to the demise of your 401(k), IRA, or other retirement savings if you're not careful.

The point of some of these questions may elude you at this stage. That's OK. What's important now is this: Going through them will start you thinking seriously about protecting your retirement money now, because depending upon your response, each situation could, by itself or in combination with others, sound the death knell for your life savings, and land Uncle Sam your pot of gold.

Here's the deal. Answer "yes" or "no" to each of these 20 questions. Give yourself five points for each "yes" answer, and five points for each "no" answer. When you're finished, tally the total number of "yes" points and "no" points in the blanks provided, then check the scoring box to find out your risk IQ—i.e., how much or how little of your retirement savings are at risk.

TEST YOUR RISK IQ

1. Do you have most of your retirement savings in a company 401(k), 403(b), or 457(b) retirement plan? _____YES _____NO

2. Do you have company stock in your 401(k)? _____YES _____NO

3. Is your retirement plan one of the largest assets you own? _____YES _____NO

4. Have you recently left your company or retired, or will you be retiring soon? _____YES _____NO

5. After you retire, will you be leaving your retirement account with your former employer? _____YES _____NO

6. Will you be taking a lump-sum distribution from your company plan at any time? _____YES _____NO

7. Will your retirement account savings pass according to the terms in your will? _____YES _____NO

8. Have you named a trust to be the beneficiary of your retirement plan? _____YES _____NO

9. Is your estate the beneficiary of your retirement plan? _____YES _____NO

10. Do you own any alternative (nontraditional market) investments like real estate, business interests, or cryptocurrency in your retirement accounts? _____YES _____NO

11. Have you put off instructing your beneficiaries about what to do—and what not to do—with your retirement plan once they inherit it? _____YES _____NO

12. Were any (or will any) of your retirement savings (be) included in a property settlement (either paid or received) as part of a divorce? _____YES _____NO

13. Will you be inheriting a retirement account from anyone? _____YES _____NO

14. Are you confident that your financial advisor, bank, broker, or mutual fund company will have all the necessary documentation on your retirement account that your beneficiaries will need? _____YES _____NO

15. Are you unsure of the exact amount that the IRS requires you to withdraw from your retirement account, and when? _____YES _____NO

16. Have you put off checking out your financial advisor to ensure that he or she has the required specialized knowledge in tax planning for retirement distributions? _____YES _____NO

17. Will you be rolling cash, stock, or other property over from one retirement account to another? _____YES _____NO

18. Has it been more than a year since you last updated the beneficiary forms for every retirement account you own? _____YES _____NO

19. Will you need to tap into your retirement savings before you reach age 59½? _____YES _____NO

20. Have you heard of the Roth IRA but taken no steps to find out more or set one up yet? _____YES _____NO

TOTAL POINTS: _____YES _____NO

SCORING YOUR RISK IQ

The total number of "yes" points represents the approximate percentage of your retirement savings that will probably go to the U.S. Treasury, and the total number of "no" points represents an approximation of how much you and your family will likely keep.

Most likely you're now reeling from shock—unless your risk IQ beat the taxman soundly, which, while possible of course, is not probable. I've given this evaluation to tens of thousands of consumers, tax professionals, and financial advisors over the years in my seminars and workshops, and most find their retirement accounts to be woefully vulnerable to extreme taxation.

But I'll give you the benefit of the doubt and say that you did come through relatively unscathed, holding on to more of your retirement savings than the government will take. If so, here's a promise. My next book will be about YOU! I'll call it *The Retirement Savings Time Bomb Survivor* and we'll sell it to Hollywood. I smell an Oscar!

As for the rest of you who are just now coming out of shock at the prospect of spending a lifetime building your savings only to wind up leaving it to the government, take heart.

As you dive into this book and sail through its five easy steps for leaving your loved ones with more and the taxman with less, dream instead about what to do with all that extra cash—and shuck off the nightmare about having your confiscated nest egg come back to you some day in the form of a meager monthly Social Security check (assuming the Social Security fund is still solvent when that time comes).

Your retirement savings is *your* money. Protect it! If you truly want you and your family to be able to enjoy the fruits of your lifetime of labor and success, turn the page *now* and start getting even with—and getting over on—the taxman!

THREE

ROLL OVER, STAY PUT, WITHDRAW, OR CONVERT?

*In all things, success depends upon previous preparation, and
without such preparation, there is to be such failure.*

—CONFUCIUS (551–479 BC), PHILOSOPHER

Worst Rollover Attempt Ever and Why We Can't Have Nice Things!

Beware the Once-per-Year Rollover Rule

When pop star Taylor Swift broke out her 2017 song, "This Is Why
We Can't Have Nice Things," she might very well have been sing-
ing about tax attorney Alvan Bobrow and his IRA. Bobrow's multiple IRA rollovers landed him in Tax Court in 2014 and ended up
ruining some very nice things for the rest of us.

Conflicting with a long-standing IRS position in private letter
rulings (PLRs) as well as earlier editions of IRS Publication 590, the
Tax Court in *Bobrow v. Commissioner (TC Memo 2014-21)* made a surprising decision. It declared that the once-per-year IRA rollover
rule applies to *all* an individual's IRAs, not to each of his or her IRA
accounts separately.

What had Bobrow done to ruin everything for the rest of us? He
took two distributions totaling $65,064 from one of his IRA ac-

counts. When he did not have the funds to complete his rollover at the 60-day mark, he took the exact same amount, $65,064, from his second IRA and rolled the funds over to his first IRA. That still left him $65,064 short in his IRAs. When he again did not have the funds to complete his rollover from the second IRA within 60 days, he asked his wife to take the exact same amount out of her IRA to put into his IRA, which is what they did. This meant that his initial distribution of $65,064 had been out of the IRA for 120 days going on 180 days. Get the picture? IRS took exception to all these transactions and wanted income tax from the Bobrows. They disagreed and went to Tax Court. The court told both parties that they had it wrong and that the law said you could only do one 60-day rollover, no matter how many IRA accounts you have. Years after the court's stricter interpretation of the once-per-year rule in the *Bobrow* case, plenty of confusion on this point remains.

Not only did Bobrow lose, but others after him have knowingly or unknowingly violated this same rule and wound up having their attempted rollover taxed, thereby ending the IRA tax shelter for funds intended to cover retirement later, not the taxman now. This is a horrible way to lose your retirement savings, and it's happening to more people now. Thanks to Bobrow trying to game the system, he ruined things for us all! Don't let this happen to you. Later in this chapter I'll give you all the details on how the once-per-year IRA rollover rule works, including some exceptions.

Do Direct Transfers!

The best way to deal with the once-per-year rule is to avoid it altogether. Do direct transfers. They are never subject to the rule! This means if you are looking to move your IRA funds, go with a trustee-to-trustee transfer instead of a 60-day rollover. What's the difference? Instead of receiving a distribution from your IRA and rolling it over within 60 days, you use a transfer to move your IRA funds directly from one IRA trustee to another, without ever touching the money in between. Keeping the whole transaction out of your hands is the key.

There are no limits on how many transfers you can do, and the best part is that the pesky once-per-year IRA rollover rule never comes into play! Having trouble getting your IRA custodian to do a trustee-to-trustee transfer? Try asking for a check made payable to the receiving IRA. Even if you personally walk the check over to the financial institution holding your IRA money, it is still considered a transfer and avoids the hassle of the once-per-year rollover rule. Just make certain the check is not made out to you personally, only to your IRA.

Making a Decision on the Biggest Check of Your Life

Picture this: You're about to retire, just retired, left a company to take another job, or have been laid off (aka downsized, rightsized, or whatever they're calling it these days), having built up a sizable retirement account. Or maybe you're among the millions who have lost their jobs and are making these tough choices right now. Consider this the first day of the rest of your life.

Now what?

You're about to get the Biggest Check of Your Life: your lump-sum distribution. Surely this calls for some forethought or pre-planning about what to do with it. And I don't mean leafing through the latest cruise brochures or inquiring about renting an armored car for hauling your money around.

Fortunately, there aren't a ton of options to make your head spin. You've got four choices for what to do with your money:

- Option #1: Roll over to an IRA.

- Option #2: Stay put in the company plan (if, or for as long as, allowed) or roll to a new employer's plan.

- ■ Option #3: Take a lump-sum distribution and pay the tax now.

- ■ Option #4: Convert to a Roth IRA or a Roth 401(k).

The choice you make here is probably the most important financial decision of your lifetime. In a way, it's like deciding where to park your car for easy access, convenience, and safekeeping. In tandem with the five simple steps for protecting your retirement savings that I'll present in Part 2, your decision here can make or break your retirement.

To gauge the tax ramifications of each option, take the following factors into consideration:

1. **When will you need the money?** Will you need it in retirement? Or sooner rather than later? Your answer will determine whether you're better off rolling your money over into an IRA (option #1) or taking a lump sum and paying tax on the distributed amount at ordinary income-tax rates or special tax-favored rates (option #3) or converting to a Roth IRA (option #4).

2. **What will your tax bracket be in retirement?** Contrary to popular belief, it is not uncommon to wind up in a higher tax bracket in retirement than during your working years. If your postretirement bracket will be significantly higher, the required annual distributions from option #1, which are tax-deferred until withdrawn, will be taxed at that higher rate, leaving you less to live on. Therefore, it might be a better long-term retirement strategy to take a lump-sum distribution and pay the tax on it now, but at a lower rate under special tax treatment (option #3) if you qualify. This could help you avoid excessive taxation. Also consider doing a Roth conversion (option #4).

3. **How is your health?** If you're seriously ill or old enough to have one foot in the grave already, it's time to start thinking about how your lifetime of savings can help your loved ones

once you shuffle off this mortal coil. You'll want to be able to extend the tax deferral on your retirement account distribution to your beneficiary. Option #1 or #4 will allow you to do just that.

4. **How much money will you need for retirement?** Maybe you have sufficient non-tax-deferred savings to support your retirement. If so, you can choose option #1 or #2. But if you predict you'll have to tap into your pre-tax retirement money now to make ends meet, option #3 may be a must.

5. **How much is the lump-sum distribution?** If it's large, taking the tax hit up front probably won't pay off because of the unlikelihood of your being able to make up the shortfall in your remaining years. Therefore, options #1 and #2 are more viable. If the lump-sum distribution is a small amount, you'll pay proportionately less in current tax under option #3, or you can convert it to a Roth account (option #4).

6. **How old are you?** The minimum age you can begin taking distributions without getting socked with a 10 percent early withdrawal penalty is 59½. (For more on this rule and its exceptions, see Chapter 4.) More to the point, however: The younger you are, the more years you will have to keep building tax-deferred money, since retirement is still a ways off. So, if you're younger than 59½, consider option #1 or #4. But if you're older, you have a lot more flexibility for avoiding taxes and penalties in all four options than those young whippersnappers.

7. **What is your estate plan?** With an IRA rollover (option #1), the money can continue building up, tax-deferred, for your heirs after your death. Or you can use distributions of those IRA monies to fund better estate-planning options such as life insurance (see Chapter 8). If you want to leave an income-tax-free inheritance to your beneficiaries, you should consider a

Roth conversion (option #4). Given the current generous $10 million estate-tax exemption ($20 million per couple)—or possibly even more since these amounts increase each year with inflation—the inherited Roth IRA is not only income-tax-free but can be estate-tax-free too! You will have to pay a tax to convert those funds, but that tax payment can be done at to-day's historically low income-tax rates, and your beneficiaries won't have to worry about future tax-rate increases. Paying the conversion tax also reduces the size of your estate, which can reduce exposure to federal and state estate taxes that would otherwise leave less for your family. The IRA rollover (option #1) also allows you to set up more flexible planning options for your beneficiaries.

8. **Who will pay the income tax?** Can taxes be shifted to your beneficiaries at lower rates (option #1), or will it be cheaper for you to pay the income tax now with the special tax treatment offered by option #3? Another option is a Roth conversion (option #4), whereby you pay the income tax on those funds upon conversion, relieving your beneficiaries of ever having to sell off key assets to settle up with Uncle Sam. Furthermore, you will have reduced the size of your estate that will be subject to estate tax by the amount of tax you paid on the conversion.

9. **Will you work again?** If there's a chance that you will wind up "unretired," option #1's portability feature—the ability to park your money temporarily in an IRA rollover account and then roll it back into your new employer's plan—may be most attractive to you. However, in most cases it is best to roll the funds to an IRA and leave them there (rather than rolling them back to your new employer's plan). If you already have a new job lined up, you may want the flexibility of option #2: rolling your money right from your prior employer's plan into your new employer's plan to take advantage of loan provisions or creditor protection (if your state does not already protect IRAs from creditors). Then again, if there's a chance

that you'll be working again, but you need the money now, option #3 may be your best choice because you may qualify for special tax treatment. If not, you may as well select option #1 and withdraw what you need from the IRA as you need it.

10. **Is creditor protection a big issue for you?** Many states afford IRAs protection from creditors. If your state does not protect IRAs from creditors, however, and this is an important issue for you, you might want to consider leaving the funds in your company plan or rolling them over to a new employer's plan (option #2). Option #3 (taking a lump-sum distribution) exposes your pension money to creditor claims, such as lawsuits, malpractice, divorce, bankruptcy, or other creditor problems. But you should not let the issue of creditor protection tip the scales and sway you, because most people do not have judgments on their retirement accounts. Give some serious thought here to which is more important to you: creditor protection or having all the advantages of the IRA rollover. Ask yourself, "Would I want to give up the opportunity to control my IRA in exchange for creditor protection I may never need?"

CAUTION!

Don't base your decision on any one factor alone unless that factor is a major issue for you.

As I delve into the details of your four options for what to do with that Biggest Check of Your Life, keep reviewing your responses to the 10 factors that you should consider—and remember that more than one road leads to Rome. Each option is not always all or nothing. You may, for example, want to roll over part of your company plan money (option #1) while withdrawing some for expenses (option #3). That's perfectly legal and doable! Remember, it's your money—and it's my job to ensure that you hold on to as much as possible, so you and your family can enjoy it for many years to come.

Option #1: Roll Over to an IRA

The IRA rollover is the best option for most people. It's the most liberal and flexible. Once your funds are rolled to an IRA, you can take advantage of everything the tax law allows. That is not necessarily true of company plans. Believe it or not, some 401(k)s, for example, impose far more restrictive rules than even the IRS!

With this option, you roll your lump-sum distribution into an IRA account and park it there until you're ready to take withdrawals. (You could also roll the distribution to your new employer's plan, but if your old plan had a lot of restrictive rules, you'll probably be subject to the same ones in your new plan—so you'll be no better off.)

When it's a valid rollover, the distribution is tax-free. Remember, it is best to do a direct rollover to avoid any 60-day rollover problems, because when a distribution is payable to you directly, the rollover must be completed within 60 days of the day you receive the distribution. Otherwise, you'll have to pay income tax on the whole withdrawal (plus that pesky extra 10 percent early distribution penalty for a withdrawal made before you are 59½ years old or before age 55, if the age-55 exception applies [see page 71]). Plus, the distribution will be subject to 20 percent mandatory withholding. This so-called 60-day rule is strictly enforced, although the IRS has the authority to waive it under special circumstances when the delay is beyond your control due to "casualty, disaster, disability, hospitalization, death, or incarceration" (though it seems to me that these last two especially would make violating the 60-day rollover rule the least of one's worries).

The 60-day rule can also be waived due to restrictions imposed by a foreign country (such as being trapped behind enemy lines if war breaks out), postal errors (inconceivable as these may seem), an error committed by your financial institution (impossible!), or any other situation where denying a waiver would be unfair or against good conscience.

Whose good conscience?

Good question.

In fact, this 60-day-rollover situation has gotten so bad that back in 2016, the IRS provided much-needed relief for those who just could not get the funds rolled over within the 60 days and risked having their retirement savings be taxed prematurely simply because the rollover wasn't completed in time. The IRS released Revenue Procedure 2016-47 to provide "self-certification" relief for late 60-day rollovers. Since 60-day violations are rampant, IRS essentially allows you to use the honor system to give yourself more time to complete your late 60-day rollover if you fall into one of the twelve acceptable excuse categories that the IRS allows. The IRS even provides a model letter you can use and, unlike the time-consuming and expensive private letter ruling (PLR) process, this is quick and free. The relief procedure applies to 60-day rollovers from both company plans and IRAs.

Here is the model letter the IRS has provided. You can also find it on the IRS website (www.irs.gov) if you search for "Revenue Procedure 2020-46" or "2020-46," and then scroll to the end of the document provided.

MODEL SELF-CERTIFICATION LETTER FROM IRS
APPENDIX TO IRS REVENUE PROCEDURE 2020-46
APPENDIX
CERTIFICATION FOR LATE ROLLOVER CONTRIBUTION

- -

Name
Address
City, State, ZIP Code
Date: _____
Plan Administrator/Financial Institution
Address
City, State, ZIP Code

Dear Sir or Madam:

Pursuant to Internal Revenue Service Revenue Procedure 2020-46, I certify that my contribution of $[ENTER AMOUNT] missed the 60-day rollover deadline for the reason(s) listed below under Reasons for Late Contribution. I am making this contribution as soon as practicable after the reason or reasons listed below no longer prevent me from making the contribution. I understand that this certification concerns only the 60-day requirement for a rollover and that, to complete the rollover, I must comply with all other tax law requirements for a valid rollover and with your rollover procedures.

Pursuant to Revenue Procedure 2020-46, unless you have actual knowledge to the contrary, you may rely on this certification to show that I have satisfied the conditions for a waiver of the 60-day rollover requirement for the amount identified above. You may not rely on this certification in determining whether the contribution satisfies other requirements for a valid rollover.

Reasons for Late Contribution

I intended to make the rollover within 60 days after receiving the distribution but was unable to do so for the following reason(s) (check all that apply):

____ An error was committed by the financial institution making the distribution or receiving the contribution.

____ The distribution was in the form of a check and the check was misplaced and never cashed.

____ The distribution was deposited into and remained in an account that I mistakenly thought was a retirement plan or IRA.

____ My principal residence was severely damaged.

____ One of my family members died.

____ I or one of my family members was seriously ill.

____ I was incarcerated.

____ Restrictions were imposed by a foreign country.

____ A postal error occurred.

____ The distribution was made on account of an IRS levy and the proceeds of the levy have been returned to me.

____ The party making the distribution delayed providing information that the receiving plan or IRA required to complete the rollover despite my reasonable efforts to obtain the information.

____ The distribution was made to a state unclaimed property fund.

Signature

I declare that the representations made in this document are true and that the IRS has not previously denied a request for a waiver of the 60-day rollover requirement with respect to a rollover of all or part of the distribution to which this contribution relates. I understand that in the event I am audited, and the IRS does not grant a waiver for this contribution, I may be subject to income and excise taxes, interest, and penalties. If the contribution is made to an IRA, I understand you will be required to report the contribution to the IRS. I also understand that I should retain a copy of this signed certification with my tax records.

Signature: _____

Caution: Relief Applies Only to *Valid* Rollovers

This letter will work in most cases, if you fit one of the twelve reasons and follow the procedure. But this self-certification is not an absolute get-out-of-jail-free card. You should know the limitations and which late rollovers cannot be waived. The IRS can always check up on you with a tax audit, just like when you file your taxes (honorably, of course!). The IRS will know this was a late rollover because they get tipped off by special reporting done by the custodian.

So, make sure you actually qualify and aren't trying to game the honor system. The IRS was careful to specify that the rollover must be a "valid rollover" to qualify for relief. This is an important point. Since not all retirement account distributions are eligible for rollover, they will not be considered valid rollovers, even if executed in a timely manner, and can result in taxes as well as penalties for early distribution and excess contributions.

ACTION PLAN TO CORRECT LATE 60-DAY ROLLOVERS USING SELF-CERTIFICATION

1. Make sure that the IRS has not previously denied a waiver of the 60-day rollover rule for your transaction.

2. Make sure that the reason for missing the 60-day deadline was one of the now twelve reasons the IRS lists in the ruling.

3. Fill out the self-certification letter (use the IRS model letter provided in the appendix to Rev. Proc. 2020-46) and give this to the plan administrator (for company plans) or the IRA custodian. Make sure the letter will be accepted. The custodians do not have to accept the late rollover, for example, if they have knowledge that you are not being truthful, or they know you don't qualify. This self-certification does not have to be filed with the IRS. The IRA custodian will eventually report the late rollover to them on Form 5498.

4. Make sure the late rollover is done as soon as possible after discovery of the problem. Getting it done within 30 days is best since the IRS says that automatically qualifies as a safe harbor to the "as soon as practicable" requirement.

5. Keep all this documentation on file since you may be questioned later on, for example, under audit, which could come a year or two later.

Once-per-Year IRA Rollover Rule

While blowing a 60-day rollover deadline can sometimes be fixed, here's a rollover rule that cannot be corrected and can cause permanent damage to your IRA. I call this a fatal error since even IRS cannot give you any relief here.

You might recall I introduced this earlier in the section "Worst Rollover Attempt Ever and Why We Can't Have Nice Things!" Let me give you the gist of this so that your IRA (or Roth IRA) continues to provide the nice things you want and need it to.

How the Once-per-Year IRA Rollover Rule Works

The bottom line is that you can do *only* one IRA-to-IRA rollover in a single 365-day period. What if you own both traditional and Roth IRAs? You are still limited to just a single 60-day rollover within 12 months.

For example, let's say that Juan is trying to change from one investment company to another. He takes a $2,000 distribution from his traditional IRA on January 10 with a plan to roll it over within 60 days into another traditional IRA. Two days later, on January 12, he takes a $30,000 distribution from his Roth IRA, with a plan to roll over that distribution within 60 days into a new Roth IRA. Bad move. Unfortunately for Juan, he is now stuck. Because the once-per-year rule limits him to only one 60-day rollover within a 365-day period, only one of the distributions he took out is now eligible for rollover. That means the other one cannot be put back (rolled over) and loses its tax-deferred status (or even worse—its tax-free status if it's the Roth IRA). Those funds will no longer be considered IRA funds. If you make this error on a large rollover attempt—maybe the entirety of your account if you're changing institutions—then say goodbye to that retirement account and hello to a gigantic tax bill, and possibly a 10 percent early distribution penalty too. Not good!

In many cases, spouses enjoy special privileges under the IRA rules, but not with the once-per-year rule. The IRS made it clear in several PLRs that this rule applies even to spouse beneficiaries. Here is an example of how a spouse beneficiary can run into trouble. Let's say that Jane is the beneficiary of both her husband's traditional and Roth IRAs and would now like to do a spousal rollover of both. If Jane receives a distribution from the inherited traditional IRA on May 10 of Year 1 and does a 60-day rollover of the funds, she cannot take a rollover-eligible distribution from the Roth IRA until May 10 of Year 2. How can Jane get around this roadblock?

Fortunately, there is a solution. Jane can *directly transfer* the funds from the inherited Roth IRA to her own Roth IRA at any time, because the once-per-year rollover rule does not apply to direct transfers.

Keep in mind that the IRS's 12-month period does not follow the calendar, so a new calendar year does not mean a fresh start for purposes of this rule. Instead, the 365-day period begins on the date you received the funds that you rolled over.

As with most IRA rules, there are exceptions. The once-per-year rollover rule applies *only* to IRA-to-IRA and Roth IRA-to-Roth IRA 60-day rollovers. It does not apply to Roth *conversions*. Since a Roth conversion is an IRA-to-Roth IRA transaction, it is not subject to the 12-month period rule.

All distributions from employer plans to IRAs, whether direct or indirect, are considered rollovers under the tax code. These do not count toward the once-per-year rule. Because the funds are going from an employer plan to an IRA or Roth IRA, the IRA-to-IRA or Roth-to-Roth transaction provisions don't apply. Rollovers from IRAs to 401(k)s or other company plans aren't subject to the once-per year rule either.

Once-per-Year IRA Rollover Rule Violations

What are the consequences of botching the once-per-year rollover rule? Let me tell you, it is not pretty. The funds that are not eligible for rollover will be considered distributed within the tax year in which they left the IRA account. Those funds may not only be fully taxable but could also be subject to the 10 percent early distribution penalty.

If those funds are mistakenly deposited into another IRA as a rollover, they generally become an excess contribution in the IRA account, subject to a 6 percent *per year* excess accumulation penalty if they are not removed from the account in a timely fashion. That penalty will continue to apply each year until the excess contribution is removed or until the six-year statute of limitations on excess contributions expires. (See Chapter 11, page 372, for more on fixing excess contributions.)

Now, would you like to avoid all this nonsense? Of course you would—especially if the solution is simple, and it is.

The best and safest way to do a tax-deferred lump-sum distribution is *directly* from one company plan to another, or to an IRA, via trustee-to-trustee transfer. The same advice goes for moving funds from IRA to IRA, or from Roth IRA to Roth IRA.

By doing a direct transfer, the distribution never winds up in your hot little hands, so you never have to worry about the unexpected coming along to gum up your ability to comply with the 60-day rule. You also don't have to worry about the once-per-year rule. Just do the trustee-to-trustee transfer instead. It's safer. Plus, you can do as many trustee-to-trustee transfers a year as you like.

The 20 Percent Tax Trap on Rollovers

Here's another reason why I recommend using the trustee-to-trustee (direct) transfer method instead of the rollover method when withdrawing money from a company plan and putting it in an IRA: If you go the 60-day rollover route, the plan is required to withhold 20 percent federal income tax from the taxable rollover amount. This means that instead of rolling over 100 percent of your account balance, your plan withholds 20 percent for taxes, leaving you just 80 percent to roll over.

Yes, I know. Rollovers are supposed to be tax-free, so why does the tax law require 20 percent—or any amount—of your distribution withheld?

Here's why: If you do a rollover rather than a direct transfer, the government is not assured that you will indeed redeposit 100 percent of that big fat check into the IRA or other retirement account. It simply does not trust you with your own money. Therefore, the government covers itself by forcing company plans to withhold 20 percent from your distribution before giving you a dime.

"But if I do the rollover and have the 20 percent withheld, I won't owe anything, so I'll get the 20 percent back as a tax refund, right?"

Right. But the problem is this: If you don't roll over the entire amount (100 percent), the amount not rolled over (i.e., the 20 percent withheld by the plan) is taxable and even subject to the 10 percent early withdrawal penalty if you're under 59½ (or under age 55, or 50, if that exception applies). "Gotcha!" says the IRS.

The 20 percent withholding tax requirement applies to 60-day rollovers from company plans to IRAs, but not to rollovers from IRAs. Nevertheless, I still advise going the direct trustee-to-trustee transfer route because you avoid the 60-day rule, the one-rollover-per-year limitation, *and* the 20 percent withholding.

The 20 percent withholding requirement also does not apply to rollover distributions of company stock in a qualified plan—when that is the only asset in the plan. (For more on this exception, see option #3.)

EXAMPLE

You have $500,000 in your 401(k) and do a 60-day rollover to an IRA. The 401(k) plan will cut you a check for $400,000 (80 percent of your account balance). The plan is required to send the other 20 percent ($100,000) to the IRS, and you'll get credit for it when you file your tax return. Unless you have an extra $100,000 under a mattress you can use to replace the 20 percent shortfall, you can't do a complete rollover (all $500,000), so you'll wind up owing tax on that 20 percent that wasn't rolled over—plus a 10 percent penalty if you're younger than 59½ (or under 55, or 50, if that exception applies). This is a killer tax trap that could cost you and your family decades of tax-deferred compounding on that 20 percent of your retirement savings. What a nightmare! That's why you should always do a trustee-to-trustee transfer (direct rollover) when moving retirement money from a company plan to another retirement account.

Allowable Rollovers

Taxable retirement account distributions from company plans such as 401(k)s, 403(b)s, and 457(b)s can be rolled over to another 401(k), 403(b), or 457(b) or to an IRA. In addition, Roth 401(k) funds can be rolled over to Roth IRAs and other Roth 401(k)s, but Roth IRA funds cannot be rolled over to Roth 401(k)s or IRAs. Only taxable amounts can be rolled from an IRA to a company plan. After-tax amounts can be rolled over to IRA accounts.

Amounts that can be rolled over are called eligible rollover distributions (ERDs), and it is the rollover that makes the distribution tax-free. Certain distributions are not eligible to be rolled over. These include:

■ Required minimum distributions (see Chapter 4)

■ Any distributions that are part of a series of substantially equal periodic payments, called Section 72(t) payments (see Chapter 11), or distributions over a specified period of 10 years or more

■ Hardship distributions: Some company plans may allow participants to withdraw to pay for a medical emergency, funeral, or other pressing needs. The reason that the IRS will not let you roll over hardship distributions to an IRA is because it feels that if you had such a pressing need for the cash, then the cash must be used for that pressing need. In other words, the IRS saw this as a potential loophole and closed it.

■ Distributions to nonspouse beneficiaries (see Chapter 6)

Rollover Rules

After-tax funds (the nontaxable amounts) from a 401(k) plan can be rolled over to 403(b) plans and vice versa, but only if done as a direct rollover (a trustee-to-trustee transfer). If after-tax funds are shifted from one 401(k) or 403(b) plan to another 401(k) or 403(b), the receiving plan must agree to keep a separate accounting of both the taxable and the after-tax funds, as well as of the income earned on those funds. Section 457(b) plans do not accept after-tax contributions, so no after-tax money can be rolled into or out of a 457(b).

A separate accounting of after-tax funds rolled into them is not required for IRAs, since that is done by the IRA's owner and re-ported to the IRS on Form 8606 ("Nondeductible IRAs"), which is filed with the IRA owner's personal tax return.

The Pro-Rata Rule

The problem with rolling after-tax money to an IRA is that you cannot simply withdraw that money tax-free from the IRA. This is because once it's in the IRA, it gets treated the same as nondeduct-ible contributions under what is known as the *pro-rata rule.*

The pro-rata rule applies to withdrawals of basis in an IRA, which, as you'll remember from "Talking the Talk," is the amount of nondeductible IRA contributions and after-tax contributions rolled into an IRA from another plan. Basis is a good thing because it's already-taxed money and, thus, can be withdrawn tax-free. The hitch is accounting for the basis in an IRA when you go to with-draw from the account—since the pro-rata rule will not allow you to withdraw just the basis and pay no tax on that money.

The rule states that distributions from your IRA represent a "proportionate share" of both basis and taxable money. The per-centage of each IRA distribution that is nontaxable is calculated by dividing the amount of nondeductible contributions (including rollovers of after-tax money from another plan) by the balance of all your IRAs, including SEP- and SIMPLE IRAs, which are IRA-based retirement plans for small businesses, including self-employed people.

For example, assume you have $100,000 in your IRA, plus a $300,000 401(k) that includes $40,000 of after-tax contributions (basis) and $260,000 of taxable funds (no basis), which you roll over. Your IRA balance is now $400,000. Then some unexpected bills ar-rive, and you need money to pay them. So, you withdraw the $40,000 of basis from your IRA. The $40,000 cannot be withdrawn completely tax-free because of the pro-rata rule. Only 10 percent ($4,000) of the withdrawal would be tax-free; you're taxed on the other $36,000. The total of your after-tax funds is $40,000 and the total IRA balance (after the rollover) is $400,000; $40,000 divided by $400,000 = 10 percent. So, 10 percent of the $40,000 IRA withdrawal equals $4,000, the amount that is tax-free, and 90 percent ($36,000) of the $40,000 IRA withdrawal will be taxable. (See Figure 1.) The end result is that you still have $36,000 of after-tax funds in your IRA.

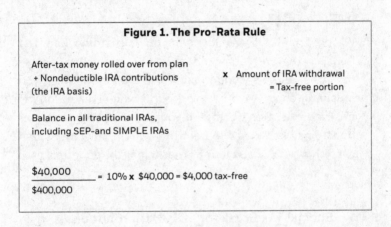

Figure 1. The Pro-Rata Rule

$$\frac{\text{After-tax money rolled over from plan} + \text{Nondeductible IRA contributions (the IRA basis)}}{\text{Balance in all traditional IRAs, including SEP-and SIMPLE IRAs}} \times \text{Amount of IRA withdrawal} = \text{Tax-free portion}$$

$$\frac{\$40,000}{\$400,000} = 10\% \times \$40,000 = \$4,000 \text{ tax-free}$$

The best analogy I can think of for the pro-rata rule is a cup of coffee and cream. The coffee is your IRA, and the cream is the after-tax money rolled into the IRA (or the nondeductible IRA contributions). Once the cream is poured into the coffee, you can't separate the two. In other words, you cannot just withdraw the after-tax funds and pay no tax. Every drop has a set percentage of both coffee and cream. The only way to change the percentage is to add more coffee or more cream.

If you have no current need for the money and your plan for the IRA is to leave it intact for your beneficiaries (except for the annual required distributions you must take after you turn 73), then it pays to roll the after-tax money to your IRA where it can continue to grow tax-deferred.

SO, YOU THINK YOU SPOTTED A LOOPHOLE?

Q: Ed, what if I withdraw the after-tax money from my 401(k) and roll it over to a separate, secret new IRA account, in a different bank, in a different state? Then I can withdraw the after-tax money I kept segregated from my other IRA funds tax-free, right?

A: Wrong! The IRS is way ahead of you on that one, bub. The Regs say that whether you have one IRA in the bank across the street and a second in a bank in a different state, you must aggregate all your IRA accounts when computing the pro-rata rule. Don't compare yourself to the big corporations. They know how to beat the system; they just shred everything. It's up to us small fries to pay the country's bills.

Special Tax Break for 401(k) Distributions = Tax-Free Roth Conversions

There is an exception to the pro-rata rule. If you wish to convert any after-tax funds from your 401(k) or other company plan to a Roth IRA, you can do it tax-free. Sound interesting? Here's how:

IRS Clarifies Tax-Free Roth Conversions of After-Tax Company Plan Funds

In Notice 2014-54, the IRS confirmed that if you have both pre-tax and after-tax money in your employer plans, like your 401(k), for example, you can allocate the pre-tax portions of your plan distributions to traditional IRA rollovers and after-tax portions to your Roth IRA as a tax-free Roth conversion. Notice 2014-54 doesn't change the way plan money is distributed. If after-tax monies are held in separate accounts, distributions are still made on a pro-rata basis from that account between after-tax contributions (which are the tax-free portion) and earnings on those funds (which are taxable).

To utilize this provision, you must first see if your company plan permits you to split your distribution into two separate accounts (meaning the pre-tax funds going to the IRA and the after-tax funds being converted tax-free to a Roth IRA). They don't have to, but you should definitely ask. What have you got to lose? Maybe they don't know the split is possible. They might even change their plan rules to benefit all your coworkers, making you a company tax hero!

Here's an example of how this tax tactic works:

Doug, whose traditional 401(k) totals $100,000, has just left his employer. His plan balance consists of $80,000 of pre-tax salary deferrals and cumulative earnings as well as $20,000 of after-tax contributions. Doug is now eligible to take a distribution of any portion or all his 401(k) funds. If Doug chooses, he could move the entire $100,000 to an IRA, tax-free, via a direct rollover. In doing so, he will retain his tax-deferral on the entire distribution, but future earnings on both the pre-tax and after-tax money in his traditional IRA will be taxable when they are distributed. Plus, his IRA distributions will generally be subject to the pro-rata rule.

Instead, Doug would probably be better off taking advantage of the guidance provided in Notice 2014-54 and splitting his distribution, having the pre-tax portion sent to his traditional IRA, while simultaneously having only the after-tax portion converted to his Roth IRA. The $20,000 of after-tax money would now be converted to a Roth IRA tax-free and could be distributed, along with its earnings, tax-free as part of a qualified distribution.

Here's what *won't* work. You cannot withdraw only the after-tax plan funds and convert them tax-free, unless they are held in a separate account. Note that the splitting strategy applies *only* to distributions from company plans. It does not apply to distributions from your IRA, where withdrawals are still subject to the pro-rata rule.

IRA Rollovers to Company Plans

Only the taxable amount (the pre-tax money) distributed from an IRA can be rolled over to a company plan. The after-tax funds (basis) in an IRA cannot be rolled over. They can be rolled into an IRA *from* a company plan, but not out *to* a company plan. They're like the guests at the Roach Motel—they check in, but never leave. After-tax funds must remain in the IRA. Also, any nondeductible contributions (which also count as basis) cannot be rolled to a company plan. But both after-tax funds and nondeductible contributions can still be rolled over into other IRAs. As with rollovers from a company plan to an IRA, the transfer is subject to the 60-day rule, unless it is made directly via trustee-to-trustee.

"Why would I want to roll over from an IRA to a company plan?" you ask.

"Because when IRA funds are rolled to a company plan, the pro-rata rule is negated!" I answer.

Here's the picture.

Let's say you have three IRAs with a total balance of $200,000. IRA #1 has a taxable (no basis) balance of $100,000. IRA #2 has a balance of $70,000 made up of $40,000 in after-tax funds (basis) rolled over from another plan, while the remaining $30,000 is taxable. IRA #3 has a balance of $30,000 including $20,000 in nondeductible IRA contributions (basis); the remaining $10,000 is taxable.

IRA #	Total IRA Amount	Basis (Not Taxable)	No Basis (Taxable)
1	$100,000	--0--	$100,000
2	70,000	$40,000	30,000
3	30,000	20,000	10,000
Totals	$200,000	$60,000	$140,000

Of the combined $200,000 balance among the three IRAs, a total of $140,000 is taxable, and a total of $60,000 is basis (nontaxable). Because the combined $100,000 balance ($70,000 + $30,000) of IRAs #2 and #3 is less than the total taxable amount of $140,000, you can roll IRAs #2 and #3 into a company plan—at which time the combined basis figure of $60,000 will be transferred to IRA #1. The money itself is not actually moved to IRA #1, as there is no money to move, since IRAs #2 and #3 were emptied when they were rolled over into the company plan.

As a result, IRA #1 has the same $100,000 balance it had before, but now only $40,000 will be taxable, and the remaining $60,000 will be basis, or nontaxable—which means that only the taxable $40,000 in IRA #1 can be rolled into a company plan.

Let's take this example a step further and say you roll the remaining $40,000 of taxable IRA money into a company plan. Now left with $60,000 in IRA #1 (your only remaining IRA), you can withdraw the entire $60,000 tax-free because it is all basis. To even greater advantage, you could then convert the withdrawal tax-free to a Roth IRA.

As you see, you need to do a bit of a rollover jig to negate the pro-rata rule. In the end it may not be worth the effort because there's this obstacle to consider: Even though the IRS allows IRA money to be rolled over to a company plan, the plan—a 401(k), for example—doesn't have to accept that money, and many company plans don't. Why? Because they don't want the additional administrative headache of having to keep track of your IRA and your 401(k) too.

CAUTION!

Think twice before rolling IRA money to a company plan. Even though this is allowable and could enable you to bypass the pro-rata rule, the best retirement distribution, investment, and withdrawal options are in the IRA. Once IRA funds are rolled to a company plan, they become plan assets and are thus subject to plan rules and restrictions.

Stock Rollovers

With all that stock building up in your retirement plan, it's likely that you may want to roll some or all of that over too.

The IRS does permit tax-free rollovers of stock—as well as other noncash property—from a qualified plan or IRA to another IRA, and vice versa. Distributions are taxed at ordinary income tax rates based on the fair market value of the stock at the time of distribution. This fair market value then becomes your foundation for computing gain or loss on the future sale of the stock.

However, if the company stock in your retirement plan (defined as stock in the company that employed you) is highly appreciated (meaning it has substantially increased in value since you purchased it in the 401[k] plan), you may not want to roll it over to an IRA (even though the conventional wisdom tells you to do so) but take a lump-sum distribution instead (see option #3).

Figure 2. Allowable Rollovers at a Glance
PERMITTED ROLLOVERS UNDER THE TAX LAW

In recent years, more liberalized rollover rules have greatly expanded portability between different kinds of retirement accounts. The chart below shows permitted rollovers. The IRA category includes SEP-IRAs. SIMPLE IRAs also are included in this category once two years have passed since the first contribution was made. For the first two years, rollovers are permitted only to and from other SIMPLE IRAs. Keep in mind that even though the tax law may permit a rollover, a company plan is not required to accept it.

Rollovers of taxable funds are permitted between all the plans listed in the chart below. The chart shows which plans can also roll over after-tax funds to other plans. The rollover of after-tax funds must be done as a direct rollover. Even though the tax law permits these rollovers, company plans are not required to accept rollovers.

ROLLOVERS FROM	ROLLOVERS TO			
	IRA	401(k) Plan	403(b) Plan	457(b) Plan
IRA	All taxable (eligible) funds can be rolled over to other IRAs. After-tax funds rolled into IRAs from plans and nondeductible IRA contributions can be rolled over to other IRAs.	All taxable (eligible) funds can be rolled over to a 401(k) plan. After-tax funds rolled into IRAs from plans and nondeductible IRA contributions cannot be rolled to a 401(k) plan.	All taxable (eligible) funds can be rolled over to a 403(b) plan. After-tax funds rolled into IRAs from plans and nondeductible IRA contributions cannot be rolled to a 403(b) plan.	All taxable (eligible) funds can be rolled over to a 457(b) plan. After-tax funds rolled into IRAs from plans and nondeductible IRA contributions cannot be rolled to a 457(b) plan.
401(k) Plan	All taxable (eligible) funds can be rolled over to an IRA. After-tax 401(k) contributions can be rolled into an IRA.	All taxable (eligible) funds can be rolled over to other 401(k) plans. After-tax 401(k) contributions can be directly rolled to other 401(k) plans.	All taxable (eligible) funds can be rolled over to a 403(b) plan. After-tax 401(k) contributions can be directly rolled to a 403(b) plan.	All taxable (eligible) funds can be rolled over to a 457(b) plan. After-tax 401(k) contributions cannot be rolled to a 457(b) plan.
403(b) Plan	All taxable (eligible) funds can be rolled over to an IRA. After-tax 403(b) contributions can be rolled to an IRA.	All taxable (eligible) funds can be rolled over to a 401(k) plan. After-tax 403(b) contributions can be directly rolled to a 401(k) plan.	All taxable (eligible) funds can be rolled over to other 403(b) plans. After-tax 403(b) contributions can be directly rolled to other 403(b) plans.	All taxable (eligible) funds can be rolled over to a 457(b) plan. After-tax 403(b) contributions cannot be rolled to a 457(b) plan.
457(b) Plan [governmental 457(b) plans only]	Section 457(b) plans do not accept after-tax funds, so no after-tax funds can be rolled into or out of a 457(b) plan. The taxable plan balance can be rolled to an IRA, 401(k), 403(b), or another 457(b) plan. The expanded rollover rules do not apply to Section 457(b) plans of nongovernmental tax-exempt organizations.			

Figure 2. Allowable Rollovers at a Glance (*continued*)
ROLLOVER RULES FOR ROTH ACCOUNTS

ROLLOVERS FROM	ROLLOVERS TO			
	IRA	Roth IRA	Non-Roth 401(k), 403(b), 457(b) Plans	Roth 401(k), 403(b), 457(b) Plans
Roth IRA	Never allowed.	All Roth funds can be rolled to another Roth IRA.	Never allowed.	Never allowed.
Non-Roth 401(k), 403(b), 457(b) Plans	See previous chart.	Treated as a taxable conversion.	See previous chart.	In-plan conversions permitted at any time if allowed by the plan.
Roth 401(k), 403(b), 457(b) Plans	Never allowed.	Roth plan funds can be rolled over to Roth IRAs.	Never allowed.	Only if allowed by the receiving plan. Five-year holding periods will be determined by the way the funds are moved.

The Same-Property Rule

The IRS lets you roll over stock or other property, but the rollover must be of the same property that was distributed from your retirement account. This is called the *same-property rule.* For example, you cannot distribute stock or substitute an equivalent amount of cash or other property and roll that over to an IRA in lieu of the stock. You must roll over stock for stock, cash for cash, bonds for bonds, mutual funds for mutual funds, blueberries for blueberries, and so on. With a distribution from an employer plan, you *can* sell the stock and roll over the cash that you received for it. But this cannot be done when rolling over from

one IRA to another. With IRA rollovers, the same property must
be rolled over.

ADVANTAGES OF ROLLING FROM A COMPANY PLAN TO AN IRA

1. Required Minimum Distribution (RMD) simplicity

■ IRAs are aggregated for calculating RMDs. You can take your
RMD from any one or a combination of your own IRAs. With company plans, you generally must take your RMD from each plan separately. Exception: RMDs can be taken from any one of a person's
403(b) plans.

2. More flexible withholding options

■ Plans are generally required to withhold 20 percent of an eligible
rollover distribution paid to an employee. With IRAs, there is no
such 20 percent mandatory withholding rule. IRA owners can opt
out of withholding, elect to have 10 percent withheld, or have an
even larger amount withheld if they wish. You have more control
over the tax to be withheld in your own IRA.

3. Smoother estate planning

■ Assets in an IRA can more easily be coordinated with your overall estate plan than assets in a company plan such as a 401(k).

■ You can name anyone you wish as your beneficiary (except in
some community property states), and even split accounts, naming
several primary and contingent beneficiaries.

■ Funds in a company retirement plan are subject to federal law that
governs 401(k)s and certain other employer plans (ERISA—Employee
Retirement Income Security Act of 1974) that, for the most part, requires you to name your spouse as beneficiary—unless your spouse

signs a waiver. However, if you want to name someone else as your beneficiary (and your spouse won't sign the waiver), you should do an IRA rollover, if available. For most plans, spousal consent to do a rollover is not necessary. Once the funds are in your IRA, you're not required to name your spouse as beneficiary. However, be forewarned that if you go too far in disinheriting your spouse, most states have "right of election" laws to make sure the spouse gets at least a legal minimum share of your estate.

4. More investment choices

■ An IRA provides a whole universe of investment options to choose from, plus the ability to customize your investments to meet your personal needs. This flexibility is especially important in economically volatile times.

■ With an IRA, you can instantly make changes that fit your risk tolerance and retirement needs rather than going through a bureaucracy where you are now an ex-employee and thus receive little personal attention.

5. Roth conversion ability

■ You leave the door open to future eligibility for converting from a traditional IRA to a Roth IRA (see Chapter 7), and to allowing income to pass tax-free to your beneficiaries.

■ You can convert company plan funds—such as your 401(k) money—directly to a Roth IRA. Just like converting from a traditional IRA, you still pay the tax on the converted funds, but this alone is not reason enough to leave funds there. The plan must allow a distribution so that you can convert that distribution to a Roth IRA. In other words, you cannot just convert your plan funds directly to a Roth IRA anytime you wish. But through the IRA rollover, you can convert to a Roth IRA at any time.

6. Qualified charitable distributions (QCDs)

▪ If you give to charity, as most people do, using a QCD is the way to go. You get the best tax break since you can exclude the amount you give from income by making a direct gift from your IRA to the charity. You can direct up to $100,000 to qualified charities each year, and this $100,000 limit will be increased slightly each year based on inflation adjustments. Since QCDs are available only from IRAs, if you have your funds in a 401(k) or other company plan, you won't qualify for a QCD. The funds would first have to be rolled over to an IRA to take advantage of the QCD tax break. It's only available to IRA owners and IRA beneficiaries who are 70½ years old or older. QCDs are another reason to do the IRA rollover. Learn more about the tax benefits of QCDs in Chapter 4.

7. Annuity investment

▪ You can invest some of your IRA in an annuity, a feature that is generally not available with other types of retirement plans. However, the SECURE Act has made changes that should make annuity options more widely available in 401(k)s. I know that everything you've read elsewhere says not to do this because the annuity is already tax-deferred. But that thinking is wrong. I have annuities in my own IRA (actually, in my Roth IRA, where distributions will be tax-free!) and if I died while the market was tanking, my beneficiaries would receive a guaranteed death benefit at the higher (stepped-up) pre-decline value. Plus, because it's a Roth they've inherited, that benefit will be tax-free to them.

▪ You've got a hedge against an unstable market.

8. Greater flexibility, availability, and control

▪ You have no withdrawal restrictions with an IRA, whereas company plans may have some—for example, a 401(k) might not release money to you, even for a personal hardship, if you're under the minimum age requirement of 59½.

■ You have immediate access to your funds, regardless of your age. Of course, you'll have to pay tax and, if no exception applies, a 10 percent penalty for the early withdrawal (see Chapter 4). But at least, in an emergency, they can't keep you from your money.

■ You are in complete control and don't have to ask anyone's permission to take your money out, whereas even if a company plan did allow you immediate access, if you're no longer working there because of a layoff or taking a new job elsewhere, getting your hands on that cash may take some time. Keep in mind that if something's happening in your life to cause you to need the cash right away, the last thing you'll need in that moment is more bureaucratic hassles or additional pressure. This exact scenario played itself out amid the COVID pandemic when company benefits departments were not available to handle emergency cash needs from employees. With an IRA, you can get to your money when you need it.

■ You exercise greater control over the amount of tax you pay by withdrawing more in low-income years—whereas with a lump-sum distribution (option #3), it's all or nothing; the entire account balance must be taken out, even if you don't need all that money, at the time of distribution.

9. Account consolidation and simplicity

■ You can consolidate all your retirement plans under a single umbrella and not have to worry about keeping track of different distribution requirements and withdrawal options for each plan.

■ You'll relieve yourself of so much paperwork. What could be better than that? People are drowning in the monthly, quarterly, and annual statements they receive along with the tax reporting required for each retirement account. And just think of all the trees you'll save! Even if you have all this online, you still must find everything on your computer.

10. Plan portability

■ If you aim to keep working, you're able to roll the taxable money that's in your IRA account back into your new company's plan if the plan allows. (But you cannot roll after-tax IRA money, which would consist of nondeductible IRA contributions and any after-tax funds rolled into an IRA from a company plan, back into a company plan.)

11. Access to professional advice

■ IRAs can be handled by knowledgeable financial advisors, whereas management of company plans, such as 401(k)s, is typically outsourced and handled by know-nothing clerks.

■ No more "one-size-fits-all" plan management; you get an advisor who works for you, not the company you work for, to help customize your plan decisions. This will allow you to formulate the long-term retirement and estate plan that's best for you and your family.

■ You'll have the capacity to work with an advisor who is a specialist in IRA distribution planning. However, the challenge here is that the *average* advisor is not an IRA distribution specialist and cannot competently address these issues. In fact, fewer than 1 percent of advisors are competent to do so. That's a problem, because you need an advisor who is *well versed* in the distribution issues covered in this book, which affect you and your family. That is why I created *Ed Slott's Elite IRA Advisor Group*^{SM}, an advanced education program for financial advisors. My firm trains advisors in the program on these issues on an ongoing basis; many people have been in the program for years and are recognized as Master Elite IRA Advisors, our highest level of achievement in this specialized field. You can find an Elite IRA Advisor in your area on our website: www.irahelp.com.

■ Bottom line case for the IRA rollover: As an ex-employee, you will always receive better service and more personal attention from your own financial advisor than from some inexperienced phone rep at the firm where the company plan has been outsourced. You're better off with someone working solely for you.

Option #2: Roll to a New Employer's Plan or Stay Put in the Company Plan (If Permitted)

This option lets you park your retirement savings with your old employer, depending upon whatever restrictions may apply. For example, some company plans don't allow this or allow it for only a set period of time.

Or you can roll your money from your old company plan to your new employer's plan. Although technically a rollover, this generally amounts to the same as staying put in your old employer's plan because your retirement money is still in a company plan and, therefore, subject to company plan rules.

ADVANTAGES OF STAYING PUT

1. Federal creditor protection

∎ You're protected against personal bankruptcy, malpractice, lawsuits, and any other bids on your assets from current or potential creditors on the federal level (whereas IRAs receive creditor protection on the state level). In addition, under the Federal Bankruptcy Law, virtually all IRA funds are creditor protected from bankruptcy but not other judgments.

2. Borrowing ability

∎ If you find yourself suddenly strapped for cash, you can get a quick loan from a qualified plan, whereas you cannot borrow from an IRA. This privilege can be an important one but, for obvious reasons, should be exercised only as a last resort. If you feel that you may need to borrow in the future, you might want to roll the funds into your new company's plan and keep that option open— that is, if the new company's plan allows borrowing. Not all company plans allow borrowing and, important to note, most do not allow loans to former employees.

3. Affordable life insurance

▪ Money in a qualified company plan can be used to buy life insurance (if offered by the plan), whereas IRAs cannot hold life insurance. Why is this important? Life insurance offered through your company plan may be the only life insurance you qualify for or can afford. Leaving the plan and trying to continue the insurance on your own may prove too costly.

4. The "still-working exception"

▪ If you're still working, you can put off the age 73 required minimum distribution (RMD) until you're fully retired (see Chapter 4). This still-working exception to the RMD rules does not apply to distributions from IRAs.

5. The "age-55 exception"

▪ If you were at least 55 years old when you left your job and need to tap your retirement funds immediately, distributions from a company plan are subject to income tax but no 10 percent early withdrawal penalty (see Chapter 4). This exception does not apply to distributions from IRAs.

6. The "age-50 exception" for public-safety employees

▪ Distributions from a government retirement plan by public-safety employees who separate from service at age 50 or older are exempt from the 10 percent penalty. "Public-safety employees" include law enforcement officers, firefighters, emergency medical service workers, certain customs officials, Border Protection officers, air traffic controllers, nuclear materials couriers, U.S. Capitol Police, Supreme Court Police, and diplomatic security special agents of the Department of State. In the SECURE 2.0 Act, Congress expanded this list to include municipal corrections and forensic security employees, as well as private firefighters. In addition, public safety workers can qualify for the exception to the 10 percent penalty after they have 25 years of service—even if that happens before age 50.

∎ For example, a firefighter retired at age 52 in 2022 and takes a distribution from his governmental defined-benefit pension plan in 2024, at age 54. That distribution is penalty-free, but he still pays tax on it.

Option #3:
Take a Lump-Sum Distribution and Pay the Tax Now

This option lets you withdraw all your pension monies in one fell swoop and get the nasty tax bite over with now. You might select this option if your retirement account balance is relatively small, and/or if you need it right away to cover living expenses, medical costs, or other pressing bills. But if the balance in your plan(s) is substantial, then you'd be better off with option #1—rolling to an IRA—and withdrawing only what you need rather than being taxed on the whole enchilada.

Option #3 comes with several choices. Each involves withdrawing the entire amount from your company plan, but two of the three offer special tax breaks, if you qualify.

The choice with no tax breaks is withdrawing your entire account balance without the benefit of any special tax treatment on the distribution. This is the most expensive way to go and should, for obvious reasons, be avoided, unless you really, *really* need all your pension money, or most of it, at once. Then you'll have to do what you have to do, of course, but it will surely cost you a bundle in taxes (maybe even a penalty for early withdrawal too).

The other two choices offer special tax breaks that may at least soften the blow of withdrawing your funds.

Special Tax Break #1: Net Unrealized Appreciation (NUA) on Distributions of Company Stock

This allows you to take company stock—i.e., shares in the company you work for—from your qualified plan and pay ordinary income tax on the original cost of the stock rather than on its fair market value at the time of withdrawal. The difference in the value of the company stock from the time it was purchased to the time of distribution is called the net unrealized appreciation (NUA). Provided you withdraw all the funds in your plan, you can then defer the tax on the NUA until you sell the stock—at which time (even if it's the day after the distribution), you get to pay tax at the long-term capital gains rate on the appreciation only. *Currently the maximum long-term capital gains rate is only 20 percent, compared to the maximum tax rate for ordinary income of 37 percent. That's a big tax savings—especially considering that the 20 percent long-term capital gains rate is the maximum. In the lower income brackets, the rate can be 15 percent or even zero!*

In addition, the long-term capital gain on the sale of NUA stock is exempt from the extra 3.8 percent tax on net investment income. That extra 3.8 percent turns most other 20 percent long-term capital gains rates to an actual rate of 23.8 percent, but not for NUA.

Bear in mind that *company stock* means shares in the company you work for. Only those stocks apply for the NUA tax break. For example, if you're a Microsoft employee, only withdrawals from your plan of shares of Microsoft qualify for NUA.

To qualify for this break, the distribution must be a lump sum, meaning the entire plan balance, not just the stock, must be withdrawn in one tax year. In addition, the lump-sum distribution must occur after a triggering (qualifying) event. Triggering events are (1) separation from service (not for the self-employed), (2) reaching age 59½, (3) death, or (4) disability (only for the self-employed). Other noncompany stock assets (cash, funds, etc.) in your plan can be rolled over tax-free to an IRA or to another qualified company plan. (All or part of the company stock can be rolled over as well, but in that case there's no need to think about NUA because there is no current tax on rollovers to an IRA.)

Now, let's hang some numbers on the words and get a picture of how the NUA tax break works.

Say, for example, the original cost of the company stock in your plan was $200,000, and its current fair market value is $1 million. At the time of distribution, you pay regular income tax on the $200,000, but the stock continues to grow, tax-deferred. You pay no current income tax on the $800,000 of NUA. The stock is now out of your company plan and in a regular taxable brokerage account. When you eventually sell it, you pay a long-term capital gains tax, currently 20 percent on the NUA. So, assume you sell the stock immediately after distribution when it is worth $1 million. This gives you $800,000 in capital gains ($1 million current value less $200,000 original cost) taxed at 20 percent, and you pay $160,000 in taxes.

On the other hand, if you were to roll the stock over to an IRA, there would be no tax on the rollover, but when the stock is eventually withdrawn, it would be taxed at its full market value as ordinary income.

> ### CAUTION!
>
> When you take advantage of the NUA tax break on company stock, there are no mandatory IRA withdrawal requirements, because the stock is no longer in an IRA. You can hold your stock well into your dotage if you like and keep it growing tax-deferred for your beneficiaries. But remember that any dividends on the stock *are* taxable!

The NUA tax break is most beneficial when the company stock in your plan has appreciated substantially from the time it was purchased. If the current value of the stock at distribution is roughly the same as the original cost, you would pay ordinary income tax on practically the whole amount of the distribution, thereby rendering the tax break virtually worthless. Taking out company stock and paying tax now rather than rolling it over doesn't pay off either if the stock has a high basis or is not highly appreciated.

Let's change the facts in the example and see why.

Say the basis is the same as before ($200,000) but the value of the shares at distribution is only $250,000. It just wouldn't be worth it to withdraw the stock and pay regular income tax now because the appreciation is not much higher than the basis. You would owe tax on the $200,000 immediately, and all of it would be taxed at ordinary income rates. Better to roll the stock over to an IRA and keep it growing, tax-deferred.

What happens, though, if you hold on to the stock rather than withdrawing it and taking distributions, and then it appreciates even more?

Let's use our example's initial figures. The stock's original cost (the basis) is $200,000 and the stock is worth $1 million at withdrawal. Now what? As before, you will pay ordinary income tax on the $200,000, but the NUA (the $800,000) isn't taxed until you sell the shares. Say you sell the stock three months after distribution, and by then it has appreciated another $100,000. You'll pay the 20 percent capital gains rate on the $800,000 (because that is the NUA), but the additional $100,000 of appreciation after the distribution will be taxed at ordinary income tax rates.

You pay the long-term capital gains rate (in this example, 20 percent) on the NUA regardless of when you sell the stock, but the stock must be held for more than one year from the date of distribution for any further appreciation to qualify for long-term capital gain tax rates. (Note: the 3.8 percent additional tax on net investment income does *not* apply to sales of the NUA stock.)

So, if you held the stock for more than one year and then sold it for $1.1 million, the additional $100,000 of appreciation would now qualify for the long-term capital gains rate as well.

OK, now let's look at another scenario 10 years later.

You've held on to the stock all that time; it's now worth $2 million, and you die without selling it, so it's part of your estate. What tax will your beneficiaries pay if they sell the inherited stock? Do they get to use the fair market value of the stock at the time of your death as the basis in figuring any NUA (or loss) between that time and when the stock is actually sold? This is called a *step-up in basis*, and the answer is NO.

Your beneficiaries will receive the same tax treatment you would have received on the NUA had you lived and sold the stock; they'll pay the long-term capital gains rate on the $800,000 of NUA. They will, however, receive a step-up in basis on all appreciation since the date of the distribution (giving them a basis of $1.2 million).

So, if they sell all the stock for $2 million the day after your death (and, unlike vultures, some beneficiaries have been known to wait a whole *two* days before swooping in and feasting), they will pay capital gains tax on the $800,000 of NUA. They will receive a step-up (increase) in basis from the $1 million the stock was worth at distribution to the additional $1 million of appreciation on the date of your death and will pay no income tax on that second $1 million. Any further appreciation on the now $2 million worth of stock, however, will be subject to capital gains tax. If the beneficiaries wait and the company stock appreciates from $2 million to, say, $2.3 million, they will pay a capital gains tax on the $800,000 of NUA plus the $300,000 of appreciation since your death. Or, to look at it another way, their basis for figuring gain is $1.2 million (the $200,000 of tax you paid when you originally withdrew the company stock from your plan, plus the $1 million step-up in basis for your beneficiaries).

TAX TIP!

If you have not yet reached age 55 in the year you leave the company, you would owe a 10 percent penalty on the cost of the company stock at distribution time but would pay the penalty only on the amount that is taxable. For NUA-qualifying stock, that amount would be the cost. You will escape the 10 percent penalty on the NUA because it is not currently taxable. But if the appreciation is high enough, it might be advantageous to pay the 10 percent penalty to preserve the tax deferral on the NUA. If instead you choose to roll over the stock to an IRA, it's true that you will not be hit with the 10 percent early withdrawal penalty, but you will eventually pay ordinary income tax on the full market value of the stock as you withdraw it. The age-55 exception from the 10 percent penalty applies only to early distributions from qualified plans after separation from service and does not apply to IRAs.

Partial Distributions and NUA

If your plan consists of employer securities and other assets (cash, funds, etc.), you can roll the noncompany stock portion of your plan (the cash and funds) into an IRA rollover account and transfer the company stock portion to your taxable (non-IRA) brokerage account. The company stock still qualifies for the tax break on the NUA. On a partial rollover, however, you will still pay ordinary income tax on the cost of your shares. You could also roll part of your company stock into the IRA if you don't want to pay tax on the entire cost of the shares.

Electing Not to Defer Tax on NUA

Deferring tax on NUA means you don't pay tax until you sell the company stock. But you can elect to take the distribution of the company stock without deferring the tax as well. Why would anyone in his or her right mind do this? Because if you qualify, you could then have the entire value of the stock (including the NUA) taxed using 10-year averaging (however, due to attrition, most people no longer qualify for this break, so first see the details explained in "Special Tax Break #2"). If there has been little or no appreciation, or if the distribution is small, the tax may be less using this strategy.

No 20 Percent Withholding on NUA, but . . .

As you'll remember from my discussion of option #1 (rolling to an IRA), generally employers are supposed to withhold and send to the IRS 20 percent of distributions from a qualified plan (unless it's a trustee-to-trustee transfer).

There is, however, a little-known exception to this rule when the only remaining asset in the plan is employer stock. Distributing $500,000 worth of NUA stock might cause $100,000 to be sent to the IRS, diminishing the amount rolled over, if the NUA stock is not the only asset in the plan at the time of the distribution. Not good! To avoid such an outcome, it pays to make certain that your employer will first send the plan's other assets (often cash) directly to the IRA custodian, which might be a bank or a brokerage firm, with nothing withheld because it's a trustee-to-trustee transfer. Then the NUA shares can be distributed "in kind," with nothing left in the account to withhold for the IRS.

Timing Is Critical

The entire NUA transaction must take place within one calendar year in order to qualify as a lump-sum distribution and thereby merit the tax advantage. An NUA transaction may take several weeks, however, from the time the employer makes the in-kind distribution to the time the transfer agent issues new shares. Whenever all reported dates must be within a given year, the IRS is a merciless timekeeper. Therefore, you should never ask for in-kind distributions of company stock after mid-December; it's better to wait a couple of weeks until the beginning of the next year.

No Mix and Match

You should not commingle NUA stock with other employer stock. For example, if you own other company stock that's not in your plan but in a separate brokerage account, you should not put distributed NUA shares into that account as well. Doing so may interfere with the record keeping necessary to ascertain the cost basis of the NUA stock, which would make it more difficult to claim the tax break.

To avoid such complications, simply set up a separate account (even with the same broker) under the same name to hold the NUA shares.

Actually Getting the NUA Tax Break May Take Work

I've given you the theory, but it's up to you to put theory into practice. Here's where you may hit some roadblocks: Many people who typically oversee company plans have never heard of the NUA tax break. So, it will probably be up to you, or the financial advisor acting on your behalf (another good reason for having one), to avoid the bum's rush.

"On paper, the NUA tax break is tremendously appealing," says Peggy Cabaniss, a top financial planner and colleague of mine in Orinda, California. "But in the 'real world,' the tax benefits may be hard to come by. For example, I have two clients, each of whom works for a very large, presumably sophisticated corporation, and they both ran into difficulties trying to use this strategy—not with the IRS, but with their own employee benefits people."

In each case, no one in human resources knew anything about the NUA tax provision or how to handle the necessary paperwork, she says. "But we persisted. For one client, we wound up talking with the firm that acts as custodian for the company's 401(k) plan. Finally, we reached a senior person in the retirement planning department who knew what to do." And how's her other client faring? "We're still working on it," Peggy tells me. "We're still hoping to find *someone* who can help."

Does going after the NUA stock break always have to be such a hassle? Not necessarily, says David Foster, a fellow CPA and ace financial planner in Cincinnati, who's an expert on this issue. "Many of my clients work for Procter & Gamble, which is very knowledgeable about NUA stock and very helpful. P&G publishes the cost basis of employer stock on each employee's annual profit-sharing statement, a practice that all companies should adopt. But many companies outsource the administration of their employee retirement plans and won't get involved at all. Even the largest brokers and mutual fund companies seem to be unfamiliar with NUA stock."

So how does he help clients overcome such situations? Here are some of David's recommendations:

Tips for Achieving NUA Success

▪ **Start early**. At least six months before retiring, begin your search for someone who can help you.

▪ **Get it in writing**. Demand formal documentation of the cost basis of your employer stock as well as your employer's promise to make an in-kind distribution of the company shares.

▪ **Be a pit bull**. Chances are, the first person you speak with won't know NUA from the NFL, but someone in the organization will. Keep saying, "This transaction is permitted by the tax code, so I'd like to speak with your supervisor."

▪ **Know the technicalities**. The greater your own familiarity with NUA issues, the more likely you'll get someone in authority to comply with your wishes.

▪ **Don't be sidetracked by IRS Publication 575**. Some employers will cite this publication as "proof" that the NUA strategy is not allowed if any part of the lump sum is rolled over. They are misinterpreting the information, which is presented in the context of discussing special averaging of lump-sum distributions.

▪ **Be persistent.** In some cases, the NUA tax benefits won't be available, perhaps because the plan does not permit in-kind distributions of company stock. If you're told that this is the case, don't give up easily. Insist upon seeing the plan provision forbidding the practice.

"In most circumstances, if you are persistent, you will be able to find someone who's knowledgeable," David says. "That person might work for your employer, the plan custodian, or the third-party administrator, but will be able to provide exactly what you need, including a properly executed Form 1099-R that reports the transaction to the IRS."

Because the issue of basis is so important, he adds, "You should consider whether it pays to limit the amount of company stock you are buying or stop buying company stock altogether inside your company plan as you near retirement."

Also, I don't advise active trading of employer shares inside a plan once you're approaching retirement. Such activities will raise their average cost per share and devalue the tax benefit.

"If you want to buy more employer stock in the last few years preceding retirement, you should do so in a brokerage account, outside of your retirement plan. 'Overloading' in employer stock can be dangerous to your wealth, as the employees of Enron and some other less infamous boom-to-bust companies learned, to their detriment," David says.

What if an employer says that it can't compute the basis of the company stock in the retirement plan? Here's your chance to help the company follow IRS rules. As David explains, "When you take a distribution from an employer-sponsored retirement plan, the employer must report your NUA in box 6 of your 1099-R, file that form with the IRS, and send you a copy as well. The IRS will use that information to see how much tax an individual must pay on in-kind distributions of company stock. So, you see, given the reporting requirements, computing your basis isn't exactly an option even if an employer says it is. They have to do it. But it's hard to get them to, so you must press them on it."

Special Tax Break #2: 10-Year Averaging

This special tax break for easing the burden on lump-sum distributions from company plans is available to fewer people each year because it was set up years ago only for those born before 1936. So, in 2024, only those over age 88, with funds still in a company plan, can benefit. For sure, this is a dwindling population, but I wanted to mention this tax break in case you are that rare bird that still might qualify.

If so, here are the basics, and the rest is explained on IRS Form 4972, "Tax on Lump-Sum Distributions (From Qualified Plans of Participants Born Before January 2, 1936)." You'll find the special 10-year averaging rates there too.

QUALIFYING FOR 10-YEAR AVERAGING

1. You must have been born before 1936. Or, if you are a beneficiary, the person you inherited from must have been born before 1936.

2. The distribution must be from a qualified plan, such as a 401(k).

3. The distribution of your entire plan balance, excluding your voluntary employee contributions, must be made in one tax

year. You cannot roll any part of the distribution over to an IRA or other company plan.

4. You must have been in the plan for at least five years before the year of the distribution.

5. You cannot have used 10-year averaging for any previous distribution after 1986.

You would use 10-year averaging to lower your liability if you need to take out your total plan balance now for living expenses, medical bills, or other pressing needs—or just because your balance is so small that you would have withdrawn it all anyway as the tax bite wouldn't be huge.

If you have a large plan balance, however, and don't need all your money now, you're better off rolling over to an IRA and withdrawing only what you require—because 10-year averaging demands that you withdraw your *entire* plan balance.

The 10-year averaging tax is figured separately from your regular tax and the income is not added to your adjusted gross income (AGI). Thus, the distribution won't cause you to lose tax deductions, credits, or other benefits keyed to AGI.

Beneficiaries and 10-Year Averaging

Your beneficiaries will qualify to withdraw and pay tax on a lump-sum distribution from your employer plan using 10-year averaging too, regardless of their age, provided you qualified for averaging at the time of your death and, of course, the distribution meets all the other requirements—such as the mandatory withdrawal of the entire balance in one tax year.

Other Property Distributions

Noncash property such as real estate or limited partnership interests can be distributed (as well as rolled over) from a company plan or IRA. Determining a value may be sticky, however.

Finding the value of listed stocks or mutual fund shares is generally easy. You can look them up online in an instant. But how do you put a value on nonconventional investments such as real estate or interests in a limited partnership? Most likely they'll need to be appraised—and that appraisal had better be a good one because it will be the foundation for determining your taxable distribution. Also, if a distribution is required, there could be a 25 percent penalty imposed by the IRS if the taxman feels your valuation falls short of the required distribution amount. (Noncash property rollovers don't pose the same problem because the shift is tax-free regardless of the property's value. Only on the day when the other property must be withdrawn from the rollover account will an appraisal be needed.)

ADVANTAGES OF TAKING YOUR LUMPS

1. Special tax breaks

▪ You may qualify for NUA stock or 10-year averaging tax relief.

▪ If your plan consists of assets (cash, funds, etc.) in addition to company stock, and you withdraw everything in a lump sum, not only are you able to defer tax on the NUA, but the taxable portion may even qualify you for 10-year averaging, giving you a double tax break.

▪ If you participated in the plan before 1974, you may even qualify for 20 percent capital gains treatment on that portion.

2. Fewer worries and restrictions

▪ You no longer need to concern yourself with future tax rates or unexpected hikes; you're paid up!

▪ You don't risk future penalties on your net after-tax distribution.

▪ Since lump-sum distributions are already taxed, you can use them any way you wish, without restrictions. For example, you could use the cash to buy a retirement home or to buy life insurance to cover the tax on your estate for your heirs (see Chapter 8).

3. Less hassle for heirs

▪ Once you elect to pay the tax on a lump-sum distribution, you save your heirs from all sorts of complexities involved in inheriting an IRA or other plan distribution; plus, they have the liquidity to offset expenses.

Option #4: Convert to a Roth IRA or a Roth 401(k)

The Roth conversion option provides a fantastic opportunity to build a tax-free retirement for you as well as a tax-free legacy for your heirs. These are powerful long-term benefits, but there's a catch: You pay for these benefits by electing to pay tax up front on the converted funds as opposed to choosing a tax-free rollover to a traditional IRA (option #1) or to another company plan (option #2). Paying the tax to convert is not an all-or-nothing choice, however. For example, you can choose to convert some funds to a Roth IRA and roll the balance over to a traditional IRA tax-free.

Company plan funds can also be converted to Roth IRAs, but as already noted, you will owe tax on the taxable amounts you convert.

The law also allows company plan funds to be converted to a Roth account within the company plan. For example, 401(k) funds can be converted to a Roth 401(k) within the plan. The same goes for 403(b) and other employer plans, as well.

Now that you know your company plan funds can be converted to Roth accounts, you have two decisions to make:

▪ *Should* you convert?

▪ If you decide to convert all or any part of your company plan funds to a Roth, then you have two alternatives: (1) convert to a

Roth IRA, or (2) convert within the plan to a Roth 401(k), Roth 403(b), or Roth 457(b), called an in-plan conversion. This decision comes down to whether you want to move your funds to a Roth inside or outside your company plan. Generally, you are better off converting outside your company plan, for all the reasons mentioned earlier in this chapter on the advantages of an IRA rollover (option #1). For a complete discussion on whether a Roth conversion makes sense for you, and for the full scoop on in-plan conversions, please go to "Step #3: Roth It" (Chapter 7).

Not Vulnerable Until Withdrawn

Remember that retirement assets aren't vulnerable to the taxman until they're transferred—from generation to generation or from tax-deferred status to a taxable position. Until distribution takes place, the taxman, like the troll under the bridge waiting to jump out and gobble up the first traveler to pass by, must control his appetite. If you haven't taken steps to protect your retirement assets beforehand, it'll be too late to stop the taxman from devouring a good chunk of it.

Always keep in mind too that the longer a retirement account can be kept intact (free of tax erosion), the more it will grow. Think of advance planning like building a retaining wall, or planting grass or shrubs to prevent a hill (your savings) from sliding into the sea. The more your account grows, the bigger the nest egg you get to enjoy in retirement, and the greater the legacy you pass on to family members and other beneficiaries.

My 5-Step Action Plan for Defusing the Retirement Savings Time Bomb

I've given you the four options on *where* to park your retirement plan assets. Now comes the Moment of Truth: doing the parking.

How to begin?

Well, relying on your brother-in-law, your hairdresser, the cab-driver, your buddies at the Raccoon Lodge, or any of the other usual "experts" for guidance is not the way, that's for sure. You need to get down to the nitty-gritty of creating a simple, workable plan you can use to protect your retirement savings from being taxed to death.

This plan will boil down to five steps that are easy to follow and easy to implement.

Step #1: Time It Smartly

By choosing the right time to start taking your money out—and the right amount to take—you can avoid racking up those huge tax bills, plus penalties, that stem from withdrawing too little, too early, or too late. You may not have a crystal ball but making some wise predictions about your future finances can save you a bundle.

Step #2: SECURE It

Don't be fooled by the name Congress gave to their recent raid of your retirement savings. They call the law the "SECURE Act" but it does the exact opposite when it comes to the retirement funds you leave to your children and grandchildren. The SECURE Act changed the game for retirement planning. The law eliminated the stretch IRA for most nonspouse beneficiaries and replaced it with a much shorter 10-year rule. Congress needed cash and did not want to wait decades to get it from your beneficiaries. Now (beginning with deaths in 2020), most of your nonspouse beneficiaries (your children or grandchildren, etc.) will have to withdraw and pay tax on the retirement funds they inherit from you by the end of that

10-year window. (And, in some cases, they'll also need to take annual required distributions during that 10-year period.) You'll need new planning alternatives to avoid the tax hit your beneficiaries may take. Not to worry. Once you take advantage of this step, you can not only avoid Congress's diabolical plan but will end up with an even better outcome that provides a larger inheritance with more control and less tax. This step is a perfect lead-in to the next three steps in my 5-Step Action Plan to protect and really SECURE your retirement savings, despite what Congress had in mind.

Step #3: Roth It

Contribute or convert your current traditional IRA to a Roth IRA, if you're able. It's the tax deal of the century that allows you to stockpile cash in your retirement account income-tax-free for the benefit of you and your beneficiaries. Years ago, there were limits on who could convert, but today everyone qualifies to convert all or part of their traditional IRA to a Roth IRA, since all conversion restrictions have been eliminated permanently. Since the SECURE Act, Roth IRAs have become an even more valuable vehicle for passing on tax-free retirement funds to your beneficiaries.

Step #4: Insure It

Congress had no idea what they unleashed when they created the SECURE Act. By eliminating the stretch IRA, they made IRAs less desirable to leave to beneficiaries, leading more people to look elsewhere for better long-term options. While IRAs may be moving to the trash heap for estate planning, life insurance gets bumped up to the top of the list of tools for creating your perfect estate plan. Life insurance may now be the new stretch IRA. With a properly set up permanent life insurance policy, you provide your beneficiaries with larger inheritances with less tax by replacing the stretch IRA with a life insurance replacement plan. OK, so you'll have to shell out a few bucks for the premiums. Don't be penny-wise and pound-foolish. Spending a little now not only prevents your life savings from being virtually wiped out every time Congress comes looking for money but can help keep those assets compounding into a tax-free fortune!

Step #5: Avoid the Death-Tax Trap

Create a perfect IRA/estate plan that will send the hungry taxman off to sniff around for other easy prey. Levied at death, estate taxes somehow never seem as permanent as their qualifying event. Congress loves to monkey with these taxes—probably because many members tend to have big estates. As a result, estate-tax laws are in constant flux. For example, thanks to new, supersized estate exemptions (over $13 million for most people), it's unlikely that you'll pay a federal estate tax. But since that law is set to expire after 2025, you do need an up-to-date estate plan that can last as long as you, and beyond. The time to revise your estate plan is now.

Nothing is certain except death and taxes—neither of which is particularly pleasant to contemplate. But I promise that my 5-Step Action Plan will diminish much of your dread of the latter (at least where your retirement savings are concerned). Of course, Murphy's Law lives on, and we can always count on the unexpected.

For now, though, let's take the first step on our journey along the Yellow (aka gold) Brick Road to success in keeping your retirement nest egg out of the maw of the IRS Cookie Monster.

PART TWO

FIVE EASY STEPS TO PROTECTING YOUR RETIREMENT SAVINGS FROM THE TAXMAN

STEP #1:

TIME IT SMARTLY

---

*I am proud to be paying taxes in the United States. The only
thing is—I could be just as proud for half the money.*
—ARTHUR GODFREY (1903–1983), TV AND RADIO PERSONALITY

You can't let your tax-deferred retirement accounts sit forever without paying tax on them. That's the bargain you made for all those years of receiving those goody-goody tax breaks from the IRS. It's payback time, or soon will be. And you know what they say about payback! Tax-free savings is like entering into a deal with the devil. You recognize there'll come a day of reckoning, but for the time being you keep focused on the perks instead.

FOUR

TIMING IS EVERYTHING

With retirement plan distributions, that day of reckoning (or pay-back time) has a name. It's called the required beginning date (RBD) when you must start taking your required minimum distribution (RMD) and pay tax on your long-deferred earnings.

For IRA holders, the RBD arrives on the April 1 that follows the year they turn 73. For example, if you turn 73 in January 2024, your RBD falls on April 1, 2025. (April 1 is only for the first year's distribution, however; each subsequent year's distribution must be taken by December 31 of that year.)

Don't forget or ignore your RBD date! If you do, you'll face a 25 per-cent penalty tax on the RMD you were supposed to take but didn't. Fortunately, you can reduce that penalty to 10 percent if you with-draw the missed RMD during a correction window. For most peo-ple, the RMD would need to be taken and a 10 percent penalty paid by the end of the second tax year following the year for which the RMD was missed.

For example, if your RMD is $40,000 and you withdraw nothing from your account by your RBD, you'll get socked with a $10,000 penalty—one-quarter of the $40,000 you didn't withdraw. Ouch and double-ouch; that's no flesh wound. If you take the missed RMD within the correction window, you can reduce your penalty payment to 10 percent, in this case to $4,000. The IRS has been known to be willing to waive the penalty entirely for good cause, but you still must take the missed distribution.

"Then what's the big deal?" you ask. "Why worry about it if the

IRS won't bother trying to catch us? Think about it, man. If there were no tax audits demanding proof of every deduction, we'd claim a zillion deductions! That's the American way."

You have a good point—except that the banks, brokers, insurance companies, mutual fund companies, and other financial institutions holding your IRA money are required to alert you, and the IRS, that a distribution must be taken (and, if you wish, even make the RMD calculation for you).

So, if you've been lax about taking your RMD, or figure on being lax when the time comes with the hope that you'll fall below the IRS radar, think twice—you're already a blip on that screen and could risk losing a fortune.

Getting It Early (Distributions Before Age 59½)

Generally, distributions taken before you reach age 59½ are subject to a 10 percent early distribution penalty. Don't ask me where Congress came up with the number 59½. Maybe we're being used as guinea pigs in a legislative experiment to see if we can still count after we turn 59. Or maybe the ½ was a typo that never got corrected. Whatever the reason, it made it into the Internal Revenue Code, which means it's the law.

The early withdrawal penalty is generally assessed on the amount that is taxable. For example, if you withdraw $5,000 from your IRA at age 40, you will have to pay income tax on that amount as well as a $500 penalty (10 percent of the $5,000 early withdrawal). If only $4,000 of the $5,000 was taxable because you had, say, $1,000 of nondeductible contributions, then the penalty is $400 (10 percent of the $4,000 taxable amount). There are some cases when even a nontaxable distribution can be subject to the 10 percent penalty. That can happen with a Roth IRA if you are under 59½ and withdraw converted funds that have been held for less than five years. While that distribution is not taxable, it is subject to the 10 percent penalty. For details on that anomaly, see "Step #3: Roth It" (Chapter 7).

The idea of penalizing us for hurting ourselves is not just ludicrous but sadistic. We should not have to pay a 10 percent penalty on money that's ours, just because circumstances compel us to dip into our own retirement accounts early. But that's the reality we face.

Typically, people withdraw money early from their retirement accounts because they need it to cover expenses. Then, after paying these expenses, April 15 rolls around, and they find themselves without the money to pay the early withdrawal penalty plus income tax on top of it. And if they can't fork that over to the government, they get hit with more penalties, plus interest on unpaid taxes and penalties. So, what do they do next? If they haven't already depleted their retirement account, they dip back in and take out more or even all that remains to cover the additional unpaid taxes, interest, and penalties. You can see where this is headed, and it ain't good.

Here's another common scenario: A couple decides to borrow from their 401(k) plan, which is allowed since it's not an IRA. They fully intend to repay the borrowed funds, but then the unexpected happens, and suddenly they can't. For example, I know a couple who borrowed from the husband's 401(k) to finance their wedding because they were out of cash from buying a house. Then they couldn't repay the money because the house wound up being a money pit in need of tons of repairs. The funds withdrawn from the husband's 401(k) became taxable and subject to the 10 percent early withdrawal penalty when they couldn't pay it back in time, so they had to dip into the 401(k) for more. It took this couple almost six years to bounce back from the vicious circle they'd gotten themselves into—and it would have taken even longer if some wonderful friends hadn't stepped in to help with loans to get Uncle Sam off their backs. In the end, tapping their retirement savings early left this couple paying a fortune in unnecessary penalties and interest, not to mention federal and state income tax. Worse, they decimated the 401(k) nest egg that they had spent years building up!

Penalty-Free Withdrawals

Some exceptions to the 10 percent early withdrawal penalty now make it a little easier—and, unfortunately, more enticing—to tap our IRA and company plan money early.

These exceptions are sometimes referred to as loopholes, but they are *not* loopholes! You still must pay income tax when you make the withdrawal, and you are still depleting your retirement money. Instead, these are *penalty-free exceptions* that should be used wisely and only as a last resort. Don't misconstrue them as a way to beat the system, or you'll only wind up beating yourself.

The SECURE 2.0 Act not only expands coverage of an existing 10 percent penalty exception but also creates a bevy of new ones. Complicating matters further, these new 10 percent penalty exceptions have different effective dates.

Three Categories of Early Withdrawal Exceptions

Not all exceptions to the 10 percent penalty apply to all plans. Many people who wind up paying the 10 percent penalty do so because the exception they used did not, in fact, apply to their distribution. For example, the age 55 separation from service exception applies only to distributions from company plans and not from IRAs.

Exception categories:

1. Exceptions that apply to distributions from *both* company plans and IRAs
2. Exceptions that apply *only* to distributions from IRAs
3. Exceptions that apply *only* to distributions from company plans

Not knowing which exception applies to which retirement plan can end up being unnecessarily costly.

CAUTION!

Be warned. Be *very warned!* It is rarely a good idea to tap your nest egg before its time. The whole concept of saving tax-free for your golden years is lost if you use your savings for purposes other than retirement. Today's liberalized early-withdrawal rules may be welcome, but they can also become an overpowering lure to spend now what should be saved for later.

IRA AND COMPANY PLAN EXCEPTIONS

1. **Death.** This is the ultimate form of early withdrawal and definitely no way to get a tax break! Nonetheless, as ridiculous as it may seem to be stating the obvious, let's make it official: The IRS does not subject the beneficiary of your IRA, or even your corpse, for that matter, to the early withdrawal penalty. But, as always, plan distributions (early or otherwise) are subject to income tax.

2. **Disability.** There is no 10 percent penalty for an early withdrawal if you need the money because *you* are "disabled"—which the tax code defines as your being "unable to engage in any substantial gainful activity by reason of any medically determinable physical or mental impairment which can be expected to result in death or to be of long-continued and indefinite duration." It's not enough to say that you fit this profile, either; the IRS requires you to prove it with a physical or psychological assessment by a doctor.

3. **Medical expenses.** Penalty-free early withdrawals can be made if the funds are used to pay unreimbursed medical expenses

exceeding 7.5 percent of your adjusted gross income (AGI). Furthermore, you do not have to itemize deductions on your income taxes to qualify for this break. That's good, since under the current tax rules most people will no longer be itemizing their deductions. Unless you have major-dollar medical expenses, you'll likely be using the increased standard deduction. To qualify for the penalty exception here, the medical expenses must be paid in the same year the distribution was taken.

4. **Annuitizing.** This tax break is referred to as the "72(t)" exception. It allows you to escape the early withdrawal penalty by taking your distributions each year in what the tax code calls a "series of substantially equal periodic payments." This process boils down to annuitizing your account balance and taking withdrawals over a 5-year period or until you reach age 59½, whichever is longer. The payout amount is determined by your single life expectancy or by the joint life expectancy of you and your beneficiary, according to IRS actuarial tables. During the payout period, you cannot change the payment schedule formula; if you do, you'll be hit with the 10 percent penalty, which will be assessed retroactively, as if you never qualified for the 72(t) exception in the first place. For company plans, this exception applies only *after* you have separated from service. For IRAs, this exception applies at any time, regardless of whether you are still working. (See Chapter 11 for extensive discussion of the 72[t] exception.)

5. **IRS tax levy.** There is no such thing as creditor protection from the IRS. If you can't pay your taxes, the IRS can legally snatch your retirement savings to cover them. This is called an IRS tax levy, and it is serious business. If the IRS does levy your retirement account, the withdrawal, if made before you turn 59½, will not be subject to the 10 percent penalty; the seizure itself would still be subject to regular income tax, however. Too bad you can't hire the IRS to collect from people

who owe you money. There would be no such thing as accounts receivable.

6. **Active reservists' exception.** Distributions to military reservists from IRAs, 401(k)s, or 403(b)s taken before reaching age 59½ are penalty-free if the reservist was called to active duty for more than 179 days, and the distribution is taken between the date of the call-up and the end of the active-duty period.

The provision also allows the prior early distributions to be rolled back (repaid) to an IRA within two years of the end of the active service. For example, a distribution taken by a qualifying reservist whose active duty ended on July 12, 2023, can be rolled back to an IRA up until July 12, 2025.

Repayments will have no effect on the annual IRA contribution limits. They can be made in addition to the regular IRA contributions for that year and will not cause an excess contribution. But the repayments are not deductible, so presumably that will create a basis to keep track of on Form 8606 so that eventual distributions of these funds will be tax-free. Given that complication, it might be a better idea to make these repayments to a Roth IRA.

7. **Birth or adoption exception.** The SECURE Act created a new exception to the 10 percent early distribution penalty for "qualified birth or adoption distributions." The exception applies to both IRA and employer plan distributions.

A distribution is qualified if it is made from an IRA or employer plan within one year of the date of birth or finalized adoption. There is a $5,000 lifetime (not annual) limit per birth or adoption on penalty-free withdrawals. The exception applies only to distributions made after the adoption of a child younger than age 18 or physically or mentally incapable of self-support. Although a qualified distribution may be penalty-free, it is still subject to tax.

A married couple can *each* take $5,000 per child. There is no requirement that the distributions be used for birth or adoption expenses, and the distributions can be repaid within three years.

Example 1:
Dan and Kim, both under age 59½, are the proud parents of new son, Jake. One month after Jake's birth, Dan takes a $5,000 penalty-free distribution from his 401(k) plan. Two months later, Kim takes a $5,000 penalty-free distribution from her IRA.

Example 2:
Mark and Maya are 55-year-old foster parents to two boys: 17-year-old Jack and 24-year-old James. James is mentally incapable of self-support. Mark and Maya decide to officially adopt both Jack and James, and the adoption process is finalized on June 1, 2024. Mark and Maya each withdraw $10,000 ($20,000 combined total) from their IRAs before June 1, 2025. Since the withdrawals are qualified, Mark and Maya will not have to pay the 10 percent early withdrawal penalty, but they will be taxed on the withdrawals.

Mark and Maya did their homework. Both Jack and James are eligible adoptees since Jack is under age 18 and James is physically or mentally incapable of self-support.

Additionally, Maya's younger brother Ray (the boys' new uncle) wants to help support the newest family members. Ray is 52. If Ray takes a $5,000 distribution from his IRA, he cannot leverage the birth or adoption penalty exception. Unless another exception applies, Ray will be subject to a $500 early distribution penalty in addition to tax on the $5,000. Even if Ray gives the money to Maya to directly help care for the adopted boys, he does not qualify because he is not the adoptive parent.

Withdrawals from an employer plan can be repaid back to the same plan (but only if the employee is still eligible to participate in the plan) or to an IRA. Withdrawals from an IRA can be repaid only to an IRA—not to a plan. Any repayments will be treated as a direct trustee-to-trustee transfer, and repayments to an employer plan will be treated as an eligible rollover distribution.

The SECURE Act does not specify the tax treatment of qualified birth or adoption distributions that are repaid. Since the taxpayer has already been taxed on the withdrawal, it can be assumed that the repayment would create basis—funds that won't be taxable when withdrawn.

As an analogy, the Pension Protection Act of 2006 created another exception to the 10 percent early distribution penalty (which we just discussed) for "qualified reservist distributions" and allowed those distributions to be repaid. If the IRS treats birth or adoption withdrawals the same way, then the taxpayer would have to keep track of basis (on Form 8606 for IRA repayments and in the employer plan for plan repayments) to ensure that the eventual distribution of the repaid funds is tax-free.

While this seems like a good idea, remember that even if the withdrawal is penalty-free, it is still taxable, which will lessen the amount parents can spend. One worry here is that parents may get the $5,000, spend it, and then not have funds left to cover the taxes the following year, when many new parents need still more money. This sounds like a good provision, but it could end up adding to financial woes. The retirement account is meant for retirement; generally speaking, it should be used only as a last resort for anything else. Other nonretirement funds should be used first if possible. But if withdrawal *is* necessary, it's a good idea to contribute those funds back to the retirement account if they become available later.

8. **Federally declared disasters.** The SECURE 2.0 Act makes permanent an exception for federally declared disasters. You may withdraw up to $22,000 (aggregate) from your IRA or

employer plan if your principal residence is located in the disaster area, an economic loss was sustained, and the withdrawal is taken within 180 days of the first day of the disaster (or when the disaster was declared, if later). In addition to these distributions being penalty-free, the income from such distribution may be spread equally over three years. Also, qualifying withdrawals may be repaid at any time during the three-year period beginning after the day of the distribution.

Historically, this type of disaster relief was administered on an ad hoc basis. While Congress has stitched together several relief packages for different natural disasters around the country, some victims, such as those of Superstorm Sandy in the Northeast, were denied assistance. This SECURE 2.0 provision should reduce the need for legislators to address every new hurricane, wildfire, or flood, while also making a uniform penalty exception available to all future qualifying victims.

Example:
Diane's home is located in a declared disaster area. A landslide destroyed her house, and her tour business took a hit when tourists stopped coming due to the damage. Diane decides to take a penalty-free qualified disaster distribution of $22,000 from her IRA. She has the option of including the income from the distribution spread equally over a three-year period. She also can repay the distribution within three years.

9. **Terminal illness.** SECURE 2.0 creates a new penalty exception for those who are certified by a physician as having a terminal illness. While the standard definition of "terminal illness" includes language dictating it is "reasonably expected to result in death in 24 months or less," this new exception increases that period to 84 months (seven years). You can repay any distribution you take under this exception within three years. There is no maximum limit on how much you can withdraw penalty-free.

Example:

Luigi, age 48, runs a highly successful contracting company that specializes in asbestos mitigation. Sadly, after years of exposure and heavy smoking, Luigi contracts cancer. His doctors all agree that he has fewer than seven years to live. Before he gets too sick, Luigi wants to take his extended family on a once-in-lifetime private cruise and Mediterranean vacation. Luigi withdraws $250,000 from his IRA to cover flights, food, wine, and the private yacht. He leverages the terminal illness 10 percent exception to avoid what would otherwise have been a $25,000 penalty if the exception had not existed. The full $250,000 will be taxable in the year Luigi takes the distribution. If he wishes to repay all or part of the $250,000 within three years, he can do so.

10. **Domestic abuse.** A new 10 percent penalty exception was created by SECURE 2.0 for victims of domestic abuse by a spouse or domestic partner that occurred within the previous 12 months. You can self-certify that you experienced domestic abuse and withdraw the lesser of $10,000, indexed for inflation, or 50 percent of the vested balance of your account.

"Domestic abuse" is defined as physical, psychological, sexual, emotional, or economic abuse, including efforts to control, isolate, humiliate, or intimidate the victim, or to undermine the victim's ability to reason independently, including by means of abuse of the victim's child or another family member living in the household. You can repay a distribution taken under the domestic abuse exception within three years.

Example:

Linda, age 36, has been stuck in an abusive relationship for years. Her live-in boyfriend abuses her physically and threatens her children. Linda's friends keep telling her to get out, but Linda has little money to escape the situation because her boyfriend strictly monitors her checking account. She does have a small 401(k) at her place of employment. Finally determined to leave the relationship, Linda meets with her plan administrator, who says her vested plan balance totals $20,000. Linda takes a full domestic abuse distribution of $10,000. She gathers up her children and escapes the abusive situation. Linda opens a new bank account and uses the $10,000 to start a new life. Linda understands that the $10,000 will be taxable in the year of the distribution, but she thinks that is a small price to pay for her freedom.

11. **Financial emergencies.** Although extremely limited, SECURE 2.0 provides an exception for certain distributions necessary to meet "unforeseeable or immediate financial needs relating to personal or family emergencies." You can self-certify as to eligibility. Distributions using the financial emergency exception are limited to a maximum amount of $1,000, once per calendar year. Additionally, you may not take any other emergency distributions in the following three years, unless you repay the original distribution or if your future employee contributions (for plans) or contributions (for IRAs) exceed the amount of the previous emergency distribution.

Example:
Melissa is a participant in a 401(k) plan at her work. In December 2024, her son breaks his leg in a sledding accident, and Melissa needs emergency funds for his surgery. She informs her plan administrator that she would like to take a $1,000 financial emergency distribution. In January 2025, Melissa needs additional funds to cover caretakers during her son's recovery. However, until she repays the original $1,000 emergency distribution in full, or until she makes enough employee contributions into the plan to replace the original $1,000 withdrawal, she cannot again leverage the financial emergency penalty exception.

IRA-ONLY EXCEPTIONS

1. **Higher education.** Early withdrawals from IRAs (including Roth IRAs) are penalty-free if used to pay expenses for higher education—college, graduate school, vocational school, or any other "post-secondary-educational schooling"—for yourself, your spouse, a child, or a grandchild. Qualifying expenses include tuition, room and board, fees, books, supplies, plus equipment used for enrollment or attendance. Additionally, funds to cover the purchase of computers and related equipment, software, and fees for internet access (if used primarily by a student during any of the years they are in school) qualify for penalty-free IRA distributions. If, for example, you're paying tuition bills for a child, he or she does not have to live with you or even be a dependent for you to take an early withdrawal from your IRA penalty-free.

This break for education is allowable only for courses being taken now or in the near future, however. The education expenses must be paid in the same year the distribution was taken. For example, if you withdraw money early from your IRA to cover some old education bills, you'll be hit with a penalty.

Also, you can take advantage of this exclusion only for education expenses in excess of scholarships that have been earned, veteran's benefits that have been received, or U.S. savings bonds redeemed for that purpose. Amounts paid for education from a Coverdell Education Savings Account (formerly called an Education IRA), tax-free scholarship, employer-provided educational assistance, and any other tax-free benefit cannot be included. Furthermore, only distributions up to the amount of the education expenses paid are exempt from the 10 percent penalty. For example, if you've got $6,000 of qualifying education expenses and $2,000 will be covered by tax-free funds paid from an employer-provided assistance plan, the remaining $4,000 can come out of your IRA without incurring an early withdrawal penalty. But if you withdraw more than that amount from your IRA, only the $4,000 would still be exempt from the penalty if no other exception applied.

CAUTION!

Although taking an early withdrawal from a Roth IRA for school expenses qualifies you for the higher-education break too, it's possible to fall into a trap here and wind up paying tax on part of the withdrawal. Here's how: Let's say you're younger than 59½ and have accumulated $15,000 in a Roth IRA as follows: $12,000 in original contributions and $3,000 of earnings. If you just need the $12,000, you don't even have to worry about qualifying for the education break because your original con-tribution (the principal) can be taken out at any time, for any purpose, tax-free. However, should you need the whole $15,000, you'd still be able to take out the $12,000 tax-free but would have to pay regular income tax on the remaining $3,000 be-cause that money is made up of earnings, not principal. The same caution flag applies to regular IRAs as well, because even if you escape the penalty, you still pay income tax on the total amount withdrawn early (unless part of that total consists of nondeductible contributions). All in all, this may not seem like a bad deal in order to gain penalty-free, early access to your account to defray education costs—but there's a major down-side you might not be thinking about: You will, of course, have emptied your entire retirement account in the process!

2. **First-time homebuyer.** You can take an early withdrawal of up to $10,000 from an IRA penalty-free to help pay for a first home. Well, strictly speaking, not necessarily the *first* home you've ever owned; the tax code defines *first-time homebuyer* as anyone who has not owned a home for two years prior to

the early withdrawal. In other words (it's amazing how often one must resort to using this phrase when explaining the tax code), if you sold your last home three years ago and have been renting ever since, then you qualify as a first-time home-buyer under the tax code and are entitled to take an early withdrawal from your IRA penalty-free. The $10,000 is a once-in-a-lifetime maximum, which is why it really doesn't pay to use this exemption to buy a home. Given today's housing prices, $10,000 would likely barely cover closing costs. And to get that penalty-free 10 grand, you'll have to pay the associated income tax, which means you'd be lucky to be left with $7,000 of the $10,000 after taxes. Plus, you'd probably end up spending the entire $10,000 on new-home-buying expenses (which never end), thereby digging yourself into a hole—because come April 15, you'd have to cough up the $3,000 owed that you've already spent. So, it's not a good idea to tap your retirement account to buy a home.

But if you must, you must. Remember, though, whatever you withdraw from your IRA for home-buying purposes must be used exclusively to "buy, build, or rebuild that first home," which the code defines as your "principal residence." If you're married, your spouse must fit the first-time-homebuyer profile as well. It may seem like a given that he or she would since you're married and, one presumes, living together, but those little devils who write the tax code try to think of every possible scenario for grabbing your money.

For example, let's say you owned a home for five years, sold it, and moved into an apartment. A few years later, you get married and move into your spouse's house. Then the two of you decide to buy a new home of your own together, tapping your IRAs early for partial financing. Under this scenario, you and your spouse wouldn't be able to take advantage of the first-time-homebuyer tax break because *each of you must qualify for it individually.*

> ## LOOPHOLE ALERT!
>
> Here's how to double your pleasure with the first-time-homebuyer tax break. If you're a qualifying married couple and you buy the home jointly, each of you can withdraw $10,000 from your IRA, bringing the penalty-free amount you can use to $20,000! So, forget the prenuptial agreement and instead make sure that you marry someone who won't blow this tax break for you!

Here's another hitch to the first-time-homebuyer tax break: You must use the IRA money toward the purchase of that home within 120 days of the withdrawal. If for some reason the deal goes south, and the purchase doesn't take place, you can put the money back in your IRA without penalty, if you do that within the 120 days.

Run that by you again? OK, let's see how this works with some numbers. Let's say you turned 40 in 2014. Assume you made IRA contributions of $2,000 a year over the subsequent 10 years. In 2024, you turn 50, and your IRA is worth $25,000 ($20,000 from contributions plus $5,000 of earnings). On May 1, 2024, you withdraw $10,000 from your IRA to use as part of a down payment for a home under the first-time-homebuyer provision, and the closing takes place on June 1. You pay regular tax on the distributed funds but no penalty, as the funds were used for their intended purpose within 120 days of the withdrawal. And under this scenario, if the account is a Roth IRA, the entire $10,000 distribution would also be income-tax-free.

Now here's another example using the same facts, except that the closing takes place on September 30. Here, the $10,000 early distribution from your IRA wouldn't qualify for the first-time-homebuyer exception because the funds weren't used within 120 days of their withdrawal on May 1. With a Roth IRA, however, the $10,000 early distribution would still be free of both income tax and penalty because it came out of your original $20,000 in contributions and didn't cut into the $5,000 of accumulated earnings. Got it? Good. Now here's hoping you've bought yourself a good one!

3. **Unemployment/health insurance.** If you're out of work, you can take an early distribution penalty-free up to the amount used to pay for health insurance. To qualify as unemployed, the tax rules say you must have received, or be receiving, state or federal unemployment benefits for 12 consecutive weeks. To get the penalty-free break, the early distribution must be used to pay your health insurance in either the year you received unemployment benefits or the year after. Self-employed individuals can also be out of work and need health insurance; if so, they can get this penalty-free break too, even though they generally do not receive unemployment benefits.

COMPANY-PLAN-ONLY EXCEPTIONS

1. **Age 55.** As you'll recall from Chapter 3, if you turn age 55 or older in the year you retire or leave your employer, withdrawals from your company plan are not subject to the 10 percent penalty. The exception does not apply, however, if you retire before age 55 but take no distributions until you reach age 55. For example, if you leave your job at age 52, but take no distributions from your company plan until you are 56, the 10 percent penalty kicks in (unless you qualify for another exception). Also, if you leave your job at age 55 and roll the company plan funds over to an IRA and then withdraw from the IRA before age 59½, you will be subject to the 10 percent penalty—because the age-55 exception applies only to distributions from company plans.

2. **Age 50.** This works similarly to the age-55 exception except that it applies at age 50 to government plan distributions taken by federal, state, and local public-safety employees (law enforcement officers, firefighters, emergency medical service workers); certain customs officials, Border Protection officers, air traffic controllers, nuclear materials couriers, U.S. Capitol Police, Supreme Court Police, and diplomatic security special agents of the Department of State; and private-sector firefighters and corrections officers who are employees of state and local governments. If that's you, then, like the age-55 exception, this applies only if you separate from service at age 50 or older. (Note that SECURE 2.0 allows the age-50 exception to be used even before you turn 50, provided that you have put in 25 years by the time you separate from service.)

Example:

Vince is a Border Protection officer. He joined the force at age 22. Now Vince is 47 and wants to retire due to health concerns, but the bulk of his assets are tied up in his workplace retirement plan. Prior to SECURE 2.0, Vince would have had to wait to separate from service in, or after, the year he turned 50 in order to access his work plan dollars without penalty. However, with the expansion of the age-50 exception, Vince can leave his job at 47 and still take advantage of the age-50 exception because he has 25 years of service with the employer sponsoring the plan.

3. **Section 457(b) plans.** Early distributions from 457(b) plans (deferred compensation plans) are not subject to the 10 percent early withdrawal penalty, but they are subject to income tax at distribution time.

SO, YOU THINK YOU'VE SPOTTED A LOOPHOLE?

Q: Since withdrawals before age 59½ from 457(b) plans are not subject to the 10 percent penalty, and the rollover rules spelled out in the last chapter say that you can roll over your taxable IRA funds to a company plan, including a 457(b), then why don't I roll over my IRA to my 457(b)? Then I'll be able to withdraw that money from the 457(b) penalty-free and beat the IRS. This sounds too easy!

A: That's because it won't work. It's true that you can roll over your taxable IRA funds to your company plan, including a 457(b), but only if the plan allows this—it doesn't have to. But even then, Tax Code Section 72(t)(9) specifically states that when IRA funds are rolled over to a 457(b) plan, any withdrawals of those funds will be subject to the 10 percent penalty (if you are under age 59½ and no other exceptions apply), the same as if you withdrew those funds from your IRA. So, rolling them over won't get you off the hook.

Q: But once the IRA funds are in my 457(b) plan, how will anyone know which funds I'm withdrawing?

A: The IRS and the plan will know because one of the conditions for the rollover is that the company plan must keep a separate accounting of the IRA funds you rolled over. In other words, Big Brother will be watching!

4. **Divorce.** If any part of your company plan is paid to an ex-spouse as an alternate payee under what is called a qualified domestic relations order (QDRO), this distribution will not be subject to the 10 percent penalty; or if the funds are transferred from your company plan to the ex-spouse's IRA, you, the plan participant, will not be taxed on either type of distribution. Instead, the ex-spouse will pay the tax (and potential

10 percent penalty) when he or she withdraws from the IRA. IRAs split in a divorce get the same treatment except that a QDRO is not the controlling document; a divorce or separate-maintenance decree would be used. Once the IRA is transferred to the ex-spouse, the IRA is treated as if it were the ex-spouse's IRA. The IRA can only be transferred either by changing the name on the IRA account from one spouse to the other spouse, or through a direct transfer. If the transfer is not done according to the divorce agreement, the withdrawal is taxable to the spouse owner who made the distribution and any funds given to the ex-spouse will be tax-free to the ex-spouse only—but the funds can no longer be transferred to the ex-spouse's IRA.

5. **Pension-linked emergency savings accounts.** A new type of account established by SECURE 2.0 called a pension-linked emergency savings account, allows distributions that are not subject to the 10 percent penalty. Optional for employers to install, these are designed to separate an employee's long-term retirement dollars from short-term emergency needs. The name is somewhat misleading, however. These new accounts are not stand-alone accounts nor are they linked to proverbial pension plans, but rather can be attached to a defined contribution plan—like a 401(k) or 403(b).

Pension-linked emergency savings accounts are available only to employees who are eligible to participate in the employer's plan and who are not "highly compensated" (meaning that they do not own more than 5 percent of the company, did not receive compensation from the business of more than $150,000, indexed for inflation, and were not in the top 20 percent of employees when ranked by compensation).

Employers may automatically opt employees into these accounts. Contributions are made on a Roth-like basis and are eligible for employer matching contributions. The amount you can contribute (not counting any match) is capped at $2,500 (or lower, as set by your employer).

6. **Qualified long-term care distributions.** This new exception created by SECURE 2.0, which takes effect December 29, 2025 (effectively 2026, though, since it's unlikely anyone will do this in the last two days of 2025), will allow you to take penalty-free distributions to pay the premiums for certain long-term care contracts. You will be limited to the lesser of $2,500 annually (indexed for inflation) or 10 percent of your vested account balance.

Of course, there are qualifying requirements. A *long-term care premium statement* must be filed with the plan, which must include the name and tax ID of the insurance company, a statement that the coverage is certified long-term care insurance, proof that the participant is the owner of the policy, what premiums are owed, and the relationship of the covered individual to the plan participant. As for "relationship," coverage for the spouse of the plan participant will qualify if the couple files a joint tax return.

THE 60-DAY LOAN

I referred to this in "Talking the Talk" and again in Chapter 3, but let's delve more deeply into "the 60-day loan." No matter how old you are, you can take money out of your IRA for a 60-day rollover once every 12 months. You can use that money for any reason, with no penalty or tax *provided that, within 60 days of the withdrawal, you return the same amount of money to the account or to another IRA account you own.* If you don't, the IRS hits you with the 10 percent penalty (assuming it was an early withdrawal) and, unless the account is a Roth IRA, you'll pay income tax on the distribution, as well. In other words, this tax break works only for those who need short-term cash and are absolutely positive they can replace that cash within 60 days—otherwise it could turn into a very expensive loan. This once-a-year rule does not apply to company plans. If the plan allows it, you can do as many company plan rollovers as you wish.

Keep in mind that you can take advantage of the 60-day, tax-free withdrawal only once a year. This one-year period is not necessarily a calendar year, unless you receive your IRA funds on January 1. The one-year period starts on the date you receive the funds from your IRA, not on the day you put them back. Be careful about going the 60-day loan route. Go back and review the 60-day and once-per-year rollover rules in Chapter 3, where they are covered in detail. I don't want you running afoul of these expensive tax traps. The rules are rigid, with little latitude other than the allowable "frozen-deposit" excuse whereby your IRA funds may become frozen because of insolvency problems suffered by the bank or financial institution holding them. The IRS has been granted authority to extend the 60-day rule in other special situations. (The 60-day rule also applies to spousal rollovers covered later in this chapter and to Roth conversions. See Chapter 7.)

The Sweet Spot: After 59½ but Before 73

This scenario is easy because there are no rules. It's an IRA free-for-all. You can withdraw any amount you wish any time you wish between the days you turn 59½ and 73 without incurring an IRS penalty of any kind.

For example, you can take a distribution of $500,000 at age 63 and then not withdraw again until your *required beginning date (RBD)* when you turn 73. Yes, you'll pay income tax on the $500,000 withdrawal, but the IRS won't pour any additional salt in that wound.

Think of this period of relatively rule-free bliss—the calm before the storm, or what I call "The Sweet Spot." Soon you'll be entering another dimension, a shadowy dimension where the shadows have shadows: the dimension of required minimum distributions after age 73, otherwise known as "the *Twilight Zone* of taxation."

Required Minimum Distributions (RMDs)

After Age 73 (Lifetime Distributions)

Remember what I wrote at the beginning of this chapter about payback? That after all those years of getting tax breaks, tax time will, indeed, come? Well, that day has arrived.

RMD Age Raised from 70½ to 72 to 73

For most of this book I have knocked Congress for changing many of the retirement tax rules to our detriment, but fair is fair. I have to say that the single best provision in the SECURE Act is finally getting rid of that half year that has confused seniors for decades. Thanks, Congress. No more half year to think about. And SECURE 2.0 raised the RMD age once again. Now, when it comes to RMDs, it's simply age 73! (Note that SECURE 2.0 stipulates the RMD age will ultimately go up to 75, but that won't happen until 2033.)

Which RMD Age Do I Use?

The SECURE Act raised the age for beginning required minimum distributions (RMDs) to age 72 for all retirement accounts subject to RMDs. SECURE 2.0 then raised the age to 73, and to age 75 in 2033. Which RMD age do you use? The best way to determine that is to look at your birthday. After all, most people know the year they were born, don't they? The first RMD can be delayed until April 1 of the year after the account owner reaches their applicable RMD age.

Which RMD age to use?

Age 72 (or 70 ½)	Born 1950 or earlier
Age 73	Born 1951–1959
Age 75	Born 1960 or later

Example:

Robert turns 73 in 2024 so his first RMD year is 2024, but for the first year only, Robert can delay his RMD until *April 1st* of the following year, which is 2025. But that is still his 2024 RMD. If he delays it until 2025, he must still take his 2025 RMD by year end. This results in two taxable RMDs coming out in the same year. This may not be the best outcome for Robert.

Unrelated to the SECURE Act, but effective as of 2022, are updated life expectancy tables for calculating RMDs, replacing the 2002 updates. You can find it on page 126.

You've turned 73. Congratulations! As a birthday present, Congress has gift wrapped for you the most complex set of tax rules ever written (assuming they *were* written and didn't just bubble up from some cauldron in the congressional kitchen). These "IRA distribution rules" (which apply to most company plans, as well) will govern the rest of your retirement savings life, and sorting them out makes deciphering the Rosetta Stone seem like a cakewalk. But you must understand these rules, or you will risk the IRS absconding with your retirement savings legally through a combination of draconian penalties, income and possible estate taxes, and your own state's punitive tax measures.

Whether you want to or not, you must start taking distributions from your retirement account as of your required beginning date (RBD), which is generally April 1 of the year following the year you turn 73.

The process of how the IRS calculates your RBD is a bit bewildering (I'll "unbewilder" it for you in a moment), but each year thereafter another distribution is required, then another—a sequence of events that won't come to an end until you do . . . unless, of course, you outlive your retirement savings.

RBD Exceptions

There are some exceptions to the rules that will allow you to delay taking your RMD after your required beginning date:

▪ **Still working.** You first heard about this provision in Chapter 3. Now let's examine the guts of it. If you are still working for a company (and own no more than a 5 percent interest in that company), you can delay required distributions until April 1 of the year following your retirement date. (While most company plans offer this still-working option, they are not required to. It's an optional provision.) There is no age limit on this exception if you are still working. You can even work just part time. Nothing in the tax code says you must work full time or for any minimum number of hours to qualify for this exception. It just says "still working."

For example, let's assume that you turned 73 in 2024 and are an employee of, say, Google. It's not your company, so you don't own more than 5 percent of it (you only wish you did!), but you're a participant in Google's 401(k) plan. Normally, your RBD would be April 1, 2025, but you figure Google's stock price is bound to go up eventually, so you keep working. This means you can delay RMDs in the 401(k) until April 1 of the year following your retirement. Fast-forward 26 years. It is now 2050 and you are 99 years old, so you hang it up finally and wheeze into your rocking chair. Your RBD for the 401(k) will be the following April 1 (2051). This means that you do not have to take any RMDs from the 401(k) until that time. Think how much your 401(k) will have grown in the interim, and how much you'll have to live on when you really get old!

> ## CAUTION!
>
> The "still-working" exception does not apply to IRAs or to plans of former employers, only to the plan of the company for which you are still working. Therefore, even though you are, in fact, still working, albeit somewhere else, you must begin distributions from those other plans by your age 73 RBD. If you do not, you will be subject to the 25 percent penalty on the amount(s) you should have withdrawn from those plans but didn't.

∎ **403(b) plans: old and new money.** You can delay taking "old-money" distributions from a 403(b) plan until you turn 75. *Old money* in this case does not mean cash passed down from J. Paul Getty, but money you put into your 403(b) before 1987. Required distributions on this pre-1987 balance can be postponed until you're 75. The remaining balance (i.e., all post-December 31, 1986, contributions, aka *new money*) must follow the required distribution rules for age 73. If the 403(b) plan contract is transferred to another 403(b) plan, the exclusion from required distributions for pre-1987 account balances is retained as long as the new 403(b) plan tracks the December 31, 1986, account balance, making it clear which funds are the pre-1987 funds. Old money that is distributed and rolled over to an IRA loses the age-75 exception, however.

CAUTION!

Delaying old-money distributions may save you in taxes in the short run but can cost your beneficiaries a mint down the road if your 403(b) plan beneficiary is not your spouse. How so? If you die before reaching 75 and your beneficiary is a nonspouse (your child, for example), he or she will be faced with the full complexity of the rules for getting the funds out of the 403(b) and into a properly titled, inherited IRA (or inherited Roth IRA).

The first issue to address is that a nonspouse beneficiary must be named on the 403(b) beneficiary form. Second, a nonspouse beneficiary must know to do a direct transfer (meaning not touch or spend the money during the transfer process) of the inherited 403(b) funds to an inherited IRA. And third, he or she must do the transfer by the end of the year after your death. Additionally, if the beneficiary is an eligible designated beneficiary* (who still qualifies for the stretch IRA), the first RMD must be taken by the end of the year after your death. Beneficiaries who miss any of these steps get stuck with whatever the 403(b) options are. So, do your nonspouse beneficiaries a favor and just transfer the 403(b) account to an IRA as soon as possible, and don't forget to complete your beneficiary form. Then, if you don't make it to age 75, all your EDB has to do is transfer your IRA funds to an inherited IRA, allowing the funds to be stretched over his or her lifetime, or more likely over 10 years (if not an EDB), which is what most nonspouse beneficiaries will end up with under the SECURE Act payout rules.

*The term "eligible designated beneficiary" (EDB) was made up by Congress as part of the SECURE Act to identify those beneficiaries who still qualify for the stretch IRA, which was eliminated for most nonspouse beneficiaries. You will find all the details in Step #2: SECURE It (Chapters 5 and 6).

▪ **Grace period.** For your first-year age 73 RMD, you're allowed a grace period to take your withdrawal. All future distributions, however, must be taken by the end of the distribution year. For example, if your 73 year is 2024, you can wait until April 1, 2025, to take your 2024 distribution, but you must also take your year-2025 distribution by the end of 2025 and so on. There is no grace period for distributions beyond the first year.

▪ **Penury.** What happens if the market takes such a dive that your retirement account balance won't even cover your required distribution? Well, in the past the IRS never considered the possibility that a retirement account could decline in value (hahahahaha!), and so it would still impose the formerly 50, but now 25 percent penalty for nonwithdrawal even if there were nothing in the account to withdraw. The IRS addressed this matter and years ago inserted a single sentence in the regulations that I call "The Enron Effect Clause," which says that if the value of your IRA or plan has dropped so much that your RMD amount exceeds your entire account balance, then you can simply empty the account without penalty. In other words, the IRS has a heart after all—it won't make you withdraw more than you actually have and penalize you if you don't. Your RMD is limited to your account balance. So, if you withdraw the remaining balance in your IRA, that will satisfy your RMD for the year—and future years, since there is nothing left. For example, say that by the time you plan to withdraw your RMD, the balance of your $1 million IRA has declined to almost nothing. The IRS says you don't have to withdraw the RMD calculated on the $1 million that's no longer there, but the RMD will be limited to the balance that's left (if anything), and you will be exempt from the RMD penalty forevermore. Of course, you will also be broke.

TAX TRAP!

If you turn 73 in 2024, your RBD is April 1, 2025. If you wait to take your first required withdrawal until 2025 (when you must also take your second), this will cause a bunching up of your first-year and second-year required distributions into one tax year (because all distributions after the first one must be taken by the end of the distribution year). The result will most likely be an overall increase in your income tax. This double-distribution situation can happen only for the first and second RMDs (required minimum distributions), and only if you wait until after your first distribution year to take your first RMD. The better route is to take your first required distribution by the end of your 73 year. This will spread your first two RMDs over two separate tax years and likely result in a lower tax bite each year.

The 3.8 percent additional tax on net investment income does not apply to distributions or any gains sheltered inside retirement plans. However, while income from an RMD is not subject to the 3.8 percent tax, that increased income could push you over the income limit and cause your net investment income to be subject to the extra tax (see "Talking the Talk").

MAJOR TAX TRAP!

Here's the biggest incentive for staying on top of the RBD rules and making sure that you withdraw the right amount at the right time from your plan: *The IRS will take 25 percent of your retirement savings if you mess up.* Even though in SECURE 2.0 Congress reduced this RMD penalty from 50 percent, it is still one of the worst tax penalties ever conceived by Congress. It subjects you to a 25 percent penalty on the amount of your RMD that you failed to withdraw. This 25 percent penalty is reduced to 10 percent if you take the missed withdrawal in a "timely" manner (generally within two years), but that is still significant. For example, if your RMD is $20,000 and you withdraw only $6,000, you will have to pay a $3,500 penalty, as you were short by $14,000, and 25 percent of $14,000 = $3,500. It's easy to see how you could wipe out a lifetime's worth of savings by falling into this tax trap alone. Even death doesn't erase the 25 percent RMD penalty. It applies to your beneficiaries as well. So, never miss a required distribution.

Calculating Your Required Minimum Distribution

Now that you know *when* you must start withdrawals after age 73, you need to know exactly *how much* you'll be required to withdraw. You can always withdraw more each year, but you cannot take less. Otherwise, you'll be left strumming those 25-percent-penalty blues.

Here's how to make the calculation.

Determine Your Account Balance

RMDs are based on your account balance as of December 31 of the year before you take that first distribution. For example, if you turned 73 in 2024, you would determine all your retirement account balances as of December 31, 2023. IRAs and other plan balances you may have inherited are figured separately and will be covered later in this chapter.

If you own a Roth IRA, that balance is not included in your total either, since Roth IRA owners are not subject to required distributions. Similarly, spouse beneficiaries who roll an inherited Roth IRA into their own Roth IRA, or who treat the inherited Roth as their own, are exempt from required distributions too, but non-spouse Roth IRA beneficiaries are not exempt from taking them.

If you have multiple IRA accounts you must compute the required distribution separately for each of them, but the total required amount can be withdrawn from any one or a combination of those accounts (see "Keeping Track of Multiple-Account RMDs," page 144 of this chapter). Withdrawing from a beneficiary IRA, however, cannot satisfy the RMD on your own IRA. The RMD on the inherited IRA must be calculated separately and withdrawn only from that account or from another beneficiary IRA that you inherited from the same person. If you have beneficiary IRAs from different decedents, you cannot combine those RMDs. Each beneficiary account from a different decedent must be figured and withdrawn separately.

Like IRAs, 403(b) RMDs can be combined for distribution, but you cannot satisfy your required IRA distribution by withdrawing from your 403(b) plan or vice versa.

If you have more than one qualified plan, such as several 401(k)s, RMDs must be figured for each plan and withdrawn respectively from that account. For example, if you have four different 401(k) plans, you must withdraw the required amount from each plan. You cannot withdraw from one plan to satisfy the RMD on another plan even though they are both 401(k)s. That aggregation can be done only with IRAs and 403(b)s. If you have several accounts within a particular 401(k) plan, however, you can withdraw the required amount from any one of those accounts.

You cannot satisfy your RMD from a traditional IRA by withdrawing from a Roth IRA or vice versa. Roth IRA beneficiaries who are subject to required distributions must withdraw from the Roth IRA. They can aggregate only Roth IRAs inherited from the same person.

Determine Your Life Expectancy

Having determined your IRA balance as of the end of the previous year, you must next determine your life expectancy based on your age in the RMD year. The greater your life expectancy, the lower your RMD will be, and the less income tax you will pay. To get your life expectancy, refer to what is known as the Uniform Lifetime Table (Figure 3, page 126). This table is used for calculating the IRA owner's RMDs no matter who your beneficiary is—unless your sole beneficiary for an entire year is your spouse and your spouse is more than 10 years your junior. This is known as the *spousal exception.*

Spousal Exception RMD Calculation

The spousal exception requires you to refer to the IRS Joint Life Expectancy Tables available online at the IRS website (www.irs .gov). To calculate your RMD, go to Publication 590-B for the combined life expectancy of you and your spouse. For example, if Mickey is 75 and his spouse, Minnie, his sole beneficiary for the entire year, is 58, the spousal exception applies, so Mickey would look up the combined life expectancy of a 75-year-old and a 58-year-old in the IRS Joint Life Expectancy Table.

When the spousal exception was first introduced in the proposed Regs, many people questioned what would happen if the spouse (and sole beneficiary) dies or gets divorced during that year. The Final Regs answered this question with a provision stating that marital status is determined as of January 1. So, if Minnie dies during the year, and a new beneficiary is named, the spousal exception still applies; Minnie will still be considered the sole beneficiary for purposes of calculating that year's required distribution, *but not the distribution for the following year.* If there is a divorce during the year, the spousal exception applies only if the beneficiary is not changed during the year of the divorce.

Recalculating RMDs Each Year

The Uniform Lifetime Table is a "recalculating" table in that you must go back to it every year to get your new life expectancy. For example, the table (see Figure 3, page. 126) shows that a 73-year-old has a life expectancy of 26.5 years, but that does not mean the plan balance must be emptied by the time he or she reaches 99.5 years (73 + 26.5 = 99.5). The 26.5-year life expectancy is for age 73 only. Every year thereafter, a new life expectancy must be calculated. Therefore, at 99, the person in our example still has a life expectancy of 6.8 more years (the lucky dog!). (Even at age 120, there's still 2.0 years of life left in the old codger yet—at least according to the table.) The theory is that if you take only the required minimum amount each year, you will never run out of IRA money—unless the market tanks, of course, and your retirement account is wiped out—because, as far as the IRS is concerned, you never run out of life expectancy. What optimism! They want to keep you alive and kicking—kicking in, that is!

Make the Calculation

OK, you've determined your account balance for the prior year, and you've determined your life expectancy according to the Uniform Lifetime Table (or the Joint Life Expectancy Table if the spousal exception applies to your situation). Now, to get your RMD, all you need to do is divide your account balance by your life expectancy. For example, let's say you turn 75 in 2024. Your life expectancy according to the Uniform Lifetime Table is 24.6 years. If your plan balance as of December 31 of the prior year (2023) is $400,000, you divide $400,000 by 24.6 years and get $16,260, which is your RMD for that account for 2024. If you have more than one account, you could combine the total balance and withdraw the entire amount or break it up into several smaller withdrawals, as long as by the end of the year all $16,260 has been withdrawn. You can always withdraw more by the end of the year without paying any penalties, but never less. And if you did withdraw more in 2024—say, $20,000 instead of $16,260—forget about having the extra $3,740 credited to you so that you could take less in 2025. The IRS doesn't work that way. The Regs stipulate that each distribution year stands on its own.

Figure 3. Uniform Lifetime Table

Age of IRA Owner or Plan Participant	Life Expectancy (in Years)	Age of IRA Owner or Plan Participant	Life Expectancy (in Years)
72	27.4	97	7.8
73	26.5	98	7.3
74	25.5	99	6.8
75	24.6	100	6.4
76	23.7	101	6.0
77	22.9	102	5.6
78	22.0	103	5.2
79	21.1	104	4.9
80	20.2	105	4.6
81	19.4	106	4.3
82	18.5	107	4.1
83	17.7	108	3.9
84	16.8	109	3.7
85	16.0	110	3.5
86	15.2	111	3.4
87	14.4	112	3.3
88	13.7	113	3.1
89	12.9	114	3.0
90	12.2	115	2.9
91	11.5	116	2.8
92	10.8	117	2.7
93	10.1	118	2.5
94	9.5	118	2.3
95	8.9	120+	2.0
96	8.4		

Most IRA owners will use this table, but there is one exception. If the spouse is the sole beneficiary for the entire year AND is more than 10 years younger than the IRA owner, do not use this Uniform Lifetime Table. In this case, use the actual ages of both spouses based on the Joint Life Expectancy Table. This will result in a longer life expectancy and a smaller required distribution.

SO, YOU THINK YOU SPOTTED A LOOPHOLE?

Q: Ed, I think I've figured a way around taking RMDs. You said to base the RMD on the prior year's balance, right? What if on December 20 I withdraw the entire amount in my IRA, and then on January 5 of the next year (well within the penalty-free 60-day period) I redeposit all the money back to my IRA? If I go back to the December 31 balance to figure my RMD, guess what? The December 31 balance is ZERO because I withdrew all the money, so there is no RMD! Cool, huh? If I do this 60-day shuffle every year, I'll never have to withdraw from my IRA, right?

A: WRONG! The IRS is way ahead of you—again. There is another little rule that says if you remove any funds from your IRA before year end and roll them back into your IRA the following year, even within 60 days, you must add the outstanding rollover amount(s) back to your account balance as of December 31 of the prior year for calculating your RMD. For example, let's say that on December 20 you withdraw your entire IRA balance of $500,000. On the following January 5, you redeposit the $500,000 back to your IRA. To calculate your distribution, you must use your prior December 31 IRA balance. That balance is zero, but the Regs say that in this case you must add the $500,000 outstanding rollover back to your December 31 IRA balance and use that $500,000 to calculate your RMD. Sorry, Charlie. Nice try.

Test Your RMD Know-How

Here are a few examples of how to calculate your lifetime RMD in a variety of situations. Let's see if you've got the hang of it.

▪ *The IRA owner is 74 years old in 2024. His beneficiary is his spouse, who is 72 years old in 2024. His IRA balance on December 31, 2023, is $425,000. What is his RMD for 2024?*

A: $16,667.

Q: How did you get that?

A: According to the Uniform Lifetime Table, the life expectancy for a 74-year-old (the spouse's age is irrelevant here because the spousal exception does not apply) is 25.5 years. You then divide the $425,000 IRA balance from the end of the prior year by the 25.5 years: $425,000/25.5 = $16,667.

▪ *The IRA owner is 74 years old in 2024. His beneficiary is his alma mater. His IRA balance on December 31, 2023, is $425,000. What is his RMD for 2024?*

A: $16,667.

Q: How did you get that?

A: The situation is exactly the same, except for the identity of the beneficiary, which makes no difference as long as the spousal exception does not apply.

▪ *The IRA owner is 74 years old in 2024. He neglected to name a beneficiary. His IRA balance on December 31, 2023, is $425,000. What is his RMD for 2024?*

A: $16,667.

Q: How did you get that?

A: The same method. The fact that there is no named beneficiary is of no consequence in computing lifetime RMDs. However, as Chapter 5 will show, naming a beneficiary is vitally important in making sure an IRA keeps growing tax-deferred for your beneficiaries.

■ *The IRA owner is 74 years old in 2024. His 15 children are equal co-beneficiaries. They range in age from 2 to 25 years old. His wife has chosen not to be named a beneficiary because she thinks her children will take care of her. (Obviously she's never heard the adage "A mother can take care of 15 children, but 15 children cannot take care of one mother.") His IRA balance on December 31, 2023, is $425,000. What is his RMD for 2024?*

A: $16,667.

Q: How did you get that?

A: Again, the same method; it does not matter how many beneficiaries there are. If the spousal exception does not apply (and it does not in this example), the number of beneficiaries and their ages are meaningless to the lifetime RMD calculation. You still use the Uniform Lifetime Table based on the IRA owner's age in the distribution year. The ages and number of beneficiaries will play an important role only in post-death RMDs (see Chapter 6).

The Spousal Exception

Use the IRS Joint Life Expectancy Table when the spouse is more than 10 years younger AND is the sole beneficiary for the entire year.

■ *The IRA owner is 74 years old in 2024. His sole beneficiary for the entire year is his spouse, who is 45 years old in 2024. His IRA balance on December 31, 2023, is $425,000. What is his RMD for 2024?*

A: $10,291.

Q: How did you get that?

A: The spousal exception applies because she is the sole beneficiary and younger by more than 10 years. Therefore, in this situation, the Uniform Lifetime Table would not be used to calculate the RMD, but rather the IRS Joint Life Expectancy Table (see IRS Publication 590-B), where you would look up the joint life expectancy of a 74-year-old and a 45-year-old, which happens to be 41.3 years. You then divide the $425,000 IRA balance by 41.3 and get $10,291.

▪ *The IRA owner is 74 years old in 2024. His beneficiaries are his spouse, who is 55 years old, and his son, who is 30 years old in 2024. The spouse will receive 90 percent of the IRA and the son will inherit 10 percent. His IRA balance on December 31, 2023, is $425,000. What is his RMD for 2024?*

A: $16,667.

Q: How did you get that?

A: The spousal exception does not apply here because even though the spouse is more than 10 years younger than the IRA owner and will inherit 90 percent of the account, she is not the *sole* beneficiary—and so the Uniform Lifetime Table is used to calculate the RMD for 2024.

▪ *The IRA owner is 74 in 2024. His sole beneficiary is his spouse, who is 53 years old in 2024. His IRA balance on December 31, 2023, is $425,000. His spouse dies in February 2024, and he names his son as beneficiary in May 2024. What is his RMD for 2024?*

A: $12,463.

Q: How did you get that?

A: Even though the spouse died in February of the distribution year and a new sole beneficiary was named, the spousal exception still applies for the distribution year because of the marital-status provision. You may recall from earlier in this chapter that marital status is determined as of January 1. So, if the spouse dies during the year, and a new beneficiary is named, the spousal exception still applies. The joint life expectancy of a 74-year-old and a 53-year-old is 34.1 years. You then divide $425,000 by 34.1 = $12,463.

- *Following up on the previous example, assuming the IRA owner does not remarry and keeps his son as his sole beneficiary, what would the RMD be for the next year (2025) when the owner is 75, and the account balance on December 31, 2024, is, say, $450,000?*

A: $18,293.

Q: How did you get that?

A: The spousal exception cannot apply because he didn't remarry, so the Uniform Lifetime Table would be used for 2025. According to that table, the life expectancy for a 75-year-old is 24.6 years. You then divide $450,000 by 24.6 = $18,293.

How Divorce Affects the Spousal Exception—Using the IRS Joint Life Expectancy Table

- *The IRA owner is 74 in 2024. His sole beneficiary is his spouse, who is 53 years old in 2024. His IRA balance on December 31, 2023, is $425,000. However, they divorced in March 2024, but he did not change the beneficiary during 2024. What is his RMD for 2024?*

A: $12,463.

Q: How did you get that?

A: Even though they divorced in the distribution year, the spousal exception still applies for 2024 because *he did not change the beneficiary during the year of the divorce.* The joint life expectancy of a 74-year-old and a 53-year-old is 34.1 years. You then divide $425,000 by 34.1 = $12,463.

This is not a good plan, though, because if he died while his ex-spouse was still named as the beneficiary, then the ex would end up with his IRA, and that is most likely not what he intended. It is more likely that the IRA owner may die soon after a divorce if the ex is still the named beneficiary . . . just sayin'. Make sure you update your beneficiary forms *immediately* after a divorce.

▪ *The IRA owner is 74 in 2024. His sole beneficiary is his spouse, who is 53 years old in 2024. His IRA balance on December 31, 2023, is $425,000. However, they divorced in March 2024 and he names his son as beneficiary in May 2024. What is his RMD for 2024?*

A: $16,667.

Q: How did you get that?

A: The spousal exception no longer applies since he changed the beneficiary during the year of the divorce. So, he uses the Uniform Lifetime Table to calculate the RMD for 2024.

As was the result in several examples above, according to the Uniform Lifetime Table, the life expectancy for a 74-year-old (the spouse's age is irrelevant here because the spousal exception does not apply) is 25.5 years. You then divide the $425,000 IRA balance from the end of the prior year by 25.5 years: $425,000/25.5 = $16,667.

Calculating RMDs for "Split IRAs"

For estate-planning purposes, splitting an IRA into two or more accounts and naming different beneficiaries for each can sometimes pay handsomely. It also pays to split IRAs to reduce current income taxes on lifetime RMDs.

For instance, in one of the examples cited previously, if instead of naming his spouse and child as 90/10 co-beneficiaries, the 74-year-old owner of the $425,000 IRA had split the IRA into two IRAs, naming his 55-year-old spouse as the sole beneficiary of one and his son as beneficiary of the other, the spousal exception would have applied to the IRA where the spouse was the sole beneficiary. Thus, the Joint Life Expectancy Table would have been used in calculating RMDs on that account, resulting in a lower required distribution.

Uh-oh. You've got a confused look on your face. OK, let's do the calculation using some actual numbers.

The 55-year-old spouse is the named beneficiary on 90 percent of the $425,000 IRA and the son is the named beneficiary on 10 percent, resulting in a total RMD of $16,667. But now the IRA is split 90/10 into two IRAs: one for $382,500 (90 percent of the $425,000) and the other for $42,500 (10 percent of the $425,000). The spouse is the sole beneficiary on the $382,500 IRA and the son is the sole beneficiary on the $42,500 IRA. This split is not set in stone. The IRA owner can change his mind at any time, transfer funds from one IRA to another, or take his RMD from one IRA and not the other if he wishes. But for our purposes here, let's assume the spouse remains the sole beneficiary for the entire year on the $382,500 IRA.

Because the spousal exception applies to the $382,500 IRA, the IRS Joint Life Expectancy Table can be used to determine the life expectancy figure—in this case, the joint life expectancy of a 74-year-old and a 55-year-old, which is 32.4 years. Divide $382,500 by 32.4 years and you come up with an RMD on that account of $11,806.

However, the spousal exception does not apply to the $42,500 IRA because the son is the sole beneficiary of that account. So, the Uniform Lifetime Table would be used instead to determine the single life expectancy of a 74-year-old, which is 25.5 years. Divide $42,500 by 25.5 years and you get an RMD on that account of $1,667. The total RMD for the two IRAs is $13,473 ($11,806 + $1,667 = $13,473), which is the minimum that can be withdrawn from any one or both of the accounts.

To sum up: Before the $425,000 IRA was split, the RMD was $16,667. After the split, it is $13,473. Subtract $13,473 from $16,667 and you get a difference of $3,194. That's how much less the owner is required to take out for the year by having split his one IRA into two and naming different beneficiaries for each. And, as a result of taking out less, the owner's income tax on that distribution will be lower. This is the main benefit of splitting accounts in situations where the spousal exception applies. But there are benefits to splitting IRAs even in situations where the spousal exception may not apply, such as when your spouse is a beneficiary and wants to take advantage of the special rules that apply to spouse beneficiaries.

So, it is generally a good idea to split accounts if you have multiple beneficiaries. This can even be done by beneficiaries themselves, but it's better that you do it, so as not to open the door to a family feud and other potential problems. (Chapter 5 gives more information about splitting accounts with multiple beneficiaries after the death of the IRA owner.)

CAUTION!

Don't mix different kinds of beneficiaries—for example, a person (or designated beneficiary) with a nonperson such as an estate, charity, or trust—as co-beneficiaries on one IRA. It won't affect calculating the RMD, but it may close the door to an eligible designated beneficiary stretching the account later on. The stretch IRA is not permitted after the owner's death in cases where one of the co-beneficiaries is not a person and the account is not split by the end of the year after death. So, for example, instead of naming your favorite charity and your three children as co-beneficiaries on one IRA, split the IRA into two IRAs, naming the charity as sole beneficiary on one of them and your children as sole beneficiaries on the other. You must be especially careful when your beneficiary is disabled or chronically ill since these beneficiaries get special treatment under the SECURE Act. (See Chapters 6 and 10 for more on planning for these beneficiaries.)

How to Reduce the Tax on Your RMDs

Now that you are well versed in how much you must withdraw from your retirement plans due to RMDs, wouldn't it be great if you could reduce those amounts and pay less tax?

Here are four ways you can do just that:

Qualified Charitable Distributions (QCDs)

The Tax Cuts and Jobs Act of 2017 did not address QCDs, but it made them *way* more valuable as a tax saver for those who give to charity. If you normally give to charity, as most do, this is the way to do so from here on in . . . if you qualify. That's the only downside: QCDs are not available to everyone—only to IRA owners or IRA beneficiaries who are age 70½ or older. *Neither the SECURE Act nor SECURE 2.0 changed this provision. The QCD age remains 70½.*

What's the big benefit? Lower taxes!

Here's how it works.

Instead of making your charitable donations the old-fashioned way by writing a check to the charity and taking an itemized deduction, you transfer the amount you wish to donate directly from your IRA to the charity. This is a QCD. When you do this, the distribution from your IRA is excluded from your income.

You'll see that this is better than a tax deduction, especially since you probably aren't getting that deduction anymore anyway. Under the current tax laws, due to eliminations and cutbacks as well as the big increase in the standard deduction, most people are no longer itemizing their deductions. For most taxpayers who are now taking the standard deduction, charitable gifts offer no tax benefit.

If you use the QCD, though, you get to use the larger standard deduction *plus* a tax benefit from your donation. You don't get the actual tax deduction, but instead you get to exclude the charitable distribution from income, which is much better taxwise. Excluding the QCD amount from income reduces your adjusted gross income, which ultimately means you pay less in income tax.

Now the even better part . . . QCDs taken from your IRA can count toward your RMD. If, for example, your RMD for the year is $5,000 and you normally give that same amount to charity, the QCD can satisfy your $5,000 RMD and you will not have to include that amount in income.

I'm not saying to give more to charity to get a lower tax bill. I'm saying to give what you normally do but do it using a QCD and your tax bill will be lower on the same exact gift amount. It will leave both your heart and your wallet feeling good.

Pay attention to the QCD rules to make sure you qualify.

- The QCD applies only to IRA owners and beneficiaries who are 70½ years old or older. It does not apply to company plans like 401(k)s.

Planning Note

Even though the SECURE 2.0 Act raised the RMD age to 73, it did not change the QCD age, which remains at 70½. Due to this age gap—age 70½ to age 73—you can use QCDs for your charitable giving even if there are no RMDs yet. You don't have to wait until you reach your required beginning date to take advantage of QCDs, if you are at least age 70½. It still pays to give to charity this way, even if RMDs have not yet begun for you.

- The donation must be transferred *directly* from the IRA to the charity. An IRA check made out to the charity (not to you!) qualifies as a direct transfer.

- Nothing can be received in return for the donation. You must receive a CWA (contemporaneous written acknowledgment) from the charity acknowledging that you didn't receive anything of value.

- QCDs can be made only with pre-tax dollars. The pro-rata rule does not apply to QCD transactions.

- Gifts to donor-advised funds or private family foundations do *not* qualify.

- The base annual QCD limit is $100,000 per person, which is enough for most givers. The $100,000 limit increases slightly each year with inflation. For 2024, the QCD limit rises to $105,000. This means that if your RMD is less than the present dollar limit, you can still give up to the annual limit. Whatever you give via the QCD is excluded from your income.

- In addition, if you are a married couple who both qualify for the QCD and each have IRAs, you can increase the tax benefit of your giving by each using your own QCD (but not each other's).

- No separate tax deduction can be taken, since you have already excluded the QCD amount from income, which is better than a tax deduction.

Funding Charitable Gift Annuities with QCDs

Prior to SECURE 2.0, QCDs could be made only to charities and not to a split-interest entity. A split-interest entity allows you to make a charitable gift and receive an income during your lifetime with the remainder going to charity after your death.

Now, QCDs can be made to a charitable remainder annuity trust (CRAT), a charitable remainder unitrust (CRUT), or a charitable gift annuity (CGA). Both a CRAT and CRUT permit income to be paid during your lifetime with the remainder going to charity after your death. A CGA is an annuity contract between you and a charity in which you receive income during your lifetime and the remainder goes to charity after your death. However, there are some significant limitations with all QCDs:

- The split-interest entity can be funded only with QCDs and no other funds.

- A QCD can be made only to a split-interest entity once in a lifetime.

- A QCD is subject to a dollar limit that's indexed for inflation. Beginning in 2023, the dollar limit was $50,000, but it will increase in future years ($53,000 for 2024).

Practically speaking, a CRAT or CRUT is probably not a great candidate for a QCD. Because these trusts are expensive to set up and administer, they're more often used for much larger sums of money. It's unlikely that the cost involved with establishing a new trust just for a $50,000 QCD would be worth the effort.

From a planning perspective, using a QCD to fund a CGA may be the best option to come out of this new provision. Many charities already offer charitable gift annuities. Now these can be funded with a QCD. Here's how the process works:

1. The IRA owner does a once-in-a-lifetime QCD of up to $53,000, based on the 2024 limit. If less than $50,000 is transferred as a QCD to a CGA in a calendar year, the remaining amount *can* be transferred later that year in a separate QCD but *cannot* be transferred in another year.

2. The charity invests the funds from the QCD in a CGA. A CGA is an annuity contract between the IRA owner and the charity, in which the IRA owner makes a gift of the QCD funds to the charity. In exchange, the charity assumes a legal obligation to provide the IRA owner with a fixed amount of monthly income that continues until death.

3. IRA owners can name only themselves and/or a spouse to receive the income payments. This rule is more restrictive than the rule that generally applies to CGAs when they are not funded by a QCD, in which the CGA can be paid over the lives of any two people (married or not).

4. The interest in the CGA must be nonassignable, meaning you cannot arrange for it to be paid to someone else or back to the charity. This rule is also different from the rules that apply to CGAs that are not funded by QCDs. Often CGA beneficiaries who do not need the money can stop interest payments by assigning their interest back to the charity. This is apparently not allowed if the CGA was funded by a QCD.

5. Because a CGA can be structured to last through the joint life span of a married couple, it appears that both an IRA owner and his or her spouse could do QCDs to the same CGA from their own IRAs.

6. The annuity payments must start no later than one year from the date of funding. Deferral is not allowed.

7. All the income payments are treated as ordinary income rather than including a portion that is tax free, which is the case when a charitable annuity is funded with non-QCD funds.

8. There is a 5 percent minimum payout for CGAs that are funded with a QCD.

Advantages of Funding a CGA with a QCD

The main reason to fund a CGA with a QCD is to use IRA dollars to benefit the charity of the IRA owner's choice. The IRA owner must be charitably inclined for this strategy to make sense, because the rates of return on investments in CGAs funded by QCDs may not be as large as other potential investments. The CGA can also count toward your RMD (since it is a QCD).

QCD Tax Tip

Structure your QCDs as the first distributions from your IRA. The first dollars out of your IRA go toward satisfying your RMD, and since RMD income cannot be offset by a future QCD, you want to have your QCDs completed first. It's best to make your QCD contributions early in the year to ensure that they offset the income from your RMD.

SECURE Act QCD Warning!

The SECURE 2.0 Act raised the age for RMDs from 72 to 73, *but the QCD age did not change*. It remains age 70½. However, Congress added a poison pill. Before I explain the evil part, let's discuss some of the benefits.

In a move that will simplify retirement accounts for older individuals, the SECURE Act eliminated the age 70½ limit for making traditional IRA contributions. This brings the IRA contribution rules more in line with those of the Roth IRA, which never had such age limits. Now, individuals who are still working, regardless of age, can contribute to a traditional IRA, if they meet all the contribution requirements.

The SECURE Act (Indirectly) Expands
the Use of the Back-door Roth Strategy

The elimination of the age restriction on traditional IRAs may open a back-door Roth opportunity to those over age 70½ with income higher than the Roth contribution limits. Maybe Congress overlooked this benefit. Don't tell them! By eliminating the age requirement for contributions to a traditional IRA, more people qualify for the back-door Roth IRA. Since more older people can contribute to a traditional IRA, which has no income limitations, if their income is too high for a Roth IRA contribution, they can make a nondeductible traditional IRA contribution and then convert those funds to a Roth IRA. For more detail on this move, see Step #3: Roth It (Chapter 7).

IRA and Roth IRA Contribution
Rules—Money Goes In . . . and Then Back Out

But what just became simpler does come with a slight complication. This new rule will create some confusion when combined with RMD requirements. Let's say you are 75 and still working. Without exception—unless you die before your required beginning date (RBD)—IRA RMDs must start by your RBD.

Your RBD is April 1 of the year after you turn age 73. So, since you are now 75, you have had to take RMDs from your IRA for the last couple of years. You are now in a position where you can make contributions *and* you must also take distributions. This "in and out" of contributions and RMDs will become commonplace.

Despite this in-and-out stuff, eliminating the age restriction for IRA contributions will still benefit older workers. Now for the evil part . . .

Because Congress couldn't just leave well enough alone, this coupled with QCDs created a big fat mess.

QCD Limitations Under the SECURE Act

Congress figured out how to take something that was relatively simple and make it more complicated. Imagine that! As a result of one of the most ridiculous provisions Congress has ever created,

QCDs have become taxable. What gives? While Congress has no problem forking over bailouts and tax breaks by the trillions to big business, CEOs, banks, and Wall Street, they took the time in the SECURE Act to make sure we peons did not overly give of our own hard-earned IRA funds to our favorite charities, just when these groups need help the most. Insane! They found a solution looking for a problem.

We cannot get into the minds of Congress here, but were they really worried someone might make a deductible IRA contribution of say $7,000 at age 73 and turn right around and do a tax-free QCD that same year? What, exactly, is the abusive result of this transaction? That the country would lose the income tax due on that $7,000 contribution. Really? This was their concern? Whatever their reasoning, Congress created a provision in the SECURE Act that would reduce the QCD exclusion from income for certain deductible IRA contributions made after age 70½. The really absurd part of all of this is that you could make that same $7,000 contribution in the year before you turn 70½ and do a QCD a year later with no effect on the QCD's exclusion from income.

Result: Congress Created Taxable QCDs!

The following formula will apply in years when you, at age 70½ or older, make a deductible IRA contribution *and* do a QCD in that year or a later year. In that case, for any year, the portion of a QCD that is taxable is the excess of:

(i) the aggregate amount of post-70½ deductible IRA contributions, over

(ii) the aggregate amount of any taxable prior year QCDs.

If the current year QCD always exceeds the IRA contribution, the rule is easy. The amount of the QCD excluded from income is reduced by the amount of the post-age 70½ deductible IRA contribution.

Example:

Joe is still working at 75 years old. Under the new law, he contributes $7,000 to a tax-deductible traditional IRA. Then, in the same year, he decides to do his first-ever QCD in the amount of $10,000. Joe thinks he can exclude the entire $10,000 QCD from his income, but he can't. Thanks to the SECURE Act, only $3,000 of the $10,000 will be excluded because he already deducted his $7,000 IRA contribution. Now Joe will actually have a taxable QCD of $7,000!

The one saving grace is that if Joe itemizes instead of using the standard deduction on his tax return, he can take that $7,000 as an itemized deduction since he received no benefit from the gift through his QCD.

This Tax Trap Can Linger to Future Years!

If Joe never ended up making a QCD that year and makes no more tax-deductible contributions, that $7,000 contribution will still loom over his shoulder forever until he does a QCD. If he does the $10,000 QCD five years later, the old $7,000 deductible contribution will still make $7,000 of the QCD taxable. The post-70½ deductible contribution will haunt him like Jacob Marley until it is used up by taxable QCDs.

Planning Note

Don't make deductible IRA contributions after age 70½ if you are also doing QCDs. This combination will reduce the QCD tax benefit while also leaving you with QCD complexities that last for years. Roth IRA contributions would be better, or backdoor Roth contributions that begin by making a nondeductible traditional IRA contribution and then converting those funds to Roth IRAs. Or, if you are married and both you and your spouse have IRAs, you could make a deductible contribution to your traditional IRA but have your spouse do the QCD from his or her IRA funds. You'll end up with the same result without the QCD tax trap.

Qualifying Longevity Annuity Contracts (QLACs)

A QLAC is a relatively new type of longevity annuity contract that you can purchase within your IRA or employer plan.

Double Benefits for You

QLACs have two major benefits. One: prior to starting payouts, they can reduce your RMD amount and, in turn, reduce your tax bill. Two: when the QLAC kicks in, usually at age 85, you are protected from outliving your IRA money, at least up to the QLAC amount you purchased.

The QLAC value can be excluded from your account balance that is used for calculating RMDs. But there are limits. Retirement account owners can purchase QLACs only up to an overall base maximum of $200,000 (2024 limit), which will increase each year by being indexed for inflation. That's still a nice chunk of change to chop off an RMD calculation, not to mention the added benefit of longevity insurance.

As with most things in life, good things come with trade-offs. Watch out for the downsides of a QLAC. Beneficiary options and payouts are much more limited, especially if you die before age 85.

Roth Conversions

For those who have not yet reached age 73:

If you still have a few years to go before you must begin your age-73 RMDs, a series of Roth conversions over the years will lower your IRA balance and can reduce or even eliminate your future RMDs. You will have to pay tax on the amount you convert, of course, but no more tax than you will have had to pay after age 73 anyway, albeit over time. The prize for a bigger tax bill now is lower RMDs for *life* (or none at all if you convert everything). That means no worry about taxes on your future distributions.

If you *have* reached age 73, those RMDs cannot be converted to Roth IRAs because a conversion is technically a rollover, and RMDs cannot be rolled over. The first dollars out of the IRA are deemed to satisfy the RMD, but after that, the remaining IRA funds can be converted. That will increase the tax for the conversion year but will reduce future RMDs. And over time, converting smaller amounts each year, filling up lower tax brackets, can ultimately put a dent in your overall future tax bill.

Rollovers to Company Plans

I listed this last since not everyone can take advantage of this one. That's because you must be both over age 73 and still working. Lately, though, this is a growing population.

If you are subject to RMDs from your IRA and still work at a company with a 401(k) plan, a rollover to the company plan can delay future RMDs. To benefit from this, first make sure the company plan allows roll-ins from IRAs. Remember that RMDs from the company plan can be delayed until retirement if you do not own more than 5 percent of the company, and if the plan allows this still-working exception for RMDs. Although they're not required to, many plans do allow this.

Before doing a rollback to the plan, you must take the current-year RMD from the IRA, since an RMD can never be rolled over. Once the IRA RMD is taken, then the balance of the IRA can be rolled over to the company plan, eliminating your IRA RMDs going forward. Although RMDs from your employer plan will be due for the year of retirement and thereafter, you might be in a lower tax bracket then. Note: Only pre-tax IRA funds can be rolled back to an employer plan.

Keeping Track of Multiple-Account RMDs

Staying on top of RMDs for one account is pretty easy, but if (like most people today) you have more than one IRA, 401(k), 403(b), or any other type of retirement account, including inherited IRAs, this task can easily become a confusing, tricky, time-consuming ordeal, especially if a person is at all disorganized (no, not you!).

To avoid headaches in dealing with multiple-account RMDs that could lead to making a costly mistake (such as missing an RMD on one account and getting hit with the RMD penalty—as high as 25 percent—for the error), take these four simple action steps:

Action Step 1: Make a List

Compile a complete list of all your retirement accounts, including company plans, 401(k)s, 403(b)s, 457(b)s, Keogh plans, traditional IRAs (including SEP- and SIMPLE IRAs), and inherited IRAs or inherited retirement accounts, including Roth IRAs. This list should include only retirement accounts that are subject to required distributions. For example, you would not include your company plan if you are still working for that company (and you do not own more than 5 percent of it) because you are exempt from required distributions on that account until after you retire. You also would not include your own Roth IRA or Roth 401(k) or 403(b) since Roth IRA owners and Roth plan participants are not subject to required distributions. Roth IRAs inherited from someone other than your spouse, however, are subject to required distributions even though the required distributions may not be taxable.

When writing down your list of accounts, include the name, age, and relationship of the beneficiary to you on each account, so that you can ascertain whether the spousal exception applies; then you can separate that account from the others.

Another good reason for writing down this information is that it forces you to check that you have named a beneficiary on each account. You might discover that you neglected to name a beneficiary in some cases. While not naming a beneficiary has no effect on *your* lifetime distributions, it's key to the beneficiary being able to maximize his or her payout options.

Action Step 2: Group Accounts by Category

Once you have accounted for all your retirement plans subject to RMDs, group them together by category. For example, all traditional IRAs, including SEP-IRAs and SIMPLE IRAs, go together. All inherited IRAs from the same person go together, but those inherited from a different person should be separated. Likewise, group all Roth IRAs inherited from the same person together, but keep Roths inherited from others separate. And if the spousal exception applies to any of your accounts, separate them from the pack too—because you will be using a different table for calculating RMDs. Apart from 403(b) plans, company retirement plans stand individually. Do not group them with other company plans. Multiple accounts in one company plan, however, can be grouped together, but here again you must keep any spousal exception plans separate.

Action Step 3: Figure RMDs for Each Group

Use the Uniform Lifetime Table (Figure 3, page. 126) or the IRS Joint Life Expectancy Table (see IRS Publication 590-B—make sure you are using the correct tables based on the RMD year, since the IRS issued new tables for 2022 and later years) to calculate the RMD for each of your retirement accounts other than those you have inherited. If you can stretch (if you are an eligible designated beneficiary) on these inherited accounts, you need your life expectancy figure from the Single Life Expectancy Table (Figure 5, page. 166). Each group, as determined in Step 2, will produce a different RMD, which is why you need to figure out each RMD separately.

Action Step 4: Take Your RMD

For IRA and 403(b) accounts, you can take the entire distribution from one account or take several distributions equal to the entire amount from a combination of accounts within that same group. For all other types of accounts, you must take each RMD separately. What you can't do, for example, is take a required IRA distribution from a 403(b) account or from a Roth IRA. Whichever account, or combination of accounts within the same group, you decide to withdraw from, make sure that your total withdrawal at least equals your RMD; otherwise you'll have a 25 percent RMD penalty to pay. Also, if you have more than one group or category of plans, make sure that you have withdrawn the minimum from each plan. You cannot satisfy one group's required distribution by taking more from another group.

Now that you've gotten the idea of how to keep track of multiple-account RMDs, let's go through the four actions using a real-world example—although if you have this many different accounts with all the bells and whistles, my hat's off to you because you're that rare bird with too much money!

Assume that you turn 73 in July 2024. You have decided to take your first required distribution by the end of 2024 so that you won't have to take your first two RMDs in 2025. Your first RMD will be based on the balance in your retirement accounts as of December 31, 2023.

Action Step 1: Make a List

1. IRA

Your account balance on December 31, 2023 $100,000
Your beneficiary: spouse, age 67 in 2024

2. IRA

Your account balance on December 31, 2023 $250,000
Your beneficiaries: three children
(one-third each), ages 42, 40, and 34 in 2024

3. IRA

Your account balance on December 31, 2023 $50,000
Your beneficiary: charity

4. SEP-IRA

Your account balance on December 31, 2023 $70,000
Your beneficiary: spouse, age 67 in 2024

5. Roth IRA

Your account balance on December 31, 2023 $65,000

Your beneficiary: spouse, age 67 in 2024
Note: Not subject to required distributions.

6. 401(k) from former company

Your account balance on December 31, 2023 $340,000
Your beneficiary: spouse, age 67 in 2024

7. 401(k) plan from company (still working)*

Your account balance on December 31, 2023 $26,000
Your beneficiary: spouse, age 67 in 2024

*Since you don't own more than 5 percent of the company, this plan is exempt from required minimum distributions until you retire.

Action Step 2: Group the Accounts by Category

Group the four IRA accounts, even though each has a different beneficiary, because the spousal exception does not apply; therefore, the Uniform Lifetime Table will be used for life expectancy. Do not include the Roth IRA in this group because Roth IRA owners are not subject to RMDs. Include only one 401(k) company plan since there is no RMD on the other 401(k), because you are still working.

GROUP 1: MY IRA(S)	BALANCE ON DECEMBER 31, 2023
Account #1 IRA	$100,000
Account #2 IRA	$250,000
Account #3 IRA	$ 50,000
Account #4 IRA	$ 70,000
Group 1 Total	**$470,000**

GROUP 2: MY COMPANY PLAN(S)	BALANCE ON DECEMBER 31, 2023
Account #6 401(k)	$340,000
Group 2 Total	**$340,000**

Action Step 3: Figure RMDs for Each Group

GROUP 1		
Life expectancy, age 73	= 26.5 years	
IRA balances on December 31, 2023		**RMD**
Account # 1 IRA	$100,000	$3,774 ($100,000/26.5)
Account #2 IRA	$250,000	$9,434 ($250,000/26.5)
Account #3 IRA	$ 50,000	$1,887 ($50,000/26.5)
Account #4 SEP-IRA	$ 70,000	$2,641 ($70,000/26.5)
Total RMD	**$470,000**	**$17,736**
GROUP 2		
Life expectancy, age 73	= 26.5 years	
401(k) balance on December 31, 2023	$340,000	$12,830 ($340,000/26.5)
Total RMD		**$12,830**

Action Step 4: Take Your RMD

RMD for Group 1 is $17,736. This amount can be taken from any account or combination of accounts in Group 1. RMD for Group 2 is $12,830. This amount must be taken from the 401(k) of the company from which you are retired but not from the second 401(k) or from any other retirement account.

Now, let's tweak the example a bit by trading your spouse in for a younger model. Everything in the example remains the same except that your new spouse is 25 years old (don't you wish!). It's just an example so it's OK to dream.

Action Step 1: Make a List

To save space, I won't bother repeating the list of accounts since nothing will have changed except the age of the beneficiary spouse on accounts #1, #4, and #6. So, let's move on.

Action Step 2: Group the Accounts by Category

As before, group the four IRA accounts, but now separate the IRAs naming your 25-year-old spouse as beneficiary. Since the spousal exception now applies to the two accounts in Group 1(a), the IRS Joint Life Expectancy Table (see IRS Publication 590-B—but make sure you are using the new 2022 tables) will be used to calculate RMDs. The Uniform Lifetime Table will be used to calculate the RMD for the remaining two accounts in Group 1(b).

GROUP 1(A): MY IRA(S)	BALANCE ON DECEMBER 31, 2023	Spousal exception applies
Account #1 IRA	$100,000	
Account #4 SEP-IRA	$70,000	
GROUP 1(B): MY IRA(S)	**BALANCE ON DECEMBER 31, 2023**	
Account #2 IRA	$250,000	
Account #3 IRA	$50,000	
GROUP 2: MY COMPANY PLAN(S)	**BALANCE ON DECEMBER 31, 2023**	**Spousal exception applies**
Account #6 401(k)	$340,000	

Action Step 3: Figure RMDs for Each Group

GROUP 1(A)		RMD
Life expectancy, ages 73 and 25	= 60.3 years	
IRA Balances on December 31, 2023		
Account #1 IRA	$100,000	$1,658 ($100,000/60.3)
Account #4 SEP-IRA	$70,000	$1,161 ($70,000/60.3)
Total RMD		**$2,819**
GROUP 1(B)		
Life expectancy, age 73	= 26.5 years	
Account #2 IRA	$250,000	$9,434 ($250,000/26.5)
Account #3 IRA	$50,000	$1,887 ($50,000/26.5)
Total RMD		**$11,321**
Combined total, Groups 1(a), 1(b)		**$14,140**
GROUP 2		
Life expectancy, ages 73 and 25	= 60.3 years	
401(k) balance on December 31, 2023	$340,000	$5,638 ($340,000/60.3)
Group 2 Total		**$5,638**

A WORD TO THE WISE

Don't wait until the last minute of the last day of the distribution year to take your RMDs. There could be a delay at the financial institution holding on to your money because of a landslide of other last-minute RMDs, or some emergency on the home front that temporarily knocks all thoughts of RMDs from your mind until it's too late to take it without incurring an RMD penalty of possibly 25 percent. I recommend taking your RMD before Thanksgiving. That way, you know that you've taken care of it in time, and you can enjoy the holidays.

Action Step 4: Take Your RMD

The $14,140 RMD for Groups 1(a) and 1(b) can be taken from any account or combination of accounts in Group 1, but not from Group 2. Similarly, the $5,638 RMD for Group 2 must be taken from that account, not from your other company plan.

By this point, you're probably wondering how you could ever have taken a distribution safely before reading this book.

Well, guess what? You're not home free yet.

There's more.

Keep reading.

STEP #2:
SECURE IT

◼

What Does This Word *SECURE* Mean?

Merriam-Webster top definitions are:

Free from danger, affording safety, trustworthy, dependable, free from risk of loss

These sound like something we'd all want from Congress for our retirement savings, right?

But here's what Congress thinks the word means: *Exactly the opposite of all of the above.*

SECURE is the word they use to describe the new ways they are finding to separate you from your retirement savings. I've said this many times, but here it is again: Our tax system penalizes savers. The SECURE Act is just the latest scheme Congress has devised to punish you for saving for your retirement and wanting to provide a legacy for your children, grandchildren, or other beneficiaries.

S.E.C.U.R.E. is the acronym Congress chose for the massive retirement tax law enacted on December 20, 2019: Setting Every Community Up for Retirement Enhancement. Most provisions affecting your retirement savings became effective just 12 days later, on January 1, 2020. Thanks for the grace period! Congress followed up the SECURE Act with SECURE 2.0, which was enacted on

December 29, 2022. While this "Son of SECURE" is not exactly the game changer for retirement accounts that its "Dad" (the original SECURE Act) was, there are still many changes that will affect IRA and plan owners and beneficiaries.

You can bet that any law Congress passes will almost always do exactly the opposite of whatever its name suggests. Remember years ago when Congress came up with the Deficit Reduction Act? LOL hahahaha how did that work out? We're broke now. So, when Congress brings us laws called the SECURE Act and SECURE 2.0, be afraid, be very afraid. And hold on to your wallet too.

The SECURE Act and SECURE 2.0 will affect both how we save for retirement and how we pass on those funds to our loved ones. So, it pays, literally, to familiarize yourself with this latest round of tax rules. Here in this section—Step #2: SECURE It—I'll make these provisions as easy as possible to understand. Then, in the following chapters on Roth IRAs, life insurance, estate planning, and the use of IRA trusts, I'll show you how to adjust your individual plans. But before we move on to those topics, let's get right into the details of what's changed and how these changes affect your retirement savings strategy.

The SECURE Act

The SECURE Act made some significant changes to the rules for retirement accounts. Did you think that things might get simplified? In some ways they have, but for your beneficiaries, things just got a whole lot worse. Some of the SECURE Act changes will upend parts of your existing estate plans.

Here are some of the SECURE Act's key changes:

- Elimination of the "stretch IRA." Now a 10-year rule applies for most beneficiaries, except for *eligible designated beneficiaries* (EDBs). This new term, made up by Congress to confuse us even more, designates a new category of beneficiaries who *can* still use the stretch IRA.

- Raising the RMD age to 72, and then to 73 by SECURE 2.0 (see Chapter 4).

- Elimination of the 70½ age limit for making traditional IRA contributions.

- Creation of a tax trap for QCDs (qualified charitable distributions). QCDs are still allowed at age 70½, but some may no longer be entirely tax free. (But you already know this from Chapter 4, where I gave you all the details.)

SECURE It—Step #2

In these next two chapters, as well as in Steps 3, 4, and 5 of the 5-Step Action Plan that follow, I will focus on the BIG change: the elimination of the stretch IRA. Fear not. I'll provide you with alternative planning solutions that actually turn out to be even better than the stretch. But before we get to that, you need to understand the problem and what's at stake. That's our first order of business.

This critical step, SECURE It (using the dictionary's *protective* meaning rather that Congress's *confiscatory* meaning), involves two parts that I've separated into the next two chapters.

The first part, *Set Up Your Beneficiary Plan*, sets the table, explaining what you need to do now, in your lifetime, to create plans and properly document them. I will show you how to ensure that the retirement savings not used by you will be received by your beneficiaries in the most favorable tax manner.

In the second part, *Payouts to Your Beneficiaries*, I focus on the obstacle course Congress and the IRS have created to thwart the plans you'd thought were all set based on all your prior strategizing. My goal is to help you understand how these new rules will apply to your beneficiaries so you can adjust your planning. This information will play a critical role in your decisions about your next course of action. I'll guide you through those decisions throughout the rest of the book. But first, let's examine the rules of the game, many of which have suddenly changed.

FIVE

SET UP YOUR BENEFICIARY PLAN

The louder he talked of his honor, the faster we counted our spoons.

—RALPH WALDO EMERSON (1803-1882)

It's imperative that you create a plan for your beneficiaries now, while you're still breathing. Otherwise, your family may be left with a tax mess that cannot be fixed.

Like many of my clients, you might be thinking, "Let my beneficiaries deal with this tax-planning business after I'm gone." But the reality is, without your intervention now, they may never get that chance. To gain the best possible post-death payout options, the IRA owner (that's you!) must put all the pieces in order before you meet your end. You can't leave this work to your beneficiaries because they won't be able to change much once you're gone. After you're dead, they can't go back and undo your decisions (or lack thereof). That's like playing your wedding video in reverse in hopes of becoming single again. What's done is done. If you don't make the right choices now, your beneficiaries will be stuck, and a good chunk of the savings you've worked for could end up with Uncle Sam. By your actions, you decide how much he gets and how much goes to your family.

So, let's begin the process of arranging your retirement savings. Think of this part as setting the table for the big feast that will, unfortunately, not include you. This is something you are doing for your loved ones so that the money you worked for and saved diligently for decades, a paycheck at a time, creates the family legacy you've envisioned. This all starts with you. So, let's arrange everything so the kids will eat well and you can have peace of mind that you've taken care of all you could.

Goodbye, Stretch IRA

Yes, the stretch IRA may have gone the way of the dodo bird, but you still have to know how to get it for your beneficiaries, since those rules still apply to certain beneficiaries.

The SECURE Act exempted from the new restrictions certain beneficiaries—specifically those that Congress calls *eligible designated beneficiaries* or EDBs. This means that EDBs *still get the stretch IRA*. Think of EDBs as first-class passengers on the plane. They get all the tax amenities allowed before the SECURE Act. Sounds good, right? Unfortunately, you'll find that most of your beneficiaries, other than your spouse, will be flying in not even coach but steerage. That's why you'll probably need to change the plans you've made, and in the chapters to come, I'll show you exactly how to do that.

NOTE FOR BENEFICIARIES WHO INHERITED BEFORE 2020

The stretch IRA still applies to beneficiaries who inherited before the SECURE Act became effective in 2020. These beneficiaries were grandfathered under the pre-2020 tax rules.

What Is the Stretch IRA?

The stretch IRA is a simple concept. It is the ability of the named beneficiary to spread (or stretch) post-death required minimum distributions (RMDs) over the beneficiary's lifetime using the IRS Single Life Expectancy Table. All that must be done to guarantee the stretch is to name an individual beneficiary on the IRA beneficiary form. Printing a name on that form is crucial.

It's the only way to establish a beneficiary as a *designated* beneficiary. And only designated beneficiaries qualify for the stretch IRA. That rule even applies to EDBs, even though they're flying first class.

Must Be a Designated Beneficiary

An individual named on the beneficiary form, as well as on qualifying see-through trusts (special trusts set up as IRA beneficiaries; see Chapter 10), is deemed a designated beneficiary. And any designated beneficiary who inherited before 2020 still gets to continue the stretch IRA.

Determining the Designated Beneficiary

Who Is the Designated Beneficiary?

In the best of all possible worlds, I would be able to say that the person you name on your IRA beneficiary designation forms will be the one who inherits your IRA. But here again, the IRS has added some twists and turns to keep us on our toes. They've made this process more complex—and for good reason. You see, the IRS realized that nothing is constant (except the IRS); things change and IRA owners need the opportunity to change with them by being able to amend and update their plans as events in their lives warrant (or as tax laws change). So, the IRS came up with an improved, albeit somewhat more involved, system to give IRA owners and their beneficiaries the maximum flexibility in beneficiary planning.

To have a designated beneficiary, you must name an individual (a person with both a birth date and a pulse) as your beneficiary on your IRA beneficiary form. (You could also name a trust, even though a trust is not a person, but let's leave that discussion for Chapter 10.) But the IRS has gone the extra mile by allowing limited changes to be made to beneficiaries, even after you're dead.

"Oh, come on, Ed. You're pulling my leg! A beneficiary can be changed after I'm dead? By whom?"

"By you."

"*Me?* Where from? The grave?"

"In a way, yes. The changed beneficiary must come from a list of candidates preapproved by you."

It's like allowing your daughter to marry only from a group of candidates you've deemed suitable—although if she's still single after your death, she can, and probably will, marry anyone she likes, whether he's on your list or not. In the case of an IRA, however, yours is the final word. No other nonapproved person can become a designated beneficiary. Beneficiaries can be changed after the IRA owner's death, but only to beneficiaries named by the IRA owner during his or her life (from the owner's preapproved list as spelled out on the plan's beneficiary form). No beneficiary can be added to the list who wasn't named by the owner—doing so would undermine the whole goal of leaving your money only to the people you want to inherit it.

In most cases, the designated beneficiary will wind up being the person you named on the IRA or company plan. But in other cases, it may not go that way. So, in fact, the actual designated beneficiary won't be known until after you're dead! The designated beneficiary on your IRA or company plan will not be determined until September 30 of the year following the year of the IRA owner's death. *Say what???*

For example, if the IRA owner (that's you) dies in 2024 (let's pray not), then the designated beneficiary will be determined on September 30, 2025. On that date, there will only be one designated beneficiary left standing, and that person (hopefully the one you named) will officially become *the* designated beneficiary.

"Could someone besides the beneficiary I name end up as the designated beneficiary on September 30 of the year after my death?"

"Easily." You see, the period between the IRA owner's death—say, June 10, 2024—and September 30, 2025 (the September 30 of the year after the owner's death), is what is commonly known as the *gap* period (see Figure 4, below) during which a variety of things can happen. A beneficiary can be changed during the gap period (but only to some other beneficiary named by the IRA owner). The change can be to another primary beneficiary or a contingent beneficiary (terms I'll get to shortly), but it cannot be changed to anyone whose name you did not put on the IRA beneficiary designation form. So, your designated beneficiary could wind up being a different person than you had in mind, but no *new* designated beneficiary can be introduced after your death. The only ones who can inherit are beneficiaries named by you, so no need to worry about having to file a complaint from beyond the grave.

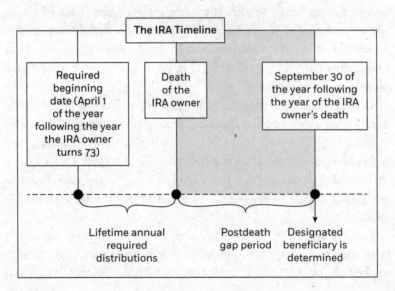

Figure 4. The Gap Period IRA Timeline

Primary and Contingent Beneficiaries

This brings us to the importance of naming contingent (also known as secondary) beneficiaries in addition to the primary (or first-named) beneficiary, who has first dibs on the account.

If he or she is living when the IRA owner or plan participant dies, the primary beneficiary will inherit the account. But the primary can also decide not to accept the inheritance and *disclaim* any right to it. Called a *renunciation* in legal parlance, this disclaimer is a written declaration that the beneficiary does not want the account he or she is to inherit. In this case, the IRA would pass to the contingent beneficiary (if there is one).

Let's say Ed named his son Bill as the primary beneficiary on his IRA. Ed also named Bill's son Jim as the contingent beneficiary. Ed dies in 2024. Although Bill is legally entitled to the IRA, he decides he doesn't need the money and would rather see his son Jim inherit it. Once Bill disclaims his interest through a renunciation, Jim, formerly the contingent beneficiary, now becomes the primary beneficiary.

To change the designated beneficiary, a disclaimer must be considered valid under Section 2518 of the tax code. A valid disclaimer is defined as a written refusal to accept property to which you are legally entitled. For an IRA, this disclaimer must be filed with the IRA custodian (i.e., the bank, broker, fund company, etc. holding the IRA) within nine months of the IRA owner's death (unless the person disclaiming is a minor, in which case the nine-month period would begin upon the minor's twenty-first birthday). The person disclaiming cannot accept any of the benefits of the property or direct who will get the property as a result of the disclaimer. This means the primary beneficiary cannot say, "I don't want it. Give it to my buddy Joe." Then the property goes to the next in line (usually the contingent beneficiary), based on the wishes of the decedent. Beneficiaries can disclaim part or all of an inheritance.

If the disclaimer does not qualify under Code Section 2518, then it is not considered to be a valid disclaimer. In this case, the designated beneficiary cannot be changed, and the transfer will be treated, taxwise, as a gift. Caution: A disclaimer is a legal document and should be drafted by a knowledgeable attorney. In other words, don't try this at home.

Had Bill not disinherited himself, he would have been the designated beneficiary. But after the disclaimer, Jim inherits and gets the nod as designated beneficiary when that is determined on September 30, 2025. Since the stretch IRA has been eliminated for both Bill and Jim under the SECURE Act, they would each have been stuck having to withdraw the inherited IRA funds within 10 years after Ed's death under the 10-year rule. This same rule will likely affect many families. In the past, a disclaimer could lengthen the payout period when a younger beneficiary, say a grandchild, ended up as the designated beneficiary through the stretch IRA. But that won't happen much anymore. These days, with no difference in the post-death payout period for most inheritors, the disclaimer decision will now most likely be made for nontax reasons based on who the family wants to receive the funds.

This post-death flexibility is only possible because the IRA owner (Ed) was smart enough to name a contingent beneficiary (his grandson, Jim). You should always name a contingent beneficiary (or several, as the case may be) on every retirement account you have. By naming a contingent beneficiary, you will have made that person an approved beneficiary in the "postseason," so to speak. Once that person is eligible through your declaration, he or she can become the designated beneficiary after your death despite not having originally been the primary beneficiary.

But, in the example I cited, if Jim *hadn't* been named contingent beneficiary, couldn't Bill, in disclaiming the inheritance, just have instructed the bank to turn the IRA over to Jim instead of him?

The answer is no. Bill can name Jim as his own beneficiary, but he has no right to name Jim as beneficiary of the inherited IRA; only the IRA owner can do that. If Bill had such a right, he could instead name Spike, Jim's stupid twin brother, who runs through money faster than Kansas can whip up a tornado—which would have been totally against Ed's wishes. Remember, Bill can only disclaim (refuse) the inheritance, nothing more.

If Bill had disclaimed his interest in the inheritance and his father had named no contingent beneficiary, then the person next in line to receive the IRA would be determined by the IRA document, which would most likely name Ed's estate. In this case, whoever is named in Ed's will would inherit the IRA. In the absence of a will, a legal procedure called *intestacy* would take over, leaving the state to decide who would inherit the asset.

If Bill's father did *not* name a contingent beneficiary and Bill disclaimed the inheritance, how would the inherited IRA then be paid out? To find out, we would have to wait until September 30, 2025, when the designated beneficiary is determined. But, of course, if there is no contingent beneficiary named, and Bill disclaims, guess what? On September 30, 2025, the envelope is opened, and oops . . . *there is no designated beneficiary!*

"But wait a minute, what if the will says Jim is to receive the disclaimed account? Won't he be declared the designated beneficiary on September 30, 2025?"

Nope. And if you've been paying close attention, you know why.

Jim can *never* be a *designated beneficiary* because his grandpa, the IRA owner, didn't *name* him as such. Jim is only a *beneficiary* because he has inherited through the will. When someone inherits through the will, the *estate* is the beneficiary. The estate is not a person and, therefore, cannot be a designated beneficiary. It makes no difference that Jim receives the IRA through the estate. The estate is still the beneficiary on the date that the designated beneficiary is determined. When that happens in this case, there is no designated beneficiary and the IRA will be paid out to Jim, but under the rules applied to a situation in which an IRA owner has died without naming a designated beneficiary. Those rules, explained in detail shortly, require you to know whether the IRA owner died before or after his required beginning date (RBD).

So, the bottom line is this: *always* name a contingent beneficiary in addition to a primary beneficiary on your beneficiary form to preserve your chance to have a say in the allocations of your assets, from beyond the grave.

How the Stretch IRA Works—for Those Who Still Qualify

The IRS does not set a dollar limit on stretch IRA growth; it only sets a time limit that governs the date by which the account must be completely withdrawn.

Consider this example: An IRA owner dies after choosing her 40-year-old daughter as the named beneficiary. Because her daughter, Milda, has a disability, she qualifies as an eligible designated beneficiary (EDB). This means that once Milda inherits the IRA, she can stretch it over her life expectancy of 44.8 years (based on her age, 41, in the year after she inherits). She needs to use the life expectancy table only once—to look up her age in the year following the year of her mother's death, which is her first required distribution year. To calculate her RMD for each successive year, Milda will subtract one year from her 44.8-year life expectancy until that set term has expired or she's withdrawn everything from the account (a beneficiary can always withdraw more than the required amount), whichever comes first.

Calculating RMDs for Inherited IRAs

This gets a little funky because of the many variables.

IRA beneficiaries are subject to RMDs, as well as to the 25 percent penalty for not taking an RMD. Calculating the RMD depends on which kind of beneficiary you are. There are different kinds (I don't mean good and evil), and in some cases the payout rules will differ depending on when the plan participant died—either before or after the required beginning date (RBD).

A *designated beneficiary* enjoys the special status of having a life expectancy—though not necessarily a "life" (even the IRS can't guarantee that). For calculating their lifetime RMDs on an inherited IRA, nonspouse eligible designated beneficiaries (who still get the stretch IRA) do not look to either the Uniform Lifetime Table or the IRS Joint Life Expectancy Table used by plan owners. Instead, they use the Single Life Expectancy Table for Inherited IRAs (see Figure 5, page 166). A nonspouse beneficiary would use this table to compute only the first year's required distribution for the inherited IRA—and only if that nonspouse beneficiary is an EDB. The life expectancy will then be reduced by one for each succeeding year.

A spouse beneficiary who is the sole inheritor and elects to have RMDs deferred until the deceased IRA owner would have turned age 73 gets to use the Uniform Lifetime Table instead of the Single Life Expectancy Table. However, in applying the Uniform Lifetime Table, the spouse must use the deceased owner's age—not the spouse's own age. (This deferral election provision was newly created under the SECURE 2.0 Act—see Chapter 6 for more details.) A spouse beneficiary who doesn't make the deferral election must start RMDs in the year after the IRA owner's death. In that case, the spouse beneficiary would use the Single Life Expectancy Table and can go back to the table each year to recalculate his or her present-moment life expectancy.

Figure 5. Single Life Expectancy Table (for Inherited IRAs)

To be used for calculating post-death required distributions to beneficiaries.

This table applies for inherited RMDs for 2022 and later years.

Age of IRA or Plan Beneficiary	Life Expectancy (in Years)	Age of IRA or Plan Beneficiary	Life Expectancy (in Years)	Age of IRA or Plan Beneficiary	Life Expectancy (in Years)
0	84.6				
1	83.7	41	44.8	81	10.5
2	82.8	42	43.8	82	9.9
3	81.8	43	42.9	83	9.3
4	80.8	44	41.9	84	8.7
5	79.8	45	41.0	85	8.1
6	78.8	46	40.0	86	7.6
7	77.9	47	39.0	87	7.1
8	76.9	48	38.1	88	6.6
9	75.9	49	37.1	89	6.1
10	74.9	50	36.2	90	5.7
11	73.9	51	35.3	91	5.3
12	72.9	52	34.3	92	4.9
13	71.9	53	33.4	93	4.6
14	70.9	54	32.5	94	4.3
15	69.9	55	31.6	95	4.0
16	69.0	56	30.6	96	3.7
17	68.0	57	29.8	97	3.4
18	67.0	58	28.9	98	3.2
19	66.0	59	28.0	99	3.0
20	65.0	60	27.1	100	2.8
21	64.1	61	26.2	101	2.6
22	63.1	62	25.4	102	2.5
23	62.1	63	24.5	103	2.3
24	61.1	64	23.7	104	2.2
25	60.2	65	22.9	105	2.1
26	59.2	66	22.0	106	2.1
27	58.2	67	21.2	107	2.1
28	57.3	68	20.4	108	2.0
29	56.3	69	19.6	109	2.0
30	55.3	70	18.8	110	2.0
31	54.4	71	18.0	111	2.0
32	53.4	72	17.2	112	2.0
33	52.5	73	16.4	113	1.9
34	51.5	74	15.6	114	1.9
35	50.5	75	14.8	115	1.8
36	49.6	76	14.1	116	1.8
37	48.6	77	13.3	117	1.6
38	47.7	78	12.6	118	1.4
39	46.7	79	11.9	119	1.1
40	45.7	80	11.2	120+	1.0

This table is for calculating the post-death distributions required for designated beneficiaries who inherited before 2020 and non-spouse eligible designated beneficiaries (EDBs) who inherit after 2019. (It is also used for spouse EDBs who do not make the RMD deferral election.) It is never to be used by IRA owners or plan participants to calculate lifetime required distributions. A nonspouse beneficiary would only use this table to compute the first year's required distribution for the inherited IRA if they qualify as a designated beneficiary (for pre-2020 deaths) or as an EDB (for post-2019 deaths). The life expectancy will then be reduced by one for each successive year. Beneficiaries subject to the 10-year payout rule under the SECURE Act will use this table only if they inherited from someone who died *after* their required beginning date, and even in that case, only for years one through nine of the 10-year term. Other than that situation, nonspouse beneficiaries will not use this table. They will simply have to withdraw all their inherited funds by the end of the 10th year after death. They can, of course, voluntarily withdraw anything they wish in years one through nine. The more they withdraw in those years, the less they will have to withdraw at the end of the 10th year. I'll expand on this rule in the next chapter (Chapter 6) on beneficiary payouts.

A *noneligible designated beneficiary (NEDB)*, aka most nonspouse beneficiaries, must use the 10-year rule for distributions from an inherited IRA. The entire account balance remaining becomes the RMD in year ten. NEDBs who inherit from someone who died *before* their RBD can still take out as much or as little as they wish in years one through nine, but still, the entire remaining balance in the inherited IRA must be withdrawn by the end of the 10th year after death. Any beneficiary who inherits a Roth IRA is also exempt from RMDs for years one through nine of the 10-year term. Because Roth IRA owners are never subject to lifetime RMDs, they are always deemed to have died before reaching their RBD, regardless of their age at death. (Once again, see Chapter 6 for more details on these special beneficiary payout rules.)

A *non-designated beneficiary (NDB)*, on the other hand—an estate, charity, or nonqualifying trust, for example—has no life expectancy.

Post-death payouts to these beneficiaries follow a separate, less favorable set of rules that I'll explain later.

Get used to these two terms: beneficiary and designated beneficiary. When I use *beneficiary*, I am referring to the inheritor of an IRA or plan who may or may not be a designated beneficiary, whereas when I use the term *designated beneficiary*, I am referring strictly to a person whom the IRA owner or company plan participant named as a beneficiary on the beneficiary form. (Go back and review the "Talking the Talk" section for a comparative explanation of these terms.)

Spouse or Nonspouse Makes a Difference Too

Another distinction among IRA inheritors is whether the beneficiary is a spouse or a nonspouse. A *spouse* is the wife or husband of the deceased IRA owner or plan participant. *Nonspouse beneficiaries* are divided into two more groups: *persons* and *other*. The former is defined as an individual who is not the legal spouse of the IRA owner or plan participant, such as a son or daughter, friend, or partner. *Other* can include an estate, charity, trust, or entity that, without a life expectancy, can never be a designated beneficiary. (Unless, perhaps, it's Pinocchio. You may recall that he becomes a real boy!)

Incorrect "Titling" Will Destroy Your Inherited IRA

Before a nonspouse beneficiary begins RMDs, the deceased IRA owner's account must be titled correctly. The IRS stipulates that the deceased's name must stay on the account. Nonspouse beneficiaries cannot retitle inherited accounts in their own name—otherwise, the account becomes taxable immediately, and *poof* . . . it disappears. Often the beneficiary, let's say a son, will say, "I inherited the account, so it's mine now; I may as well put it under my name." Sounds logical; after all, it does belong to him. The IRS, however, deems this action to be a rollover (even though no money is actually withdrawn from the account) and subjects the entire account balance to income tax. To avoid this costly mistake, make sure the deceased owner's name remains on the account forever.

Here's a tale that might have turned into a horror story, had I not been able to save this inherited IRA from becoming taxable before its time.

When her mother died unexpectedly in a tragic car accident, a client of mine, age 40, and her brother learned that their mother had named them as beneficiaries on her $500,000 IRA account. My client and her brother live in New York State, but their mother had lived in Florida, so they retained their mother's Florida attorney to handle the estate. Luckily for them, they asked the estate attorney to check with me on any tax issues. The attorney dutifully touched base and, figuring it would be the same as deeding the mother's house to the children, suggested casually, "Why don't I just go ahead and put the IRAs in the beneficiaries' names and get that out of the way."

I rocketed up in my chair with a thundering "NOOOOOOO!" Then I composed myself and explained in a quieter tone that an IRA is a completely different animal from a house. It is loaded with unforgiving tax traps if not handled properly; changing the name on the inherited IRA would make it a rollover and the children would wind up owing taxes on the whole $500,000 that tax year.

"But if the law denies rollovers for inherited accounts, how can a spouse roll over? That's an inherited account, isn't it?" the attorney asked.

"No, it isn't," I replied. "At least for tax law purposes, it isn't. Under the tax code, an inherited account means a retirement account inherited by someone other than a spouse. That's because when a spouse—a wife, say—rolls the IRA over to her own IRA, it becomes *her IRA* and is no longer inherited."

The attorney asked for the specific tax law so she could brush up on it. For you Code nerds out there who may be wondering, "Yeah, Ed, where does it say that?" here's where to look: IRC Section 408(d)(3)(C), "Denial of Rollover Treatment for Inherited Accounts." Doesn't beat around the bush, does it?

Satisfied, the attorney then asked, "Well, how should the account be titled?"

The tax rules offer no official titling language. So, let's assume that the name of the deceased IRA owner was Roberta Smith and the named beneficiary is Elizabeth Smith. Here's what other advisors and I would recommend as an acceptable way to title an inherited IRA: **"Roberta Smith IRA (deceased May 12, 2024), F/B/O (for the benefit of) Elizabeth Smith, Beneficiary."** If there were more than one beneficiary named on the IRA, then the IRA would be split and the other beneficiaries' names would go at the end of the account set up for them. If the account were left to Elizabeth Smith and her brother, James Smith, then James Smith's beneficiary IRA would be titled: **"Roberta Smith IRA (deceased May 12, 2024), F/B/O James Smith, Beneficiary."**

Keep each inherited IRA separate. Typically, each financial institution has its own verbiage for this, but the important thing is that the account is identified as a "beneficiary account" and that the deceased IRA owner's name stays on it. The financial institution may use the words *inherited IRA* instead of *beneficiary account.* That's OK too. The "F/B/O"—which, as just noted, means "for the benefit of"—is sometimes written out rather than abbreviated. That's just fine too.

It is not unusual for a financial institution to make the uninformed (to put it mildly) mistake of transferring the title of a nonspouse beneficiary's inherited IRA to the beneficiary's name in the honest belief that it is doing the right thing. If your bank or brokerage suggests this, persuade the uninformed employee—or, even better, the employee's supervisor—that the account must stay in the deceased owner's name or you'll get robbed. If you have to, give them the section of the tax code I cited above. Remember, it's your own money at risk now.

Although the IRA owner's name must remain on the account, the Social Security number must be changed from the deceased's to the beneficiary's. The IRS goes by the Social Security number on the account to determine who will pay tax on any distributions, and it frowns upon having to collect from beyond the grave. Therefore, for tax-reporting purposes, I recommend changing the Social Security number on inherited accounts as soon as possible after the owner's death. Then it won't later slip your mind and incur the IRS's wrath.

If I hadn't alerted the Florida attorney to the grave (no pun intended) mistake she was about to make, my client and her brother would have found themselves paying tax on the $500,000 instead of being able to grow the account tax-deferred and spread distributions over many more years. Back then, before the SECURE Act took that away, they qualified for the stretch IRA. Had things gone differently, they might have slapped the attorney with a lawsuit for costing them a bundle. But instead there were smiles all around.

While the tax code considers taking the decedent's name off an inherited account to be the same as a taxable withdrawal of the entire account balance, this doesn't mean a nonspouse beneficiary can't change the account's location via a direct transfer from one bank to another without being taxed if, say, the investments are performing badly. The IRS rules allow this. The transfer can be made for any reason, not just to change investments. The bank holding the account must be willing to make the transfer to the receiving bank, however, and some banks aren't. They will say, "We don't do trustee-to-trustee transfers, but if you are unhappy, here's your money." So, you're stuck—because once funds are distributed, they're taxable. Thus, an uncooperative financial institution can hold your inherited IRA hostage. Of course, depending on the size of the account, you may have greater leverage than you know because the bank will not want to lose such a valuable customer.

What if you take the check and, within the allotted 60-day period for tax- and penalty-free withdrawals, transfer it to a correctly titled inherited IRA account at the mutual fund company where you want it? No good. The 60-day rule applies only to eligible rollovers, and a nonspouse beneficiary cannot roll over an inherited IRA without killing the account taxwise. I cannot emphasize this enough.

Where There's a Will . . .
It Still Won't Help Your IRA

When I ask people, "Who will get your IRA after you die?" what typically pops out of their mouths is "I don't know. But it's in my will." They figure it *must* be covered in their will. "Isn't that what a will is for? To say who gets what?" That's true—of property that is meant to pass through the will. But . . .

Most couples own their home jointly. They have joint investment, bank, and brokerage accounts. They also have life insurance, pensions, and IRAs or other retirement accounts. That list of property is the typical estate of every American couple. Well, guess how much of that typical estate is typically covered by every typical American couple's typical will (assuming the will is perfect in all respects)?

None of it!

People are shocked when I tell them this. They react with "I just paid thousands of dollars for a will, with trusts and a complete estate plan, and you're telling me it hardly covers any of the assets I own?" For many people, indeed most, that's right.

Most property today passes *outside the will*. In other words, the will is overridden. For example, if you own your home jointly with your spouse and one of you dies, the house goes to the surviving spouse who is the joint owner, regardless of what the will says. It passes by operation of law that trumps any conflicting provision in your will.

The same is true of property that passes by beneficiary designation, such as an IRA, a company retirement account, or an insurance policy. All these items are spoken for, so to speak. They have assigned destinations and are transferred according to the designated beneficiary form, not the will. The form overrides the will. So, if your IRA or other retirement account is one of the larger assets in your estate, as it is for many people, then your beneficiary form is the essential document. It controls the distribution of the money you worked for and saved all your life. It is, in effect, the will for your IRA that assigns the funds directly to your beneficiaries.

You can use the designated beneficiary form supplied by your bank, brokerage, or mutual fund company—in fact, some insist upon this—but if the form doesn't provide enough space to fit all the pertinent information about your beneficiaries that's necessary, attach a separate sheet. Here's why . . .

When you have many beneficiaries and contingent beneficiaries, it is unlikely that the name, share, relationship, Social Security number, etc. for each beneficiary will fit in the small amount of room the typical beneficiary forms provide. Most forms give you room for two or three beneficiaries and that's it. Don't write smaller to cram the information in or include some names but not others. Write, "See attached list of primary and contingent beneficiaries" or "See attached rider listing all beneficiaries" and clip the list(s) to the form. The idea is to *force* the reader (the financial institution) to look elsewhere for the complete list of beneficiaries rather than assume that the only beneficiaries are those listed on the front page of the form. Therefore, both your "See attached" note and your attached lists of names and information should appear to be obviously part of the document. This is an important tip. Follow it, or else.

These days, more and more beneficiary information gets collected digitally in online forms (that you should still check for accuracy!), where you should have plenty of room to enter all of your beneficiary info. But I still see lots of forms requiring handwritten info. Either way, check and recheck these listings because your choices will be etched in stone once you're gone.

If the financial institution will accept your own customized designated beneficiary form, that's OK too, but institutions often prefer having the information on their own forms.

Items to discuss with your financial institution include:

▪ Your beneficiary's ability to name a beneficiary. This can avoid the beneficiary's estate becoming the beneficiary. When the estate is the beneficiary, the IRA will have to go through probate, resulting in possible delays plus additional fees and expenses, and it could end up handed to someone you never intended.

▪ Your nonspouse beneficiary's ability to move the inherited account to another financial institution via a trustee-to-trustee transfer. This is important because a nonspouse beneficiary cannot do a rollover. That would cause all the funds to be subject to tax and end the inherited IRA.

∎ A "per stirpes" payout in case your beneficiary dies before you do. *Per stirpes* means that if a beneficiary who is one of several beneficiaries on an inherited account dies, then that person's share goes to his or her descendants and not the other co-beneficiaries.

∎ The default provisions of your IRA agreement (more about this later in the chapter).

∎ Procedures for keeping track of beneficiary forms. You don't want to use a bank or other financial institution that has none or won't reveal what its procedures are. Today, many of these forms can be reviewed online.

∎ Whether the financial institution will provide you with an "acknowledged copy" of your designated beneficiary form. By an "acknowledged copy" I mean a copy signed by someone at the company so that in the event that the firm loses the form after your death, your beneficiaries can present this acknowledged copy and know that it will be accepted. Who at the bank or financial institution should sign the acknowledged copy? Anyone with a title, even if it's "chief janitor" (who is probably a vice president in disguise anyway). This is a precautionary measure, but one that could settle any potential family feuds.

Who Gets What?

There is another important but obvious item that should go without saying, but I'll say it anyway because I take nothing for granted. You must spell out who gets what—in other words, clearly state each beneficiary's share. I know this sounds like a no-brainer, but it isn't. Most beneficiary forms get no respect (not to mention time or attention) and get filled out carelessly. If you have four children and want them to inherit equally, then say that. Use the term *equally* or *25 percent each* or *one-quarter each* so that it is clear what percentage or fraction you want to go to whom. The same goes for contingent beneficiaries. Say who gets what, or there could be big problems ahead for your beneficiaries. Don't believe me? Just ask Janice.

Janice came to me for tax advice after the death of her mother. She and her five sisters had inherited their mother's IRA account, which had amassed about $600,000. Most of the funds had come from a rollover that Janice's deceased father had left to her mother. Janice told me about the trouble she was having with the bank. She knew her mother's intention had been for all six sisters to share the IRA equally. However, there was no instruction included on the bank's form to indicate the desired allocation of IRA account shares. As a result, the bank would pay only Janice, the eldest, whose name was listed first on the form. Absent any instructions to the contrary from the deceased, the bank took the position that sister number one was the primary beneficiary, and sisters two through six were all contingent beneficiaries. This meant that sister two could inherit only if Janice had died before the IRA owner, their mother; sister three could only inherit if sisters one and two had died before their mother; sister four could inherit only if sisters one, two, and three had died before their mother; and so on.

Had she been a creep, Janice could legally have taken the entire $600,000 with the bank's blessing, leaving her sisters high and dry, and taking off on a hell of a vacation somewhere (although, ultimately, she might have wound up on a permanent vacation to hell). But she wasn't that type. She wanted the account divided equally among all six sisters, as her late mother had wanted. If only Mom had spelled out her intentions . . .

The only way to uphold the mother's wishes to have the IRA shared equally was for Janice, deemed the primary beneficiary, to withdraw the entire $600,000 IRA, pay the income tax on it, and then divide the remainder equally among her sisters as gifts. (Of course, she could also have gone through the disclaimer process, but she and her sisters were already disgusted with having to deal with so many legal complexities arising from their mother's death and didn't want to go through more.) The income tax turned out to be over $240,000. Only Janice could take the distribution, so she was responsible for the tax. And because the distribution was reported on one single tax return instead of six different tax returns, the tax levied was much higher than it would have been had each sister been able to report one-sixth of the distribution on her individual tax returns. (Under our graduated tax rate system, six people who report $100,000 of income each will pay less tax than one person reporting $600,000.)

Although the even split that the mother had wanted was ultimately achieved, almost half the IRA was lost to taxes. This outcome would easily have been avoided had the mother added just two measly little words to the designated beneficiary form: "equal shares."

Estate as Beneficiary

The last thing you want is for your IRA to pass through your estate. Once the IRA is paid to your estate, the account cannot have a designated beneficiary. And without a designated beneficiary, there is no life expectancy, which means any stretch IRA opportunity that your eligible designated beneficiaries had under the SECURE Act has been lost. (Remember, even EDBs must first qualify as designated beneficiaries.) This seems obvious, but even the best and brightest have trouble understanding it. Here's what I mean:

A few years ago, I gave a lecture at the Wharton School of Business alumni dinner in New York City. Before I spoke, the person running the event told me that this was an extremely intelligent audience, so I should not be hesitant to speak on a highly advanced level. He made his point. They weren't dummies.

I reached the part of the lecture where I said, "Don't let the IRA pass through your estate, because your best option is to have a living beneficiary who can take distributions after your death." Then I asked the audience, "What's the life expectancy of your estate?" The response was a flurry of activity as everybody pulled out their phones to start crunching numbers. Since an estate is not a person, it cannot have a life expectancy, but I guess that was too simplistic a concept for this clever crowd.

When you name your estate as your beneficiary, you are turning your retirement plan into a probate asset like anything else that passes through a will. So, in addition to the tax ramifications, which can be hefty, probate costs will gnaw away at all the funds you worked so hard to save. If you have a large retirement plan, the combination could add up to a substantial amount of money, depending on lawyer and court filing fees. And if the will is contested, even more—perhaps most—of the IRA could get eaten up.

But the worst thing of all about naming your estate the beneficiary of your IRA—which you should never, NEVER do—is that your heirs could lose the possibility to stretch it, even if only for 10 more years.

Even if a living, breathing human being inherits through your estate, the IRA distribution rules say that an estate cannot be a designated beneficiary because it is not a person. *The beneficiaries who eventually receive the funds will receive them as an NDB—non-designated beneficiary.*

And if the estate becomes the beneficiary, for whatever reason, the distribution options are limited. For good. Into eternity. Forevermore.

OK. Point made, I hope? Let's move on.

How Does the Estate Become a Beneficiary?

When you open an IRA with a bank, broker, mutual fund company, or insurance company, one of the forms you sign is an IRA agreement. You'll recognize the IRA agreement. It's the document with the smallest possible writing and the most pages. Only the people who write them actually read them . . . maybe.

This document can kill your IRA, but only with your help. If you do not name a beneficiary, or if your beneficiary (or the financial institution holding the account) cannot find the beneficiary form, then you are subject to the default provisions of the IRA agreement, whether you read them or not. Generally, the default provisions will do in your beneficiaries, because most agreements say that if no beneficiary is named, then the IRA will be paid to your estate. And once that happens . . . say it with me now: out the window goes the possibility of being a designated beneficiary.

If you're lucky, despite your gaffe, your IRA may also get a second crack at life. If your financial institution is among those that recognize how most people are their own worst enemies when it comes to naming beneficiaries, they might just use an IRA agreement that allows for the creation of a designated beneficiary despite your forgetfulness and neglect.

For example, some IRA agreements state that if you die without a beneficiary named on your IRA, then the beneficiary will be your spouse. If you are single or divorced or your spouse is dead, then it goes to your children. If there are no children, then it goes to your estate. This creates two lines of defense before your estate can ever become the beneficiary. If your institution has this type of IRA agreement, that's great, but ultimately, it's not the institution's job to name your beneficiaries. You should do that—because the people named by the company may not be the beneficiaries you would choose. Here's such an example:

John was married to Mary for 40 years and they had three children. After Mary died, John remarried. John's understanding with his new wife was that after he died, his IRA would go to his children and not to her. But when John died, his children could not find his IRA beneficiary form. They went to the bank, but the bank couldn't locate it either. This meant the IRA would be treated as if there had been no named beneficiary. In this case, the IRA agreement was one that sought to save people from themselves, protecting inheritances by naming a real, live human instead of the estate. Imagine John's children's dismay when their stepmother became the designated beneficiary by default, despite John's wishes. Without paper proof naming his children, the IRA plan agreement kicked in. The fact that his children couldn't lay their hands on the beneficiary form when it mattered made it as if John had never completed it.

Where's the Designated Beneficiary Form?

If at this very moment you had to put your hands on the beneficiary form for every IRA or retirement account you own, could you? For most people, the answer is no, followed by "It's OK, though; the bank will have them." Sorry, but the chances of that are about equal to the chances of the IRS closing up shop. The bank may simply have lost the forms. Or it may have destroyed them for any number of reasons—including making space for more forms—or purged them in the latest merger.

Think I speak with a forked tongue? Consider this true story:

Many years ago, a tax client of mine who was a local bank teller asked if I would prepare her son's tax return. (She said he was a student and had only one W-2 from a summer job, so the return would be easy. All clients say that . . . and I fall for it every damn time.) I saw from her son's W-2 that he'd worked at her bank over the summer, so I asked her what job he'd done. She explained that the bank had been taken over by another bank, requiring a name change. So, a crew of people—her son among them—had been hired to destroy bank documents bearing the old letterhead.

"What kind of bank documents?" I asked suspiciously.

"Blank forms, stationery, beneficiary forms, and other old or unimportant items like that," she answered.

Trust me on this. Anyone with an IRA in a bank (including me!) had better have a copy of his or her IRA beneficiary forms because, likely, the bank won't.

OK, so you can't count on banks, but since you have your IRA with a financial advisor firm, not a bank, the firm will certainly have copies, right? Probably not. Advisors move around a lot, and when they switch to a different firm, their old paperwork often gets lost in the shuffle.

Should you look for missing beneficiary forms? No! Don't waste your time. All prior choices can be changed. Fill out new beneficiary forms, keep them in a safe place, and let your beneficiaries know where that safe place is so they don't have to have your home bulldozed after your death in hopes of finding them. You doubtless think I'm exaggerating, but I'm not. I had a case where this almost happened. Two sisters called me. They were fifty-ish and their parents were in their eighties. The sisters were worried because all their lives their father had been hiding things in the house—literally in the walls, under the floors, in false panels, or under the property. Their father had somewhat of a checkered past during which he'd accumulated lots of cash and other assets, including bearer bonds, as well as numerous retirement accounts that he'd stashed, along with other important documents, at his home. (No, I won't tell you the address because I'm buying the house as soon as the parents pass away so I can go on a treasure hunt!) The sisters called because they wanted to have an updated estate plan for their parents. It was an emergency, they said, because their father (the only one who knew where all the gems were buried) was losing his memory and deteriorating fast. We were able to track down most of the investments and contacted the various banks and brokerages, most of which had nothing on file as far as beneficiary forms were concerned. So, we requested new forms and had the parents fill them out. The parents also agreed to fill out powers of attorney allowing the daughters to handle their financial affairs. Fortunately, the daughters had enough foresight to act fast when they realized the writing was on (and in) the wall. They eventually found most of the financial information they needed, but that is not the case with many beneficiaries.

The mutual fund companies have a pretty good record on beneficiary forms. Some even print the beneficiary and contingent beneficiary names right on the quarterly or annual statements. But again, it's your job to check that these beneficiary designations are current.

What do I mean by *current*?

Even if the financial institution has a beneficiary form on file (or online), it has no way of knowing if your beneficiary has died unless you update your form with this news. That's what I mean by keeping the form current. Most of the beneficiary forms I see include dead beneficiaries because they haven't been touched since the account was opened in, say, 1986. Having a dead beneficiary is the same as having no beneficiary, which is almost always the same as naming your estate as beneficiary. Capisce?

Under the IRA rules, you can change your beneficiary at any age, any time you wish, except after you're dead. I mention this because for some strange reason there is so much confusion about these rules. Under the rules now in effect, nothing is locked in until you die.

When I tell this to my older clients who thought they were locked into poor, unchangeable choices they'd made in the long distant past, they are absolutely thrilled. They love the fact that they can make changes anytime they want. One client told me he calls this new freedom of choice his "IRA leverage." I asked him what he meant by that. And he explained, "Well, it's like this. I can change my IRA beneficiaries any time and as often as I want now. Last week I had my 80th birthday party and two of my kids didn't show up. So, they're out!"

Got it. Attention, prospective IRA beneficiaries: Better be good to your parents. They can, and will, eliminate you in a heartbeat.

Life Events

Pay attention to what I call *life events* that may require appropriate changes on all your beneficiary forms.

By "life events," I mean the following:

▪ Changes in the tax laws seem to occur every time Congress meets. (Stay up to date on how these laws could affect your IRA by visiting my website, www.irahelp.com, or with my monthly IRA newsletter, *Ed Slott's IRA Advisor*, see page 438.)

▪ The birth of a new grandchild may lead to your wanting to add that child as a beneficiary.

▪ If you're getting married or remarried, you may want your spouse-to-be to inherit your IRA, or maybe you don't. Whichever the case, make the appropriate changes immediately after the nuptials. (Although if you want your spouse-to-be to get your IRA and he or she is 30 years younger than you are, maybe waiting until after the honeymoon to make the changes is a safe move—just to make sure they really want you, and not just your big IRA).

▪ A divorce would certainly require beneficiary changes (if your ex-spouse was your beneficiary)—unless you are out of your mind and *want* to leave your retirement savings to your ex!

About half of the states now automatically remove your ex-spouse as your beneficiary after a divorce through what are known as *revocation upon divorce* laws. In 2018, the U.S. Supreme Court upheld those laws as constitutional in an almost unanimous ruling (eight to one) in a Minnesota case (*Sveen v. Melin, U.S. Supreme Court, No. 16-1432, June 11, 2018*). Here, an ex-wife was never removed from the beneficiary form of a life insurance policy. The court ruled that under Minnesota's revocation upon divorce statute, she (the ex-wife) would not be entitled to the funds even though she was named on the beneficiary form. After seven years in court, the deceased husband's children were awarded the money. But who knows what he'd intended? He had never revised his beneficiary form. The point is that all of this could have been avoided had the beneficiary form been kept up to date. Then the funds would have been allocated according to *his* wishes, not a court's. Although this was a life insurance beneficiary form case, the court said that this ruling could apply to IRAs since they also pass by beneficiary designation. Meanwhile, if the account had been a 401(k), the ex-wife would have won and received the money since the federal ERISA (federal retirement law) governing 401(k)s overrides state laws, such as Minnesota's revocation upon divorce law.

The moral of the story? Always update retirement plan beneficiary forms after a divorce!

∎ You named your spouse, but now your spouse has died and probably won't need your retirement account wherever he or she is headed. Similarly, the death of any named beneficiary would require an update to your beneficiary form.

Keep your antennae tuned for any such events that would necessitate a change in the beneficiary form for each retirement account you have. And make the change right away. Don't leave the updating to next week or next month to be forgotten about until you die and your beneficiaries realize the changes went unmade, at which point there is no designated beneficiary and your heirs may have to empty the inherited account much quicker than they might have otherwise.

So, don't think of this form as a stale old document to be filled out once and never revisited. Think of it as something that needs constant attention, just like you.

Planning for Multiple Beneficiaries on One IRA Account

Separate Account Rules

What Are Separate Accounts?

Separate accounts (also referred to as the "separate account rule" or "separate share rule") are necessary when a single IRA has multiple beneficiaries. This is a common occurrence since IRA owners often name several children as beneficiaries on their IRA. But when more than one person inherits a single IRA, distribution complications can arise.

The idea is to create separate accounts or shares by splitting the IRA into one account for each beneficiary. You can split the IRA during your lifetime, or the beneficiaries can split it after your death. The beneficiaries can never split an IRA while you are still living. After all, it's not theirs to split until you are gone.

The SECURE Act changes the way you need to evaluate splitting IRAs into separate accounts for multiple IRA beneficiaries. Before the SECURE Act, it always made sense to recommend splitting accounts so younger beneficiaries could stretch required minimum distributions (RMDs) over their own longer life expectancy. With the demise of the stretch IRA for most beneficiaries, splitting IRAs for that purpose alone is no longer necessary for nonspouse beneficiaries who inherited *before* the IRA owner had reached his or her RMD required beginning date (RBD). Those beneficiaries will only be constrained by the 10-year payout rule. However, creating separate accounts is important if the IRA owner died *on or after* the RBD because that requires the beneficiaries to also take annual RMDs over the 10-year period. In any case, there are more practical reasons to continue recommending that separate accounts be created.

Separate Account Deadlines

When you leave your IRA to multiple beneficiaries, they will most likely need (or want) to split the account. To do this, they need to know the rules and deadlines.

The first deadline comes when the identity of the beneficiaries is determined by *September 30 of the year following your death.* (Remember, we covered that earlier in this chapter.) The beneficiaries identified as of September 30 are the only ones considered when determining the required distribution rules. In some cases, it will be helpful to the remaining beneficiaries if another beneficiary is paid out before that date and therefore can be disregarded for required distribution purposes.

The second deadline arises when the account must be split. Even though the IRS requires beneficiaries to be identified by that September 30, beneficiaries have three more months—until the December 31 following the year of death—to actually split the account. But they are better off not counting on that extra time. That's because it may take a while for the custodian to open separate accounts, and—especially near the end of the year—you don't want to be scrambling to meet a December 31 deadline. Instead, be safe and get the split done by the September 30 of the year after the IRA owner dies.

Non-Designated Beneficiary (NDB)

As was true before the SECURE Act, if one of the beneficiaries is a non-designated beneficiary (NDB)—i.e., not human, such as a charity, an estate, or a nonqualifying trust—each beneficiary may be forced to take distributions faster than otherwise required. The exact timing depends on whether you die before or after your required beginning date (RBD). (The RBD is generally April 1 of the year after the individual reaches age 73.)

Except in the case of a split, all the beneficiaries must be paid out by December 31 of the fifth year following death if the IRA owner dies before their RBD. If the owner dies on or after his RBD, all the beneficiaries (without a split) must be paid over the remaining life expectancy of the deceased IRA owner (had he or she continued to live). Only in tax law can a deceased person still have a life expectancy! Sometimes this life expectancy is referred to as the "ghost life expectancy." For good reason.

What can the beneficiaries do to change this outcome? They can either ensure that the NDB is paid out by the September 30 deadline or split the account in a timely way. That would allow the individual beneficiaries to reap the benefits of the more advantageous payout rules—either the stretch IRA (if an eligible designated beneficiary) or the 10-year payout rule (if a noneligible designated beneficiary).

Take Ann, who named both her adult son, Brian, and her favorite charity as 50/50 beneficiaries of her IRA. Ann died on May 15, 2023, at age 64. If the charity, a non-designated beneficiary, is paid out its share by September 30, 2024, only Brian will be left as a designated beneficiary. This will allow him to use the 10-year payout rule. However, if the charity is not paid out by September 30 and remains a beneficiary, Brian's payout period will be cut in half from 10 years to 5. Because Ann died before her RBD (age 73) the 5-year rule will apply to her son.

MEMORY JOG

Remember that each inherited IRA must be correctly titled (as discussed earlier in this chapter) after the IRA owner dies or risk being immediately taxed as a complete distribution. Here is how, in the case of Brian's IRA, the inherited account would be titled after the split: "Ann Smith IRA (deceased May 15, 2023), F/B/O Brian Smith, Beneficiary."

Practical Reasons for Separate Accounts

The SECURE Act changed the purpose of separate accounting in some cases of post-death planning, but it didn't eliminate the need. In some cases, each one of an IRA owner's beneficiaries will be considered a noneligible designated beneficiary (NEDB) and will only be subject to the 10-year payout rule (and not the requirement to take annual RMDs during the 10-year period). In those cases, creating separate accounts to allow a younger beneficiary to use a longer life expectancy would be of no value. However, there still may be practical reasons to split the account.

When an estate or charity or other nonliving entity is named as a beneficiary, splitting accounts in a timely manner may allow a 10-year payout to a living beneficiary instead of a 5-year payout. Also, when one of your multiple beneficiaries is an EDB, separate accounting is still necessary to preserve the stretch for the EDB.

Providing each beneficiary with a separate IRA account allows you to allocate specific investments for each beneficiary rather than leaving a certain percentage to each. Splitting accounts also allows each beneficiary to control the investment of her share after death. Finally, creating separate accounts would give each beneficiary who is subject only to the 10-year payout rule (and not the annual RMD requirement) the freedom to take a portion of her account anytime within the 10-year period.

But probably the biggest reason for beneficiaries to split an inherited IRA is one that is mandated by the IRA custodian. Generally, there can be only one tax ID for each inherited account, therefore each beneficiary must have his own inherited IRA.

> ### TIP!
>
> If you're an IRA owner, you're probably thinking, "No way am I trusting my kids to complete the split on time. I'll just split it now and deal with the extra paperwork. At least I will know for sure that after I die each will be entitled to use his or her own applicable rule to keep the IRA going." You're right. That's probably the best course of action—especially if the co-beneficiaries don't get along or have different ideas and goals. By splitting the account before they inherit, you turn your wishes into a sure thing.

Disaster-Proof Your IRA with These New Year's Resolutions

What's great about these resolutions is that they're easy. They don't involve going to a gym to work out, eating tasteless food just because it's "healthy," or cleaning out three decades worth of junk from the garage. Keeping these resolutions only requires a bit of organization when it comes to your retirement accounts.

This New Year's I will . . .

■ Name a primary beneficiary for each IRA I own.

■ Go one step further and name a secondary or contingent beneficiary (in case my primary beneficiary dies before I do) to take advantage of post-death estate-planning and disclaimer opportunities available under the IRA rules.

■ Obtain copies of the beneficiary forms outlining my wishes for each IRA I own.

■ If there are multiple beneficiaries on one IRA, make sure that each beneficiary's share (including contingent beneficiaries) is clearly identified with a fraction, a percentage, or the word *equally*, as applicable, to eliminate any confusion about who gets what.

■ Make sure that the financial institution or my financial advisor has my beneficiary selections on file and that their records agree with my choices. (At many institutions you can check this online.)

■ Keep a copy of all my IRA beneficiary forms and give copies to my financial advisor and attorney.

■ Let my beneficiaries know where to find my IRA beneficiary forms. I will give them details on all the retirement accounts I have and where the beneficiary form for each is located.

■ Advise them on how the payout rules will apply to their share of any retirement accounts they inherit from me. (Or maybe just give each of them a copy of this book.)

■ Review my IRA beneficiary forms at least once each year to make sure that they are correct and reflect any changes due to new tax laws or major life events such as a death, birth, adoption, marriage, remarriage, divorce, or *somebody forgetting my birthday!*

SIX

PAYOUTS TO YOUR BENEFICIARIES

Money is always there, but the pockets change.
—GERTRUDE STEIN (1874-1946)

Post-Death Distributions

Stein was right. The pockets will indeed change after your death, so make sure to prepare your beneficiaries with the information they need so that more money stays in their pockets and less lines the deep pockets of the IRS. This requires following strict rules that spell out the amounts your beneficiaries must take, and by when.

Now that you know about the different kinds of beneficiaries, plus the ins and outs of beneficiarydom, it's critical to understand the payout periods that will affect each type of beneficiary. This is tricky terrain. Lots of different variables determine real-life payout outcomes, so pay close attention. Once you grasp the rules that will govern payouts for your beneficiaries, you might even discover details that have you rethinking some of the beneficiary choices you've already made. The good news is, you're still alive! So, it's not too late to make changes. This chapter will give you all the information you need to help you advise your loved ones about what to expect when they're expecting . . . an inheritance, that is.

Three Beneficiaries Categories

Payout rules are determined by multiple factors, but three over-arching beneficiary categories define the different outcomes. To know what payout periods will apply to your beneficiaries, it's critical to understand the three beneficiary categories that determine the schedule.

While you can pick who you want to inherit your accounts, you can't decide how the IRS categorizes those individuals into three different types:

- Noneligible designated beneficiaries (NEDBs)

- Eligible designated beneficiaries (EDBs)

- Non-designated beneficiaries (NDBs)

Noneligible Designated Beneficiaries (NEDBs)

These individual designated beneficiaries are either people, like your adult children and grandchildren, or qualifying trusts. Most nonspouse beneficiaries fall into this category, and they will be subject to the 10-year rule for post-death payouts, regardless of when they inherit or whether you reached your required beginning date (RBD) before you died. With the SECURE Act, they are no longer eligible for the stretch IRA. The new rules covered here apply to anyone who has inherited retirement funds in 2020 or later. Beneficiaries who inherited in 2019 or earlier can still use the old stretch IRA rules.

Eligible Designated Beneficiaries (EDBs)

I like to call this category *beneficiary royalty*. These people include the account owner's surviving spouse and minor children up to age 21, people with disabilities or chronic illness, and individuals not more than 10 years younger than the account owner. The elite of beneficiaries, they fly first class and don't mingle with the other riffraff. Because they are exempt from the SECURE Act's 10-year rule, they are the rare birds who qualify for the stretch IRA no matter when they inherit.

Non-Designated Beneficiaries (NDBs)

If EDBs are the royalty, these are the serfs. NDBs are nonhumans with no life expectancy. They include estates, charities, and non-qualifying trusts. Most of you won't have beneficiaries in this category because *you've been reading this book* and have, of course, heeded my warnings against winding up without a designated beneficiary. You've carefully filled out your beneficiary forms listing named beneficiaries and contingent beneficiaries to make sure your retirement savings don't end up in this third-tier class, right? Right??? NDBs definitely don't qualify for the stretch.

Having Designated Beneficiaries Still Matters!

Even though most designated beneficiaries will still be subject to the 10-year payout rule after your death, naming an individual or qualifying trust as the designated beneficiary of your retirement account brings advantages. At a minimum, having a designated beneficiary can lock in the 10-year rule. In cases where your inheritors would qualify as EDBs, it's crucial to take care of the *D* part of that acronym. Remember, to get the stretch, EDBs must be *designated*, meaning you named them on the beneficiary form.

Advantages for Designated Beneficiaries

Even with the 10-year rule in effect, there are still plenty of good reasons to have a designated beneficiary (instead of having the IRA or retirement plan pass through your will or worse, through intestacy if you have no will).

Naming direct beneficiaries *can avoid potential disinheritance where an unintended beneficiary inherits through the estate (through the will).* Directly named beneficiaries will be the ones who receive the funds.

Reasons to designate beneficiaries include the following:

- To make sure that eligible designated beneficiaries get the stretch, since EDBs must also be designated beneficiaries.
- To avoid the 5-year rule when the account owner's death occurs before the RBD.
- To qualify as a see-through trust for trust beneficiaries.
- To avoid probate, longer estate administration, legal fees, and disputes among beneficiaries.

A Note on Proposed IRS Tax Rules

In February 2022, the IRS issued "proposed regulations" on how the RMD rules under the SECURE Act will work, and some big surprises are covered in depth in this chapter. Many of the RMD rule changes, especially for beneficiaries, are based on these proposed regulations. Although dubbed "proposed," these regulations are the only rules we have, so the safest route is to follow them as though they are "official." Yes, at some point the IRS will issue final regulations. (And who knows? By the time you read this they may already have been released.) But until then, the RMD rules from the proposed regulations are the ones I'm referring to in this chapter, and they are the ones you should follow. For updates on these and other important IRA tax rule changes, visit our website, www.irahelp.com. We are constantly posting updates there.

Post-Death Payout Rules for NEDBs: The 10-Year Payout and the ALAR Rule

Let's begin with the category likely to include most of your (non-spouse) beneficiaries: NEDBs. When IRA owners name individuals who are not their spouse (an adult son or daughter, for example), those beneficiaries are usually considered NEDBs. NEDBs are bound by the SECURE Act's 10-year rule, but with an extra layer of complication. In the proposed regulations, the IRS has taken the position that annual RMDs are *sometimes* required during the 10-year rule, depending on whether the account owner dies before or after their RBD. As you learned earlier, RBD stands for the required beginning date for taking distributions. But as you'll see in this chapter, RBD also means "really big deal" when it comes to payouts to your beneficiaries. (Note: Since lifetime RMDs are not required from Roth IRAs, all Roth IRA owners are deemed to have died before their RBD. This means Roth IRA NEDBs are never subject to annual RMDs in the 10-year period. However, inherited Roth IRA funds must still be fully withdrawn by the end of the 10th year after death.)

When an IRA owner dies *before* their RBD, there is no RMD for years one through nine after their death. The first, and only, RMD comes in year 10, when the remaining account balance must be taken. In other words, at the end of the 10 years, the inheritor is required to take a *100 percent RMD*—withdrawing the entire balance. If not, any remaining balance will be subject to a 25 percent penalty for not taking an RMD. Ouch!

When the account owner dies on or after their RBD, the story is very different. In its proposed SECURE Act regulations, the IRS took the position that when death occurs on or after the RBD, an NEDB must also take RMDs in years one through nine of the 10-year period. This requirement of annual RMDs within the 10-year period stems from an old rule in the tax code called the "at least as rapidly rule" (ALAR). While many originally thought the SECURE Act had done away with this rule, the IRS brought it back in the proposed regulations. The ALAR rule is tricky! It does not require the beneficiary to take the same RMD amount as the IRA owner, but it does require the beneficiary to keep taking RMDs. This is a key point. ALAR is not a function of amount, it is a function of frequency.

Here's an easy way to understand this: once RMDs have been "turned on" (by the owner reaching his or her RBD), they cannot be turned off. If the original IRA owner died before the RBD—he or she was not yet required to take lifetime RMDs—then the NEDB does not need to take RMDs in years one through nine. Why? RMDs were never "turned on." However, if that same IRA owner died on or after his or her RBD, that same NEDB would be required to take RMDs in years one through nine of the 10-year period, because RMDs had been "turned on." (Whatever is left in the account at the end of year 10 is considered the total final RMD.)

Word to the wise: *The IRA custodian is not required to notify your beneficiaries of these rules, and many will not.* It's up to you to let your heirs know about these requirements so that they don't make an error and get stuck with unnecessary missed RMD penalties.

Just think of poor Brad. His father, Sam (the IRA owner) died in 2023 at age 65 (before his RBD), having named Brad, age 38, as the beneficiary. Because he is a living, breathing human and not Sam's spouse or his minor child, Brad becomes an NEDB. As such, he has no RMDs until 2033 (the 10th year after his father's death). Brad can take out any amounts he wants in years one through nine.

Let's say the IRA balance in year 10 is $200,000. That becomes Brad's RMD, and if that entire amount is pre-tax dollars, Brad will need to report $200,000 of additional ordinary income for the year. If Brad misses that RMD, the 25 percent penalty applies, just as it does for lifetime distributions missed by IRA owners. This means that not only will Brad owe income tax on the $200,000 but he'll also owe $50,000 ($200,000 x 25 percent) for missing the deadline to take the RMD. If the account that Brad had inherited was a (post-tax) Roth IRA, there would be no income tax, but he would still owe the $50,000 penalty. Don't let your NEDBs end up like Brad. Make sure they know the 10-year rule backward and forward!

Keep in mind that the 25 percent penalty applies to all retirement accounts, *including inherited Roth IRA accounts.* Imagine owing a 25 percent penalty on a distribution that should have come income-tax-free! Make sure your beneficiaries, especially your Roth IRA beneficiaries, fully understand this rule and all its implications.

Take note: If the IRA owner took no year-of-death distribution (or just a portion of it), then the designated beneficiary would have to take it (or the rest of it) by the due date, including extensions, of the beneficiary's income tax return for the year of death and pay the income tax. The year-of-death RMD that the IRA owner did not take is paid directly to the beneficiary, and the beneficiary pays the income tax. Only if the estate is the beneficiary does the distribution get paid to the estate of the IRA owner.

For NEDBs who inherit from account owners who die on or after their RBD, the ALAR rule creates more complications. Compare Zoe's situation to Brad's from our prior example. Zoe's father, Lenny, age 80, died in 2023. Zoe is the beneficiary of his traditional IRA. Zoe is an NEDB and must take annual RMDs from the inherited IRA for years 2024–2032 (years one through nine of the 10-year period). Also, the entire remaining inherited IRA balance must be distributed by December 31, 2033. Zoe will use the IRS Single Life Expectancy Table to calculate her initial RMD factor. Since she is age 56 in 2024, her corresponding factor is 30.6. Zoe will subtract one from this factor in each successive year. Zoe's RMDs will be less than Lenny's, but this is of no consequence. The ALAR rule simply dictates that RMDs must continue annually.

"Hey, Ed. You keep saying, '10-year rule,' but I'm also always hearing about a 5-year rule. Can the 5-year rule ever apply when there's an NEDB named on the account?"

The short answer is no. Don't let anyone tell you the account has to be withdrawn in 5 years. That's just not true. The only exception arises if the custodian of the account (the bank, broker, fund company, or other financial institution) has written those terms into the IRA document. If, regardless of federal tax law allowing otherwise, *their* rules require you to withdraw the account within 5 years, then it's time for a direct transfer to a new custodian.

Old Rules vs. New Rules:
Payout Rules When the Beneficiary Dies

Old Rules: When the Beneficiary Died Before 2020

If the beneficiary died before 2020 and there was still a balance in the IRA, then the successor beneficiary (the beneficiary's beneficiary) can continue the stretch IRA for the years remaining on the original schedule.

New Rules: Under the SECURE Act,
If the Beneficiary Died/s in 2020 or Thereafter

If the beneficiary died in 2020 or thereafter and there is still a balance in the IRA, then the successor beneficiary is subject to the 10-year rule from the SECURE Act. When a beneficiary names his or her own beneficiary, the remaining IRA balance will go directly to that beneficiary with no probate, claims, or other legal obstacles.

TIP!

The SECURE Act Impacts Rules for Trusts

Prior to the SECURE Act, when an IRA was left to a trust, and the trust qualified as a "see-through" trust, the inherited IRA funds could be stretched over the oldest trust beneficiary's life expectancy. This was possible because the trust beneficiaries were considered designated beneficiaries for IRA distribution purposes. The SECURE Act eliminates the ability to stretch post-death RMDs for most beneficiaries, including most trusts. Instead, most trusts will now be considered NEDBs and are subject to a 10-year payout period. There are some exceptions, and I'll cover all that in Chapter 10.

Post-Death Payout Rules for Eligible Designated Beneficiaries (EDBs)

Here we've reached Wonderland, the enchanted forest, Shangri-la: the realm of the eligible designated beneficiary (EDB). Congress created this new category of beneficiaries under the SECURE Act, declaring these beneficiaries as the only ones eligible to stretch distributions over their life expectancy. They will generally have to take an RMD each year based on their own life expectancy. The stretch is not required, however. If the account owner died before their RBD, an EDB can elect the 10-year rule instead of the stretch.

The 10-year rule automatically kicks in if a beneficiary no longer qualifies as an EDB (such as when a minor turns 21). And when an EDB dies, the 10-year rule will apply to their beneficiaries (the "successor" beneficiaries). Since the EDB had been taking RMDs (RMDs have been "turned on"), the IRS says that the ALAR rule also requires annual RMDs during any subsequent 10-year period.

Extended Effective Dates

The effective date for the elimination of the stretch and the new 10-year rule generally applies to deaths after December 31, 2019. But that effective date was extended for two years (effective for deaths after December 31, 2021) for governmental plans, including 403(b) and 457(b) plans, and the Thrift Savings Plan. It was also extended for as long as two years for collectively bargained plans, depending on the expiration date of the union contract.

Keep in mind that an EDB *must* be a designated beneficiary—a person who is named on the beneficiary form and is alive at your death. EDB status is *determined at the date of your death* and cannot be changed, unless the beneficiary no longer qualifies—for example, when a minor child reaches age 21. The rules spell this out pretty clearly.

From the Act:

> *Time for Determination of Eligible Designated Beneficiary—The determination of whether a designated beneficiary is an eligible designated beneficiary shall be made as of the date of death of the employee.*

So, who qualifies for this elite class of beneficiaries? In addition to being alive, your loved ones must fall under one of these five classes:

1. Surviving spouse
2. Minor children of the account owner, up to age 21—but *not* grandchildren
3. Disabled individuals—under the strict IRS rules
4. Chronically ill individuals
5. Individuals not more than 10 years younger than the IRA owner (those older than the IRA owner also qualify)

In addition, trusts for the sole benefit of any of these EDBs should qualify as an EDB.

I want to give you some more detail about each class of beneficiaries. But since the surviving spouse is like the queen on a chess board, with the power to move in just about any direction she wants, I'm going to save that beneficiary class for last.

2. Minor Children

This category only applies to *your* minor children, so grandchildren are excluded. (Before the SECURE Act, grandchildren got the longest stretch IRA period because of their young age. Now they will mostly be subject to the 10-year rule.) Because this category applies only to the IRA owner's or plan participant's own minor children, few minors will qualify here, unless maybe a parent died young leaving minor children inheriting their IRA. But since most IRA owners die, say, at age 80 or older, most won't be leaving their IRA to their 14-year-old child—except for Tony Randall, or Billy Joel, who began RMDs in 2021. Yikes! Say it ain't so.

So, who qualifies as a minor? This definition is pretty simple: A minor EDB is a child of the deceased IRA owner who has not yet reached age 21. Once the minor child reaches age 21, the payout period from the inherited IRA reverts to the 10-year rule. But since the child had been taking stretch RMDs (RMDs have been "turned on"), the IRS says that the ALAR rule also requires annual RMDs during that 10-year period.

3. Disabled Individuals

When the IRS uses the term *disabled*, the definition is quite strict. Usually, I do my best to try to spare you the legalese, but in this case, I think it's important for you to see for yourself just how specific this class is.

From Tax Code Section 72(m)(7):

> *Meaning of Disabled—For purposes of this section, an individual shall be considered to be disabled if he is unable to engage in any substantial gainful activity by reason of any medically determinable physical or mental impairment which can be expected to result in death or to be of long-continued and indefinite duration. An individual shall not be considered to be disabled unless he furnishes proof of the existence thereof in such form and manner as the Secretary may require.*

You must not only be unable to work for a long or indefinite period, but you also *must be able to prove it.* In fact, the IRS-proposed regulations say that individuals must provide proof of their disability to the IRA custodian or plan by October 31 of the year after the year of death.

4. Chronically Ill Individuals

To qualify as a chronically ill individual under the SECURE Act, a person would need certification (by a licensed health-care practitioner) specifying that they are unable to perform at least two activities of daily living for at least 90 days—or—require "substantial supervision" due to a "severe cognitive impairment." Here again it's important for you to read the language in the law.

These specifications come directly from Tax Code Section 7702B(c)(2):

> (2) Chronically ill individual
>
> (A) In general
>
> The term "chronically ill individual" means any individual who has been certified by a licensed health care practitioner as—
>
> (i) being unable to perform (without substantial assistance from another individual) at least 2 activities of daily living for a period of at least 90 days due to a loss of functional capacity,
>
> (ii) having a level of disability similar (as determined under regulations prescribed by the Secretary in consultation with the Secretary of Health and Human Services) to the level of disability described in clause (i), or
>
> (iii) requiring substantial supervision to protect such individual from threats to health and safety due to severe cognitive impairment.
>
> Such term shall not include any individual otherwise meeting the requirements of the preceding sentence unless within the preceding 12-month period a licensed health care practitioner has certified that such individual meets such requirements.
>
> (B) Activities for daily living
>
> For purposes of subparagraph (A), each of the following is an activity of daily living:
>
> (i) Eating.
>
> (ii) Toileting.
>
> (iii) Transferring.
>
> (iv) Bathing.

(v) Dressing.

(vi) Continence.

A contract shall not be treated as a qualified long-term care insurance contract unless the determination of whether an individual is a chronically ill individual described in subparagraph (A)(i) takes into account at least 5 of such activities.

Here again, proof of chronic illness must be given to the IRA custodian or plan by October 31 of the year following death.

Individuals who are either disabled or chronically ill, as defined under the tax code, on the death date of the IRA owner qualify as eligible designated beneficiaries and are permitted to stretch inherited RMD payments over their life expectancy.

Technically speaking, if their status changes, and they're no longer considered disabled or chronically ill, they revert to the 10-year rule. But given the strict health requirements, many beneficiaries who qualify as either disabled or chronically ill are less likely to lose disability or chronically ill status. In fact, their condition may preclude their ability to inherit IRA or plan funds directly. Many of these beneficiaries will need trusts to help them protect and use the funds they inherit. Luckily, Congress included provisions for this in the SECURE Act, allowing the use of the stretch IRA through an *applicable multi-beneficiary trust,* another term made up by Congress, which I cover in more detail, with examples, in Chapter 10.

5. Individuals Not More Than 10 Years Younger Than the IRA Owner

A nonspouse beneficiary who is not more than 10 years *younger* than you is an eligible designated beneficiary under the SECURE Act and can use his or her own age to stretch inherited IRA RMD payments. This provision will most likely apply to individuals like a sibling, partner, or friend who is around your age or older. Congress put this exception in here because they figured most of these beneficiaries, unlike children or grandchildren, will not have a long stretch period anyway since they are relatively close in age to the IRA owner.

If your beneficiary is older than you, then, by definition, he or she is not more than 10 years younger than you. As an EDB, he or she also qualifies for the stretch IRA. Turns out some older beneficiaries get an even better deal. If you die after your age-73 RBD, an older beneficiary gets to stretch the IRA they inherit from you over *your* longer life expectancy, rather than theirs. This will give the beneficiary a longer life expectancy (at least in terms of payout period—we can't guarantee they'll actually live longer!) than he or she would by using his or her own life expectancy listing.

But wait . . . that's not the end of the story yet. IRS has added new rules here, and now the RMD saga gets very weird!

Monitoring Concurrent Life Expectancies for Older EDBs

In what may be the craziest section of the IRS-proposed regulations, there is a situation in which an EDB can use the life expectancy of another individual to calculate RMDs (as explained above), but at the same time need to monitor his or her own life expectancy to determine when the inherited account would need to be emptied.

Let's look at an example to see how this can play out . . .

Example:

Robert dies at age 74, which is after his RBD. Robert's beneficiary is his older sister, Sally, age 80. Since Sally is not more than 10 years younger than Robert (she is older), she is an EDB and can stretch RMD payments. However, since Robert died after his RBD, and Sally is older than Robert, Sally is permitted to use Robert's single life expectancy to calculate RMDs. Robert's life expectancy in the year of his death is 15.6 for a 74-year-old. For subsequent years, Sally subtracts one each year. As such, the IRA should last for 15 years, until Sally is age 95.

And here is where things go off the rails. From the Explanation of Provisions of the proposed regulations, page 48:

> . . . *these proposed regulations require a full distribution of the employee's remaining interest in the plan in the calendar year in which the [life expectancy factor] would have been less than or*

equal to one if it were determined using the beneficiary's remaining life expectancy (even though the [life expectancy factor] for determining the required minimum distribution is based on the remaining life expectancy of the employee).

Translation:

Although Sally is using Robert's life expectancy factor (15.6) to calculate her annual RMDs as an EDB, she must also monitor her own life expectancy factor to determine when she must empty the account. Had Sally used her own life expectancy to calculate RMDs, she would have started with 10.5 (the factor for Sally's age in the year after Robert's death—age 81*). Eleven years later, Sally's own life expectancy factor would drop down to 0.5. Since 0.5 is less than one, Sally is required to empty the inherited IRA at age 91. This is true even though Robert's life expectancy still had four years remaining and was the life expectancy factor Sally had been properly using to calculate her RMDs from age 81 to 91.

Sally's Age	Using Robert's Life Expectancy	Using Sally's Life Expectancy
81	14.6	10.5
82	13.6	9.5
83	12.6	8.5
84	11.6	7.5
85	10.6	6.5
86	9.6	5.5
87	8.6	4.5
88	7.6	3.5
89	6.6	2.5
90	5.6	1.5
91	4.6	0.5
92	3.6	
93	2.6	
94	1.6	
95	0.6	

This new rule will be incredibly complicated for custodians, advisors, seniors, and other reasonable people to administer. It is difficult to understand what abuse the IRS was looking to prevent here. Can you imagine explaining this to someone in their nineties?

*Note: While the example in the regulations uses the life expectancy of 11.2 in the year of death, we chose to use the life expectancy in the year after death for our example.

1. Surviving Spouse

And now, let's talk about the star of this regal category of EDBs, the surviving spouse. Your spouse is the person to whom you are legally married at the time of your death. Just so there is no question about this, you can have only *one legal spouse* under federal law. I put that in here because there is at least one tax court case (and probably more) in which a husband had two wives. When he died, the court ruled that, under federal law, only one could qualify as his legal spouse and inherit his company retirement account. In case you were wondering, his first wife won, because when he left her for wife number two, he'd never legally divorced. The court ruled that wife one was the legal heir even though he'd been with wife number two for more than 30 years building a retirement account at his job that she thought she would inherit. Wife number one somehow heard about his death and went after his retirement savings in court—and won. Advice: Check whether your new spouse is really single! Don't rely on Facebook status.

Your spouse receives the same inheritance benefits that he or she had before the SECURE Act. That's good, since most people name their spouse on their IRA accounts. But things take a turn for the worse after your spouse dies, since the stretch IRA elimination rules take full effect for the nonspouse beneficiaries who inherit next—the successor beneficiaries.

10-Year Payout Rule for Successor Beneficiaries

Successor beneficiaries—*the beneficiaries of the beneficiary*—are bound by the 10-year rule no matter their relationship to the previous account owner or their physical condition. It does not matter if the successor is a spouse or disabled or could otherwise qualify as an EDB and therefore be able to stretch RMD payments. If the original beneficiary was using the 10-year rule, the successor can only continue whatever time remains on that existing 10-year period. If the original beneficiary was stretching inherited account payments over his or her own single life expectancy, the successor will continue that same payment structure, but will also overlay the 10-year rule. If RMDs were turned on at any point prior to the successor beneficiary acquiring the account, those RMDs cannot be turned off.

Consider Florence, age 55, who died in 2020. She named her son Gary, age 30, as beneficiary of her traditional IRA. On that date, Gary qualified as a chronically ill EDB under the tax code definition, so he began taking stretch RMDs based on his own single life expectancy.

If Gary dies in 2028 with his son, Jay, named as primary beneficiary, Jay becomes the successor beneficiary. Jay must receive the remaining IRA portion by the end of the 10th year following his father's death (December 31, 2038). Even though Florence had not yet started taking RMDs, since Gary "turned on" RMDs as an EDB, the ALAR rule dictates that Jay cannot turn RMDs off. He must take RMDs for years one through nine within the 10-year period, and those RMDs must be based on Gary's RMD schedule.

When Your Beneficiary Is Your Spouse

Now we're in variable Heaven—or Hell, depending upon one's point of view.

When you name a spouse (and I mean your spouse, not someone else's) as your IRA or company plan beneficiary, the spouse has great freedom of choice for how to handle his or her inheritance. Each choice will have different ramifications.

Option #1: Rollover

The most common and practical option for your spouse is called the *spousal rollover*, which makes the account the spouse's own. (No, it does not mean your spouse has to physically roll over or play dead to inherit your retirement money.) The spousal rollover provision allows your spouse to transfer your IRA to his or her IRA after your death. Your IRA then becomes your spouse's IRA, and he or she follows the rules for calculating RMDs based on the Uniform Lifetime Table, the same as any IRA owner. The spousal rollover can be accomplished in two ways:

1. Rollover: where your spouse withdraws the balance from your IRA or company plan and deposits it in his or her IRA within 60 days.

2. Direct transfer (also known as a *direct rollover* or a *trustee-to-trustee transfer*): where the funds go directly from your retirement account to your spouse's, without your spouse touching the money in between. This is the preferred method for transferring funds from your IRA or plan to his or her IRA.

Your spouse could also roll over your IRA or plan to his or her own company plan—provided the company the spouse works for agrees to accept the funds in its plan.

Hypothetical RMDs . . . Yes, It's Really a Rule!

There is no deadline for completing a spousal rollover. A spouse beneficiary could wait for many years before doing so. If a spousal rollover is executed before the end of the year when the surviving spouse turns 73, or before the end of the year following the year of the IRA owner's death, there is no issue. However, if that is not the case, the proposed SECURE Act regulations include a special rule that creates the need to calculate "hypothetical RMDs" for previous years. These "hypothetical RMDs" would need to be taken prior to the spousal rollover. This is one of the crazier and more complex rules to come out of the proposed SECURE Act regulations. What is its purpose? What was the IRS concerned about? Answer: A perceived RMD loophole, where RMDs could be avoided when a spouse elects the 10-year rule. At its core, this rule closes the loophole that would otherwise allow a surviving spouse to choose the 10-year payout rule, avoid RMDs for most of that period, and then do a spousal rollover in year nine.

Option #2: Elect to Treat the IRA as His or Her Own

In this case, instead of moving the money from your IRA to his or hers, your spouse can simply put his or her name on your account. Now it's the spouse's IRA and is treated the same as if it had been rolled over, subjecting the spouse to RMDs when he or she reaches his or her RBD. If the spouse is already past his or her RBD when the account is inherited, the spouse, whether treating the account as his or her own or rolling it over, must begin distributions from the IRA by the end of the year after your death. Treating an inherited IRA as his or her own IRA is the same as a rollover, since in either case the spouse becomes the IRA owner and is no longer considered the beneficiary.

The spouse must be the sole beneficiary to elect to treat the IRA as his or her own. But if he or she is one of several beneficiaries, the account can be split, and the spouse can still be the sole beneficiary of his or her share of the account. The only difference is that with the spousal rollover, the funds must be physically moved from the deceased IRA owner or plan participant's account to the spouse's IRA. By electing to treat the IRA as their own, spouse beneficiaries do not have to move the money. They can just retitle the account in their name as their own IRA. (Nonspouse beneficiaries can never retitle an account in their own name.) The spouse can be deemed to make the election to treat the account as his or her own by not taking a required distribution or by making an additional IRA contribution to the account. The IRS figures that these two actions mean that the spouse beneficiary is treating the account as his or her own IRA.

Under the proposed IRS regulations, the deadline for a spouse treating the IRA as his or her own is the later of: (1) the end of the year in which the surviving spouse reaches age 73, or (2) the end of the year following the year of the IRA owner's death.

Spouse Rolls Account Over (Option #1) or Treats It as His or Her Own (Option #2)

A spouse beneficiary rollover or a spouse's decision to treat the inherited IRA as his or her own without rolling it over yields the same outcome: The spouse is no longer the beneficiary but is instead the *owner* of the account and treated by the IRS as if he or she had *always* been the owner.

For example, Peter dies in 2023 at age 70 (before his RBD), designating his 65-year-old spouse, Blanche, as beneficiary of his IRA. Blanche rolls the IRA over (or elects not to roll it over but to treat the account as her own) and becomes the account owner. But because she is 65, she can delay taking her first-year RMD until April 1, 2032, which is the April 1 after the year—2031—she turns 73 (although, as we've discussed previously, she would probably be better off taking her first RMD by the end of 2031 to avoid paying tax on both first- and second-year RMDs in 2032).

OK, let's use the same example but make Blanche 74. As before, she can roll over the entire IRA account balance to her own IRA (or elect to treat it as her own) and not have to take an RMD for Peter's year of death because he died before he was subject to RMDs. Since she herself is past 73, however, after the rollover, her first distribution year becomes 2024 when she turns 75. As the IRA is now hers, she'll look to the Uniform Lifetime Table for her life expectancy factor at age 75, which is 24.6 years. She then divides the December 31, 2023, IRA balance by 24.6 to arrive at her RMD for 2024. For 2025 and later years, she will simply repeat the process of looking at the Uniform Lifetime Table to determine the new life expectancy factor for each year's RMD.

Now, let's look at a few "after-RBD" scenarios where the spouse is beneficiary of the IRA.

Sheila died in 2023 at age 76 (after her RBD), leaving her IRA to her 63-year-old husband, Ralph. If Ralph rolls over the IRA (or elects to treat the account as his own), he becomes the IRA owner. Just as in the first "before-RBD" example I gave you, since he is 63, he does not have to begin RMDs until he reaches his RBD at 73, which will be in 2033 (although, again, he could delay to April 1, 2034, if he wanted).

In our new scenario, however, Sheila, at 76, was past her RBD and already taking her required distributions. If she died without taking her 2023 RMD, however, Ralph must take and pay tax on the distribution she would have taken had she lived, even though he is not yet subject to RMDs until his own first distribution year of 2033. He cannot roll over that amount too because rolling over a required distribution is disallowed. (But he could transfer it directly and later take it out of the new IRA.) So, if the IRA balance on December 31, 2022, was $400,000, then Sheila's RMD for 2023 (based on the Uniform Lifetime Table life expectancy factor for a 76-year-old of 23.7 years) is $400,000/23.7 = $16,878. If she died before taking it, Ralph would have to take it. If she withdrew only part of it, he would have to withdraw only the remainder. If she withdrew only, say, $10,000 in 2023, he would have to withdraw the remaining $6,878.

Now, let's make Ralph 73 years old instead of 63. Otherwise, the facts are the same: His wife, Sheila, died in 2023 at 76 (after her RBD) and left her IRA to him. As before, she went to her great reward before taking her 2023 distribution, so he must take it, and then he can roll the remainder of the IRA into his own account. Since he's over 73, however, he must begin RMDs the year after Sheila's (the IRA owner's) death; in this case he must begin in 2024. Once rolled over, however, he becomes the IRA owner and so he will use the Uniform Lifetime Table for calculating his first-year (2024) RMD. In 2024, he'll be 74, so that's the age he will use to get his life expectancy factor, which is 25.5 years. Then he divides the December 31, 2023, IRA balance by 25.5 to arrive at his RMD for 2024. For later-year RMDs, he just repeats the process.

> ### TIP!
>
> As soon as a spouse rolls over or redesignates the account as his or her own, the Social Security number on the account should be changed to the spouse's number because it is now his or her account and the spouse will pay the income tax on distributions. Many people neglect to make that change. If a 1099-R is issued with the deceased IRA owner's Social Security number, this can result in needless tax reporting problems. To avoid complications, address this immediately after the IRA owner's death. Even if the spouse chooses not to roll over and instead remains a beneficiary, the Social Security number on the IRA account should be changed to his or her number.

Option #3: Spouse Chooses to Remain a Beneficiary

The spouse can choose to neither roll over the account nor treat it as his or her own. If the spouse chooses, he or she can remain a beneficiary and be subject to the same general rules as nonspouse EDBs. Why would a spouse want to do this instead of going the typically more advantageous rollover route? If the spouse is older than the deceased, this choice might be best because the spouse could hold off on distributions for longer (as we shall soon see). But the main benefit of a spouse remaining a beneficiary comes if the spouse beneficiary is younger than 59½—the age for eligibility to withdraw penalty-free.

For example, when Sadie was widowed at the young age of 40 (she may be the only 40-year-old in the world named Sadie, but play along with me here—it was a family name), she inherited the IRA and rolled over the funds so that the account then became hers. At that point she was no longer treated as a beneficiary but became an owner. If she wants to take any money out, she must pay the 10 percent penalty assessed to retirement plan owners who tap into their retirement plan accounts before age 59½. (This 10 percent penalty does not apply to company retirement plan or IRA beneficiaries, only to owners, which Sadie has now become.) And so, in cases like Sadie's, where the spouse beneficiary is much younger than 59½, it could pay to remain as beneficiary. This way, if she needs some of that IRA cash to live on, she can tap it penalty-free. Furthermore, choosing to remain a beneficiary does not restrict her from being able to roll it over later. Therefore, when she does hit 59½, the spousal rollover option, with its attendant advantages, is still available.

If the spouse is the sole beneficiary and chooses to remain so rather than rolling over, then he or she must begin taking RMDs by whichever is later: December 31 of the year the IRA owner would have turned 73, or December 31 of the year following the IRA owner's death.

This is an interesting provision because it can be used to delay RMDs when the IRA owner dies before reaching 73. But it can be used only if two conditions are met: the spouse is the sole beneficiary, and the spouse makes an election to defer RMDs. (If there are multiple individual beneficiaries, the account may be split so that each beneficiary becomes the sole beneficiary of that share. In such situations, the spouse would again qualify as a sole beneficiary—but only of his or her cut.) But even if the spouse is the sole beneficiary, if he or she doesn't make the RMD deferral election, RMDs must begin in the year following the IRA owner's death—just like for nonspouse EDBs. The deferral election is a new and complicated requirement that is part of SECURE 2.0.

The real benefit of this provision comes when the IRA owner dies before reaching 73, especially if it's well before. In such cases, if the spouse chooses to remain as beneficiary and elects to defer (instead of rolling over), he or she does not have to begin RMDs until the year the deceased would have turned 73. That means if the deceased died at age 50, for example, the spouse could delay RMDs—and keep growing the account tax-deferred—for more than 20 years! (When the RMD age goes up to 75 in 2033, the period during which a spouse can delay RMDs will extend even further.) If the surviving spouse were younger than the deceased IRA owner, he or she could roll over the IRA just before the year the deceased would have turned 73 and delay distributions even longer—because once the rollover occurs, the spouse beneficiary is deemed to be the IRA owner and can, under the rules, wait until he or she reaches 73 to begin RMDs.

> ### CAUTION!
> #### Another Fine Mess That Congress Has Gotten Us Into. . . .
>
> Most people don't seem to know or understand the widespread impact of this new surviving spouse's RMD deferral election provision. As of 2024, the rule as written will technically impact the options available when a spouse is the beneficiary, which is a very common situation. However, practically speaking, most inheritors won't be in the situation where a younger spouse dies first. Before you make decisions based on this new complication, visit our website, www.irahelp.com.

An Older Spouse Inherits an IRA and Wants to Delay RMDs for as Long as Possible

In most cases, an older spouse will die before their younger counterpart. Most cases, though, are not *all* cases. Occasionally, an older spouse will inherit an IRA from a younger spouse. If that happens when the younger deceased spouse was not yet 73 and the surviving spouse wants to delay RMDs for as long as possible, then it may pay to remain a beneficiary and make the RMD deferral election. By doing so, the surviving spouse can delay RMDs until the younger spouse would have been 73.

Example:
Ken, 75, is married to Rachel, 65. Rachel dies, leaving her IRA to Ken, who has plenty of other assets and wants to minimize his income as much as possible to reduce his tax liability. If Ken does the spousal rollover, he will need to begin taking RMDs the following year, since the funds will be treated as if they were always in his account, and

he is already over 73. Thus, the better course of action—contrary to conventional wisdom—may be for Ken to remain a beneficiary and make the deferral election. By doing so, Ken can take advantage of the special rules for spouse beneficiaries and delay RMDs until Rachel would have been 73, giving him eight more RMD-free years. But if Ken remains a beneficiary and doesn't make the election, he'll need to start RMDs in the year after Rachel's death.

Calculating RMDs When the Spouse Remains a Beneficiary

A spouse who chooses to remain a beneficiary and makes the deferral election (instead of rolling over the IRA or treating it as his or her own), can take beneficiary payouts using the Uniform Lifetime Table (also used by IRA owners). But in applying the table, spouses must use the age of the deceased IRA owner—not their own age. Is this a good thing or a bad thing? It depends.

It's a good thing if the spouse beneficiary is older than the IRA owner, as in the earlier Ken and Rachel example. Recall that Ken can delay RMDs until he turns age 83 (when Rachel would have been 73). He would utilize the Uniform Lifetime Table to calculate RMDs, but he would use Rachel's age—not his own. So, his first RMD would be 26.5 (the factor for a 73-year-old)—not 17.7 (the factor for an 83-year-old). That will mean lower RMDs for Ken.

By contrast, being required to use the deceased's age isn't such a good thing if the spouse beneficiary is younger than the IRA owner. Consider the married couple of Randall and Jen. If Randall dies at 67 when Jen, his sole IRA beneficiary, is 50, Jen can do an immediate spousal rollover or treat the IRA as her own. But if she does either of these things, she will have to pay the 10 percent penalty if she needs the IRA funds before she turns 59½. If Jen remains a beneficiary and makes the deferral election, she can delay RMDs until Randall would have turned 73 (when she is 56). Once RMDs start, she can use the Uniform Lifetime Table. But Jen must use the age Randall would have reached had he lived (73), not her own age (56). This means that Jen's first RMD, in the year she turns 56, will be based on a 26.5-year life expectancy (the factor for a 73-year-old under the Uniform Lifetime Table). In the following year, it will be 25.5 (the factor for a 74-year-old). Had Jen been able to use her own age, her first RMD would have been based on a 42.6-year factor. Jen using her own age would have made that first RMD and all subsequent RMDs much smaller.

A WORD TO THE WISE

Whether the spouse beneficiary elects to roll over the inherited account or remain a beneficiary, he or she should *immediately* name both a beneficiary and a contingent beneficiary on the account. As you saw in Chapter 5, neglecting to do this is the number one mistake made by spouses who inherit. This is the key to the survival of the account after the spouse's death, and it's the key to keeping it in the family.

NDB (Non-Designated Beneficiary): A Nonperson Beneficiary

Now that you've witnessed the beneficiary magic of being an EDB, imagine the disappointment of becoming an NDB. Remember (for the zillionth time) that having a beneficiary does not mean the same thing as having a *designated* beneficiary. A *designated* beneficiary is an *individual*—a human being, who is still alive at the time of your death—named on the beneficiary form or is the beneficiary of a qualifying see-through trust. All other beneficiaries and nonqualifying trusts are *non-designated* beneficiaries. A living, breathing human becomes a *non-designated beneficiary* when he or she inherits an account through a nonqualifying trust or estate.

If you're reading this and your account doesn't have a designated beneficiary, act now! All you need to do is fill out a beneficiary form for the account. Sounds easy, and is easy, but still people manage to avoid taking this simple step to protect their savings.

If you don't designate a beneficiary, the inheritor of your account(s) becomes a non-designated beneficiary (NDB), which has the least tax advantage. To understand why, let's take a moment to refresh your memory.

Unlike for NEDBs or EDBs, payout rules for NDBs are divided into two different tracks, the "before" and the "after" tracks. The distributions change depending on when the IRA owner dies, since their age at death determines whether they've reached their required beginning date (RBD) for distributions. If the owner dies *before* his or her RBD, then the NDB must take disbursements from the account under what is called the *5-year rule.*

The 5-year rule requires the beneficiary to withdraw the entire inherited IRA or company plan by the conclusion of the fifth year following the IRA owner's death. It does not matter how much the beneficiary withdraws yearly during the 5-year-rule period as long as the account is emptied by the end. And just like a missed 100 percent RMD under the 10-year rule, any balance the NDB leaves in the inherited IRA after 5 years is subject to the 25 percent penalty. But the 5-year rule applies *only* when the IRA owner dies before his or her RBD and has named no designated beneficiary.

It's called the 5-year rule, so of course the IRS means 5 years, right? Ha! Things are never that simple.

The 5-Year Rule Becomes a 6-Year Rule

As you might recall, 2020 was a pretty rough year for a lot of Americans. To ease the financial strain of the pandemic, Congress passed the Coronavirus Aid, Relief, and Economic Security (CARES) Act, which waived RMDs for 2020, including RMDs for IRA beneficiaries. This means beneficiaries subject to the 5-year rule got to add an additional year to their distribution schedule, making it a 6-year payout period. Because the year 2020 was left out of the 5-year payout period calculation, NDBs who inherited between 2015 and 2019 enjoy a 6-year run.

Case in point: Liz inherited an IRA through the estate of her uncle Lou, who died at age 57, before his RBD. Liz was required by the 5-year rule to empty the inherited IRA account. When Uncle Lou died in 2018, Liz calculated that she had to empty the account by the end of 2023. But because of the CARES Act RMD exemption for 2020, Liz gets to add an extra year onto the 5 years. She now has until the end of 2024 to empty the account.

Keep in mind that the 5-year rule applies *only* when the IRA owner dies *before* his or her RBD. Given the widespread confusion over this point, I want to emphasize that fact until it's coming out of your ears. I hear too many stories of beneficiaries and designated beneficiaries being told by their banks and advisors that they must withdraw the account over the 5-year-rule period, when for most of them that's simply untrue.

An IRA owner's RBD is April 1 following the year of his or her 73rd birthday. Even if the IRA owner dies on the eve of that date, the death is viewed as occurring before the RBD even though the IRA owner is, in fact, past the required minimum distribution age of 73. So, for example, if an IRA owner is 73 in 2024, his or her RBD would be April 1, 2025. If the owner dies on March 30, 2025, he or she will be treated as having died before the RBD, and the beneficiaries will follow those distribution rules.

Say, for example, a beneficiary inherits through an estate of an IRA owner who died at 75. Will the 5-year rule apply? NO! Even if there is no designated beneficiary (as is the case here because the estate is the beneficiary), the 5-year rule can never apply when the IRA owner dies at 75 because that's well after his or her RBD. Instead, the IRA will be paid out to the NDB over the IRA owner's remaining single life expectancy (had he or she lived), based on the IRA owner's age in the year of death—less one for each future year's distribution. Remember how this rule is known as the "ghost life" rule? That's because you are calculating RMDs using the life expectancy of a ghost. Only in tax law can a deceased person have a remaining life expectancy!

As I mentioned earlier, unless the IRA custodian itself (your bank, broker, fund company, or other financial institution) requires a 5-year payout period in its IRA document, the NDB is not under that time constraint. In that case, despite the tax law allowing otherwise, your beneficiaries will be stuck abiding by the 5-year terms, unless the inherited funds can be directly transferred to a custodian that allows for a longer payout.

The IRA Owner's Post-RMD Death

What if the IRA owner dies *on or after* his or her RBD and there is no designated beneficiary? Then the 5-year rule does not apply. Instead, as I just stated above, the IRA will be paid out over the IRA owner's remaining single life expectancy (had the owner lived—the "ghost rule") based on his or her age in the year of death—less one for each future year's distribution. And if the IRA owner had not yet taken a year-of-death distribution (or took just a portion of it), then the beneficiary must take it (or the rest of it) and pay the associated tax.

Interestingly, for some who die in their seventies, this can now produce a post-death payout period exceeding 10 years. That means your non-designated beneficiary might get a better deal than your noneligible designated beneficiary who can only stretch disbursements for 10 years, max. Under this payout period, the NDB must take an amount equal to the RMD each year, but the beneficiary can take more in any given year if he or she so desires.

Example:

If George died in 2021 at age 78 with no designated beneficiary, the IRA must be paid out over 11.6 years. The first distribution year was 2022, the year after George's death. The first distribution needed to be taken by December 31, 2022, and then by each December 31 thereafter until the 11.6-year term is up (unless the account is emptied before then). Where did I come up with an 11.6-year set term? The life expectancy factor of a 78-year-old (from the Single Life Expectancy Table, Figure 5, page. 166) is 12.6 years. For 2022, the first distribution year, you would reduce the 12.6 factor by one, yielding 11.6. You then divide the December 31, 2021, IRA balance by 11.6 to arrive at the RMD for 2022. For the 2023 distribution, the factor was 10.6 years. You then divide the December 31, 2022, IRA balance by

10.6 to arrive at the RMD for 2023. For 2024 it is 9.6 years, for 2025 it will be 8.6 years, and so on. George's beneficiary reaps the benefit of a quirk in the tax code and gets more than a 10-year payout.

Pop Quiz!

A Review of SECURE Act Distribution Rules

Have you been paying close attention? Hope so, because we're about to explore some examples to see how much you've absorbed from this chapter. Keep in mind that eligible designated beneficiaries (EDBs) can stretch RMD payments over their life expectancies, but noneligible designated beneficiaries (NEDBs) cannot. NEDBs will be subject to the 10-year payout rule (and in some cases the requirement to take annual RMDs in years one through nine).

<u>Example 1</u>: NEDB—Child (over age 21, so not a minor) inherits

Tom, age 32, inherits a Roth IRA from his father. He is a designated beneficiary, but he is not an EDB, because he is not under age 21.

The Stretch or the 10-Year Rule?

Tom is subject to the 10-year rule. He can take as much or as little out of the inherited Roth IRA each year during the 10-year period, but he must withdraw the entire Roth IRA balance by the end of the 10-year period, or he will be subject to the 25 percent penalty on the amount not taken. Tom is not subject to annual RMDs for years one through nine of the 10-year payout period. This is because, like all Roth IRA owners, Tom's father is considered to have died before the RBD. If, instead, the account that Tom inherited had been a traditional IRA and his father had died on or after his RBD, then Tom would need to take RMDs during the 10-year payout period.

Example 2: EDB—Spouse is the beneficiary and son inherits after the beneficiary's death

Jim dies at age 75 (after his RBD) and leaves his IRA to his wife, Joann, age 57. Because she needs access to the funds, Joann elects to remain a beneficiary by doing an inherited IRA.

The Stretch or the 10-Year Rule?

Joann will have an RMD, but by choosing to remain a beneficiary, she can take distributions without incurring the 10 percent early distribution penalty. Her RMD will be based on her single life expectancy, recalculated each year. Once Joann does a spousal rollover of the inherited IRA at age 60, her inherited IRA RMDs stop.

Joann dies two years later, at age 62, and leaves the IRA to her son, Jeffrey, age 30. Jeffrey cannot be an EDB because he is not under age 21, disabled, or chronically ill. He is also more than 10 years younger than Joann (of course). Because the SECURE Act requires a 10-year term to pay out the inherited IRA, Jeffrey must deplete the account by the end of the 10th year following his mother's death.

Example 3: EDB—Beneficiary is a child under age 21

Lisa, age 10, inherits an IRA from her mother. Lisa is an eligible designated beneficiary (EDB) because she is under 21.

The Stretch or the 10-Year Rule?

For the next 11 years, Lisa can stretch distributions over her single life expectancy. On Lisa's 21st birthday, the 10-year rule will apply. This means that Lisa will need to empty the inherited IRA by the end of the 10th year after she reaches age 21. But it also means that Lisa must continue taking annual RMDs during years one through nine of the 10-year period under the ALAR (at least as rapidly) rule.

Example 4: Two children as co-beneficiaries— one an EDB, one an NEDB

Kristy, age 45, dies and leaves her IRA to her two daughters, Alexa, age 25, and Zoey, age 15.

The Stretch or the 10-Year Rule?

First, the account should be split so each beneficiary has her own inherited IRA and can use the rules that apply, otherwise Zoey will not be able to use the stretch IRA. Since Alexa is over age 21, she will use the 10-year payout. She will have no annual RMDs because Kristy died before her RBD, but her inherited IRA will need to be emptied by the end of the 10th year after her mother's death. Zoey, on the other hand, is under 21. She can temporarily stretch the inherited IRA based on her single life expectancy. On her 21st birthday Zoey becomes subject to the 10-year payout rule and must empty the remaining account by the end of the 10th year after her 21st birthday. During the 10-year payout period, annual RMDs must continue to Zoey because she was already taking them to use the stretch. Under the ALAR rule they cannot stop.

Example 5: EDB—Chronically ill or disabled beneficiary

Grandma Gertrude dies. She had named her grandson Gary, age 30, as her primary beneficiary. On her death date, Gary qualifies as "chronically ill" under the tax code definition.

The Stretch or the 10-Year Rule?

Because he is an eligible designated beneficiary due to his medical condition, Gary *can* stretch the RMD payments, if he provides proof of his chronic illness to the IRA custodian by October 31 of the year following the year of death. Gary is required to take an annual RMD until the account is depleted or until he no longer meets the definition of chronically ill. If we change the scenario and make Gary disabled, the results would be the same.

Example 6: Two siblings as co-beneficiaries—one an EDB, one an NEDB

Three sisters are a tight group. Sandra is the eldest at 70. Sheri is 61, and Celeste is 59. Sandra dies and leaves an IRA to each of her younger sisters.

The Stretch or the 10-Year Rule?

Once again, with multiple beneficiaries, the account should be split into separate inherited IRAs so that each beneficiary can take advantage of the rules that apply to them. Since Sheri (61) is fewer than 10 years younger than Sandra, she qualifies as an eligible designated beneficiary and can stretch RMD payments over her single life expectancy (around 25 years) for a 62-year-old—her age in the year after death. Under a special rule, Sheri can also elect the 10-year payment rule since Sandra died before her RBD. That might be appealing to her, because she wouldn't be required to take annual RMDs during the 10-year period.

Younger sister Celeste is only 59. She is more than 10 years younger than the IRA account owner. Therefore, she is not considered an eligible designated beneficiary and is bound by the 10-year payout term. Celeste's inherited IRA must be emptied by the end of the 10th year following Sandra's death.

This means that if middle-sister Sheri only takes the RMD, she can continue to stretch her inherited IRA RMD payments for more than another decade beyond when younger sister Celeste had to empty her account, even though these two sisters are only two years apart.

Example 7: NEDB inherits but becomes disabled in a later year

John dies, naming his son, Jerry, age 30, as his primary beneficiary.

The Stretch or the 10-Year Rule?

Bound by the SECURE Act, Jerry must use the 10-year payout for his inherited IRA. Six months after his father's death, but before

Jerry had gotten around to titling the IRA in his [own] name as an inherited IRA, Jerry gets into a car accident. Jerry is now fully disabled under the tax code rules. Does his disability qualify Jerry for the stretch? Unfortunately, no. He cannot qualify as an EDB because he was not disabled on the date of his father's death. Remember that EDB status is determined at the date of death, even if circumstances change afterward.

Example 8: NDB—Estate is the beneficiary

Allen dies at age 65 (before his RBD) and leaves his IRA to his estate (a non-designated beneficiary). When Allen's son, David, inherits through the estate, he becomes a non designated beneficiary.

The Stretch or the 10-Year Rule?

Neither. RMDs to David would be based on the 5-year rule. The entire inherited IRA account balance must be withdrawn by the end of the fifth year after Allen's death, because the IRA owner died before his RBD and with no designated beneficiary. Even though David eventually inherited through the estate, the estate was still the beneficiary, so David is stuck with the rules that apply when there is no designated beneficiary, which in this case is the 5-year rule, since death occurred before the RBD.

Example 9: NDB—Estate is the beneficiary:
Life expectancy rule #1

Anthony dies at age 87 (after his RBD) and leaves his IRA to his estate (a non-designated beneficiary). Anthony's son, Chuck, age 40, inherits through the estate, so he becomes a non-designated beneficiary.

The Stretch or the 10-Year Rule?

Neither. RMDs to Chuck would be based on Anthony's remaining life expectancy, had he lived (the "ghost rule"). In this case, Chuck loses out since Anthony's life expectancy is less than the 10-year payout that Chuck could have had if he'd been named as a designated beneficiary.

Example 10: NDB—Estate is the beneficiary: Life expectancy rule #2

Archie died at age 74 (after his RBD), leaving his IRA to his estate (a non-designated beneficiary). Archie's son, Hamilton, age 40, inherits through the estate, so he becomes a non-designated beneficiary.

The Stretch or the 10-Year Rule?

Neither. RMDs to Hamilton would be based on Archie's remaining life expectancy, had he lived. The first RMD in the year following the year of death would be based on Archie's 14.6-year remaining single life expectancy (15.6 for a 74-year-old, minus one). In this case, Hamilton makes out better than a designated beneficiary. He has a 14.6-year payout instead of a 10-year payout. A strange result, but this happens only when the IRA owner dies soon after his or her required beginning date.

Example 11: NEDB—Grandchild inherits

Grandpa Thomas dies at age 80, having named his granddaughter Susan as the primary beneficiary of his traditional IRA.

The Stretch or the 10-Year Rule?

The 10-year rule. Susan is not an eligible designated beneficiary under the SECURE Act because she is not *his* child, so Susan must use the 10-year rule for her distributions. As such, Susan, age 35 in the year after death, establishes an inherited IRA and must empty the account by the end of the 10th year after Grandpa's death. She must also take annual RMDs for years one through nine during the 10-year payout period, under the ALAR rule.

Example 12: NEDB—Successor beneficiary (the beneficiary's beneficiary)

Ann died in 2015. She named her daughter, Bea, age 48 at the time of Ann's death, as her primary beneficiary.

The Stretch or the 10-Year Rule?

Bea gets to use a stretch IRA since her mother died in 2015, before the SECURE Act was in effect. But then Bea dies after 2019, the effective date of the SECURE Act, having named her own child (Ann's grandchild), CeCe, as beneficiary. CeCe must receive the remaining IRA by the end of the 10th year following Bea's death. Bea had been taking RMDs while using the stretch so the ALAR rule applies. CeCe must continue to take RMDs based on Bea's life expectancy in years one through nine of the 10-year period.

<u>Example 13</u>: EDB dies

Grandma Gertrude dies, having named her grandson Gary, age 30, as her primary beneficiary. On the date of Grandma's death, Gary qualifies as "chronically ill" under the tax code definition.

The Stretch or the 10-Year Rule?

Gary can begin taking stretch RMDs. Gary later dies, with his minor child, Jay, named as his beneficiary. Jay must receive the remaining IRA portion by the end of the 10th year following his father's death because he is a successor beneficiary. The ALAR rule applies because Gary was an EDB taking RMDs to use the stretch. Jay must continue to take RMDs based on Gary's life expectancy in years one through nine of the 10-year period.

Did you pass the test? Good! Now I know the last thing you want to hear about at this point is more rules . . . but here is one more oddball that just might come into play for you and your family. It occurs when your spouse decides to remain a beneficiary on your IRA rather than make it his or her own. Maybe it's because he or she inherited before age 59½ and wanted to avoid the 10 percent early distribution penalty. Because the spouse is an EDB, the circumstances create a bit of an overlap situation between the old pre-SECURE Act rules and the new rules.

Here goes.

Special SECURE Act and SECURE 2.0 Rules for Successor Beneficiaries—When a Spouse Inherits an IRA and Forgoes the Spousal Rollover, Electing to Be Treated as the Account Owner

SECURE 2.0 allows a spouse beneficiary to elect to be treated as if he or she were the account owner. If this election is chosen and a surviving spouse beneficiary dies *before* the deceased spouse would have turned 73 (had he or she lived), then the spouse beneficiary's *own beneficiary* is treated not as a successor beneficiary but as if the account was inherited directly from the original IRA owner. In most cases that distinction won't make much of a difference. Under the SECURE Act, the 10-year rule would apply to the spouse's beneficiary regardless—*unless that successor is an EDB.* If the successor is an EDB, *the successor would still get the stretch.*

If a surviving spouse beneficiary dies *after* the deceased spouse would have turned 73 (had he or she lived), then the spouse beneficiary's *own beneficiary* is treated as a successor beneficiary and remains subject to the 10-year rule. The entire inherited IRA balance will have to be withdrawn by the end of the 10th year after the spouse's death.

Example 14: Spouse inherits and elects to be treated as the account owner (no spousal rollover)

Married couple Mike and Sabrina are both 45 years old when Sabrina passes away. Mike elects to be treated as the account owner of Sabrina's IRA and names their child, Maggie, as his beneficiary. Tragically, Mike dies five years later, when Maggie is 10 years old.

Maggie will be able to calculate RMDs using her own life expectancy (the stretch IRA). That's because she qualifies as an EDB. At age 21, she will become subject to the 10-year payout rule but must continue RMDs for years one through nine of the 10-year period.

No Stretch IRA? No Problem–for Many

Yes, I've been complaining about Congress ending the stretch IRA throughout this chapter and in many other parts of this book. But for some of you it won't be a problem. If you find yourself in these situations, you can find other things to worry about. Here's why:

Five Reasons Why Stretch IRA Elimination Is Not the End of the World

The stretch IRA is dead, and everyone (including me) is writing about how this is the apocalypse for IRA planning. But, in truth, it isn't. Let's all take a deep breath. Yes, the stretch has been minimized and this does affect some of you—particularly those with the largest IRAs. But for many of you it's really no big deal.

When we look at the larger picture, we see five main reasons why losing the stretch is no problem:

1. The stretch only affects the largest IRAs.

How many IRAs even reach the beneficiary with a balance large enough to justify stretch payouts? The Treasury Department estimates only about 20 percent of all individuals required to take RMDs will stick to the schedule and take the minimum. That means that four out of five IRA owners withdraw more than required, thereby reducing the account balance quicker, leaving less for beneficiaries, reducing and maybe eliminating the impact of a stretch IRA.

2. Spouses remain unaffected by the change.

Most married people leave their IRAs to their spouses, and surviving spouses are exempt from the new stretch restrictions. Spouses who inherit still have all the options they had before the SECURE Act and can continue to take RMDs as before.

For example, the surviving spouse could do a spousal rollover and delay the "no-stretch problem" until the next generation, thereby postponing the start of the 10-year payout rule and consuming more of the IRA funds during his or her lifetime. Again, leaving less to beneficiaries and less concern about the stretch IRA.

However, once the surviving spouse dies, then yes, most non-spouse beneficiaries will be subject to the shorter 10-year rule.

3. Most beneficiaries don't stretch anyway.

Windfalls don't last long. How many beneficiaries will wait patiently for 30, 40, or 50 years to deplete their inherited IRAs? Very few. For many beneficiaries, the new 10-year rule may be a more realistic strategy. As for the smaller inherited IRAs, it might be logical to empty the account with a lump sum distribution, especially if it is split among several beneficiaries in low tax brackets. Of course, if the inherited IRA is a Roth, it would pay to hold it for the full 10 years and gain all the tax-free build up.

4. The 10-year rule may provide better planning opportunities for beneficiaries when death comes before the RBD.

The new 10-year payout rule is different from the old stretch IRA. Under the previous system, beneficiaries generally had to begin withdrawing in the year after death—and every year thereafter—regardless of their own tax situation. Now, when a traditional IRA owner dies before his or her RBD or a Roth IRA owner dies at any age, the 10-year rule can provide more fertile planning territory because there are no annual RMDs during this window. This gives the beneficiary enhanced flexibility to take distributions when they need them, or to refuse distributions in the years when they don't. Yes, they must withdraw the entire inherited IRA balance by the end of the 10th year after death, and this could result in a sizeable tax hit in that 10th year, but proper planning over the preceding decade can soften the blow. With a Roth IRA, however, the beneficiary is better off holding on to the inherited Roth until the end of the 10th year to take advantage of the full tax-free build-up over the 10 years. Yes, the inherited Roth funds still must be withdrawn by the end of the 10 years, but the withdrawal, including all that accumulation, will be tax-free.

5. Most beneficiaries are in lower tax brackets.

Grandchildren are popular IRA beneficiaries. However, grandchildren are (for the most part) bound by the 10-year payout rule and cannot stretch inherited IRA payments over their lifetimes. But 10 years is a long time. A minor grandchild will not be a minor forever. And many grandchildren are already in their twenties and thirties when they inherit. Yes, they will be forced to deplete the inherited IRA within 10 years, but younger people are typically in the lower tax brackets. While the inherited IRA payout now works on an accelerated 10-year period, the tax hit to the younger generation will not typically be as difficult to handle. Plus, naming multiple grandchildren beneficiaries means the original account can be spread over multiple tax returns, thereby further reducing the tax impacts.

So yes, the stretch IRA has been minimized, but there is still plenty of upside to work with. Or you could just spend your whole account to finance your own retirement years and remove the problem altogether for your beneficiaries.

Suffice it to say, the SECURE Act has changed the game when it comes to retirement and estate planning. With all this information, you are now better positioned to ensure that you take advantage of the breaks while avoiding the pitfalls.

You now know the options available to your beneficiaries and how the post-death payout rules work. Give some serious consideration to how the elimination of the stretch for most beneficiaries will impact you and your family. Reconsidering your beneficiary designations for your IRA, converting traditional IRAs to Roth IRAs, and increasing the use of life insurance are all strategies to evaluate in the wake of the SECURE Act. Each of those planning alternatives will be coming right up in the chapters that follow. Now that you have a grasp of the problems, read on so we can get to the solutions.

STEP #3:
ROTH IT

The point to remember is that what the government gives it must first take away.

—JOHN STRIDER COLEMAN (1897-1958),
AMERICAN BUSINESS EXECUTIVE

The Big Picture

The Roth IRA is the single best gift Congress has ever presented to the American taxpayer. It allows us to build retirement accounts that, over the long haul, will grow to an incredible size—and remain free of income tax forever. There is only one catch: You must pay the income tax up front. Many people run screaming when they hear that. But the big changes in the recent tax laws have even made paying the tax palatable for most. When it comes to retirement planning and account protection, keep focused on the big picture.

SEVEN

CONGRESS'S SINGLE BEST GIFT

The Roth IRA works the opposite way from the traditional IRA and other tax-deferred retirement accounts such as the 401(k). With tax-deferred accounts, you get a tax deduction when funds are put into the plan and you pay the tax when you withdraw later, usually at retirement. With the Roth IRA, however, you pay the income tax when you put in the money and receive no tax deduction—but after that, all future growth and withdrawals are tax-free to you and your beneficiaries.

I prefer the Roth IRA approach hands down. Here's why:

While a current tax deduction will save you money now, withdrawals on earnings from a deductible IRA are eventually subject to tax. Many people believe that they will be in a lower tax bracket in retirement so the tax on withdrawals from a traditional IRA will be less. But that's a myth. Most people are in a higher tax bracket in retirement given the combination of their retirement income, including those increasing RMDs from IRAs not converted to Roth IRAs, Social Security, and investment income. Therefore, a Roth IRA can save even more money over the long run because withdrawals of earnings are completely tax-free and remain tax-free for your beneficiaries. And all you need to do to snag this marvelous tax break is have the account a minimum of five years and avoid taking distributions until after age 59½. As with a traditional IRA, you can withdraw before 59½, but you may face a 10 percent penalty for doing so—unless the early withdrawal is for death, disability, education, medical expenses, or first-time home-buying expenses, etc. (see Chapter 4).

Unlike with a traditional IRA, Roth IRA owners are not subject to a required beginning date (RBD) or required minimum distributions (RMDs). That's right. You *never have to take the money out* if you don't want to, not even after you turn 73. You can just let it grow and grow and grow. In fact, with a Roth IRA, you can keep making contributions (if you qualify and have the earnings) even after age 73. Thanks to a change in the SECURE Act, you can also keep contributing to a traditional IRA at any age. But remember that those traditional IRA funds will soon be forced out with RMDs, and future distributions will generally be taxable at whatever the future tax rates will be. Roth IRAs avoid these tax risks.

Only when you die, and the money is left to a nonspouse (a child, for example) must Roth IRA withdrawals begin—because beneficiaries are subject to RMDs; but with a Roth, the RMDs are almost always income-tax-free to beneficiaries, as well!

With the elimination of the stretch IRA under the SECURE Act, most of your nonspouse beneficiaries will have to withdraw their inherited Roth funds by the end of the 10th year after your death. But the funds withdrawn will remain income-tax-free at that time. Also, because all Roth IRA owners are considered to have died before their RBD, there are never RMDs during the 10-year payout period, regardless of the age of the deceased Roth IRA owner. This makes the Roth IRA an even more valuable asset to leave to your children or grandchildren.

Paralysis by Analysis

Anyone eligible to start a Roth IRA (I'll get to the requirements shortly) should do so. Now!

So, why isn't there a stampede?

Is the Roth IRA too good to be true?

Is it that we don't trust Congress to keep its mitts off the Roth?

Is it that you still aren't sure that it really, truly, absolutely, positively pays to take the tax hit now with a Roth rather than later with a traditional IRA?

I'm not being flip here. Millions of Americans have expressed these same concerns as the primary reasons they've yet to hop on the Roth IRA bandwagon. Are their worries legit? Let's examine them, along with some others, to separate truth from baloney.

∎ **It's too good to be true; Congress will water it down or snatch it away.**

Don't worry about Congress—it certainly isn't worrying about you!

Whenever I discuss Roth IRAs, the number one question I get from people just like you is:

Can I trust the federal government to keep its word about tax-free withdrawals?

My answer? Of course NOT! Look what happened with the SECURE Act. Congress took away the long-established stretch IRA that many IRA owners had put at the center of their estate plans.

Remember the CPA Mantra: Tax Laws Are Written in Pencil!

The future offers no guarantees, but we've got good reason to believe that Roth IRAs won't be taxed. First off, levying such a tax would be politically risky since voters would perceive it as Congress reneging on their promise of a tax-free retirement savings account.

Secondly, because Roth IRAs are funded with after-tax dollars, the federal government takes its cut up front. If taxes were imposed on Roth IRAs, investors would have no motivation to fund them, and the government would lose the associated tax revenues.

Even if the government somehow changes the rules on Roth IRAs to make them less appealing, existing accounts might be grandfathered. Many people do not trust Congress to keep their word 20 or 30 years from now, so the sooner you get in on this Roth deal, the greater your chance of qualifying for any grandfathering.

Look to History for the Future of Roth IRAs

Congress created the Roth IRA in 1998 and its political popularity may make it the most secure of tax programs benefiting savers. Congress is always looking for quick cash, caring far less about future revenue losses.

One illustration of this approach was a 2017 tax-reform-debate proposal to increase revenue by reducing maximum deductible contributions to 401(k)s while pushing savers toward nondeductible Roth 401(k)s. While this particular proposal did not become a reality, the trend toward so-called Rothification seems to be accelerating as Congress looks at any and all immediate revenue sources. The SECURE 2.0 Act of 2022 includes numerous new Roth provisions, both expanding tax-free retirement savings opportunities and feeding Congress's addiction to immediate revenue.

Another point to keep in mind is the 2018 tax law change that made it even easier to convert to a Roth IRA by providing most people with lower tax rates. This is precisely the time to strike, before rates go back up, as history has shown us they will.

Here's the bottom line: Roth IRAs are now even more attractive as a savings vehicle, since all indicators suggest they are here to stay.

■ **But I'll be paying the tax now!**

True. And you've had it drummed into you that tax deferral is the name of the retirement game, haven't you? Well, I have to face the fact that my profession is largely to blame for such arbitrary thinking. We accountants are too often taught to tell our clients never to pay a tax before they have to. But that's wrongheaded, if paying tax now will lead to your prospering later, which is the case with a Roth IRA, where you'll be paying *zero percent* tax on withdrawal! How much better can you do than that? Take my word. It's true. I'm an accountant. Would I lie?

■ **What about all the money I could have made investing the funds I am now turning over to IRS to pay the tax on my Roth conversion?**

This is a common question, even from accountants! This, the so-called opportunity cost, is another of the more common arguments against doing a Roth conversion. The idea is that using funds now to pay the tax up front on a Roth conversion means that the future earnings that those funds could have produced is a lost opportunity. It's time to debunk this financial myth. It's simply not true.

The number one factor here is taxes, meaning the difference between the tax rates paid up front (now, at conversion) vs. the projected tax rates later, either during your retirement or when your beneficiaries withdraw the funds. If tax rates will remain the same or increase during your retirement, then a Roth conversion will pay, despite using funds up front to pay the taxes. It's all about the tax rates, not inflation, not earnings, and certainly not "opportunity cost." If the tax rates are the same both at conversion and later in retirement, the end financial result will be *exactly the same*, and this is true regardless of how long the funds are invested before being withdrawn in retirement.

"Ed, I'm still not sold," you might be saying. "How can there be no opportunity cost if I am laying out money now that I could have been investing instead? Prove it to me!"

Okay. Let's do the math. Here's a simple proof for you.

Assumptions:

$100,000 IRA balance; lifetime investment earnings rate of 200% (over, say, 20 or 30 years); and assume a tax rate of 30%

Results:

No Roth conversion—the funds remain in the traditional IRA

$100,000 after 200 percent lifetime earnings = $300,000

$300,000 x 30 percent tax rate = $90,000

Net after-tax balance = **$210,000**

Roth Conversion:

$30,000 tax paid up front ($100,000 x 30 percent)

Net amount converted = $70,000

$70,000 after 200 percent lifetime earnings = **$210,000**

In each case, the net result is *exactly the same*.

Asked about whether factors such as "the length of time the money [would be] invested, or inflation, or investment asset class" should affect the decision to go Roth, Joel Dickson, Vanguard Group's global head of Enterprise Advice Methodology, replied: "These facts make not an iota of difference" (*The Wall Street Journal*, May 31, 2019).

Bottom line: taxes now vs. later is the key factor in determining the ultimate benefit of a Roth conversion. But one worry that can be eliminated is the opportunity cost. It's all about the tax rates.

Since it's impossible to predict future tax rates, a series of annual partial Roth conversions to hedge against future higher taxes and provide tax-risk diversification might be the smartest option.

Worst-case scenario: Let's say you converted to the Roth and later on in retirement it turned out for whatever reason that your tax rate was lower. So what! You've still locked in a ZERO percent tax rate on your Roth funds forever. No matter how low your tax rate turns out to be in retirement, it will never be less than zero, and you can't beat a zero percent tax rate. With a Roth IRA you'll never have to worry about the uncertainty of what future tax rate increases might do to your life savings and spending ability. That's what I call peace of mind. That's why I am a Roth IRA fan.

Reasons NOT to Convert to a Roth IRA

To review, I am a big Roth IRA believer, given the two biggest long-term benefits:

- Tax-free distributions in retirement (including tax-free Roth IRAs for heirs)

- No lifetime required minimum distributions (RMDs) at 73

But Roth IRAs aren't for everyone—except younger savers who have the benefit of decades of tax-free compounding. Here there is no exception!

To provide you both sides of the issue so you can make the

decision that is best for you, here are 10 reasons NOT to convert to a Roth IRA:

1. The Up-Front Tax Bill

Anyone who just can't write that check should not be doing a Roth conversion. Let it go. Making the choice to pay the tax is even more important now that the Tax Cuts and Jobs Act (TCJA) eliminated the ability to undo a Roth conversion for 2018 and future years.

Make sure you understand that once you convert, you have committed to the tax bill. Roth conversions may not be right for those worried about being locked into paying a tax up front, without knowing the true cost, which won't happen until tax time the following year. This is especially true in times of economic uncertainty, when you may require that money for more pressing needs.

2. Tax Rates

The fundamental principle of tax planning is to always pay taxes at the lowest rates. In an optimal scenario, you take deductions when rates are higher, and pay taxes when rates are lower. The core issue for planning a Roth conversion is whether retirement will put you in a lower or higher tax bracket. If the most likely answer is a lower tax bracket, then avoid a Roth conversion now.

However, most retirees I work with are shocked when their taxes *increase* in retirement. How can that be? First, even if you have less income, you're still at risk of higher future tax rates. And the fact that your IRAs are subject to required minimum distributions after age 73 will add to your annual tax bill.

The Widow/er's Penalty

Most married couples leave everything to each other in an effort to ensure that the surviving spouse has continued financial security. But this plan comes with a hidden cost—what I call the "widow/er's penalty." When the first spouse dies, the surviving spouse generally inherits the IRAs, 401(k)s, and other property. If the survivor inherits all the property, does the widow/er end up with less than the couple had together? No. The survivor now owns all the couple's shared assets—plus more if the deceased had life insurance.

Consider a client of mine. We'll call him Harry. Together he and his wife, Jane, had an income of $100,000. When Harry died, Jane inherited his IRA, along with all his other property. Jane's income decreased slightly with the change in Social Security benefits. But the real problem came at tax time. Now that she was widowed, Jane could no longer file a joint tax return. As a single taxpayer, she now had to pay *higher taxes on less income*. That's the widow/er's penalty. Harry never considered that he would leave his wife an even bigger tax problem, which she now has for the rest of her life. Every year her required distributions increase and so does her tax bill. She got hit hard. Had Harry made a Roth conversion he would have saved Jane more than $100,000 in taxes over the years. It's too late now. Instead, she is stuck paying taxes at the *highest* rates. What a waste!

The widow/er's penalty is yet another way that your retirement savings wind up at the mercy of future higher taxes. And keep in mind that higher taxes will hit your retirement savings the hardest because most of those funds haven't yet been taxed. When trying to predict what your future tax rates might be, it pays to look at the long term, especially after the death of a spouse.

3. Beneficiary's Tax Rates

In addition to projecting your future tax rates, look farther down the road into the tax rates of your beneficiaries. If, collectively, the beneficiaries will be in lower tax brackets, a conversion may not be warranted. You might have to look at each beneficiary separately. One child might be in a very high tax bracket and would benefit from inheriting a Roth IRA. For another child, in a low bracket, paying the tax on the RMDs from a traditional inherited IRA may be insignificant. Note: The conversion decision must be made by you, the IRA owner, since nonspouse IRA beneficiaries cannot convert an inherited IRA to an inherited Roth IRA. However, in a tax law quirk (of which there are *many*), named beneficiaries who inherit company plan funds, like 401(k)s, can convert them to an inherited Roth IRA. Go figure.

Multiple Beneficiaries = Less Tax on Distributions

When looking ahead at multiple beneficiaries' future tax brackets, consider the benefit of each beneficiary being able to take advantage of their own lower tax brackets, spreading the collective tax over each of their returns. With multiple beneficiaries, the funds are split among them, so they will pay less tax overall. For example, one person who reports a $30,000 taxable IRA distribution will likely pay more tax than three people who report $10,000 each, since they can each use their lower brackets, thus lowering the overall tax.

4. Side Effects of Roth Conversions—Stealth Taxes

A Roth conversion increases AGI (adjusted gross income). This may, in turn, trigger other "stealth taxes" in the form of tax bill increases from losing tax deductions, credits, or other benefits tied to AGI. Some examples include: medical deductions, child tax credits, taxation of Social Security benefits, or even the potential loss of the 20 percent deduction for qualified business income (the Section 199A deduction). Increased income can also increase Medicare premiums or impact education tax benefits.

These amount to short-term blips since the additional taxes would only apply in the year of the conversion. Are these reasons to avoid a Roth conversion? I would say, look at the bigger picture—at the long-term benefit of the Roth IRA. The tax cost is a onetime, short-term expense to gain a greater benefit throughout retirement.

5. Financial Aid

Financial aid may be impacted by a spike in income from a Roth conversion, so timing here is critical, especially when a large chunk of much-needed money might be at risk. While retirement accounts are generally excluded from financial aid consideration, income is not. Depending on your situation, a Roth conversion may have to wait until assistance is no longer needed.

6. When Will You Need the Money?

If you need to access Roth funds sooner rather than later, that's a vote against a Roth conversion. The tax cost may not be worth the benefit if the funds won't have time to grow. One good tell: If you are thinking about how soon you can access the Roth funds, then you are not a good candidate for a Roth conversion. The big Roth benefit comes through tax-free compounding over time. Roth conversions are not for the short term.

7. Where Will the Money to Pay the Tax Come From?

So, you've decided you want to convert. Great! Have you made sure you'll have the money to pay the tax bill once it comes due? Again, this conversion is permanent. There's no going back. If the only funds you'll have available to cover the taxes come from the IRA itself, then don't do the conversion. This would immediately diminish the amount converted. Plus, IRA funds used to pay the tax would themselves become taxable, and if you're not yet age 59½ when they're withdrawn, those funds would also be subject to the 10 percent early distribution penalty (unless you're able to apply an exception).

8. Over 73 and Subject to RMDs

In general, older folks should avoid a Roth conversion. The tax cost vs. the tax benefit in your remaining lifetime is not worth it, except if you plan to leave that Roth to younger beneficiaries. Even so, once you reach age 73 and become subject to RMDs, it's more expensive to convert to a Roth IRA. That's because the first dollars distributed from your IRA are deemed to satisfy the RMD, and RMDs *cannot* be converted. The only IRA funds eligible for conversion would be those remaining after you withdrew the RMD amount. This increases your tax cost because you must pay tax on the RMD amount that will not end up in the Roth IRA. Unless you had large deductions or losses to keep your taxes low on the Roth conversion, this choice would not be cost effective. Remember, the additional tax cost of making a Roth conversion is a key factor in deciding whether a conversion will be tax-efficient over the long haul.

9. QCD Effect

Qualified charitable distributions (QCDs) are donations made directly to a charity from your IRA. These save taxes for eligible IRA owners or beneficiaries, age 70½ or older, by increasing the tax benefit of giving. If you are using your IRA for making donations via the QCD, it's better not to convert to a Roth IRA. This is because the QCD itself removes taxable IRA funds at no tax cost. If you plan to use your IRA primarily for making donations (and that's a good tax-planning strategy!), then the QCD is the better move, and you should avoid a Roth conversion. One exception comes if you wish to carve out a portion of your IRA to leave to children or grandchildren. Then a Roth IRA conversion would work for those funds.

10. Future Medical Expenses?

We can't predict the future, of course, but one reason to avoid a Roth IRA conversion is if IRA funds could be needed to pay heavy out-of-pocket medical expenses in retirement (those not reimbursed by insurance). The medical expense deduction may be used to offset the tax on future IRA distributions. This, of course, assumes that the medical bills wind up high enough to itemize, given the expanded standard deduction.

A Roth conversion would waste those medical deduction options. Even worse, if you covered such costs from a Roth IRA, you'd be using after-tax funds. With a little advance planning, you might be able to anticipate some of the bigger medical expenditures necessary for when you get older. You may already know that you will need to make major investments in medical equipment or home improvements specifically for medical care, such as an elevator, stairlifts, widening hallways and doorways for wheelchairs, or other wheelchair-access renovations, like exit ramps. You might need additional outlays for railings, support bars, or bathroom modifications, to name a few. These big-ticket items could easily offset the tax on even larger IRA distributions.

Home improvements (generally not deductible) become deductible if their main purpose is to provide medical benefits—so long as these modifications do not increase the value of the home. More often, these renovations reduce home values. Medical modifications in rental units are fully deductible since the apartment is not owned.

These same tax considerations apply if you may have to pay medical expenses for a dependent besides a spouse, like a parent, child, or other qualifying relative.

Of course, each person faces a different tax and financial situation. This makes a personalized evaluation necessary. Some of you may, in fact, have a lower tax rate in retirement. Or maybe you'll be able to withdraw IRA assets at low or no tax in retirement using QCDs or heavy medical deductions. Each of these cases would eliminate the value of a Roth conversion for those funds.

Now let's move on to your next excuse . . .

■ **But I'll get no tax deduction!**

True again. So what? Big deal! Even if you are in the 32 percent federal and state income-tax bracket, a tax deduction on a $7,000 traditional IRA contribution is worth just $2,240 a year. That's about 43 bucks a week. You probably blow more than that at Starbucks to feed your flat-white, half-caf, two-pumps habit. On the other hand, if you give up the $43, and BYOC from home in a travel mug, wouldn't you say you're trading up to a much better deal (along with keeping all those paper cups out of the landfill)?

The tax deduction you receive for contributing to an IRA is really just a loan you are taking from the government. It will have to be paid back in retirement via RMDs for the rest of your life—including the tax bill on earnings from those contributions. The deduction is just a short-term gain, leading to long-term tax pain.

In addition, you can participate in a Roth IRA even if you are active in a 401(k) or other company plan—where deducting your traditional IRA contribution may not be possible anyway, due to income limits. And if you can't deduct contributions to your traditional IRA, you'll be stuck with a nondeductible traditional IRA, which, as you'll recall from Chapter 4, is one big pain in the neck when it comes to figuring out taxes on distributions under the annoying pro-rata rule. The tax-free Roth IRA wins out handily over a traditional nondeductible IRA and all its related tax-deferral reporting (Form 8606) headaches. So, forget the instant gratification of getting a tax deduction and instead focus on the enormous long-term advantages of tax-free growth!

▪ **Roth IRAs are overly complicated.**

If anything is overly complicated, it's the RMD rules for traditional IRAs and company plans! Sure, the Roth IRA has its share of tax rules, but if you hold the account for the minimum five years and until you turn 59½, those rules are easy. Then all the distributions are tax- and penalty-free forever. It's that simple! Complications arise only when you withdraw before the 5-year holding period expires or before you turn 59½. Pay attention: DO NOT DO THIS! Leave the money alone, and no distribution rules apply until you die and your beneficiaries start RMDs—but even those rules are simple because distributions are income-tax-free.

▪ **My money will be tied up!**

Not true! But wait a second, didn't I tell you earlier that you cannot touch your money for five years or until you are 59½ years old? No, what I said is that the distribution rules become more complicated if you tap Roth money early. But the same is true of traditional IRAs—except it's much more expensive to get at your traditional IRA money because you must pay the income tax on the deferred amount on top of a 10 percent penalty. With a Roth IRA, however, what you've put in has already been taxed, so it won't be taxed again if you withdraw early. And you can even avoid paying a 10 percent penalty if the funds you withdraw are your original contributions and not earnings. You see, you can take out your original contributions to your Roth IRA at any time for any reason, tax- *and* penalty-free. Now, I ask you: How great is *that*?

No More Excuses

Don't buy into all the nebulous rationales, or knee-jerk resistance to any thoughts of change that could cause you to stick with your traditional IRA or company plan status quo. Many of the people who refuse to make the shift are just tightwads who simply don't want to pay tax now—even with the prospect of a huge tax-free gold rush later.

Likewise, don't fall into what athletes call "paralysis by analysis" from overstudying the issue. By the time you're satisfied, the opportunity to Roth it may have passed you by. Look at Moses. He spent 40 years searching for the Promised Land and wound up picking the only spot in the whole Middle East with no oil! So, put up your hand and promise me: *No more analysis!*

There is nothing more to analyze. The Roth IRA works. The only way it might not work for you as a tax-saving strategy is if you haven't the cash to pay the tax up front (but if you're that short of cash, then income and estate taxes are probably not an issue for you, and neither is planning to leave the lion's share of your IRA to your beneficiaries). Another way it may not work for you is if there's a chance that you might withdraw from your Roth within five years of opening it or before you turn 59½. To gain the most from a Roth, you want to keep it long-term or at least for those five years and until you hit 59½.

So, stop looking for a reason not to Roth it. You simply can't beat this strategy for building tax-free long-term wealth. It's the opportunity of a lifetime, especially if you're young—because it gives you, among whatever other assets you may possess, the greatest asset of all . . . time.

Two Flavors

Roth IRAs come in two flavors: *Roth IRA contributions* and *Roth IRA conversions*. The big-money flavor is the Roth IRA conversion—but first, here's a short primer on Roth IRA contributions.

Roth IRA Contributions

You are limited to contributing up to $7,000 (for 2024) annually per person to a Roth IRA ($8,000 if age 50 or over) if your yearly income is below $146,000 (for single taxpayers) or $230,000 (for married couples filing jointly). These income eligibility limits are for 2024 and increase each year. The annual contribution limit can be apportioned any way you want. At a minimum you should make a token contribution to start the clock running on the 5-year holding period. For details on the 5-year holding period rules, see the box on page 254. For example, a 2024 Roth IRA contribution made as late as April 15, 2025, starts the 5-year holding period as of January 1, 2024.

Contributions can be increased each year by $1,000 for taxpayers who are at least 50 years old. Contribution limits phase out for singles with 2024 incomes between $146,000 to $161,000 and for married couples filing jointly with incomes between $230,000 to $240,000. In most cases, married persons who file separate returns cannot make Roth IRA contributions.

Back-Door Roth IRAs

Even if your income places you over the Roth IRA contribution eligibility limits, there may still be a way to stuff money into your Roth. The tactic, known as a *back-door Roth*, is to instead make a nondeductible contribution to a traditional IRA, for which there are no income limits, and then convert that money to a Roth IRA. For years, some questioned whether this was a legal workaround, but both Congress and the IRS have since approved this transaction. You must still meet the traditional IRA contribution qualifications, however, and when you convert the funds to the

Roth IRA, you must follow the pro-rata rule (see Chapter 3 and later in this chapter). That means some portion of the conversion will be taxable if you have other pre-tax IRA funds. But after the smoke clears, you'll have the funds in your Roth IRA as if you had been eligible to make the Roth IRA contribution all along. The only difference is that the funds go into the Roth as a conversion.

Roth contributions are permitted without regard to age. Thus, children with summer jobs can fund a Roth IRA based on their earnings. And even individuals in their seventies or eighties who are still working can continue to fund a Roth IRA, as long as they've got the dollars.

Roth IRA contributions are also permitted without regard to participation in a qualified retirement plan.

529 Plan-to-Roth IRA Rollovers

A 529 plan is a tax-advantaged savings account designed to encourage saving for future education costs. As long as the funds are used for qualified education expenses, the earnings can be withdrawn tax- and penalty-free. However, sometimes parents (or other account owners) wind up not using the entire 529 account balance because, for example, their child gets a scholarship or doesn't attend college. If you withdraw funds and don't use them for educational expenses, the earnings in your account will be subject to income tax and a 10 percent penalty.

In the past, the risk of unused funds has caused many parents to fund 529 plans conservatively or not at all. The SECURE 2.0 Act of 2022 addresses this problem by allowing tax-free rollovers from 529 plans to Roth IRAs. However, there are strict guidelines that you must follow:

- The maximum amount that can be rolled from a 529 account to a Roth IRA is $35,000.

- The Roth IRA must be in the name of the 529 beneficiary—not the 529 owner (if different).

- The 529 plan must have been open for more than 15 years.

- Rollover amounts cannot include any 529 contributions (and earnings on those contributions) made in the preceding five-year period.

- Rollovers are subject to the annual Roth IRA contribution limit. Further, any actual Roth IRA (or traditional IRA) contributions made by the 529 beneficiary would count against the permitted rollover amount. The effect of this rule is that a full $35,000 529-to-Roth IRA rollover would need to be completed over several years. It also means the 529 beneficiary doing the rollover must have compensation in the year of the rollover at least equal to the amount being rolled over.

- The rollover from the 529 plan to the Roth IRA is a nontaxable transaction.

- When former 529 dollars are ultimately distributed from the Roth IRA, Roth IRA ordering rules will apply. Contributions are tax- and penalty-free, and earnings are tax- and penalty-free if the distribution is qualified.

There are no income limits restricting the 529-to-Roth IRA rollover. In fact, both the account owner and the 529 beneficiary could have income that exceeds the annual IRA contribution limit, and they would still qualify for the 529-to-Roth IRA rollover. This could be considered another backdoor Roth IRA opportunity for high earners.

Roth Conversions for All!

Just a reminder . . .

There are no income limits for Roth conversions. Everyone who has a retirement account that is eligible for a distribution, like a 401(k), or an IRA can convert all or any part of that account to a Roth IRA. No limitations or restrictions.

Roth IRA Conversions

Roth IRA conversions can help you stockpile tax-free cash, but you need to be able to pay the conversion tax first, of course. This upfront tax payment is the biggest roadblock for most people. But it needn't be. If you do not pay the conversion tax now, you or your beneficiaries will pay more income tax later, because all the growth in your traditional IRA will eventually be taxed anyway, and withdrawals from that account must begin after your RBD. That is not the case with a Roth IRA.

The costliest tax blunders occur because people refuse to spend now to gain later. I understand their feelings that "a bird in the hand is worth two in the bush." But parting with some money now is the best way to leverage your assets for future growth. In effect, you're paying for seed so the crop can grow freely. If there is one overriding message to this book, it's this: Doing nothing because you can't part with a buck is the surest way to build up your retirement savings account only to hand it over to Uncle Sam.

CAUTION!

Your taxes may be slightly higher the year you convert. For example, the tax on Social Security benefits may apply solely due to the Roth conversion. The Roth conversion could also cause the following AGI-based deductions and credits to be reduced or lost completely: medical expenses, tax credits, and other benefits. The conversion could also trigger an increase in Medicare surcharges for higher-income individuals.

The 3.8 percent additional tax on net investment income could be triggered by a Roth conversion. Although the IRA income or gains are not subject to that additional tax, the income recognized from a Roth conversion could push you over the income limit and cause your net investment income to be subject to the extra tax. But don't shy away from the Roth because of this. The tax hike and loss of benefits, if any, are for one year only—whereas your Roth lives on for decades tax-free.

Here's the incredible thing about a Roth IRA conversion: There is no limit, no cap, no ceiling on the amount that can be converted—as long as you're willing to pay the income tax. You can convert $10 million if you have it. You'll owe close to $4 million in income tax (but if you've got the $10 million in the first place, this should be easy), and it would still pay to do the conversion because growth on the back end is practically limitless and all tax-free.

Convert Before You Reach 73

Converting before you're 73 avoids the minimum distribution problem.

Until you've satisfied your required minimum distribution, all money withdrawn in your 73rd year up to that amount will not be eligible for conversion. It will be treated as part of your RMD—and remember that RMDs can never be converted to a Roth! Any amounts more than the RMD can be converted.

With this strategy, you can ignore all those darn after-73 distribution rules that attach themselves to traditional IRAs like flies on s***. In fact, many people convert to Roth IRAs for that reason alone.

A Deathbed Roth Conversion

The up-front tax you pay to convert to a Roth IRA reduces your taxable estate, so, in effect, the government is paying for a good part of the cost of your conversion. Although most people will no longer be subject to federal estate tax given the current high exemption amounts, there are still a handful of states that have much lower exemptions. That could expose you to state estate taxes, and, in some cases, the tax you pay on a Roth conversion could reduce your estate to the point that you can save on state estate taxes. That's a big break, especially for older converters with large estates. Nevertheless, many older traditional IRA owners are convinced that the Roth conversion is not for them, because they will not have enough years to make up the conversion's out-of-pocket tax cost. But I've gotta tell you, the "too-old" excuse generally holds no water.

Some years ago, I had a client who was terminally ill—and one doesn't get much more "out of time" than that. It took some convincing, but I eventually persuaded his family to persuade him to convert his $1 million traditional IRA to a Roth IRA, which he did, paying about $400,000 in income tax for the conversion.

When he died soon after (long before the recent increased estate-tax exemptions), his estate was subject to an estate tax of around 50 percent. But because he had paid $400,000 in income tax on the Roth conversion, his estate included $400,000 less than it would have, so, at the 50 percent rate, his estate tax was immediately reduced by $200,000 (50 percent of $400,000 = $200,000)!

If my late client had not converted, he would have died with $400,000 more in his estate and lost $200,000 more in estate tax. But, instead, the government wound up paying half the cost of his Roth conversion (through lost tax revenue), and my late client's heirs inherited his $1 million Roth IRA, from which they can withdraw income for the rest of their lives, tax-free. (This was before the SECURE Act established the 10-year rule, so the Roth IRA beneficiaries in this case were grandfathered under the old stretch rules.)

How to Convert to a Roth IRA

You convert when you transfer (deposit) funds from your traditional IRA to your Roth IRA. If you are converting IRAs that contain nondeductible contributions, or after-tax funds rolled over from a company plan, then you must use the pro-rata rule (see Chapter 3) to determine how much of the converted funds will be taxable.

Nondeductible contributions and after-tax funds are basis (already-taxed money) and can be withdrawn tax-free, but under the pro-rata rule each dollar converted is deemed part taxable and part tax-free based on the percentage of the basis (the nondeductible and after-tax contributions) to the balance in the traditional IRA.

For example, let's say you have $300,000 in your traditional IRA and you convert $30,000 of it to a Roth IRA. If there are no nondeductible contributions, then all $30,000 is taxable. But if the $300,000 IRA balance included $30,000 of nondeductible contributions and you converted $30,000, only $3,000 would be tax-free and $27,000 would be taxable.

One might think that if there is $30,000 of basis in the IRA, one could convert the $30,000 and pay no tax. But that's not the way it works. The pro-rata rule requires that each dollar converted includes a percentage of taxable and tax-free money. In this example, the basis is $30,000 and that is 10 percent of the $300,000 IRA balance. Under the pro-rata rule, 10 percent of each distribution (or conversion) will be tax-free and 90 percent will be taxable. So, when you convert the $30,000, 10 percent (or $3,000) will be tax-free (a return of part of the basis) and 90 percent (or $27,000) will be taxable and included in the current year's income. All of this must be reported on Form 8606 for the year you convert.

Basically, a Roth IRA conversion is the same as a rollover because you're shifting funds from one type of account to another. As you recall from Chapter 3, rollovers are accomplished in one of two ways—a direct trustee-to-trustee transfer or a withdrawal and deposit within 60 days. For a typical rollover, the direct transfer is the preferred method of the two.

The once-per-year IRA rollover rule that applies to rollovers (see Chapter 3) does not apply to Roth IRA conversions, even though a conversion is basically a rollover. You can convert as many times as you wish during the year. The 60-day rollover rule (see Chapters 3 and 4) does apply to Roth conversions, however, but only when you withdraw the funds yourself to redeposit in the Roth account. (There is no 60-day rule with a direct transfer.)

Paying the Income Tax on Conversion

As you're aware by now, you must pay income tax when you convert to a Roth. Ideally, that money should not come from your traditional IRA or other retirement accounts.

If you use your IRA money to pay the conversion tax, you won't be able to convert as much, and you could incur a 10 percent penalty on the amount used. More important, you'll have less money working and growing for you tax-free in the Roth IRA!

For example, Bob wants to convert his $100,000 IRA to a Roth IRA, but the only money he has available to pay the income tax is the IRA money itself. So, he'll probably only be able to convert about $75,000 because he'll need $25,000 (depending on his tax bracket) to pay the tax. The $75,000 would go into the Roth and there would be no 10 percent penalty on that money—because the 10 percent penalty does not apply to amounts converted, regardless of the convert's age. However, the penalty does apply to amounts *not converted*. In this case, let's say Bob is younger than 59½ years old; therefore, he would owe a 10 percent penalty on the $25,000 that was used to pay the tax because that money was never converted but instead was considered a regular taxable distribution. Now Bob is paying a 10 percent penalty on top of the conversion tax in order to convert—and not getting the full $100,000 IRA into the Roth, just $75,000 of it. This is why funds other than those from your IRA should always be used to pay the income tax on a Roth conversion if you are under 59½ years old. The extra 10 percent penalty tips the scales and makes the conversion too costly.

But if you simply don't have other money to draw on, then what do you do? Forget the idea of converting? Not at all. Just convert a little less. Remember, you don't have to convert all your traditional IRA all at one time all in one year. You can convert a smaller amount each year. This way you can structure your conversions so that you can afford to pay the tax from non-IRA money and avoid having your Roth IRA growth cut down before it even gets started.

Roth IRA Conversions Are Permanent

But what if you convert to a Roth IRA and then your financial situation changes and you cannot afford to pay that tax, or you simply change your mind and no longer want to pay it? Or what if you have already paid the tax and now wish you had that tax money back? Houston, we have a problem. Roth conversions are permanent. They cannot be undone.

The Tax Cuts and Jobs Act eliminated the ability to undo a Roth conversion. What was technically called a "recharacterization" once allowed you to undo a Roth conversion for any reason at all. After you reversed your conversion, you would no longer owe the tax on the amount undone. But Congress got a bug in them that people were gaming the system by converting and reversing Roth conversions as values changed. (Really? Somehow this is where Congress decided to focus their concern about being taken advantage of, rather than targeting Cayman Islands tax havens, evasive Swiss bank accounts, carried interest, or Wall Street tax scams—never mind all the big corporations that pay little or no U.S. taxes because their headquarters are located in a post office box in Liechtenstein! But I digress.)

Anyway, Congress lowered the boom on recharacterizations of any Roth conversions completed after 2017. So, Roth conversions are now permanent. Once you convert, you will owe the related income tax, even if the stock market crashes the day after you convert. But this is no reason to avoid the incredible long-term, tax-free benefits of a Roth conversion—remember that even when you could undo Roth conversions, it was only for a set time limit. After that, they were permanent anyway.

The difference now, though, is that before you go all-in you need to make a solid prediction about your total conversion tax bill. One way to deal with this is to make a series of small annual conversions to spread the tax hit over a few years. Or wait until later in the year to convert when you'll have a better idea of what your income will be so you can better project your tax bill.

Whatever you do, don't let the permanency of the Roth conversion deter you. The tax-free buildup once the funds are in your Roth IRA is also permanent, for you and your beneficiaries, not to mention the lack of RMDs during your lifetime. That's an annual tax saver for life. Just be careful.

Recharacterizations Are Still Available for IRA Contributions

Unlike Roth conversions, Roth IRA and traditional IRA contributions can still be recharacterized. For example, say you contributed to a Roth IRA but later found out your income exceeded the limit, and you are not eligible to make a Roth contribution. If you still qualify for a traditional IRA contribution, you can recharacterize your Roth contribution to a traditional IRA. The process works in reverse too. Let's say you made a contribution to a traditional IRA, but due to income limits and plan participation you could not deduct the contribution. Assuming you qualify to make a Roth IRA contribution, you could recharacterize it to a Roth IRA contribution.

When Is the Conversion Effective?

The day the funds are removed from your traditional IRA to go to the Roth determines the year of conversion, even if those funds are not actually deposited in the Roth until the following year.

Here's another creative strategy for "Roth-ing it" even when you think you don't have the money to pay the tax on the conversion: use life insurance! Let's assume that you have a $1 million traditional IRA for which the conversion tax would come to $400,000, and you would rather have your children inherit than your spouse. Here's what to do:

Buy a $1 million life insurance policy and name your spouse as beneficiary of the policy and the IRA. When you die, your spouse will receive both the $1 million of tax-free life insurance and the IRA, which your spouse can then roll over to his or her own IRA. Now, he or she can convert that $1 million traditional IRA to a Roth IRA, using money tax-free from the life insurance policy to pay the $400,000 conversion tax.

Once he or she has a Roth IRA, your spouse is no longer subject to required IRA distributions. Your spouse never has to withdraw that money, and if he or she does, the withdrawals will be tax-free. Of course, the Roth may grow so large that it becomes subject to estate tax in your spouse's estate. If so, there is no problem. Your spouse just uses some of the remaining life insurance money to buy another policy on his or her own life that's set up outside the estate and names the children as beneficiaries. When your spouse dies, the children will inherit the Roth IRA and withdrawals can remain income-tax-free for 10 years after death (under the SECURE Act 10-year rule). The children will also inherit the new life insurance money estate- and income-tax-free and can use some of those funds to pay any estate tax due on the Roth IRA that they just inherited.

TWO 5-YEAR RULES

There are two 5-year rules governing Roth IRAs. The first one determines whether your Roth distribution is a qualified distribution and, therefore, free of income tax. The 5-year holding period starts on the first day of the year for which the Roth IRA contribution is made, even if the actual contribution is made in the following year. You have until April 15 after the year for which you want to contribute to make the contribution. For example, if you make a 2024 Roth IRA contribution in March 2025, the 5-year holding period begins on January 1, 2024, the first day of the year for which the Roth IRA contribution was made, even though it was actually made in 2025. For Roth IRA contributions, the 5-year rule does not restart for each contribution.

The second 5-year rule applies only to Roth IRA conversions, and only if you are under 59½ years old. It says that if you are younger than 59½, you must hold the converted funds for five years. Distributions of converted funds not held for five years will be subject to the 10 percent penalty if the funds are withdrawn before you reach age 59½. A new 5-year holding period is applied to each new conversion.

Taking Your Money Out of a Roth IRA

Withdrawals from a Roth IRA are tax-free if they are *qualified distributions*. What the heck does that mean? It means they must pass a few tests.

To be a qualified distribution, the funds must have been held in the account for more than five years AND conform to one of the following other stipulations:

- Be taken at or after 59½ years of age.

- Be taken upon death of the owner.

- Be taken for owner disability reasons. (The definition of *disability* is the same as that for the traditional IRA.)

- Be taken under the first-time-homebuyer-exception rules ($10,000 lifetime limit—see Chapter 4).

If you do not hold the Roth for more than five years, then even if you are 59½, dead, or disabled, or use the money for a first home, your Roth distribution could still be subject to tax.

After 5 years, the 10 percent early withdrawal penalty does not apply to the amounts converted from the traditional IRA to a Roth IRA, even if you are under 59½. But if you use some of the IRA assets to pay for the conversion taxes at the time of the conversion, that amount will be subject to early withdrawal penalty tax. The reason is that the amount withdrawn for taxes was not converted to a Roth IRA.

There are no lifetime-distribution rules for Roth IRA owners. You can withdraw as much as you want anytime you want, which is one of the great beauties of this tax-free vehicle over other types of retirement plans.

But if you start taking your money early because you can't wait for that five-year minimum or until you turn 59½, you'll face two kinds of distribution rules: aggregation rules and ordering rules.

Aggregation Rules

Under the aggregation principle, all your Roth IRA accounts, whether conversion or contributory, are treated as one pot of money, even if you have them in different places. So, for figuring taxation on early withdrawals, all your accounts are simply added together. But your withdrawals must be taken in a specific sequence that's governed by ordering rules.

Ordering Rules

These special rules tell you which funds must come out first by dividing the aggregated money in your Roth IRA accounts into three distinct groups:

1. Annual Roth IRA contributions
2. Roth conversions on a first-in-first-out (FIFO) basis

   a. Taxable amounts first, then
   b. Non-taxable amounts (from after-tax contributions)

3. Earnings on Roth IRA contributions or conversions

If you tap your account(s) early, the first dollars out are deemed to come from your annual Roth contributions. This money can be withdrawn tax- and penalty-free at any time for any reason. After the Roth IRA contributions are withdrawn (or if there are no Roth contributions), the next in line are the Roth-conversion funds, which must be taken out on a first-in-first-out (FIFO) basis, meaning conversions from the earliest years must be withdrawn first. These withdrawals will be subject to the 5-year-rule/under-59½ 10 percent early withdrawal penalty (but no tax because you paid it when you converted). (This rule was put into effect to close a perceived loophole that would have allowed individuals under age 59½ to conspire to convert from their traditional IRA and then immediately withdraw from the Roth IRA with no penalty.)

A further complication arises at this time if you have converted nondeductible traditional IRA money to a Roth IRA—because every time you withdraw from a traditional IRA that has nondeductible contributions, you need to use that darn pro-rata rule.

Beware of the Inherited Roth IRA Tax Trap

Don't fall into the trap some Roth-eligible designated beneficiaries do when they say, "If the RMD on my brother's Roth IRA is not taxable, then why should the IRS care if I take the distribution or not? After all, the IRS receives no tax on the distribution so why would it care if I take it?" Trust me on this. The IRS does care! It is not going to let you stockpile that tax-free account forever. That's why there are all these RMD rules for eligible designated beneficiaries and the 10-year rule for noneligible designated beneficiaries . . . and the rules DO apply to inherited Roth IRAs. In fact, under the SECURE Act, most beneficiaries are now subject to the 10-year rule. Instead of annual RMDs, the entire inherited Roth IRA balance must be withdrawn by the end of the 10th year after death. At the

10-year mark, the total balance becomes your RMD—in essence a 100 percent RMD. You must take the full distribution even though it's not taxable. If you don't, the balance will be subject to the 25 percent RMD penalty. Can you imagine how awful it would be to pay a 25 percent penalty on a total account balance distribution that would have been tax-free? The SECURE Act makes this penalty way more severe due to the 100 percent RMD in year 10, so keep track of your 10-year RMD due date.

When withdrawing early, the group of funds that's off limits until last is earnings. This is what makes me so vehement about keeping your hands off your Roth for the minimum five years and until you reach age 59½ (or not converting in the first place if you think you'll succumb to this temptation). Earnings will be subject to both tax and 10 percent penalty (unless you qualify for any of the exceptions I described earlier: first-time homebuyer, disability, etc.). That is to say, you've lost all the benefits of the Roth!

Inheriting Roths

When a Roth IRA owner dies, the RMD rules that apply under the SECURE Act are pretty much the same as with a traditional IRA. The only difference is that the withdrawals taken by the beneficiary are tax-free—unless the deceased did not hold the account for the required five years.

A WORD TO THE WISE

Here's one final note for nonspouse Roth IRA beneficiaries: Because you cannot roll over or treat inherited Roth IRAs as

your own (as with inherited traditional IRAs, only spouse beneficiaries can do that), the deceased Roth IRA owner's name
must remain on the account and it must be titled the same
way as outlined for traditional IRAs in Chapter 5.

When a nonspouse (i.e., a child) inherits a Roth IRA, the same distribution rules that apply to a traditional IRA inherited from an
owner who died before his or her required beginning date (RBD)
must be followed. As there is no RBD for Roth IRAs, it is a date that
can never be reached, and so, for distribution purposes, all Roth
IRA owners are deemed to have died before it (even if they're 95
when they pass away).

A nonspouse beneficiary can never roll over or contribute new
funds into an inherited IRA or Roth IRA account, whereas a spouse
can inherit a traditional IRA and convert that to a Roth IRA, but
only if rolling it over or electing to treat it as his or her own (see
Chapter 6). A nonspouse IRA beneficiary cannot convert an inherited IRA to a Roth IRA.

If the Roth IRA owner neglected to name a beneficiary or did
not name a designated beneficiary, the inherited Roth IRA must be
paid out under the 5-year rule, regardless of the Roth IRA owner's
age when he or she died. Therefore, it is even more critical to make
sure you have a designated beneficiary with a Roth IRA than it is
with a traditional IRA. At least with a traditional IRA, if you die
after the RBD with no designated beneficiary, the IRA can still be
paid out over the IRA owner's remaining single life expectancy,
which is usually more than five years. There is no such safety valve
for an inherited Roth IRA because there is no such thing as dying
after your RBD.

To make matters worse, if there is no designated beneficiary, the
estate may become the beneficiary, which—as you'll remember
from Chapters 5 and 6 (and you'd better remember!)—is the WORST
of all inherited IRA or Roth IRA scenarios.

Which Funds **Can** Be Contributed to In-Plan Roth Accounts?

- Elective salary deferrals
- Catch-up contributions (age 50 or over)
- Automatic enrollment deferrals
- Rollovers from other Roth 401(k) plans
- In-plan conversions from a 401(k)
- Employer matching contributions

Which Funds **Cannot** Be Contributed to In-Plan Roth Accounts?

- Forfeitures allocated to employees
- Rollovers from Roth IRAs
- Conversions (rollovers) from IRAs or other employer plans

The Roth 401(k)

The Roth 401(k) (as well as other Roth employer plans) provides you with a quick way to supersize your tax-free retirement savings since you can contribute much more to them than you can to a Roth IRA. (From here on, I'll be using the term "Roth 401(k)" when referring to any of these plans.) The Roth 401(k) is part of a company plan and cannot be offered alone. It must be paired with a 401(k) plan, and your employer is not required to offer a Roth option to its employees. This means you cannot have a Roth 401(k) if your company does not already have a regular 401(k) plan. The Roth 401(k) is governed by the same rules as other 401(k) plans. It must meet the nondiscrimination tests, contribution limits, and distribution restrictions to which other funds in a 401(k) plan are subject. Unlike

Roth IRA contributions, there are no income limits for making Roth 401(k) contributions. But like Roth IRAs, Roth 401(k)s have no lifetime RMDs, beginning in 2024. Before that, Roth 401(k)s were subject to RMDs, but SECURE 2.0 eliminated that problem.

Contributions to the Roth 401(k) are salary deferrals but, unlike those made to a traditional 401(k) (which are not taxed), these are made after tax and the amount deferred to the Roth 401(k) is subject to the same income tax withholding as the employee's take-home pay.

For example, Lou's employer has a traditional 401(k) plan and is now offering a Roth 401(k) option. Lou earns $50,000 a year and currently has 5 percent of his salary deferred to the traditional 401(k) plan. With the traditional 401(k), the deferral of $2,500 is pretax. It reduces Lou's take-home pay amount by $2,500 and the employer does not take any federal withholding taxes out of the $2,500. It is as if Lou were only earning $47,500 a year, since he only pays tax on $47,500. But if Lou decides to change his 5 percent salary deferral to the Roth 401(k), the $2,500 is now taken after-tax. His employer will have to calculate federal withholding on Lou's full salary of $50,000. Lou pays tax on his full $50,000 salary, even though he only receives $47,500. Lou is actually paying more taxes on the money he takes home each year.

Roth 401(k) contribution limits are the same as the elective contribution limits for the employer plan. And just as the contribution limits for a traditional IRA and a Roth IRA are combined so that you cannot contribute more than $7,000 to all your IRAs if you are younger than 50, the Roth 401(k) and the 401(k) limits also are combined. For 2024, the maximum contribution amount is $23,000 plus a $7,500 catch-up contribution if the employee is age 50 or older.

Here's another example. In 2024, Mike is younger than 50 and does not qualify for catch-up contributions. His traditional 401(k) plan will let him defer $23,000 of his compensation and it offers him a Roth 401(k). The total deferral cannot exceed $23,000 for 2024. This year, Mike decides to defer the maximum to his retirement account, electing to defer $10,000 to the Roth 401(k) account and the balance of $13,000 to the traditional 401(k) account.

Contributing to a Roth 401(k) in no way affects or limits your ability to contribute to a traditional or Roth IRA. However, being covered by a company plan could affect your ability to deduct a traditional IRA contribution, depending on your income. If you qualify, you can contribute to both Roth 401(k)s and Roth IRAs to quickly build your tax-free retirement savings.

For example, John and Nancy are married and file a joint return on their combined income of $125,000, so they each qualify to make Roth IRA contributions. They are also both older than 50 years old, so they qualify to make catch-up contributions as well. If John and Nancy each work for companies that offer Roth 401(k)s, they can contribute a total of $77,000 to their Roth IRAs and Roth 401(k)s for 2024. (I know this sounds far-fetched, but the tax law allows us to dream big here. Just imagine what a giant, tax-free nest egg they can build in only one year—if they have enough cash flow to permit squirreling away such a large percentage of their income to achieve this.)

Here is how they get to the $77,000 total contribution amount for one year.

2024 Roth 401(k) contributions:
$23,000 plus $7,500 catch-up = $30,500 each

2024 Roth IRA contributions:
$7,000 plus $1,000 catch-up = $8,000 each

Total = $38,500 each, or $77,000 for both, all in one tax year!

Elective salary deferrals, employer matching or other employer contributions, and rollovers from other Roth employer plans can all go into the Roth 401(k). However, the Roth 401(k) account can accept employer contributions or rollover contributions from another Roth employer account *only if the plan allows this*. Remember, the election to make after-tax Roth 401(k) contributions is irrevocable. You can't change your mind.

An employee can also convert other amounts currently held in the 401(k) plan to the Roth 401(k). This is commonly called an "in-plan" Roth conversion. Like a regular Roth conversion, you pay tax on the taxable amounts converted from the 401(k) to the Roth 401(k), and it can't be reversed.

SECURE 2.0 requires certain plan participants who want to leverage age 50 or older catch-up contributions to make them as Roth contributions. This rule applies if your wages from the plan sponsor (your employer) exceed $145,000 (indexed for inflation) in the previous year. This provision was set to be effective in 2024, but the IRS has extended the effective date two years, to 2026.

Roth Conversions of Company Plan Funds

Up to this point I have been talking almost exclusively about converting your IRA funds to a Roth IRA, but company plan funds like your 401(k) can also be converted now—in two ways. The choice comes down to whether you want to move the funds *out* of your company plan—a Roth IRA conversion—or keep the funds within your company plan—a Roth 401(k) conversion. Here are the details on those choices.

Conversions of Company Plan Funds to Roth IRAs

Employees can convert their company plan funds, such as 401(k)s, directly to a Roth IRA. The ability to do so is not an all-or-nothing proposition. For example, you may want to convert some 401(k) money directly to a Roth IRA and then roll the rest over to a traditional IRA.

If funds are converted from the company plan, make sure the transfer is done as a direct transfer (aka a trustee-to-trustee transfer) to avoid having 20 percent federal withholding taken from the distribution. This would leave only 80 percent of the funds converted and could result in tax and a 10 percent penalty (if under age 59½) on the withheld amount if you do not have other funds available outside of the plan to complete the conversion. To qualify as a trustee-to-trustee transfer and avoid the 20 percent withholding rule, the distribution check(s) from the company plan for the funds to be converted should be made payable to the *custodian* of the Roth IRA you are converting to—*not to you!*

While the IRS allows you to convert company plan funds to Roth IRAs, you may not be eligible to do this. Not surprisingly, this confuses some people. The company plan itself must permit the distribution. Some plans allow "in-service distributions" that can be converted directly to a Roth IRA. But if in-service distributions are not available, then you must wait until the date(s), spelled out in the plan agreement, that your company plan will allow plan funds distribution, which is usually upon reaching retirement age or upon separation of service.

As you may recall from Chapter 3, in certain situations, after-tax funds can be converted directly to your Roth IRA tax-free. See the section "Special Tax Break for 401(k) Distributions = Tax-Free Roth Conversions." Of course, as in most cases, you first need to see if your company will allow you to do this, as they are not required to.

To review, if you have both pre-tax and after-tax funds in your company plan, like your 401(k), instead of rolling all your plan funds over to your traditional IRA, you can split that rollover. First, you can directly roll over the pre-tax funds (these are the funds that would be taxable if withdrawn) to your traditional IRA as a regular, tax-free, direct IRA rollover. Then that would leave only your after-tax plan funds. These are funds that would be tax-free if withdrawn, but instead of withdrawing them, you can convert them to your Roth IRA in a tax-free conversion. This maneuver is an exception to the pro-rata rule that applies when you convert IRA funds to a Roth IRA. What you cannot do, though, is convert only the after-tax funds and pay no tax.

Conversions of Company Plan Funds to Inherited Roth IRAs

Back in 2008, the IRS ruled that nonspouse beneficiaries (like your child or grandchild) of inherited company plans could convert plan balances to inherited Roth IRAs—a move that had not been previously permitted. (For some strange reason, though, no similar rule change was made for nonspouse IRA beneficiaries; they still cannot convert inherited IRAs to inherited Roth IRAs. Sorry, Charlie.)

Now nonspouse beneficiaries who inherit your company plan balances can convert those funds to an inherited Roth IRA if they wish. Or they can choose to do a tax-free direct transfer to an inherited traditional IRA instead. To accomplish either of these, the nonspouse beneficiary must do a direct rollover of the inherited plan balance by the end of the year after your death.

For nonspouse beneficiaries choosing to convert the inherited plan balance to an inherited Roth IRA, RMDs will generally be tax-free. But they must pay income tax on the funds converted just the same as any other IRA owner or plan participant who converts to a Roth IRA. This also applies when qualifying trusts are named as the plan beneficiary, since a trust is also a nonspouse beneficiary. The post-death transfer (Roth conversion) must be done as a direct rollover (trustee-to-trustee transfer) from the plan to an inherited Roth IRA. Once the funds make it into the nonspouse beneficiary's inherited Roth IRA (or traditional IRA), the beneficiary will generally be subject to the 10-year payout rule, unless he or she qualifies under the SECURE Act as an eligible designated beneficiary for a stretch IRA (see Chapter 6).

Conversions of Company Plan Funds to Roth 401(k)s

Plan participants can convert their company plan funds to a Roth 401(k), Roth 403(b), or Roth 457(b) within the plan. (To avoid my ticking off all these different plans over and over again, please note that whatever I say about a Roth 401(k) also applies for a Roth 403(b) and a Roth 457(b), since the tax rules governing all three are generally identical. I will point out any differences that may exist.) Plans are not required to allow this but, over time, most have come around and offer the Roth 401(k) as well as the ability to convert within the plan—that is, from your 401(k) to your Roth 401(k).

Bottom line: If your company plan's rules allow you to convert at the plan level, in many cases you can take a distribution of the funds and roll it to an IRA or convert it to a Roth IRA. This begs the question: Which is more advantageous—a Roth IRA or a Roth 401(k) in the plan?

Roth IRA vs. Roth 401(k): Which Roth Is Better?

Summary: Why the Roth IRA Is Better

More Investment Flexibility

Funds converted to an in-plan Roth account are stuck with the same dozen or so investment options available under that plan. On the other hand, if you convert to a Roth IRA, the investment world is your oyster, outside of a few prohibited investments (i.e., life insurance, collectibles, and S-corporation stock). With a Roth IRA, you can fully tap the earnings potential of stocks, bonds, mutual funds, real estate, and more—whichever is most appropriate given your situation!

No Multiple Clocks

When you establish a Roth IRA, a 5-year clock begins to tick. Once the 5 years are up, and as soon as you reach age 59½, all distributions are completely tax- and penalty-free. The same cannot be said for Roth 401(k) accounts. Each plan you are in has its own 5-year clock. If you have multiple company plans with Roth funds in them, you will have to keep track of each clock separately. Further complicating matters, the 5-year clock that applies when you transfer Roth 401(k) funds depends not only on the plans themselves but also on how the funds have been transferred (i.e., by 60-day rollover or direct transfer). As if this weren't complex enough, whenever Roth 401(k) funds are moved to your first Roth IRA, regardless of how long they were held in the plan or how the funds were moved, a new 5-year clock begins. Plus, depending on whether the Roth 401(k) plan distribution is qualified, the earnings in the account (prior to the transfer) will be classified differently (either as basis or earnings) when moved into the new Roth IRA. If, after all that, you're not succumbing to brain freeze of the sort that follows downing an entire Slurpee within minutes, you should consider pursuing a position on the House Ways and Means Committee. For everyone else, perhaps you should consider just converting to a Roth IRA, where all accounts share one clock, as a more practical solution.

Summary:
Why the Roth 401(k), Roth 403(b), and Roth 457(b) Are Better

Federal Creditor Protection

Perhaps the biggest reason for converting at the plan level (inside the plan) is if you are concerned about creditor protection. Creditor protection for IRAs (including Roth IRAs) is based on state law. In some states, like my state of New York, for example, that protection is very strong. In other states, however, there is less creditor safeguarding, and sometimes none at all. On the other hand, employer plans (that cover employees beyond the business owner, and spouse) enjoy very strong creditor protection courtesy of the Employee Retirement Income Security Act of 1974 (ERISA). This federal-level protection shields the assets in your plans from creditors regardless of what state you call home. ERISA also offers greater protection in bankruptcy than most states offer for IRAs. However, sole proprietor plans have no ERISA protection and are covered by state law, just like IRAs.

Plan Loan Option

Another reason you may want to consider converting at the plan level is so that you have the option to take loans from that plan, if the plan allows. Generally, a retirement account is the last place you want to borrow money from—and if you think you may have to, you're probably not a good Roth conversion candidate in the first place. But if this is a serious consideration, the Roth 401(k) account may represent the better option.

Qualified Roth 401(k) Distributions

A qualified distribution is not subject to taxes or penalties. The distribution is qualified if the Roth 401(k) account is held for more than five years *and* any one of the following applies:

1. The employee has reached 59½ years of age.

2. The employee dies.

3. The employee becomes disabled.

A qualified distribution is considered to consist entirely of *basis*. When these funds are transferred to another employer's Roth 401(k) or to an individual Roth IRA, they go into the new account as basis and are available for distribution income-tax-free.

Rollovers

Roth employer accounts can be rolled to individual Roth IRAs, but individual Roth IRAs cannot be rolled to Roth employer plans. Employee deferrals to the Roth 401(k) are after-tax contributions, but they are different from traditional non-Roth after-tax contributions because earnings on Roth 401(k) funds can be distributed tax-free if qualified. Roth 401(k) funds can be rolled to another employer's Roth plan only if the receiving plan allows it. And the amount rolled over depends on whether the transfer was done as a direct rollover (a trustee-to-trustee transfer) or a 60-day rollover.

- Direct rollover (trustee-to-trustee transfer): the entire plan balance can go to an employer Roth plan or to an individual Roth IRA

- Rollover (60-day rollover): only taxable amounts can be rolled over to another Roth employer plan, or the entire plan balance can go to an individual Roth IRA and the rollover must be completed within 60 days

Allowable Rollovers from Roth 401(k)s

Direct Rollover (trustee-to-trustee transfer)	All or any part of the plan balance can go to another Roth 401(k), if the receiving plan allows, or to a Roth IRA.
Rollover to Employee (60-day rollover)	All or any part of the balance can be rolled over to a Roth IRA. Only taxable amounts (earnings) can be rolled over to another Roth 401(k), if the receiving plan allows.

The 5-Year Clock for Qualified Distributions

The 5-year clock determines when you can access your Roth 401(k) funds tax-free. So, you'll want to keep track. Roth 401(k)s have their own 5-year holding rules. Unlike individual Roth IRAs, where there is only one 5-year period that starts with the establishment of the owner's first Roth IRA, Roth 401(k)s have a separate 5-year holding period for each employer's Roth account. If you work for two different companies and participate in the Roth 401(k) plan at each company, you will have two separate 5-year periods, one for each plan.

Rollovers from Roth 401(k)s to Roth IRAs

The 5-year holding period is never carried over to an individual Roth IRA. Instead, the Roth 401(k) funds will be governed by the 5-year rule applicable to the Roth IRA. So, if the Roth IRA has already satisfied the 5-year period, then the employer funds are deemed to also have met the 5-year period, even if they were only in the Roth 401(k) for a year.

If you qualify, open a Roth IRA as soon as you can to start the 5-year clock for withdrawing qualified distributions tax-free. This also will start the 5-year clock for Roth 401(k) funds that are subsequently rolled into your Roth IRA.

If you cannot open a Roth IRA now (because of income limitations), then plan to convert your funds from a traditional IRA to a Roth IRA to start your 5-year clock.

When Does the 5-Year Holding Period Begin If Roth 401(k) Funds Are Transferred to a Roth 401(k), Roth 403(b), or Roth 457(b)?

Qualified Distribution	Direct Rollover (trustee-to-trustee transfer)	The 5-year holding period in the receiving plan will begin with the earlier date of either plan. All funds go into the new plan as basis.
	Rollover to Employee (60-day rollover)	Not allowed; only pre-tax amounts can be rolled over, and the funds distributed in a qualified distribution are all after-tax.
Nonqualified Distribution	Direct Rollover (trustee-to-trustee transfer)	The 5-year holding period in the receiving plan will begin with the earlier date of either plan.
	Rollover to Employee (60-day rollover)	The 5-year holding period will be the period applicable to the receiving plan. Only pre-tax amounts (earnings) can be rolled over.
Nonqualified In-Plan Conversion	The 5-year holding period for penalty-free distributions of each conversion amount follows the converted amount to the receiving plan.	

**When Does the 5-Year Holding Period Begin
If Roth 401(k) Funds Are Transferred to a Roth IRA?**

Qualified Distribution	Direct Rollover (trustee-to-trustee transfer)	The 5-year holding period will be the period applicable to the Roth IRA.
	OR Rollover to Employee (60-day rollover)	All funds go into the Roth IRA as basis and are available for distribution tax-free.
Nonqualified Distribution	Direct Rollover (trustee-to-trustee transfer)	The 5-year holding period will be the period applicable to the Roth IRA.
	OR Rollover to Employee (60-day rollover)	After-tax funds (deferrals) go into the Roth IRA as basis and pre-tax funds (earnings) go into the Roth IRA as earnings.
Nonqualified In-Plan Conversion	The 5-year holding period for penalty-free distributions of each conversion amount follows the converted amount to the receiving Roth IRA.	

Since the Roth 401(k) is an employer plan, nonspouse beneficiaries may not be able to use the 10-year rule under the SECURE Act. The plan might require a 5-year payout instead. But the tax law now requires company plans to allow nonspouse beneficiaries to transfer their inherited plan balances to properly titled inherited IRAs (or convert them to inherited Roth IRAs). However, nonspouse beneficiaries who do not do a direct rollover by December 31 of the year after the death of the plan participant will be limited to the distribution options available in the plan (5 years or a lump-sum distribution are common options for nonspouse plan beneficiaries). In other words, if they don't follow the rules, they could lose out on the 10-year rule.

Perfect Plan Protection Is Near

If you follow the steps outlined in the previous chapters, you will now have created what I consider to be the almost-perfect retirement account.

You will have a solid game plan for that Biggest Check of Your Life.

You will know how to set up and secure your retirement funds (with a beneficiary form), including the post-death options under the SECURE Act, and how to Roth it (if you qualify) to be tax-free.

However, you will also need to know how to protect it (with insurance) and how to pass it on to your beneficiaries in the most cost-efficient way. Next up . . . strategies for doing just that.

STEP #4:
INSURE IT

I've got all the money I'll ever need—if I die by four o'clock.
—HENNY YOUNGMAN (1906-1998), COMEDIAN

Even if you're not a baseball fan, the name Bill Buckner might ring a bell. And if you do follow the game, you'll surely recognize it as one of the most ignominious names in the history of baseball.

Bill Buckner was the first baseman for the Boston Red Sox in the 1986 World Series when the Sox were matched against my favorite team, the New York Mets. It was Game 6, the 10th inning. The Red Sox were one out away from securing their first World Series win in 68 years. The pitcher hurled the ball. The Mets batter swung and connected. With a thunderous *c-r-a-c-c-k-k-k*, the ball shot straight to first base and the outstretched arms of Bill Buckner, who somehow managed to flub the play before the stunned but elated crowd in New York's Shea Stadium. The ball rolled between his legs!

Thanks to this colossal error, the Mets were able to pull their collective fanny from the fire, win the game that night, and go on to win Game 7 and the World Series title. Faced with death threats, Bill Buckner moved his family to Idaho, which apparently still wasn't far enough for Boston fans, who continued to scorn him. To Boston fans in particular, and baseball fans in general, Bill Buckner had become but one thing: the Man Who Dropped the Ball.

Now, what if I told you that Bill Buckner was also one of the best baseball players . . . *ever*? Would you be shocked? Disbelieving? I know I was when I heard that exact statement made in a Fox Sports

Network show about Buckner called *Beyond the Glory*. Being an accountant, I couldn't resist doing my own audit of Buckner's statistics to see if the superlative was true.

A quick Google search confirmed that the show was right. Buckner's numbers were astounding!

He had played 22 seasons. Only 25 players in the history of baseball have played more games than he did. He had more hits than 70 percent of the players currently in the Baseball Hall of Fame, including such superstars as Mickey Mantle, Ernie Banks, Reggie Jackson, Johnny Bench, and even Ted Williams (pre-thawed). He had 500 more hits than Joe DiMaggio!

When Buckner played for the Chicago Cubs, he won a National League batting title. In fact, if you visit the Cubs' home, Wrigley Field, his star is emblazoned on the concrete Walk of Fame outside the stadium. Throughout his career, Buckner also was an exceptional fielder. He genuinely was one of the greatest players the game of baseball has ever had. And yet that one slipup that cost the Red Sox the World Series had kept him locked in the Baseball Hall of Shame.

Years later, Buckner was at last forgiven. On April 8, 2008, he threw out the first pitch at the Red Sox home opening day as fans celebrated their 2007 World Series championship. The sold-out crowd gave him a two-minute standing ovation. Eight years later, the team marked the 30th anniversary of that dropped ball back in 1986 by honoring him with another extended ovation. Forgiveness is a beautiful thing, isn't it?

As I pondered Buckner's pockmarked career, I said to myself, "It's a lot like what happens to a mismanaged IRA. A long, brilliant career, accumulating so much, can be blown so easily as the result of a single error."

Now think: is that how you want your family to remember you? As the one who dropped the ball?

EIGHT

THE POWER OF LIFE INSURANCE

Larger Inheritances, More Control, Less Tax

Most people don't think about it much, but the combination of estate and income taxes can easily eat away at an IRA of any size. In addition, Congress is constantly hovering over your IRA with a knife and fork, ready to dig in, as evidenced by every new tax law—like the SECURE Act, which ended the stretch IRA to more quickly extract tax money from your heirs. Given today's historically low tax rates, you need to focus on what future tax rates will be and how much of your IRA they will consume. While we don't know for sure what the future will bring, we can apply a little common sense and make a pretty good guess. Given the sad state of our national economy (we're broke!), tax rates will likely climb higher. Right now, the estate-tax exemption of $10 million ($20 million per couple—plus even more after you tack on the IRS's annual tax inflation adjustments) would pretty much exempt most of us from federal estate taxes, but again, this is only the current exemption level. Remember what Mark Twain said: "History doesn't repeat itself, but it rhymes." So now is the time to take advantage of this incredible low-tax environment and protect your nest egg against a likely future of confiscatory levies.

When it comes to retirement accounts, it's not enough to earn great investment returns. Yes, that's important for building the account, but even if you earn 30 percent a year, every year, for 30 years, what good is it if, at the end of the line, 50 percent or more of the account's value is lost when your savings pass to your heirs? That's exactly what can happen without sufficient funds to pay what could soon be the combined estate and income taxes on an inherited IRA. Remember the Bill Buckner story? It's the score at the end of the game that counts, and that score is what you keep after taxes!

Who Is Most at Risk?

The people most in danger of losing their savings due to the combination of taxes I've described are those who don't have much in the way of assets beyond their retirement accounts, along with those who have million-dollar IRAs.

If a beneficiary must tap an IRA to pay taxes when the IRA owner dies, the resulting cycle of taxation won't stop until the beneficiaries are so punch drunk that they won't know what's hit them, let alone what's happened to the IRA they inherited.

Why do IRA owners let their life savings fall into such an abyss? The reason can be summed up in a single word: *admiration.*

Rather than doing whatever it takes to keep their accounts from being sacked and pillaged by Congress and the IRS after they've joined the ranks of the dearly departed, they just sit there admiring how big the balance is.

For example, I have a client with a $16 million IRA (no, he's not a crooked inside trader or an absconding CEO; hard to believe, but he made it the old-fashioned way: honestly). When he proudly shows me his account statements, mesmerized by the mushrooming size of the single most valuable asset he owns, I have to snap him out of the trance with a harsh dose of reality. "This isn't your money in these statements," I tell him. "You're not going to keep any of this. This money is only temporarily attached to your letterhead. If you just sit there looking at it without taking any measures to protect it, it'll be lost after you die. Do something now while you are still alive and have options to protect that money for your heirs."

Many people with retirement accounts, especially large ones, believe the money in these accounts is sacred and should never be touched until you're absolutely forced to at age 73.

That's wrong. You can, and should, touch it. Real wealth is built by leveraging what you have to prevent an ultimate loss.

Congress has changed the rules. Now you must change your plan!

"In times of rapid change, standing still is the most dangerous course of action."

—Brian Tracy, renowned self-improvement author and speaker

The SECURE Act: Congress's Trojan Horse

After more than 30 years of consulting with people just like you, I have found that when I ask the "Why are you here?" question, I always get the same response: I want more control and less tax, plus I want to leave larger inheritances to my heirs. Congress wants the opposite. They want Uncle Sam to be your number one beneficiary. (And he's not even your real uncle!) In their never-ending search for revenue, they just can't quit salivating over your retirement savings. Congress used to try to hide that fact, but no more. They tipped their hand when they brought us the Trojan Horse called the SECURE Act in late 2019.

The SECURE Act really had less to do with keeping your retirement savings secure and more to do with securing government coffers at your family's expense. We saw what Congress was really after when they included the elimination of the stretch IRA so the retirement funds you leave to your heirs will be taxed sooner and maybe at higher tax rates to boot.

But here's the good news: Remember what I said before. It's the score at the end of the game that counts, and the game is far from over. You're on the home team and get the last at bat. Yes, Congress has changed the rules, so now you must adjust your strategy. The plan you had before may not work anymore, but options still exist that can deliver the result you want: larger inheritances, more control, and less tax. The vehicle that gets you there may have to change, but that's OK.

Upgrade to a New Model!

It's easy to get stuck in our old ways of doing things. But digging in your heels could cost you—big time. Instead, keep your eyes on the prize. As you consider your options, remember these three key estate-planning objectives:

- Larger inheritances

- More post-death control

- Less tax

Now let's help you do what it takes to get there.

Here's the deal: You are not married to your IRA. You want your plan, not the government plan, and it doesn't matter what vehicle gets you to your desired destination, especially if that vehicle can enhance your plan with less tax complexity and worry about changing tax rules. Think about it this way: You're turning in your old beat-up IRA jalopy for a spiffy new limo to take you the rest of the way. You worked hard for this money, and you deserve that new limo. But don't wait too long. Hop in before you wind up taking your very last ride—get it?

Traditional IRAs and other retirement plans are no longer a good option for leaving funds to your beneficiaries. To keep your estate plan intact, you'll probably have to replace your IRA. We've already talked about using Roth IRAs as a tax-free alternative, but now it's time to look at what may be an even better idea: *The Life Insurance Replacement Plan*, which means replacing your IRA (a poor estate-planning asset) with life insurance (an excellent estate-planning asset that is now even more valuable after the SECURE Act). Before we continue, you should know that I do not sell life insurance. I also do not sell stocks, bonds, funds, or annuities—never did. I am a CPA and tax-planning advisor, and as a tax advisor I can tell you that the single biggest benefit in the tax code is the income tax exemption for life insurance. You should know about how to use it to reach your goals, especially now that Congress has declared war on your retirement savings.

Life Insurance: Your Retirement Account's Best Defense

The single best, most cost-effective yet amazingly underutilized strategy for protecting retirement account balances, especially large ones, from being decimated by the highest levels of combined taxation is to buy life insurance to offset the tax burden that beneficiaries may face. In other words, leverage your retirement savings, rather than letting the funds sit there waiting to be decimated by future taxes. Bottom line: You want more! More money for you to enjoy now, more for your retirement, and more for your loved ones once you're gone. More, more, more, and less in taxes. That's the plan—and it is absolutely attainable.

As a tax advisor, I'm always helping families after the loss of a loved one to sort out their post-death-tax filing, so they can move ahead with their lives. And all too frequently I run into situations where families are financially devastated by taxes because of what was left undone. This should never happen—because it can almost always be avoided. That's why life insurance exists. And yet so many people ignore it, put it off, see it as an unnecessary expense, until suddenly they're gone, leaving their family members helpless to do anything more than watch the taxman snatch away a huge chunk of their inheritance.

Life insurance offers the best defense against confiscatory taxation for your family since it won't be subject to *any* post-death SECURE Act limitations. The guarantees of long-term stability and tax-free payouts that life insurance offers grant both certainty and simplicity.

This strategy became even more valuable after the 2018 tax law changes that lowered the tax rates for many through the Tax Cuts and Jobs Act. But many of those provisions are temporary. They expire after 2025, so you should take advantage of these low rates now.

Life insurance is tax efficient. Life insurance proceeds will be income-tax-free to your beneficiaries. They can also be estate-tax-free if paid to an irrevocable life insurance trust (ILIT).

Life insurance is also more flexible when trusts are needed for post-death control. A better, more flexible, and more customizable asset to leave to a trust, it can simulate many aspects of the stretch IRA without the tax complications of an IRA trust. You can set the schedule and the terms of the trust by which you would like your beneficiaries to have access to the life insurance funds. And, unlike with an IRA trust, there is no worry about who the trust beneficiaries or contingent beneficiaries are, or their ages. In this way, a life insurance trust can be focused on *your* wishes, and you will not have to deal with the array of tax rules that you would have to work around with an IRA trust. It's simpler and more effective, with less tax intrusion. You get to focus on the plan you desire without worrying about stumbling around in the quagmire of IRA trust tax rules.

Life insurance is reliable, offering you more certainty in a fast-changing world. Congress has historically changed tax laws more often than it has changed the treatment of insurance benefits.

Life insurance provides leveraged wealth transfer. In most cases, more funds will go to the eventual beneficiaries, and with fewer taxes, than if the IRA was left directly to the beneficiaries or to an IRA trust subject to taxation. While IRA funds are vulnerable to potentially higher future tax rates, tax-free vehicles like Roth IRAs and life insurance generally avoid that risk.

In case you were wondering, I practice what I preach by carrying a substantial amount of life insurance to provide for my family in that critical area. And you should too! Consider permanent, cash-value life insurance as the new vehicle that will help you reach your estate-planning promised land: larger inheritances, more post-death control, and less tax. That's what I recommend across the board.

How Can I Get In on This?

Here's what you need to do. Begin by working with your financial and tax advisors to draw down IRA funds. Sure, these distributions are taxable, but keep in mind that you're paying taxes now as part of executing a more tax-efficient long-term estate plan. These funds will be used to build tax-free assets inside a permanent, cash-value life insurance policy (as opposed to term insurance, which expires at the end of the term and builds no cash value). To ensure the lowest possible tax cost, take smaller distributions over the course of several years. Spreading out distributions will allow you to take advantage of lower tax brackets.

Then use the retirement funds you've withdrawn (that were earmarked for beneficiaries) to purchase a permanent life insurance policy. If a trust is needed for post-death control, the life insurance can be owned by a trust—an irrevocable life insurance trust (ILIT).

But Wait. If I Take Distributions, Won't I Be Subject to Penalties?

So, you *have* been paying attention. Good for you! Yes, you are correct—if you've not yet reached age 59½. Before that point, funds you withdraw are subject to a 10 percent early distribution penalty. If you haven't yet reached age 59½, the Life Insurance Replacement Plan strategy is not for you. (Isn't it nice to be considered too *young*, for once?) Either investigate a Roth conversion, which may be a better option, or wait until age 59½, when there is no penalty.

The Sweet Spot for Planning: Ages 59½ to 73

If you're between ages 59½ and 73, you are in what I call the "planning sweet spot." Take advantage of this window while IRA distributions are penalty-free but RMDs are not yet required. This period, when you have maximum flexibility with your IRA, is the optimal time for taking IRA withdrawals to fund your Life Insurance Replacement Plan.

To be absolutely clear, in case you read the preceding paragraphs with blinding enthusiasm, you cannot actually buy life insurance with IRA money. Tax law prohibits this. When I say, "Use the IRA to buy life insurance," I mean you must withdraw first and pay the income tax due on the withdrawal. Then you are free to use the after-tax amount to pay the insurance premiums. Don't just sit there admiring your balance, afraid to touch it, like the fellow in this true-life horror story from my file drawer marked "penny-wise and pound-foolish."

Rob and his wife, Sue, came to me some years ago for help with estate planning. Rob's estate consisted largely of an IRA (about $6 million) plus some other assets. My advice was straightforward: Buy life insurance to protect the IRA from estate tax. I recommended $3 million worth (approximately half the value of the IRA).

"Absolutely, positively, categorically NO," Rob said, putting his foot down literally and figuratively.

"Why not?" I asked.

"First, because I hate insurance companies. They're thieves," he answered. "And second, because it isn't necessary. I'm leaving the entire IRA to my wife, and you told me spouse beneficiaries are exempt from estate tax."

"True enough," I replied. "But what if Sue dies first?"

He had no answer to that except that statistics were on his side, and he remained adamant about "not spending a dime extra that can be saved."

Sue, on the other hand, could see what I was driving at; she realized that the insurance was necessary to protect what they had earned for their four children. So, she decided she would buy her own policy, about $2 million worth, even though she knew the premiums would be high because she was not in the best of health at the time. But she had the money and went ahead on my recommendation, correctly setting up the policy outside her estate so that none of the insurance money would be subject to estate taxes. It could be used instead by her children to offset the estate tax bill on the $6 million IRA and other assets she inherited from Rob (assuming he did die first) that would be due when she passed away.

As fate would have it, Sue passed away first, and her four children inherited the $2 million worth of life insurance she'd bought, each receiving a $500,000 check, estate- and income-tax-free.

No longer hating insurance companies, Rob opted to heed the advice I'd given him when he and his wife had first come to me, five years earlier. He tried to get that $3 million life insurance policy I'd recommended.

Unfortunately, it was too late.

Had he applied five years earlier, he'd have had no problem, but in the meantime, Rob had become quite ill, and no insurance company would cover him at any price.

All I could do was advise his four kids to hold on tight to the $2 million they'd received from their mother's death, because when Rob dies and his IRA passes to them, they will need every cent of it—and more!—to pay for his mistake.

Poor Rob. He thought he was saving money.

How Much Life Insurance Should You Have?

At a minimum, you should have enough to cover the taxes and other expenses that must be paid on your estate after you're gone. To do that you will need to know the balance in your account at the time of your death, which means you will have to project that balance. You cannot go by today's market or values—because if you have an IRA that's worth, say, $1 million right now and you are only 60 years old, that IRA could easily be worth $5 million or more over the long term given today's long life expectancies.

A good rule of thumb is to buy enough life insurance to cover at least 50 percent of the projected value of your estate at your death. This may seem like a lot of insurance to buy now, but remember what happened to Rob. As you and your account grow older and fatter, not only will purchasing more life insurance become an increasingly expensive proposition, but if your health deteriorates, you may become uninsurable.

A quick way to estimate the value of your IRA (without taking into account withdrawals or taxes) is to use the "rule of 72." This is a little math trick that shows how many times over the years your retirement account money will double at a given interest rate. Don't panic. You don't have to have Nobel laureate John Nash's *Beautiful Mind* to manage the calculations. Just divide 72 by an estimated average interest rate. For example, if you use a conservative interest rate of, say, 6 percent, that means your money will double every 12 years (72/6 = 12). An 8 percent rate would double your money every 9 years (72/8 = 9), and so on.

Let's use the rule of 72 with some dollar figures, and say your IRA isn't a million but $300,000, and you're not 60 years old but 50 (with a life expectancy of 86).

Using an average 8 percent interest rate for the rest of your life (that may not seem like a very conservative average to you, but over the long haul it is), the value (straight growth excluding withdrawals or taxes) of your $300,000 IRA will double every nine years (72/8 = 9), so that by the time you reach 86, your $300,000 IRA will have doubled four times and be worth $4.8 million! The first time it doubles, it will go to $600,000, then, after another nine years, to $1.2 million, then to $2.4 million, and finally to $4.8 million. If you start with a $500,000 IRA at age 50 and use the same 8 percent interest rate, your IRA would grow to $8 million by the time you reach 86. And a $1 million IRA would grow to a staggering $16 million! Now that is what Warren Buffett means by growing a big snowball. But don't forget that if no planning is done, the tax bill on that IRA expands as well, melting the heck out of that snowball. The math works both ways.

Compound interest can have an absolutely astounding impact, especially in a tax-deferred account such as an IRA. This is why I am so insistent that even people with modest retirement accounts need life insurance. Through the magic of compounding, even the smallest accounts can wind up exceeding the estate-tax exemption (currently at $10 million, plus inflation additions) come inheritance time.

TIP!

I have a credo: "Don't shop for bargains in parachutes, toilet paper, or life insurance. They're too important for cutting costs." Forget about the latest cut-rate deals at "Policies-to-Go.com." Find yourself a living, breathing, professional insurance agent to advise and guide you and your family. They should represent a brick-and-mortar insurance company with a solid reputation. (Think about it: Who will your family call when they have to collect on a dot-com policy—especially if the dot-com is dot-gone by then?) Ask friends or business associates to refer an agent they trust and respect. That's the best way to find someone. But if that doesn't pan out, look for an agent who is a member of the Million Dollar Round Table (MDRT), a top-of-the-line insurance industry group made up of the finest insurance professionals in the world. Check out the group's website at www.mdrt.org.

In addition, you can go to our website, www.irahelp.com, and find an advisor who is a member of **Ed Slott's Elite IRA Advisor Group**ᔆᴹ. We train these individuals on estate and tax planning for IRAs and other retirement accounts, and many are also insurance professionals who can apply their specialized IRA-planning knowledge to your situation, helping to integrate life insurance into your tax planning.

What Kind of Life Insurance Should You Buy?

OK, this is where I draw the line. Before I start sounding like a shill for the insurance industry, let me explain that you must rely on your own professional insurance advisor for guidance here.

Whatever kind you buy, though, I can tell you this: The policy should be set up so that it pays off when funds are needed after death.

"But don't all insurance policies pay off at death?" you ask.

No, they don't, because some people buy survivorship life insurance (also known as second-to-die insurance), which insures both spouses at the same time but only pays off once both spouses are deceased.

A second-to-die policy is usually much less expensive than a single-life policy, but it may cause problems if you need cash after the first death. Here's why:

When one spouse dies and leaves everything to the other spouse, there is generally no estate tax regardless of how much the spouse inherits. But even if there is no estate tax due, when the first spouse dies, the second spouse will still need cash to continue the premiums on the second-to-die policy, which does not pay off until he or she dies. If there is no other cash available, the surviving spouse may not be able to maintain the policy. So, if you buy a second-to-die policy, it might be best to couple it with a single-life policy on each spouse for a smaller amount. That way, there is at least enough cash available at the first death to continue the premiums on the larger second-to-die policy.

Second-to-die policies can also be a good option if one spouse is uninsurable. Since qualifying for coverage is based on two lives, a couple might be eligible for a policy even if one individual doesn't qualify for coverage on their own.

Keeping Life Insurance Estate-Tax-Free

Life insurance money is already income-tax-free, but if you're not careful, it could be subject to estate tax. You should set up the policy, as Sue did, so that it is not included as an asset of your estate. If it is included, its value can be effectively reduced by a third. Here's how:

If you own the policy yourself and it is worth, say, $1 million, then when you die, that $1 million will be included in your estate, entitling Uncle Sam to roughly 40 percent of it (if your estate becomes subject to federal estate taxes), with the remaining $600,000 going to your actual beneficiaries (e.g., your family). Not only is that highway robbery, it's inefficient. Nevertheless, that is how most people set up life insurance—but only because they do not know any better.

The better strategy is *not to own your own life insurance.* Think about it. Why would you want to own your own life insurance, seeing as how it pays off only after you die? What are you going to do with it then? Why own a policy you can't benefit from? Just to control where it goes? That can be done without owning it!

OK, if you shouldn't own it, who should?

Your beneficiaries!

Have them own the policy (which you will set up for them) and pay the premiums from money you give to them. If your beneficiaries are young, or if you want some post-death control on how the money is spent, you can set up an irrevocable life insurance trust

(ILIT). That's what I have for my family. The trust owns the policy and my trustee pays the premiums from money I deposit into the trust.

Whether you choose beneficiary direct ownership or an ILIT, the main point is that you do not own the insurance when it pays off; therefore, the proceeds will be excluded from your estate.

What If There Is No Estate Tax?

Never assume anything. And remember—you cannot trust Congress not to find a way to change the estate-tax exemptions and make your estate taxable in the future. Never forget how hungry Congress is for your money.

Even the current large estate exemptions are set to revert to half those amounts after 2025, and who knows what a future Congress, desperate for revenue, might do. Your estate is always at risk. Remember that and plan for it.

Even if estate tax is completely eliminated, your beneficiaries may have to deal with income taxes on the buildup of appreciated assets in your retirement accounts. Unlike many other assets, IRAs and 401(k)s do not receive a step-up in basis, where capital gains on the lifetime appreciation are eliminated after death. In other words, anyone who inherits your IRA will still have to pay income tax on the gains in the IRA that they inherit from you. Under the SECURE Act, that income tax will likely have to be paid within 10 years of your death, and possibly when your beneficiaries may be in their own peak earnings years, increasing their tax bill. Life insurance can be used to pay that tax.

If you have no retirement account, the life insurance can also serve as a pension alternative, providing your beneficiaries with a tax-free stream of cash for the rest of their lives. And if you are young and have not yet built up a substantial retirement account, life insurance can provide instant cash for your family. That can be essential if you have small children—because even a small life insurance policy can be a big help when the worst happens.

As I mentioned earlier, there are generally two ways in which people remove life insurance from their estate: They either create a special type of life insurance trust or they have the beneficiaries of the policy own the policy directly. In either case, though, the *owner* of the policy must be the one paying the premiums. Even if the policy says otherwise, if it's your policy and you pay the premiums, the IRS can treat the policy as if *you* were the owner and therefore as a part of your estate. (BAD!!!) That now begs the question: Where does a brand-new trust get the money to pay for a life insurance policy? Or what about your kids, who are busy trying to support their own children: How are they going to get the money to pay for what is, for all intents and purposes, your policy? That's easy. *From you*. That's right, you simply give them the money. "But Ed," you say, "if I give them the money and then they use it to pay the premiums, aren't I really paying for the policy?" Yes and no. And that's the point. You're paying for the policy in the sense that the money is yours, but once you make a gift to someone, the money is theirs to do with what they want. And if they *happen* to use it to pay the premiums on a life insurance policy, that's their business and not the IRS's.

A WORD TO THE WISE

If you are going to give money to children with the intention that they will use the money to pay for the premiums on an insurance policy that insures you, make sure they are responsible enough to do so. Once you gift them the money, it's theirs, and there is nothing you can do to force them to use it to pay for the life insurance premiums. Of course, hopefully your kids will realize that this is for their benefit in the end. But if you have any doubts, you may favor funding a life insurance trust instead of giving the money directly to your children.

There is, of course, a limit to how *much* of your money you can give away without triggering tax. Today, however, this is no longer an issue for virtually everyone reading this book. Here's why. For 2024, the annual-gift exclusion is $18,000. This means that you can give $18,000 to every person you wish without incurring any gift tax or using up any of your gift/estate-tax exclusion (more on this later in "Step #5: Avoid the Death-Tax Trap"). If you're married, you can double that figure to $36,000. This, on its own, can allow you to shift large chunks of assets outside your estate that can be used to create vast sums of completely tax-free wealth for your beneficiaries.

For example, let's say that you and your spouse create a life insurance trust to serve as the owner and the beneficiary of a new policy you wish to purchase (which is often the best approach when dealing with a large policy). And let's say that the trust beneficiaries are your two children and four grandchildren. That's a total of six people. And since you are married, you can gift each of them (either directly or through a trust) $36,000—for a grand total of $216,000 per year. Now I may not be a life insurance professional, but I'm pretty sure that $216,000 usually buys a pretty big death benefit. But what if you don't want to be bothered making gifts each year? Or what if you aren't married and have only one beneficiary—and therefore can only make $18,000 in annual gifts? Not to worry—at least not today. The gift-tax exemption is set at $10 million (plus annual inflation additions). That means, in addition to the $18,000 per year you can give away per person, you can also gift another $10 million plus to any combination of persons (or a trust) without having to pay a single dime of gift tax. With the gift exclusions as high as ever and the tax rates as low as they will probably ever be during your lifetime or mine, there has probably never been, nor will there probably ever be, a better time to turn your income- and estate-tax-vulnerable IRAs into tax-free wealth that can last generations. (For more about using the gift-tax exclusion to gift other assets, see Chapter 9.)

Leverage It or Lose It

It is important to look at life insurance not as an expense that must be suffered to achieve a desired end but as a solution to a problem. You can set up a policy in any number of creative ways to provide the funds needed to protect your retirement account from the tax-man, leaving it free to grow tax-deferred for years.

Consider this scenario that shows how life insurance can provide leverage and tax-free cash for a surviving spouse.

Ralph and Sadie, a married couple, have few other assets besides their home, which is worth $500,000. Ralph has a $1 million IRA. They have a 40-year-old daughter, Ruby.

I suggest to Ralph that he leave the $1 million IRA not to his wife, Sadie, but to their daughter, Ruby, instead. This way, when Ralph dies, Ruby will receive the $1 million IRA estate-tax-free because it passes under the estate-tax exemption (currently at $10 million, plus inflation adjustments, but remember, that ceiling could always change).

"Hey, wait a minute, Ed," Sadie says, looking steamed. "I see our daughter getting rich on this suggestion, which is OK by me, but what the heck am I supposed to live on?"

Yes, that is a problem, I tell her. "How much do you need?"

"Well, I need the $1 million IRA, don't I?" she replies.

I make another suggestion. "How would you like $1 million tax-free instead? There would be no age-73 distribution rules; anytime you need money, you just withdraw it, tax-free. That's better than a tax-infested IRA, isn't it?"

"Of course! But where do I find that pot of gold at the end of the rainbow?" she asks.

"Life insurance," I answer.

I advise Ralph to buy a $1 million life insurance policy and name Sadie as beneficiary. He can set it up as a plain vanilla policy and even own it himself with no need for a trust. There will be no estate tax upon his death since his assets will pass to his spouse, Sadie. Ralph will pay the premiums using funds withdrawn from his IRA.

After Ralph's death, their daughter, Ruby, will receive what's left in the IRA free of estate tax (up to the estate-tax exemption that exists at the time of her father's death, of course) as before. This way, the family as a whole receives more tax-free life insurance and less in taxable IRA funds that will be more vulnerable to higher taxes.

Meanwhile, Sadie receives Ralph's $1 million tax-free life insurance policy to spend as she wishes—a much better alternative than inheriting and paying income tax on the IRA. So, together Sadie and Ruby wind up with more than the family started with, and their cash needs are solved for life, estate-tax-free.

But it gets better.

After Ralph's death, I suggest that Sadie use some of that tax-free life insurance money to buy a $1 million policy of her own, naming her daughter, Ruby, as beneficiary. During Sadie's lifetime she will have unrestricted use of the tax-free life insurance money she inherited from her husband. After Sadie's death, Ruby will receive her mother's life insurance policy, inheriting potentially another $1 million of tax-free money.

When all is said and done, this family will have both protected and leveraged a single IRA into a tax-free family fortune. How? With plain old life insurance, that's all!

Life Insurance Has Lifetime Benefits

Question: Can you be the beneficiary of your own life insurance . . . *without dying?*
Answer: YES!

Most people value life insurance for the tax-free death benefit. But life insurance can provide benefits while you're still living too. If you have a permanent life insurance policy with a cash value, like a whole life policy for example, then you can become the "beneficiary" of your own life insurance policy. Did you know that, with some plans, the cash buildup in these policies can be accessed tax-free during your lifetime, should you need the funds? Pretty neat, huh? And you can even make a withdrawal without increasing your taxable income—a fact that removes the risk of what future higher income-tax rates could do to your savings in retirement. Plus, some newer policies now available can include chronic care or long-term care riders that can pay for health services needed during life. These life insurance funds can offer a helpful alternative to taking withdrawals from taxable IRAs.

Warning: Not all policies have these features, and there may be limitations on employing these strategies, such as with policies owned by an insurance trust, for example. Before you embark on this type of planning, contact a qualified life insurance professional to guide you through the morass of rules and regs. That's what I did for myself, precisely because I am not a qualified life insurance professional. I'm just opening the door here to let you know how valuable life insurance can be as part of an overall plan to protect your savings from confiscatory taxes and other risks that can erode what you have.

Life insurance has many other uses beyond the scope of this book, so I'll leave it at this: Tax-free cash is always the best source of money, and it solves a lot of problems, tax and nontax alike.

The "Rollback" Strategy

Remember at the beginning of this chapter where I wrote that you can't use IRA money to buy life insurance directly—how you must first withdraw the funds, pay the income tax on the withdrawal, and then use what's left to pay the insurance premiums? Well, nothing's changed since you read that part. It's still true. But wouldn't it be great if you could use the IRA money to buy the life insurance without having to withdraw it first and pay the income tax? Imagine how much more money you'd have available to buy life insurance if you didn't first have to pay that pesky income tax on the withdrawal.

Well, check this out.

One crazy tax law provision allows some people who have a company retirement plan to do just that! Technically speaking, you cannot use money within your IRA to buy life insurance, but as you'll recall from Chapter 3, taxable IRA funds can be rolled over to a company plan—and company plans *can* purchase life insurance!

Are you thinking what I'm thinking?

If your company plan—your 401(k) plan, for example—allows you to purchase life insurance and you have lots of cash in your IRA, then you can roll the pre-tax IRA funds over to your 401(k) plan and use that money to buy the life insurance without paying the income tax. No, you're not hallucinating. This is a legitimate strategy, called a *rollback*. Not every company plan will allow it (most big company plans won't), but if you have your own company, or are a partner in a law firm, medical practice, accounting firm, or other business where you can customize your own plan, the rollback strategy is doable.

In effect, what you're doing is using your IRA money to buy life insurance, but it's not prohibited in this case because the insurance is actually being purchased with company plan funds rolled over from your IRA.

You cannot play games with this strategy, though. There are, of course, rules to follow. For example, you cannot create a dummy company just to have a vehicle for rolling the IRA funds as a means of buying insurance. That's a sham and against the law.

Life Insurance Drawbacks

Life is not perfect. Everything has a cost or downside, and you need to know both the pros and the cons before you make any financial decision. Life insurance is a long-term commitment, so doing a thorough evaluation and analysis is critical. Your family may be relying on this plan for decades. You should review all the information that goes into this decision with your professional financial, tax, legal, and insurance advisors before taking any action.

Using this Life Insurance Replacement Plan as an alternative to the stretch IRA (which was largely eliminated by the SECURE Act) may not be for everyone. Here are some things to remember:

▪ This strategy assumes that your IRA funds will not be needed during your lifetime, which is often the case for the larger IRAs. Other (non-IRA) funds will need to be available for lifetime use.

▪ Not everyone is insurable. You must medically qualify for insurance coverage. No plan fits everyone, so this particular planning should be evaluated based on your personal financial situation and should be implemented only with professional guidance.

▪ Using IRA money to fund an insurance policy will incur income tax expenses now. Planning for better long-term tax benefits often requires a current investment. Keep in mind today's low tax rates could increase soon. If you don't act now, your IRA funds will be forced out later through RMDs and may be more heavily taxed at that time if rates do rise. Using IRA funds now will reduce your IRA balance and, in turn, reduce your future income taxes by eliminating required minimum distributions on IRA funds.

▪ Life insurance is a long-term planning vehicle. You must pay policy premiums consistently to keep the policy in force.

▪ Although it can take several years to build up substantial policy cash value (that's the savings account that's part of your life insurance policy), the death benefit is there from day one. Lifetime policy withdrawals reduce the death benefit and available cash surrender value. Policy loans will also accrue interest at the current rate as well as reduce the death benefit and available cash surrender value.

So, there you have the "Insure It" step. Isn't it amazing to see how powerfully a simple, yet creative life insurance plan can build tax-free wealth? Can you imagine choosing tax confiscation of your retirement account when this alternative exists? And yet, despite professional advice, many hundreds of thousands continue to do just that.

But you're not going to be one of them, are you?

You've seen the light!

You want more . . . and now you have the plan to get it:

- *Larger* inheritances

- *More* post-death control

- *Less* tax

The bottom line is this: Life insurance solves family money problems, without any of the tax restrictions that apply to IRA funds.

"Life insurance takes care of families, without going through the government first."

—Ed Slott

STEP #5:
AVOID THE DEATH-TAX TRAP

I can't die. I'm booked.

       —GEORGE BURNS (1896–1996), COMEDIAN AND "DEITY"

It's Not a Trap Anymore

It used to be that the surest way to avoid the death-tax trap was to live forever. Fortunately, immortality is no longer required for most people now that legislators have defanged the death-tax trap—at least for a time. With the SECURE Act, however, Congress has also managed to create a new version of the death-tax trap by eliminating the stretch IRA for your beneficiaries. This will impact most IRAs left to beneficiaries, and especially those IRAs left to trusts. Given these changes, you'll need to create new strategies for ensuring that your beneficiaries receive the payouts you want for them. Accomplishing this just might require an estate plan overhaul in the form of more effective alternatives, like the Roth IRA or the Life Insurance Replacement Plan, covered in previous chapters.

Taxes are a big deal. The more funds you fork over in taxes, the less money will stay in your family. However, estate planning is about more than just trying to avoid estate taxes. It's about taking the right steps during your lifetime to make sure that your wishes regarding the disposition of your assets are carried out after you're gone. For example, who are your intended beneficiaries? How much do you want to leave them? Which of your assets do you want to go to whom? For your wishes to be followed, all these questions—and many more—will be answered by an effective estate plan.

There are a host of reasons why people sidestep the issue of estate planning. It's too complicated, for instance. (This is a myth; it's easy, especially now.) Or, it's too expensive, because you have to hire a lawyer, CPA, insurance agent, or other financial services professional. Or, maybe you think your estate isn't large enough to warrant estate planning. (Think again.) Or—and this is usually the biggest reason of all—it's just too disturbing for most of us to contemplate the prospect of our own demise.

"If I start thinking about estate planning, I'll jinx myself, and I may die," people say. Well, guess what? There's no "may" about it. You *will* die. Someday. And it'll happen regardless of whether you jinx yourself or not. I've done some informal research on the subject, and three out of three people will eventually die whether or not they do any estate planning first. The only difference is that those who die with an estate plan pass on more of their hard-earned wealth to their families and disinherit Uncle Sam a lot more successfully than people who die without one.

This book is not about talk, but action. And that's particularly true of this step. Ask most estate-planning attorneys, and they will tell you that many of their clients *talk* a lot about estate planning but never really *do* anything about it. Insurance agents who know that their clients need life insurance tell me that same thing. Their clients say, "I'll think about it." What's to think about? That's just an excuse to do nothing. You must make a decision and implement it. This is even more critical now that Congress has made some big changes to the tax rules that could have a significant negative impact how your retirement funds will be taxed after you're gone. We'll revisit the SECURE Act again here in this chapter as it applies to any estate or trust plan you may have.

Most decisions can be changed, so don't wait to make the perfect choice. That will never happen. As General Ulysses S. Grant said when asked if he was sure of a decision he had just made, "No, I am not, but . . . anything is better than indecision. We must decide. If I am wrong, we shall soon find it out and can do the other thing. But not to decide wastes time and money and may ruin everything."

By now it should be clear that I have little patience with people who are "all talk, no action." I could fill another three books with stories about them—people who gave most of their money to the IRS, not because taxes were so high but because they did nothing to avoid paying more than their fair share of those taxes.

Many of the steps in this book involve spending relatively small amounts of money now to secure a windfall later. Don't be one of those people who wind up leaving your money to the IRS due to being penny-wise and pound-foolish. Remember, whatever you don't pay now, your heirs will pay later.

Welcome to Step #5: Avoid the Death-Tax Trap. This had to be our last step, of course. After all, it's the end of your story, and all worthwhile planning begins with the end in mind. I've broken down this step for you in the following two chapters:

Chapter 9: Estate Planning for Your Retirement Savings
Chapter 10: The New Realities of Naming Trusts as IRA
    Beneficiaries

The first, Estate Planning for Your Retirement Savings, has all the basics on how to create the perfect estate plan for your IRA and other retirement plans that will hold up over time. This plan will pay off over decades, maybe even generations.

The second chapter in this step, The New Realities of Naming Trusts as IRA Beneficiaries, is for those of you who may need some level of control to help protect your funds for your heirs. Perhaps you have a large IRA. Maybe your beneficiaries are too young to inherit, or you're worried about them squandering your hard-earned savings. Maybe they have financial problems, lawsuits, or creditors after them. Or perhaps they're simply unable to handle money and need professional management. As you saw in Chapter 6, the SECURE Act and the related IRS regulations have jeopardized this type of planning with the elimination of the stretch IRA. This elimination also applies to trusts that inherit an IRA.

If you are looking to use trusts for post-death protection and control, this chapter will be invaluable to you and your family. I'll go over all the new obstacles, tax traps, and potential minefields. I'll also explain the better planning approaches you'll need to take to make IRA trusts work. And I'll cover alternatives, in case you decide that the latest IRA trust-planning restrictions are too prohibitive. These next two chapters will show you how to create a rock-solid plan that maximizes inheritances and control, while paying less tax.

Now, let's begin at the end—your end—with Step #5 and avoid the death-tax trap.

NINE

ESTATE PLANNING FOR YOUR
RETIREMENT SAVINGS

Your Estate May Be Larger Than You Think

People tend to believe that the estate tax applies to anyone with an estate. In truth, it applies to anyone the government decides has too much money. How much is too much—aka the federal estate-tax exemption, or your "credit shelter amount"—is the government's call.

Estate tax laws always seem to be in flux, which makes keeping up with the latest version of the tax law a crucial part of effective estate planning. Congress loves to tinker in this area, often leaving us with death-tax rules that end up being only temporary. That's odd, since death is by nature permanent. Here's what I mean. A little history . . .

In 2010, Congress passed the Tax Relief, Unemployment Insurance Reauthorization, and Job Creation Act of 2010 (more commonly referred to as the 2010 Tax Act). This law made significant changes to the estate-planning landscape, increasing exemptions, decreasing rates, and even adding brand-new features to the law. Of course, as is generally the case when Congress acts some bad news comes along with the good—mainly that they leave us wondering what the laws will dictate when the bells toll for us.

Consider this: In 2010, there was no estate tax at all. So smart, rich people, like New York Yankees owner George Steinbrenner and Texas billionaire Dan Duncan, made sure they died that year. Mr. Duncan reportedly saved $4 billion in estate tax by dying in 2010. Now that's some A+ tax planning!

Since then, the estate tax has returned, all gussied up with some new bells and whistles. From 2011 through 2017, the estate tax exemption was raised to *$5 million per person (indexed for inflation)*— the highest exemption ever (except for 2010, when there was no estate tax at all). And that $5 million limit is *in addition to* the continued existence of the *unlimited marital deduction*, which, as the name implies, allows you to pass an unlimited amount of assets to a spouse (if he or she is a U.S. citizen) without triggering *any* estate tax.

At the same time, the top estate-tax rate was reduced to just 35 percent. To modern ears that number may not exactly sound like much of a bargain, but the last time the top estate-tax rate was lower was in 1931! It didn't stay at 35 percent, though. In 2013 the estate-tax rate rose to 40 percent, which is where it remains . . . for now.

Then, beginning in 2018 under the Tax Cuts and Jobs Act, the estate (and gift) exemptions doubled from $5 million a person to $10 million, plus a yearly increase based on the inflation factor. For example, in 2024 those exemptions total $13,610,000 per person or $27,220,000 for a married couple.

But don't hold your breath, because after 2025 these giant exemptions may revert to their former amounts—$5 million per person and $10 million per couple (plus the annual inflation additions for each year up to 2025). See what I was saying about temporary?

With all this back-and-forth, how is a person supposed to know when to die?

But wait . . . there's more. Back in 2010 Congress threw in a bonus—a new feature that provided married couples with an even greater ability to avoid federal estate tax altogether. The bonus, and what was perhaps the biggest "game changer" made by the 2010 Tax Act, was that the estate- (and gift-) tax-applicable exclusion amounts became *portable between spouses*. That's a mouthful, I know, but it's actually a pretty simple concept. It just means that any of your unused exemption can be transferred to, and used by, your surviving spouse. This benefit, known as the DSUE (deceased spouse's unused exclusion), is referred to as "portable" because the DSUE can be carried over to the surviving spouse.

For example, let's say John and Mary are married. To keep things simple, we'll just use the basic $10 million federal estate exemption without the annual inflation increases. John dies, leaving $1 million to his children and everything else to his wife. John made no taxable lifetime gifts. Therefore, John had $9,000,000 of unused estate-tax exclusion left at his death, which by law passes to Mary. If Mary dies later, her estate can exclude up to $19,000,000 from federal estate tax by using her own $10,000,000 exclusion plus the $9,000,000 that John did not use. In essence, the DSUE gives married couples up to $20 million of federal estate tax exclusion (and more if you add in IRS's inflation adjustments for that year). That's hardly chump change. This valuable tax break should never be lost or wasted, but you don't get it automatically. Instead, you must elect it.

For most couples it makes no difference which spouse dies first or how the assets are distributed after the first spouse's death. But while the ability to add a deceased spouse's remaining exemption to a surviving spouse's own exemption now exists, many people may fail to take advantage of this potential opportunity. Why? Because for a surviving spouse to transfer their deceased beloved's remaining exemption, they must elect to do so on the dearly departed's federal estate-tax return (IRS Form 706). Unless a person dies with a taxable estate (an estate that's subject to estate tax), there is generally no requirement to file an estate-tax return. But if no estate-tax return is filed, there's no way to transfer a deceased spouse's remaining exemption. So, in some cases, when the surviving spouse dies, there may be a major estate-tax issue that could have been avoided with the filing of that single document.

Take this example. When Julie died, she left everything to her husband, Dan, making her estate nontaxable. Given all the other paperwork Dan had to deal with following her death and considering the fact that Form 706 wasn't required, he neglected to file that return. Big mistake. By doing so, Dan forfeited his ability to add any of Julie's unused estate-tax exemption to his own. If he lives a long time and his estate grows beyond the value of his own estate exemption, this could end up costing his heirs dearly in taxes that could otherwise have been avoided.

Estate and Gift Exemption Amounts*

Estate Tax	$10,000,000
Generation-Skipping Transfer Tax	$10,000,000
Gift Tax	$10,000,000
Annual Gift-Tax Exclusion	$18,000

*These amounts are indexed for inflation, so they will either stay the same or go slightly higher. For example, the Estate-, Gift-, and Generation-Skipping Transfer Tax exemptions for 2024 increased to $13,610,000.

Figure 6. Estate, Gift, and GST Tax Changes
Effective 2018 Through 2025

- Effective from 2018 through 2025 (unless extended by Congress), the estate-, gift-, and generation-skipping transfer (GST) tax exemptions and the gift-tax exemption have all been set at $10 million per person and $20 million per couple, plus annual inflation additions.
- The estate, GST, and gift tax rate is 40 percent.
- The unused exemption is *portable* to the surviving spouse—meaning the deceased spouse's unused exemption may be transferred to, and used by, the surviving spouse's estate to reduce an estate-tax obligation.
- Unlike estate and gift tax exemptions, the GST tax exemption is *not* portable.
- There is a step-up in basis for qualifying estate assets—but not for IRAs, 401(k)s, or other tax-deferred retirement accounts.
- The current estate-tax rules allow more IRA funds to pass free of federal estate taxes due to the increased exemption amounts. Individuals can pass up to $10 million ($20 million per couple), plus inflation increases, of Roth IRA funds, income- and estate-tax-free to those beneficiaries.

At this point, given the huge federal estate-tax exemptions, many of us mortals might be thinking "and this would affect me how?" Maybe you're thinking, "Gee, that's all well and good, but I don't have an estate anywhere near $10 million, let alone $20 million. There's no way I'll have an issue." Perhaps. But, given all that's gone on before, why assume that the current rules, including the $10 million exemption, will stay in place? Even if the exemptions do, indeed, drop back down to $5 million and $10 million after 2025, these amounts are still way more than most of us need. But what if Congress lowers the exemptions even further or even *increases* the estate-tax rates? Don't think it can't happen. Back in 2001, the federal estate-tax rate was 55 percent. A Congress looking to plug the deficit could certainly decide that estate tax is one way to do it. Here's my point: History has shown us that you cannot rely on current estate tax laws because they are always changing. So, it's important to plan for the unknowns as well as the knowns.

For example, assume you have the money to make large gifts to family members and you do so to reduce your estate. Assume you made $10 million in gifts and used up your entire gift tax and estate tax exemption. When you die, you will have no exemption left, but at least you put it to good use before it reverted to half that amount. What if you died after the exemption went back down to, say, $5 million, but you had already taken advantage of the full $10 million? Would the IRS claw back the excess you'd already used? Nope! In late 2018, the IRS issued a release stating that making large gifts now won't cause any harm to estates after 2025.

In other words, even the IRS is saying "use it or lose it" when it comes to benefiting from the current exemption before it expires. So, by all means (if you have the means), go ahead and use these large exemptions while you can.

I realize that this large gifting example is beyond the wildest dreams of most of us, but it demonstrates the point I'm trying to make about taking full advantage of the bountiful exemption "buffet" before the brunch hour ends. I believe that a bird in the hand is worth two in the bush. So, going back to estate portability (something that more of us can use to our advantage), you should file for it even if you think you'll never need it, because you never know. I'd rather you had the greatest estate protection available. If it turns out you didn't need it, so what? Nothing lost. That's why you should elect estate portability by filing a timely estate-tax return, typically due nine months after death even if there is no federal estate tax to pay. Then your heirs will be able to take maximum advantage of the combined exemption amount—which for many people could prove to be well worth the effort and the expense of filing that election form.

It's pretty simple, really. Let me repeat: All you need to do to get the portability tax benefit of using the DSUE is to elect it by filing the federal estate tax return of the first spouse to die.

Despite this simplicity, so many people missed this big estate tax benefit that the IRS generously (and rarely do you see these two words together) gave estates an extension of five years from the date of the first spouse's death to make the portability election by filing their estate tax return. But don't count on IRS's continuing benevolence on this (or pretty much any) matter. File the estate tax return and claim the deceased spouse's unused exclusion (DSUE) before it goes the way of the brontosaurus.

On the other hand, maybe you're one of the fortunate few who, along with your spouse, has amassed an estate greater than $20 million, which would be subject to estate tax even after combining both $10 million exemptions. In that case, federal estate tax would still be a major concern for you and your family.

You might be tempted to think, "Well, I've got a $10 million exemption transferred from my last deceased spouse; maybe I should go out and get married again to get another $10 million exemption" on the assumption that the new spouse would again predecease you. Imagine the type of madness that might ensue? I can see the ad in the paper now: "Single woman in her 80s seeks older man with *big* exemption. Size matters." Unfortunately (or fortunately, if you happen to be the older man), Congress foresaw this as a possibility and included a provision in the portability rules robbing folks of this potential for macabre comedic gold. Under the law, only the exemption of your *final* deceased spouse may be added to your own. Therefore, under the current law the maximum estate-tax exclusion you can have is still set at $20 million. But nice try.

Review Your Current Estate Plan

So, what does all this mean for IRAs and other retirement assets? For most people reading this book, especially those who are married, federal estate tax is no longer an issue (although it could become one again if Congress changes the rules one day—don't put it past them). Therefore, from a federal estate-tax planning perspective only, most married couples can now name each other as their sole IRA beneficiary. With $20-plus million in combined estate-tax exclusion available, there is a much lower probability that the estate of your surviving spouse will owe federal estate tax, even with an inherited IRA.

This might make you want to run out and update your beneficiary forms to name your spouse as the sole beneficiary of your IRA instead of designating a credit shelter trust as the IRA beneficiary. (You'll find additional information on credit shelter trusts shortly.) But although the current law reduces the federal estate-tax risk of naming a spouse as an IRA beneficiary, and may provide additional tax advantages to future heirs, you should still take a closer look at all the variables, beyond the estate tax. In some cases, the simplicity of just naming your spouse as the direct beneficiary of your accounts may pay off, but in other cases, more elaborate estate planning will still be appropriate. Remember, estate planning is more than just planning to avoid estate tax. Consider the following examples:

▪ Alan and Ann Smith have been married for more than 40 years. They both have sizable IRAs, and their total net worth is $7 million. Neither Ann nor Alan has children from a previous marriage. They are both financially astute and neither believes that the other will remarry after the first death. The Smiths had been exploring sophisticated estate-planning strategies to help them avoid "wasting" the estate-tax exemption of the first spouse to die. Since that's no longer a risk, and given that they have few other concerns, the Smiths might prefer to simply name each other as sole IRA beneficiary.

▪ Bill and Barbara Jones have recently married. This is not the first marriage for either, and they both have children from their previous marriages. Bill has become careless in handling his own finances while Barbara has already married three times and is likely to walk down the aisle again if she survives Bill. For such a couple, naming each other as sole IRA beneficiary might *not* be desirable. Instead, they may want to leave their IRAs to their respective children or name a trust that can be used to benefit the surviving spouse during his or her lifetime while ensuring that whatever assets remain after the second death will pass to their respective children.

While these examples are probably more cut-and-dried than your own situation, I'm sure you get the point. Estate taxes might not be the only factor determining how you should set up your plan—assuming you have one.

For example, when the estate-tax exemptions were much lower and not portable, more people were subject to estate taxes. Back then it was common for an estate plan to include a credit shelter or family trust, to make sure that each spouse used his or her exemption; otherwise, it could be lost. The credit shelter trust was often used for tax reasons, but now that the estate-tax exemption is portable between spouses, and the surviving spouse can use his or her deceased spouse's unused federal estate-tax exemption, there's no need to use a credit shelter trust to secure that exemption. But there are still personal reasons (as opposed to tax reasons) to consider using a credit shelter trust even with the new and more generous estate-exemption amounts.

The reasons for needing a plan more complex than simply naming your spouse as the sole beneficiary of all your assets are virtually endless. Here's a short list of some of the most common reasons such a plan may still be necessary:

1. Asset Protection

If protection from creditors or bankruptcy is a major concern, a credit shelter trust can still be an effective planning option. Creditor protection laws vary significantly from state to state, with some

ESTATE PLANNING FOR YOUR RETIREMENT SAVINGS ▌ 309

offering virtually ironclad protection and others offering no protection at all. Despite a beneficiary's creditor issues, a trust can help
limit creditor access to the inherited funds, because trusts act like
middlemen of sorts between the creditor and the ultimate beneficiary.

2. Post-Death Management

Often in a marriage one spouse is the dominant decision-maker
when it comes to financial matters. (This has become less common
with younger couples, but there continue to be situations where it
still applies.) In some cases, surviving spouses may not have any
experience at all managing an IRA or other sizable account. Are
they capable of suddenly stepping into that role? Are they comfort-
able doing so? If the answer to either of these questions is no, a
credit shelter trust may still be needed. By using a credit shelter
trust, a trustee—hopefully someone more experienced with these
financial matters—can take ownership over the IRA management
decisions.

3. Concerns Over Remarriage of Your Surviving Spouse (QTIP Trusts)

When you name your spouse as your sole IRA beneficiary, he
or she has the special option of rolling over your IRA account into
an IRA in his or her own name. If the surviving spouse is over
59½ when he or she inherits the account, that's generally the best
option, since it allows him or her to withdraw any needed funds
from the account penalty-free. Once the IRA has been rolled into
an IRA in the surviving spouse's name, it's treated as if it were always the spouse's. As such, the spouse can do whatever he or she
wants to with it, including naming whichever beneficiaries he or
she chooses.

This may not sound like a big deal at first glance, but what if the
surviving spouse remarries down the road? The surviving spouse
might decide to name his or her new spouse as the beneficiary of
the IRA (formerly *your* IRA). How does that sit with you? If "not too
well" are the words that spring immediately to mind, a special type
of trust known as a QTIP (qualified terminable interest property)

trust may be necessary. QTIP trusts are not credit shelter trusts, since the trust property ends up being taxed in the surviving spouse's estate, but the remaining trust property will still go to the heirs you select (such as your children) after the death of your surviving spouse. Unfortunately, there are a slew of drawbacks when it comes to using a QTIP trust as the beneficiary of your IRA. These trusts are complex and require both careful planning and ongoing monitoring—even more so now after the changes made by the SECURE Act.

4. Keeping Post-Death Appreciation Out of Your Surviving Spouse's Estate

If you leave your IRA directly to your spouse and it's rolled over into his or her own name, the ultimate value that will be included in the spouse's estate is unknown. That's because the value to be included in the surviving spouse's estate is determined at *his or her death*, not yours. So even if your IRA is not large enough now to trigger federal estate tax (whether the exemption remains at $10 million), it might become so later, given ample time to compound and grow.

For example, suppose that Eric and Andrea are married. Eric has a $3.5 million IRA and Andrea owns a business valued at $12 million. Suppose Eric dies, leaving his IRA to his wife, and that a proper election is made at Eric's death to transfer his $10 million (plus inflation-adjusted additions) estate-tax exemption to her. There is no estate tax due since the property passed to a surviving spouse and qualified for the unlimited marital deduction. Eric used *none* of his $10 million federal estate-tax exemption, so his entire $10 million exemption will pass to Andrea after the election is made on Eric's estate-tax return. In addition, if Andrea were to die shortly after Eric, her total estate would likely still be close to $15.5 million, representing the value of her business plus the IRA she inherited from Eric. Since this total is below the $20 million of cumulative exclusion (Andrea's own $10 million exclusion plus Eric's transferred $10 million exclusion), there would be no federal estate tax owed.

Note: I am using $10 million/$20 million exemption amounts in these examples but remember these amounts have increased over the years due to inflation adjustments. For example, the 2024 federal estate exemptions are up to $13,610,000 per person, or $27,220,000 for a married couple.

Now suppose Andrea lives another 20 years. During that time, it's likely that the value of both the IRA and Andrea's business would increase. For argument's sake, let's assume that the IRA is now worth $12 million, and Andrea's business is worth $16 million. If Andrea still had the same $20 million of estate-tax exclusion available, her estate would exceed that total by some $8 million. Depending on the estate-tax rate in effect at the time of her death, it's likely that such an overage would cost Andrea's beneficiaries millions.

This situation could have been entirely avoided, however, if Eric's IRA had been left to a credit shelter trust at his death, where the appreciation of Eric's IRA after his death would be excluded from Andrea's estate, eliminating any estate-tax concerns for that asset.

A WORD TO THE WISE

At first glance, the growth of the assets in this example may seem unrealistic to you, but it's a far more reasonable estimate than you think. In fact, the increased values for Eric's IRA and Andrea's business both represent less than a 6.5 percent compound rate of return. See, I told you compound interest was powerful!

Beware of *State* Estate Tax

While the current federal estate-tax exclusion is $10 million, this has nothing to do with the estate taxes that are levied in many individual states. Many states that impose a *state* estate tax still have their own exclusions set at much lower levels. For instance, in my state of New York, we have around a $7 million *state* estate-tax exemption, and it's not portable like the federal exemption. Each state is different (and only Hawaii and Maryland have portability as of this writing), so it's important to know the *state* estate-tax exemption where you live, to plan accordingly.

If you live in a state that imposes a *state* estate tax, you can set up a credit shelter trust for that lower tax level to make sure that you and your spouse each maximize your allowed *state* estate-tax exemption. If everything is left to each other at the first death, the first to die's state estate-tax exemption will be wasted.

For example, Rick and Angela live in New York, where the *state* estate-tax exemption is $7 million. The couple's only asset is Rick's $8 million IRA. If Rick dies and leaves his IRA to Angela, she will have an estate of $8 million. At her death, and assuming no growth in the IRA, although there would be no federal estate tax owed, the New York State estate tax would amount to about $770,000 of unnecessary taxation. That's a huge amount of money—even in New York!

But let's say that instead of leaving his entire IRA to Angela, Rick had used a credit shelter trust as part of his planning. At Rick's death, $4 million of his IRA could have gone into his credit shelter trust (using up his *state* estate-tax exemption) and the remaining $4 million could have passed to Angela estate-tax-free, using the marital deduction. Then, at Angela's death, the $4 million she inherited directly could have passed *state* estate-tax-free to her beneficiaries using her own exemption.

Generation-Skipping Tax Planning

As noted earlier in Figure 6, the generation-skipping transfer (GST) tax exclusion has also been increased to $10 million (plus the annual inflation increases). The GST is an additional tax (on top of the gift or estate tax) on assets that skip a living generation of beneficiaries, such as children, and pass instead to individuals of the next generation of beneficiaries, such as grandchildren. The tax is also imposed on transfers to unrelated persons who are more than 37½ years younger than the transferor (known as a *skip* person).

Like the estate- and gift-tax exemptions, the increased GST exemption may only be effective through 2025, but unlike the exemptions for estate and gift taxes, the GST exemption is not portable. Any amount that goes unused during your lifetime (or after death) is irrevocably lost.

For example, if you were to leave all your assets to your spouse, he or she would be able to take advantage of a $20 million exemption from federal estate tax (assuming your exclusion was transferred after death), but only a $10 million exemption from the GST tax. Even though this exclusion is not portable between spouses, the larger exclusion might generate more gifts and bequests to grandchildren, great-grandchildren, or other skip persons.

Since the $10 million GST exemption is not portable, if you intend to leave significant portions of your assets to grandchildren or other skip persons, it may pay to keep a credit shelter trust as part of your overall estate plan to secure both spouses' GST exemptions.

Gift-Tax Changes

Another key change that was made by the 2010 Tax Act is that the gift-tax exclusion has been *reunified* with the federal estate tax. This means you can give as much away during your lifetime as you can after death without incurring any transfer (estate or gift) taxes.

The gift-tax exclusion, like the estate-tax exclusion, is $10 million, plus inflation adjustments, through the end of 2025, and any unused amount can pass to your surviving spouse. Of course, in addition to your $10 million exclusion, you can also make annual gifts of $18,000 to each person you desire without eating into your exemption. Married couples can gift up to $36,000 to each person without affecting either exemption. In addition, you can make unlimited direct gifts to institutions for education or medical bills, which do not count against either the $10 million ($20 million per couple) gift-tax exemption or the $18,000 annual gift exclusion.

However, if you're thinking that you can give away $20 million gift-tax-free to beneficiaries now during your lifetime, and then leave them another $20 million estate-tax-free after you're gone, I've got some bad news for you. The gift-tax exclusion and the estate-tax exclusion are inextricably linked to each other. Any gift-tax exemption used during your lifetime reduces the amount of estate-tax exclusion you have left at your death dollar-for-dollar. For example, whatever amount you gift during your lifetime (other than annual exclusions and other gifts that don't count against the gift and estate exemption) reduces your remaining exemption.

The relatively high gift-tax exclusion lends itself to any number of planning strategies. For example, a parent might make a large gift to a child to use to pay the tax on the child's own Roth IRA conversion. Of course, while making gifts can be an effective strategy, you should pay special attention to IRAs and other retirement accounts because of the unique transfer issues they present. For example, unlike nearly all other assets, *IRAs and other retirement accounts cannot be transferred (gifted) to another person, including a spouse or a trust, during your lifetime.* They can only be transferred upon death.

While it's true that the changes to estate, gift, and GST taxes are set to expire at the end of 2025, Congress has not lowered these exemptions at all in recent years, so there's at least a chance that even if they are not increased, they may be extended. But who really knows? *Don't let the fact that this law is temporary delay any planning that needs to be done now to take advantage of these incredibly generous tax provisions. If not used now, these benefits could be lost to you.*

More About Credit Shelter Trusts

If you're married and have already set up a typical credit shelter trust as part of your estate plan (also known as a *bypass trust,* or *A-B trust,* or *family trust*), it's time to review the terms. These days, the increased exemption could have some unintended negative consequences.

When using a credit shelter trust as part of an estate plan, amounts up to the federal estate exemption ($10 million, plus inflation adjustments, through 2025) will go to the credit shelter trust, and any excess over that amount will go either directly to your spouse or to a marital trust for your spouse's benefit. In a perfect estate plan, each spouse would use their entire exemption amount, paying the lowest possible estate tax after both spouses die. But for many couples, their trust terms were set up back when the estate exemption was much lower.

Many estate plans have credit shelter trusts that were set up when the exemption was $2 million. (Some people still have plans that were set up back when the exemption was $600,000!) If your plan was set up when the exemption was $2 million and your estate was $4 million, that would have been perfect, since $2 million would have gone into the credit shelter trust (using your $2 million exemption) and the other $2 million would have gone directly to your surviving spouse. Later, when the surviving spouse died (assuming his or her estate was worth $2 million at death, just to keep our ideal example), that spouse's $2 million exemption would kick in. In this way, as a couple, you could have passed down to your heirs your entire $4 million estate totally free of federal estate tax.

But what would happen now if you had the same $4 million estate with your typical credit shelter plan? Well, believe it or not, the increase in the federal estate-tax exemption could disinherit you or your spouse completely if you're not careful. How so? Well, many estate plans are written so that a credit shelter trust can always take advantage of the maximum amount that can pass federal estate-tax-free. For instance, your estate plan might include a provision that says something like: "An amount equal to the maximum amount that can pass estate-tax-free under federal law shall first be used to fund the credit shelter trust, after which any remaining assets shall be left directly to the surviving spouse." If that's the case, since your entire $4 million estate is less than the amount that can currently pass federal estate-tax-free ($10 million), everything could go into the credit shelter trust. And that could leave your surviving spouse with *NOTHING!*

It's true that many credit shelter trusts are drafted so that the surviving spouse will receive all the income from the trust annually, but he or she may not be able to access any of the principal. And even if he or she does have access to some of the principal, the access must be somewhat limited to preserve the estate-tax benefit. This may not be exactly the type of plan you thought you were getting yourself into, now, is it?

Not to worry, though. I've got some excellent news for you. If you're reading this book, *you are alive*! That means there's still time to update your estate plan and arrange things so that the beneficiaries you want to receive your assets will do so, even with the recent changes in the law. How? In any number of ways, really. You could revise your plan so that a specific amount will go into the credit shelter trust. For example, you could simply say $2 million will go into the credit shelter trust and anything over that will go to your surviving spouse. That would work for now but might limit the desired effectiveness of your credit shelter trust down the road. (Remember that since the federal estate-tax exemption is now portable between spouses, you no longer need a credit shelter trust to secure the exemption in the estate of the first spouse to die. Instead, you must be using a credit shelter trust for personal, nontax reasons.) Perhaps a better option might be to engage in some crafty disclaimer planning.

Disclaimer planning can be used to put the surviving spouse in control and seize the opportunity to maximize estate-tax savings. Using a disclaimer plan you can name your spouse as the beneficiary of all your assets and then, upon your death, your spouse would be able to disclaim any amounts not needed or that he or she preferred to go into your credit shelter trust. Amounts disclaimed up to the federal and/or state estate-tax exemption amount would then pass to contingent beneficiaries free of estate taxes.

This can provide your surviving spouse with greater financial security and can avoid his or her having to worry about needing to ask a trustee to dole out money later. This disclaimer strategy allows the surviving spouse to change the plan after the first spouse dies, accounting for the needs of the surviving spouse and whatever the estate-tax exemption is at that time. *Naming contingent beneficiaries (say, the children, grandchildren, or a credit shelter trust) is essential for this disclaimer strategy to work. Allow me to explain.*

First, let's start with a definition. Just what exactly is a disclaimer anyway? It's basically the legal equivalent of "playing dead." When a person properly executes a disclaimer, the law treats that person as though he or she died before the original owner of the assets. Therefore, the assets pass to the next person in line—which is why naming those contingent beneficiaries is so important.

For example, Willy and Wanda, both in their early forties, are married with two children. Amazingly, Willy has already accumulated $6 million in his IRA. Willy's IRA beneficiary form names Wanda as the primary beneficiary of his IRA and his children as contingent beneficiaries. When Willy dies, Wanda will have a lot of control over his IRA. If she decides she'll need the full $6 million, she can roll the whole thing over to her own IRA. Of course, depending on the growth of the account, that might create an estate-tax problem at Wanda's death.

On the other hand, Wanda may feel like she does not need the entire IRA. She can then determine just how much she wants, disclaiming all or any portion of it. If, for instance, she determines that she needs only $4 million of the IRA, she can disclaim $2 million of the total account. The disclaimed $2 million would then pass to the next-in-line beneficiaries (using some of Willy's estate-tax exclusion), which in this case would be the couple's children.

Disclaimer planning can be particularly useful given its low cost, the relative ease of its implementation, and the amount of flexibility it provides. There are, of course, still a number of rules you must follow to effectively implement a disclaimer—so you should be sure to consult with your estate-planning specialist.

For Your IRA Beneficiaries: Don't Miss This Deduction!

Back in 1918, every asset in an estate received a step-up in basis, which meant that beneficiaries paid no income tax on the value of property they inherited. Can you imagine that? (If this were the system today, no beneficiary would pay tax on an inherited retirement account.) So, in 1934, our nation's lawmakers decided certain income items should not receive a step-up in basis and defined these items as *income in respect of a decedent (IRD)*. (There were no IRAs then, so they did not foresee the amount of income tax revenue that would one day be generated by their IRD concept.)

Step-up in basis works this way: If a person dies with a stock portfolio or a home, the beneficiary will receive a step-up in basis and be able to use the fair market value at the date of death as his or her cost for determining any gain or loss on a future sale of the asset. So, if a stock was bought by the decedent for $1,000 and was worth $100,000 at death, the beneficiary would receive a step-up in basis and be relieved from reporting the $99,000 gain the decedent would have been taxed on had the stock been sold by the decedent before he or she died.

But IRD items receive no such step-up in basis. Instead, the beneficiary receives what is called a "carryover" basis, which means *the same basis as the decedent.* In other words, IRD is income the decedent earned but did not yet pay tax on. So, when the beneficiary inherits and collects the income, the beneficiary will owe the income tax. (IRD items include money owed to the decedent at death, such as wages, accounts receivable from a business, installment-sale income, rental income, and even lottery winnings, as well as, of course, retirement and annuity income.)

A WORD TO THE WISE

The key word in the federal IRD deduction equation is "federal," because there is no deduction for any *state* estate tax paid. So, on the state level, double taxation still exists.

Recognizing that the IRD concept effectively causes double taxation (estate and income tax), our lawmakers, rather than junking the concept, chose instead the Band-Aid approach to fixing it and created an income tax deduction for beneficiaries to offset this double taxation. It is called the "IRD deduction" (or estate tax deduction), and it's the government's way of throwing us a bone.

Today's increased federal estate-tax exemption means that fewer beneficiaries will be able to take an IRD deduction than in years past, but that's not necessarily a bad thing. If you inherit an IRA and can't take an IRD deduction, it's almost certainly because no federal estate tax was paid when you inherited your account. And paying no estate tax beats an income tax deduction any day.

Of course, this can be a double-edged sword. With the estate-tax exemption so high, and fewer beneficiaries qualifying for the IRD deduction, it's possible that some tax preparers will just assume there was no estate tax paid, making those who are still eligible for the deduction more likely to miss out on using it.

Perhaps you've been reading this section on IRD and have been thinking to yourself, "Yikes! I never knew to claim the IRD deduction on the account I inherited. I've probably lost thousands by now! I wonder if it's too late to stop the bleeding?" In most cases the answer is no. You can go back and amend three years of tax returns and claim the deduction for each year. You'll even receive interest on your tax refund. Don't forget to also amend your state tax return and get any refunds due if you paid state income tax on the distributions from your inherited IRA. Plus, if you still have any of the IRA (or other items of IRD) remaining, you can continue to take the balance of any unused deduction in future years.

Now that you've tripled your tax savings, you can host an IRD deduction party to tell your friends! (Be sure to invite your accountant.)

Don't Just Sit There. Put Your Estate Plan to Work!

By this point you have all the information you need to pass on your IRA to your children or grandchildren at the lowest possible estate tax. Now all you need to do is to actually create an estate plan and put it to work. Here is where most people stop. They procrastinate and never get around to it because of all the excuses I rattled off at the beginning of this chapter.

As an advisor, I can attest to the fact that getting my clients to actually implement their estate plans is one of my biggest challenges. So, when this happens, I hit them with the following true story:

A couple came to my office after attending my seminar on estate planning. At 78 and 79 years old and not in the best of health, the couple had a $6 million estate yet had done no estate planning. I first told them, "Give some money to your kids." That was a mistake. As soon as I said it the father just flipped. He shouted angrily, "Give it to my kids? They'll just piss it away!"

I sat quietly for a second, giving his inner Bruce Banner a chance to return following his whole Hulk outburst. Then I looked him in the eye and said, "Here's the way it is. You either give it to your kids, you spend it, or you fork it over to the government. You pick the pisser!"

And that's really what estate planning comes down to.

See, I told you it was easy.

TEN

THE NEW REALITIES OF NAMING TRUSTS AS IRA BENEFICIARIES

When do you name a trust as a beneficiary? When you don't trust. They should have called it a "don't trust" because if you trusted them, you wouldn't need a trust!

—ED SLOTT

Most people don't need to name trusts as their IRA beneficiaries. It's costly (you'll need an attorney and perhaps even a tax advisor who specializes in the complex area of IRA trusts, and they don't come cheap), it's cumbersome, and there is no tax benefit that can be gained with a trust that cannot be gained without one! Stop right now and read the last part of that sentence again . . . and again, until you've committed it to memory.

The only reason to name a trust as the beneficiary of your IRA (or Roth IRA) is for personal (nontax) reasons, such as restricting access to the buildup by beneficiaries who might be too young (i.e., a minor child), mentally incompetent, or prone to squandering it on a hot Ferrari or a cool vacation. But these are all reasons why you would leave *any* property in trust, including an IRA!

In the past, savers chose to name a trust as their IRA beneficiary to gain IRA advantages unavailable to other assets, such as the stretch IRA. However, since the SECURE Act eliminated the stretch IRA for most nonspouse beneficiaries, the bigger advantage now will be the post-death control. An IRA trust can be a wise choice if you want to make sure that the IRA you leave to your beneficiaries is protected for them (and from them). For example, if you want your beneficiaries to take only certain limited amounts each year so that the IRA is available to support them over their lifetimes, you can guarantee that kind of post-death control. In an IRA trust, your wishes will be upheld. But keep in mind that this kind of protection and control may come at a prohibitive tax cost. (More on how to solve that issue later in this chapter.)

Let me be very clear about this: When I say "IRA trusts" that's exactly what I'm referring to—a trust named as an IRA (or Roth IRA) beneficiary. I do not mean regular estate planning trusts used for passing non-retirement-account assets such as a house or bank account to beneficiaries. Regular estate-planning trusts are fine, and I recommend them. But an IRA often does not mesh well with the rules of a trust. An IRA is like the character Pig-Pen in the *Peanuts* comic strip. He always has a circle of dust around him; wherever he goes, the dirt goes with him. Wherever an IRA goes, the RMD rules go too, and integrating them with the trust provisions often causes conflict.

For example, RMDs must still be paid out of the IRA and into the trust. That defeats the purpose of the trust, or throws a big monkey wrench into it anyway, if the trust's purpose is to preserve trust property for an ultimate beneficiary down the line. And if an RMD is missed, the same 25 percent penalty that applies to all other IRA owners and beneficiaries who miss an RMD gets levied. Because of the RMD rules, no other asset in a trust creates the problems that an IRA does. If you put a house in a trust, there are no rules that say, "The first year, the kitchen must come out; the second year, the dining room; the third year, the bathroom; the fourth year, the bedroom; and so on." You get the point. But when an IRA is left to a trust, the RMD rules can force a part of the IRA out each year. And now with the SECURE Act eliminating the stretch IRA for most trusts, that dust circle gets even messier. To return to our house example, the SECURE Act requires that the whole house come out within 10 years after death (since most trusts will be subject to the 10-year payout rule you recall from Chapter 6).

Using Trusts for Protection

Naming a trust as an IRA beneficiary to exercise control over the funds your beneficiaries inherit may be useful for larger IRAs—especially in cases when you worry about beneficiaries who are minors or disabled, or who face the following complications: poor money-management skills, creditor or financial problems, lawsuits, bankruptcy, divorces, second marriages, or circumstances that may make beneficiaries vulnerable or easily preyed upon.

Creditor Protection

It's an odd phenomenon, but there are numerous cases of retirement account beneficiaries having creditor issues or even filing for bankruptcy protection. I say odd, since these people just inherited IRA or 401(k) sums that are often large, yet they somehow end up going through that money and even more. This is one reason you might want to leave your IRA to a trust for them. Each year, the courts further chip away at creditor protection for retirement accounts, especially when it comes to bankruptcy. The big shift began in 2014 when the U.S. Supreme Court ruled unanimously that inherited IRAs would not be protected in bankruptcy. The decision in the seminal case (*Clark v. Rameker, 134 S. Ct. 2242, June 12, 2014*) essentially said that even though IRAs are generally protected from bankruptcy under federal law, that protection will not extend to beneficiaries. The court took the view that since the beneficiary didn't contribute that money but instead inherited it, the account beneficiary does not get the federal bankruptcy protection that the original IRA owner would have had. An IRA trust may help here. Parents want to leave their children prosperity, not problems. And when it comes to preserving IRA funds, a trust can sometimes help accomplish that.

Second-Marriage Risks

The desire to exercise control from beyond the grave over the ultimate disposition of your IRA in the event of a second marriage is another motivation for naming a trust as beneficiary—in this case, a qualified terminable interest property trust (QTIP). As mentioned earlier, this is a special trust created to qualify for the marital deduction while also giving you (the IRA owner and trust creator) control over the trust principal (the IRA) after your death. For example, a spouse (say, your second wife, who has kids from another marriage) can have the IRA income or RMDs each year to live on, but after her death the remaining trust assets will go to your children and not hers. Here again, RMDs are the fly in the ointment. If she lives long enough and receives the RMDs each year, your children will be disinherited until she dies. This is a recipe for disaster (or a good Lifetime channel movie).

There is often some type of tension or adversarial relationship in many second or later marriages between the second spouse (let's say a stepmom) and the adult children from the earlier marriage(s), especially if they are older than the stepmom. If the children must wait for the stepmom to die to receive anything, they are effectively disinherited. That was probably not the intention of Dad (the IRA owner) when he was advised to set up the QTIP trust. He was probably told that his new wife would receive income for life and his children would get the principal when she dies. Well, guess what? If she lives long enough, taking RMDs each year, there won't be any principal left for the children (or their children)! The entire IRA could end up in the stepmom's family, not in Dad's, contrary to his wishes (and expectations) when he set this all up. Bottom line: if the QTIP trust is the beneficiary of the IRA, the kids won't see a dime until their stepmother dies.

Seriously, QTIP trusts create unique problems, which is why I generally advise against naming them as IRA beneficiaries. My only purpose in making you aware of their existence is, frankly, so that you'll stay away from them. You should never name a trust as the beneficiary of your IRA just because it's an IRA (even if your attorney tells you that's the reason to do it). That's wrong—because even when they're executed perfectly, trusts as IRA beneficiaries create unique problems and tax complications.

Now that you know the reasons people name trusts to inherit their IRAs, you are in a better position to understand why they may not work.

Trust Qualifications

IRA trusts cannot provide the panacea of tax and personal solutions that many IRA owners are looking for. In reality, there are trade-offs and consequences. Consider this paragraph a disclaimer and warning: Don't name trusts as IRA beneficiaries unless you know what you are doing and it's the only solution.

If an IRA trust is the only solution for you, make sure it qualifies as what the IRS refers to as a "look-through" or "see-through" trust so that trust beneficiaries are treated as designated beneficiaries. While the inherited IRA funds will likely have to be paid out under the SECURE Act's 10-year rule, if the trust does not qualify, beneficiaries won't even get the 10 years and the inherited IRA funds might have to be paid out sooner, causing tax to be paid even earlier. Here are the necessary qualifications:

- The trust must be valid under state law.

- The trust must be irrevocable at death.

- The beneficiaries of the trust must be identifiable.

- The trust's trustee must provide to the financial institution holding the account a copy of the trust instrument by October 31 of the year following the IRA owner's death.

In addition, all the trust beneficiaries must be individuals—that is to say, *people*—because only they have a life expectancy; otherwise trust beneficiaries won't qualify as "designated" and the stretch IRA will be lost to the special group of eligible designated beneficiaries (EDBs) who still qualify for that benefit. (There are some exceptions where certain trust beneficiaries can be excluded to avoid losing the stretch for remaining trust EDBs. We will discuss this later.)

If the trust fails to qualify as a look-through or see-through trust, then there is no designated beneficiary at all. In that case, the trust beneficiaries will be subject to the rules that apply when there is no designated beneficiary. Strangely enough, these rules were unaffected by the SECURE Act. Under those rules, the IRA will be paid out either under the 5-year rule (if the IRA owner dies before his or her RBD) or over the remaining life expectancy of the deceased IRA owner (if the IRA owner dies on or after his or her RBD). In another strange twist from the SECURE Act, that remaining life expectancy could actually exceed the 10-year term by a few years, if the IRA owner dies in his or her seventies.

A WORD TO THE WISE

Another problem with a trust is that after the IRA owner dies, trust tax returns will have to be filed each year for the life of the trust. This can get expensive and creates even more paperwork and possible IRS problems if the IRS decides to audit your trust tax returns. If you are audited, you had better hope the IRA trust was correctly drafted, particularly with respect to the IRA tax rules. Also, depending on the flexibility of the trust, the IRA trust beneficiaries (your children) are generally locked into the trust terms for life. As a result, there may be some family resentment against you for leaving your IRA beneficiaries with this kind of legacy, even if you'd intended it for their own good.

RIP IRA Trusts

I might sound like a broken record, but I want you to understand how completely the SECURE Act has upended IRA trust planning. If you named a trust as your IRA beneficiary, your plan needs an immediate review and probable overhaul. Of course, this involves coordination with your legal, tax, and financial advisors.

Congress has decided that IRAs and other tax-favored retirement accounts are for retirement and not to pass on to heirs, so they gutted the so-called stretch IRA option for all but a few exceptions. Now, designated beneficiaries, including qualified trusts, are subject to a 10-year payout period. If the IRA owner died on or after his or her RBD, there are also annual RMDs during years one through nine of this 10-year period. Then, any funds remaining in the inherited IRA (or plan) account must be emptied by the end of the 10th year after death. All those funds would be taxed by that time (except for tax-free Roth IRA distributions). This is exactly what Congress wanted. They wanted to downgrade IRAs as an estate-planning vehicle, and the new tax rules do just that.

As I explained in detail in Chapter 6, the law exempts five types of beneficiaries from these new rules, permitting these individuals to get the stretch IRA like under the old rules. Those exempted achieve royalty status as EDBs.

Memory Jog

The five classes of eligible designated beneficiaries (EDBs):

1. Surviving spouses
2. Minor children of the IRA owner, up to age 21—but *not* grandchildren
3. Disabled individuals—under the strict IRS rules

4. Chronically ill individuals

5. Individuals not more than 10 years younger than the IRA owner (generally siblings, partners, or friends around the same age)

Although these beneficiaries are unaffected by the new rules, once they either no longer qualify as EDBs, or die, the 10-year rule kicks in for them, or for their beneficiaries.

The 10-year payout rule is why naming trusts as IRA beneficiaries no longer works as planned and could result in either large taxable distributions if IRA funds are paid to trust beneficiaries, or high trust tax rates if the funds remain in the trust. The trust could still be used to protect the retirement funds for your heirs, but that protection and control may now come at a prohibitive tax cost.

With the elimination of the stretch, someone must pay the tax on the *entire taxable* IRA balance after 10 years:

■ either the trust, at high trust tax rates (if the funds are held inside the trust to be protected), or

■ the individual trust beneficiaries at their own rates, in which case the funds are no longer protected in trust.

Once the taxable inherited IRA funds are distributed to the trust, they are taxable the same as any IRA distribution to a beneficiary. The only difference with a trust as beneficiary is who pays the tax—the trust or the trust beneficiary? That's easy. It's the one who gets the funds. If the inherited IRA funds pass through the trust and are distributed from the trust to the trust beneficiaries, then the beneficiaries pay the income tax at their own personal income tax rates. If instead of paying out the funds that amount is accumulated in the trust, then the trust pays the income tax on those funds at trust tax rates.

Trust tax rates are the highest in the land. Accumulate around $15,000 of income, and trust tax rates jump to the highest bracket.

(Adding state income tax to the mix could result in a combined tax rate of 40 percent or more!) By contrast, an individual doesn't jump to the top tax bracket until he or she earns more than around $600,000 of income. That's a big difference!

NOTE: Roth IRAs will work better here since there will be no tax when the funds go to the trust or to the trust beneficiaries.

Pre-2020 Deaths Are Grandfathered

The SECURE Act changes are effective for those who die after 2019. Those who died in 2019 or earlier are grandfathered under the old rules. Those stretch IRAs will continue, so beneficiaries can have two sets of payout periods depending on when they inherit. To understand the gravity of this change, let's first review the old rules for inherited IRAs.

Pre-2020 Tax Rules for IRA and Plan Beneficiaries

Under the old rules, designated beneficiaries could "stretch" required minimum distributions (RMDs) from the inherited IRA (or company plan) over their lifetimes, possibly over decades, depending on their age. "See-through" trusts also qualified for the stretch IRA, so a person with a large IRA could name a trust for the benefit of a grandchild, and RMDs could be spread over 50 years or more, depending on the age of the grandchild.

Qualifying "see-through" trusts under the old rules could often accomplish both key estate-planning objectives—post-death control and tax minimization—but not anymore after the SECURE Act.

Here's why:

There are two types of IRA trusts: conduit and discretionary (accumulation) trusts.

Assuming they each qualified as designated beneficiaries by meeting the conditions of a see-through trust, payouts from the inherited IRA to the trust under the old rules could be stretched over the lifetime of the oldest trust beneficiary.

Conduit Trust

With a conduit trust, the annual RMDs get paid out from the inherited IRA to the trust and from the trust to the trust beneficiaries. No funds remain in the trust. All funds received by the beneficiaries are taxed at their own personal tax rates.

Discretionary Trust
(for When More Post-Death Control Is Desired)

With a discretionary trust, the annual RMDs are paid out from the inherited IRA to the trust, but then the trustee has discretion over whether to distribute those funds to the trust beneficiaries or retain them in the trust. This provides the trustee with greater post-death control of what gets paid to the trust beneficiaries, as compared to the conduit trust, which automatically pays out all annual RMDs to the trust beneficiaries. Any funds retained in the trust, though, would be taxed at high trust tax rates.

If the discretionary trust meets the four requirements to qualify as a see-through trust, then you must use the age of the oldest of the trust's beneficiaries to calculate RMDs on the inherited IRA. But with a discretionary trust (as opposed to a conduit trust), you must consider the ages of both the income and remainder trust beneficiaries when you look to see who the oldest beneficiary is (i.e., which beneficiary has the shortest life expectancy). That is the beneficiary whose life expectancy will be used to calculate RMDs on the inherited IRA.

Exceptions—Disregarded Beneficiaries

The proposed regulations provide exceptions where certain beneficiaries of accumulation trusts can be disregarded. A remainder beneficiary, for example, inherits trust assets only when income beneficiaries die or their interest in the trust ends. This means that in an accumulation trust, a remainder beneficiary can be disregarded if this beneficiary could only receive payments from the trust after the death of another beneficiary whose sole interest is a residual interest in the trust. One type of remainder beneficiary is called a *residual beneficiary*. This is a beneficiary who receives all the property left in the trust that is not received by anyone else. For example, assume an accumulation trust provides that if the residual beneficiary of the trust predeceases the primary trust beneficiary, then the funds are to be paid to a charity. The charity can be disregarded as a beneficiary. This allows the trust to satisfy the see-through-trust rule that all trust beneficiaries must be individuals.

A remainder beneficiary can also be disregarded when the trust terms require a full distribution to a minor child trust beneficiary of any IRA funds by the end of the year when he or she reaches age 31. The only way the remainder beneficiary would be entitled to those funds would be if the minor child trust beneficiary died before age 31.

Let's take Roger, who named his see-through trust as the beneficiary of his IRA. This accumulation trust requires a full distribution of all trust assets when the beneficiary of the trust, his son James, reaches age 31. If James dies before this scheduled full-distribution date, then any funds still in the trust would be paid to Roger's brother Gene. Gene can be disregarded as a beneficiary when it comes to determining the payout period for the trust. Since James is an EDB, distributions to the trust can be made over his life expectancy. However, should James die before turning 31, the 10-year payout period would apply to Gene.

Identifiability of Beneficiaries

The proposed regulations also address the see-through trust requirement that all beneficiaries be "identifiable." The regulations make it clear that the addition of another member of a class of beneficiaries would not cause the trust to fail the identifiability requirement.

For example, Larry designated his see-through trust as his IRA beneficiary, naming his grandchildren as the beneficiaries of the trust. The birth of another grandchild would not mean that the trust would fail to meet the see-through rules.

Example of Discretionary Trust for Children— *AFTER* the SECURE Act

Knowing her adult children could be irresponsible with money, Annie named a discretionary trust as beneficiary of her IRA. Because she died in 2020 after her RBD at the age of 75, the trust was subject to the 10-year rule and to RMDs for years one through nine. Depending on the terms of the trust, the trustee had the discretion to either retain these RMDs in the trust for further protection or pay all or part of the RMDs to the trust beneficiaries (the children). However, any funds remaining in the inherited IRA must be emptied—that is, paid into the trust—by December 31, 2030.

Taxes must either be paid by Annie's children as the funds are distributed to them or by the trust at high tax rates if the funds remain in the trust for continued protection. The trustee has discretion to pay out the trust funds to Annie's children at any time, even well beyond the 10 years—for example, after they reach the specific age at which Annie had determined she wanted them to have access to the funds. Annie's trust provisions could even specify that the trustee pay out earmarked funds to her children to cover specific needs such as health, education, or other necessary support.

The 10-year term only specifies the year by which the funds must be paid out from the inherited IRA to the trust. They will be taxed when they are paid into the trust, but once those funds are in the trust, they can remain there for protection well beyond the 10 years—for decades if desired. That protection is a good option. But it comes at a high tax cost, thanks to the limitations under the SECURE Act. Read on . . .

The SECURE Act's Effect on IRA Trust Planning

Two words: Not good! Under the new law, a conduit trust will no longer work to accomplish either of our two objectives: post-death control and tax minimization. Since the SECURE Act does away with annual RMDs for years one through nine of the 10-year term in some situations (like when a person dies before their RBD with a noneligible designated trust beneficiary), the trust could end up with no payouts until the end of the 10 years, when all the funds get released to the trust's beneficiaries—exactly what the client with a large IRA wanted to avoid.

The IRS-proposed regulations for post-death RMDs add to the trust tax problem when RMDs are required in years one through nine under the 10-year rule, and the inherited IRA funds are retained in a discretionary trust for protection. This would generally be the case when death occurs on or after the RBD. Any annual RMDs that are kept in the trust would be protected, but subject to high trust tax rates.

100 Percent RMD at the End of the 10 Years

Under the 10-year rule, most of the taxes will get bunched into the last year, unless the trust has language allowing distributions throughout the 10 years to spread out the income, or if RMDs are required for years one through nine. Either way, at the end of the 10 years the entire account will be released to a beneficiary who may squander the funds or lose them, and the inherited IRA funds will all be taxed by the end of the 10 years. See why this is a lousy estate plan?

SECURE Act Example of a Conduit Trust for a Grandchild

Prior to the SECURE Act, Alexander set up a trust for his grandson, Jake, then age 30. The trust is a conduit trust with language carefully crafted to say that the amount of the RMD must be paid out from the inherited IRA and then distributed to Jake. Alexander intended to have RMDs stretched out over Jake's lifetime. Unfortunately, Alexander died in 2020 without revising his trust in the wake of the SECURE Act. Now the trust will not work as Alexander had planned. The 10-year rule will apply, requiring the entire IRA balance to be distributed to the trust and then to Jake in 2030.

The conduit trust will generally only work now for EDBs who can still stretch payouts over their lifetimes, but even then, once the EDB no longer qualifies as an EDB (for example, when a minor reaches age 21), the 10-year payout rule kicks in.

If a trust is still deemed necessary, then a discretionary trust would work somewhat better since inherited IRA funds can still be retained and protected in the trust, even after the 10 years. But all those funds will be taxed at high trust tax rates. Providing the trust protection desired may come at too steep a tax cost for this to be a viable plan.

Special Trusts for Beneficiaries Who Are Disabled and Chronically Ill

Disabled or chronically ill individuals are considered EDBs and still get the stretch IRA, even after the SECURE Act. The tax law additionally created the ability to set up special trusts for these beneficiaries.

Who Is a Disabled Individual?

To qualify, the individual must meet this strict IRS standard of Tax Code Section 72(m)(7):

> *Meaning of Disabled—For purposes of this section, an individual shall be considered to be disabled if he is unable to engage in any substantial gainful activity by reason of any medically determinable physical or mental impairment which can be expected to result in death or to be of long-continued and indefinite duration. An individual shall not be considered to be disabled unless he furnishes proof of the existence thereof in such form and manner as the Secretary may require.*

You must be unable to work for a long or indefinite period and you *must be able to prove it.*

Who Is a Chronically Ill Individual?

Under the SECURE Act, a chronically ill individual is determined based on the definition under Tax Code Section 7702B(c)(2), under the tax rules for defining Long-Term Care Services under Long-Term Care Insurance Policies.

The terms seem similar to disability but extend further in some respects since the definition considers activities of daily living. To qualify as a chronically ill individual under the SECURE Act, an individual must be certified (by a licensed health-care practitioner) to be unable to perform at least two activities of daily living for at least 90 days—or—require "substantial supervision" due to a severe "cognitive impairment."

Under the SECURE Act, the ability to use the stretch for chronically ill or disabled beneficiaries is available to an "applicable multi-beneficiary trust" or (AMBT), another term made up by Congress. An AMBT can have other beneficiaries besides the disabled or chronically ill individual. These other beneficiaries do not have to be EDBs, but they all must be designated beneficiaries. That would include living individuals with a life expectancy but would exclude entities like an estate.

For these special needs trusts, the SECURE 2.0 Act now says that a charity (qualified under the regular IRS rules) will qualify as a designated beneficiary.

Consider this example. Brian names as the beneficiary of his IRA a special needs trust for the benefit of his disabled son, Christopher. After Christopher's death, any remaining funds from the IRA are to be paid to a local charity. This is OK since under SECURE 2.0 the charity is a designated beneficiary, and the trust will still qualify as an applicable multi-beneficiary trust. This means that stretching the RMDs over Christopher's life expectancy will still be allowed.

Additionally, to qualify as an AMBT, the trust would have to be established in one of two ways. It can provide that it is to be divided immediately upon the death of the IRA owner into separate trusts for each beneficiary. Or it can provide that no beneficiary, other than the EDB, has any right to the IRA funds until the death of the EDB.

If the trust is divided upon the death of the IRA owner into separate trusts, only the EDB will be able to use the stretch for RMD payouts. Any other trust beneficiary would be subject to the 10-year rule.

Here's another example. Mitch names his trust as the beneficiary of his IRA. At Mitch's death, the trust is to be split into two trusts, one for each of his daughters. His daughter Page, age 32, is chronically ill and qualifies as an EDB at Mitch's death. Payments from the inherited IRA to the trust for Page can be made over Page's life expectancy. Mitch's other daughter, Patty, age 28, is not disabled or chronically ill. Payments from the inherited IRA to Patty's trust are subject to the 10-year rule.

If the trust is drafted so the EDB is the sole beneficiary of the IRA funds during her lifetime, RMDs can be stretched over her single life expectancy. However, any beneficiary who has a right to the funds upon the death of the EDB must use the 10-year rule.

Consider this different scenario. Cathy names a trust for her disabled daughter, Emily, age 43, as the beneficiary of her IRA. The trust provides that any funds left in the trust at Emily's death will go to her younger sister, Amanda, age 41. Amanda is not disabled or chronically ill. During Emily's lifetime, RMDs may be paid from the inherited IRA to the trust based on Emily's single life expectancy. However, at Emily's death, payments from the inherited IRA to Amanda would be subject to the 10-year rule and would need to be paid out by December 31 of the 10th year following the year of Emily's death.

Trusts for Other EDBs

The IRS-proposed SECURE Act regulations make clear that, in addition to disabled and chronically ill EDBs, other categories within this subgroup of beneficiary royalty are still eligible to stretch IRA trust payouts. For instance, a large IRA left in trust to a minor (who is an EDB) is still eligible for the stretch IRA. A *conduit trust for minor children* (but not grandchildren) is one such example, although once the minor reaches age 21, she or he would no longer qualify as an EDB, and the 10-year rule would kick in.

Consider this example. Rick named as the beneficiary of his IRA a qualified conduit trust established for the benefit of his minor daughter, Ava. She was 12 years old when Rick died in 2020. Until Ava reaches the age of majority (age 21, regardless of state law), RMDs from the inherited IRA to the trust can be stretched over Ava's single life expectancy. However, once Ava reaches age 21, the 10-year rule will apply. This means that after 10 years all the remaining inherited IRA funds will be paid to her while she's possibly still too young to manage a large sum. In addition, under the proposed regulations, RMDs may have to continue (from the inherited IRA to the trust and from the trust to Ava) for years one through nine of the 10-year term (when she is no longer an EDB). Since RMDs had already begun, they cannot be stopped or put on hold until the account is emptied at the end of the 10-year term.

Another example of a trust that's eligible for the stretch is a *conduit trust for a surviving spouse*, including a conduit/QTIP trust for a surviving spouse, as long as all annual RMDs (or income, if higher) are paid out to the spouse with no accumulation in the trust. After the spouse dies, the 10-year rule would apply.

For example, when Loretta died in 2020, the beneficiary of her IRA was a qualified conduit trust for her surviving spouse, Lou. Because Lou was an EDB, the stretch could still apply and RMDs paid to the trust each year based on Lou's remaining single life expectancy.

Similarly, a *conduit trust for a beneficiary who is not more than 10 years younger than the IRA owner* would be eligible for the stretch, but only until the death of this beneficiary, after which the 10-year rule would apply.

NOTE: Just like under the old rules, these trusts must qualify as see-through trusts to be eligible for the stretch IRA.

The Bottom Line About IRA Trusts

These days, most IRA trusts are now more complex and problematic and less likely to accomplish the protection and control you want for your beneficiaries. They can also result in high taxes. I gotta break it to you: Since leaving an IRA or plan to a trust will generally not constitute wise estate planning, it's time to consider other options.

Alternative 1: Spouse as Beneficiary

Since the surviving spouse is an EDB (exempt from the 10-year rule), it may pay to change beneficiaries from children or grandchildren to your spouse. This could extend the time before an inherited IRA will have to be fully taxed and distributed. The law inverts the tax planning here since now a 75-year-old spouse can have a longer life expectancy for payouts than a 25-year-old grandchild, who would have to withdraw within 10 years after death.

Alternative 2: Roth Conversions

If the funds need to be left to a trust, a Roth IRA will likely prove to be a better choice. Begin a plan to draw down the taxable IRA funds at today's low tax rates and convert those funds to Roth IRAs. Then leave the Roth IRA funds to a discretionary trust providing the post-death control, while eliminating trust or personal taxes. The inherited Roth IRA funds will still have to be paid out to the trust by the end of the 10 years, but at least the distributions to the trust or the trust beneficiaries will be income-tax-free, since you will have paid the tax up front when you converted.

Remember Annie from our earlier example? She named a discretionary trust as her IRA beneficiary because she was concerned about her adult children's ability to manage money. Suppose Annie survived 2020, and in 2021, in response to the SECURE Act and historically low tax rates, she decided to convert her traditional IRA to a Roth IRA. She died later in 2021 after naming as her Roth IRA beneficiary a trust for her adult children. The trust will still be subject to the 10-year rule, but big tax bills (if paid to the children) or high trust tax rates (if kept in the trust) are avoided. This is because the Roth IRA funds are tax-free when paid to either the trust or the trust beneficiaries. Even if the Roth IRA funds are left directly to a beneficiary (not in trust), the funds can keep growing for at least 10 years after death. Because, as you know, all Roth IRA owners are deemed to die before their required beginning date, no RMDs will be required until the end of the 10 years, when all the funds must be withdrawn. A Roth IRA account can accumulate tax-free for a decade and then be withdrawn tax-free at the end of the 10 years. It's no stretch IRA, but still not a bad deal.

Alternative 3: Life Insurance

We covered this in Chapter 8, but now life insurance can also resolve the post–SECURE Act trust problems explained above. Life insurance will likely be the big winner here, especially for those of you who wish to leave your funds in trust to keep them protected for your beneficiaries. Once again, the IRA funds can be withdrawn at low tax rates over several years and the after-tax funds can be put into a permanent, cash-value life insurance policy that will satisfy both of your likely estate-planning objectives: post-death control and elimination of taxes, not to mention *larger inheritances* for your beneficiaries.

Life insurance is a much more flexible asset to leave to a trust as there are no RMDs or complex tax rules to worry about, and the proceeds are tax-free. Life insurance can be retained in the trust for the beneficiary or paid out over time, simulating the best parts of the stretch IRA, but without all the tax and trust complications. Of course, you should only do this with funds earmarked for your beneficiaries that you won't need during your lifetime. Even if you do end up needing the funds, though, you could withdraw the cash value tax-free during your lifetime.

Special Needs Beneficiaries

Life insurance can be an effective vehicle for special needs beneficiaries, where funds can remain in the trust to avoid the loss of potential benefits without being taxed.

Second Marriages

Life insurance can also be an excellent option for second-marriage estate planning, where you may want to use a trust to better control the payouts to your current spouse and beneficiaries after that spouse dies. With a life insurance trust, you can more easily arrange it so that after you die the income is payable to your spouse for his or her lifetime, but then after he or she dies, the remainder is paid to beneficiaries that *you* choose (say, children from your first marriage), rather than beneficiaries your spouse might choose (say, his or her children, leaving children from your first marriage disinherited). This is the QTIP trust I referred to earlier in this chapter, commonly used in second or later marriage situations. The QTIP trust generally does not work well with IRA funds because rigid IRA post-death RMD rules collide unfavorably with the complex trust provisions. Life insurance can help address this problematic situation, with better tax results.

Alternative 4: Charitable Remainder Trust (CRT)

If you are charitably inclined, you can leave your IRA to a charitable remainder trust (CRT). The funds transferred from your IRA to the CRT after your death are not taxed, so more of your funds wind up working for the charity and for your beneficiaries. CRTs can simulate the stretch IRA, with yearly payouts to your beneficiaries for a term of years or life. Your beneficiaries will generally need to pay taxes on those payouts. The longer your beneficiary lives and receives payments from the CRT, the greater the CRT benefit.

Here's how to accomplish this: First, seek professional legal and tax advice. Next, make sure you understand exactly how the process works. The funds will go to the charity after your beneficiary dies. If your beneficiary is in poor health or dies early, the funds may go to the charity earlier than planned. There is no payout to a successor beneficiary. But this problem can be avoided by coupling the CRT with life insurance on your beneficiary.

The CRT/life insurance strategy goes like this: The CRT funds that will go to the charity after the death of the beneficiary can be replaced tax-free with life insurance on the beneficiary. After the beneficiary dies, the remaining inherited IRA funds go to the charity, but the family of the beneficiary can receive the life insurance, tax-free, either paid directly to the next-in-line beneficiaries or, if necessary for continued protection, paid to a life insurance trust for their benefit.

Caution: CRTs provide no lifetime access for lump-sum payouts. Your beneficiaries receive only annual distributions and won't have access to lump sums, even for emergencies. That said, some people use CRTs because they want that level of strict protection for their beneficiaries, to avoid large sums being squandered. In addition, CRTs have ongoing trust-administration costs. They are generally only worth it to those charitably inclined who have larger IRAs.

Alternative 5: Leave Your IRA Directly to a Charity

If you wish to leave something to a favorite charity, you can leave your IRA funds directly to the charity without a CRT. Traditional IRAs are the best funds to leave to a charity since they, unlike your beneficiaries, don't pay taxes when they inherit. By leaving a portion of your taxable IRA funds to charity, your beneficiaries will become heir to less of an inherited IRA tax problem and more of better, non-IRA assets that can receive a step-up in basis, allowing them to inherit the appreciation on those funds income-tax-free. Everyone wins. (Except for Uncle Sam. Boo-hoo.)

The Take-Home Message

Now you have the information you need to understand how the SECURE Act affects IRA trusts. You can see that in most cases the trusts will no longer work for you and your family. However, if worry about your beneficiaries receiving money that they may not be able to handle leads you to believe you still need to name a trust as your IRA beneficiary, get informed. To protect your hard-earned retirement savings for your beneficiaries, review this chapter with your tax, legal, and financial advisors. Evaluate the types of trusts that may still work for certain beneficiaries, but also consider the alternative solutions I have proposed here, many of which can accomplish better results.

Remember, the vehicle you use to get the plan you want doesn't matter, as long as you reach the estate-planning promised land: *larger* inheritances for your beneficiaries, *more* control, and *less* tax.

Just one thing before we move on . . . Don't tell Congress, or they'll ruin this too! Let's keep these new and better planning strategies between us!

PART THREE

WHEN THINGS DON'T GO AS PLANNED

ELEVEN

WHAT TO DO WHEN
STUFF HAPPENS

Experience is a good school. But the fees are high.
—HEINRICH HEINE (1797-1856), GERMAN POET

Wouldn't it be great if everything always worked out just the way it was supposed to? In a perfect world, it does. But, as Tokugawa Ieyasu once said, "Persuade thyself that imperfection and inconvenience are the natural lot of mortals, and there will be no room for discontent, neither for despair." In other words, brace yourself: stuff happens—frequently.

Therefore, I have saved this chapter for last. You might call it an unofficial sixth step to my 5-Step Action Plan for protecting your retirement savings. It deals with the mother(s) of all IRA problems—the unforeseen as well as those issues and situations for which there seem to be no clear-cut rules.

For example, "What if I lose my job and need to take a series of early distributions to keep afloat? Will I have to pay the 10 percent penalty over an extended period of time?"

Or, "What if I screw up and miss a required distribution? Is there no last-minute reprieve from the IRS to the missed RMD penalty?"

Those situations and others are what this chapter is for—emergency use only. Hopefully, you'll never need to know any of what follows. But if stuff happens, as it's been known to do, luckily, this chapter provides a heads-up.

"Oh, Crap. I Need It *Now!*"

The combination of people retiring early (by choice or involuntarily) and money building up in retirement accounts is causing more plan owners to look for ways to tap into their plans before they reach the magic age of 59½. Withdrawing early usually means paying a 10 percent penalty, but not always. As you learned in Chapter 4, there are exceptions.

One exception growing in popularity these days is known as *annuitizing*. It's also called *SEPPs* (taking a *series of substantially equal periodic payments*). But that acronym can be confused with SEPs (simplified employee pensions), which is altogether different. So, I refer to the process as "annuitizing" or, as tax geeks (like me) call it, "72(t)," for the section of the Internal Revenue Code where the exception is found. Try out that nomenclature at parties with accountants and actuaries. What a hit you'll be!

72(t) Basics

The general purpose of annuitizing is that you can tap your IRA before age 59½ without a 10 percent penalty. This can be done by committing to a plan of withdrawals according to the rules set out in Section 72(t)(2)(A)(iv) of the Internal Revenue Code. You can begin a 72(t) payment schedule at any age. There is no required starting age. While annuitizing a company retirement plan requires that you first have terminated your employment with that company, that rule does not apply to IRAs. The 72(t) payments from an IRA qualify at any age even if you are still working.

The payments must continue for five years or until you reach 59½, whichever period is longer. During the payment period, the withdrawals cannot be "modified," meaning the method you elect for calculating the payments cannot be changed. Once you commit to 72(t)s from an IRA, you must continue with your chosen payment schedule from that IRA until you reach the end of the 5-year period or age 59½. If you do not stick with your chosen method of payments, you will no longer qualify for the exemption from the 10 percent penalty. Actually, it's even worse: The penalty will be reinstated retroactively.

Say, for example, you (the IRA owner) were 42 years old when you began your 72(t)s. You must continue your chosen withdrawal plan for 17½ years, until you reach age 59½. Assume you are now 57 and you have been sticking to the plan for the past 15 years; you've withdrawn $10,000 per year ($150,000) during that time. You have only two and a half more years to go. But your IRA has grown substantially and next year, at age 58, you decide to withdraw $50,000 instead of the usual $10,000. You figure, "What the hell, the IRS won't care; it'll be getting more tax dollars from me, faster."

Wrong! The IRS will consider that extra withdrawal a modification of the payment schedule and you will blow your penalty exemption. Because the 10 percent penalty is triggered retroactively, that means you will owe the penalty on the $150,000 of previous withdrawals plus the $50,000 withdrawal from the current year. You'll owe $20,000 in penalties ($200,000 of withdrawals x 10 percent = $20,000). The penalty, plus interest, is all due in the year of the modification—i.e., the year you fell off the 72(t) wagon. Furthermore, you would owe interest on that penalty amount figured back to each year's 10 percent penalty. The entire amount would be due on the tax return for the year that you changed the schedule and withdrew the $50,000. In addition, the tax on the $50,000 would be due in that year. It's a veritable domino effect of penalties! This is why it is so important not to stop the payments and not to increase or decrease them during the 72(t) payment period.

Here's another side of the coin: If during the 72(t) payment term it turns out that your financial situation changed and you do not need as much as you thought you would, you cannot contribute the money you do not need back to your IRA. That's because payments that are part of "a series of substantially equal periodic payments" (now you know why it's easier to call them 72(t) payments) are not eligible to be rolled over. This also means that these payments cannot be converted to a Roth IRA, because only eligible rollover distributions can be converted to a Roth. (The IRA account balance itself can be converted to a Roth during the 72(t) term, but the 72(t) distributions cannot.) If you wish to convert to a Roth IRA during your 72(t) term, you will remain exempt from the 10 percent penalty as long as the 72(t) payments continue (unchanged) from the Roth IRA. If you are annuitizing a traditional IRA and want to convert it to a Roth IRA during the payment term, you should convert the entire IRA, not just a portion of it. This way, you won't have to maintain two 72(t) payment schedules—one for the Roth and one for the balance remaining (the part not converted) in the traditional IRA.

If you do convert, Roth IRAs can be annuitized in the same manner and under the same rules as traditional IRAs. But the only situation where you would find yourself annuitizing your Roth IRA would be if you needed to withdraw from it within the first five years of the conversion. Otherwise, all withdrawals of converted Roth funds are tax-free, and if they are tax-free, they cannot be subject to the 10 percent penalty (because that applies only to taxable distributions and to withdrawals of converted funds if they have not been held for five years). Therefore, if you needed to withdraw from your Roth IRA before age 59½, you would first simply withdraw your contributions tax- and penalty-free (see Chapter 7).

If you have withdrawn all your contributions, and you still need more money, you could then set up a 72(t) schedule for the Roth IRA earnings. But that seems a little ridiculous unless the earnings are huge and you need to tap into those earnings—in which case, you probably should not have converted in the first place. But if you already have, you are probably better off simply taking what you need from the Roth IRA, paying the tax and penalty on the earnings, and not bothering to maintain a 72(t) schedule for Roth IRA earnings, which are likely minimal at this point and would result in equally minimal 72(t) payments. Even though the 72(t) payments on the Roth earnings will be penalty-free, they will still be subject to income tax, since you have not yet reached age 59½.

Death and Disability Exceptions

If the payment schedule is interrupted during the 72(t) term due to death or disability, the 10 percent penalty does not apply. For the disability exception to apply, however, the disability must be serious and qualify under IRS guidelines (as defined in Chapter 4). If the IRA owner is disabled, then any distribution, even a lump-sum distribution of the entire IRA during the 72(t) payment term, will be exempt from the 10 percent penalty. Under the disability exception, the 72(t) payment schedule can be either stopped or accelerated penalty-free.

Another (Possible) 10 Percent Penalty Exception

Another possibility for withdrawing more than the 72(t) schedule amount without causing a modification arises out of a 2009 case (*Gregory T. and Kim D. Benz v. Commissioner; 132 T.C. No. 15; No. 15867-07, May 11, 2009*) in which the U.S. Tax Court ruled that Kim Benz's 72(t) payment plan had not been modified when she took an additional distribution from an IRA that was making distributions under a 72(t) payment plan and used it for education. Although the IRS sought to have the 10 percent early withdrawal penalty assessed, the court ruled that the extra distribution did not, in fact, trigger the 10 percent penalty.

This single court decision does not guarantee that this strategy will work from here on out, but it does offer interesting information about what might be possible.

72(t) Planning Opportunities Using Multiple IRAs

Taking 72(t)s from one IRA has no effect on your other IRAs. If you have several IRAs and only annuitize one of them, then you are only committed to the 72(t) payment schedule for that particular IRA. Since each IRA is treated separately, it's important to learn how to take advantage of savings opportunities and to avoid tax traps associated with multiple accounts.

If you have one IRA and are considering annuitizing to generate monthly or annual income, first calculate how much you will need. If you will need more income than your IRA will pay out using the 72(t) payment schedule, then there is nothing else you can do but annuitize that entire IRA. But if you need less cash than your IRA will pay out, you should consider splitting your IRA into two or more separate IRAs, enabling you to annuitize one IRA and leave the other IRAs alone. If it turns out that you require more income later, your other IRAs are still available for 72(t) withdrawals. You can have an unlimited number of payment schedules ongoing at the same time or at different times, providing you with the most flexibility.

Even though you must commit to a payment schedule, by splitting IRAs you can be a little more conservative and take only what you need currently from one IRA. If your cash needs increase, you can always start a new 72(t) plan with IRA #2. But before you begin annuitizing IRA #2, you might consider splitting *that* IRA, leaving you with still another IRA (IRA #3). You should always try to keep some IRA money free from a 72(t) commitment. This way, if your financial situation changes and you no longer need that much income, you still have an IRA that remains intact. If it turns out that you need more income, you will still have an IRA to deploy with a new 72(t) schedule. Or you can simply withdraw from that IRA and pay the one-time expense of taxes and penalty without having to urgently pull extra from an IRA that is already being annuitized, which would cause a retroactive 10 percent penalty.

Figure 7. IRS Guidelines for Taking 72(t) Payments

This is the official IRS explanation of what constitutes "a series of substantially equal periodic payments." IRS Notice 2022-6 reproduced here describes the three acceptable methods for taking 72(t) payments. The notice, as well as Revenue Ruling 2002-62, allows a onetime switch from either the amortization or annuity factor methods to the minimum distribution method, providing some relief for those whose retirement account balances have declined and who would have been forced by the 72(t) amortization or annuity factor methods to take payments that were disproportionately large, given the size of their account balance.

IRS Notice 2022-6
IRS Guidance for Taking 72(t) Payments

01 *General rule.* Payments in a series are considered substantially equal periodic payments within the meaning of section 72(t)(2)(A)(iv) if they are determined in accordance with one of the three methods described in section 3.01(a) through (c) of this notice (which are based on the three methods described in Rev. Rul. 2002-62).

(a) *The required minimum distribution method.* The annual payment for each distribution year is determined by dividing the account balance for that distribution year by the number of years from the chosen life expectancy table in section 3.02(a) of this notice for that distribution year. Under this method, the account balance, the number of years from the chosen life expectancy table, and the resulting annual payments are redetermined for each distribution year. This redetermination of the annual payment is not considered a modification of the series of substantially equal periodic payments, provided that the required minimum distribution method continues to be used and the same life expectancy tables continue to be used, except to the extent required in section 3.02(b) of this notice.

(b) *The fixed amortization method.* The annual payment for each distribution year is determined as the amount that will result in the level amortization of the account balance over a specified number of years determined using the chosen life expectancy table under section 3.02(a) of this notice and an interest rate that is permitted pursuant to section 3.02(c) of this notice. Under this method, once the account balance, the number of years from the chosen life expectancy table, and the resulting annual payment are determined for the first distribution year, the annual payment is the same amount in each succeeding distribution year.

(c) *The fixed annuitization method.* The annual payment for each distribution year is determined by dividing the account balance by an annuity factor that is the present value of an annuity of $1 per year beginning at the employee's age and continuing for the life of the employee (or the joint lives of the employee and designated beneficiary). The annuity factor is derived using the mortality rates in § 1.401(a)(9)-9(e) and an interest rate that is permitted pursuant to section 3.02(c) of this notice. Under this method, once the account balance, the annuity factor, and the resulting annual payment are determined for the first distribution year, the annual payment is the same amount in each succeeding distribution year.

72(t) Payment Options

Neither the tax code nor the regulations explain how annual 72(t) withdrawals should be calculated. Internal Revenue Code Section 72(t)(2)(A)(iv) states only that the series of payments must be "part of a series of substantially equal periodic payments (not less frequently than annually) made for the life (or life expectancy) of the employee or the joint lives (or joint life expectancies) of such employee and his designated beneficiary."

Like our Constitution, these words are ripe for interpretation; they can mean many things, depending upon the interpreter. IRS Notice 2022-6 (see Figure 7), IRS Revenue Ruling 2002-62, and Notice 89-25 provide the only official guidance that all IRA owners can rely on as to what is an acceptable 72(t) payment plan for withdrawing before age 59½ penalty-free.

All 72(t) payment methods are based on the IRA owner's single life expectancy (or on the joint life expectancy of the IRA owner and his or her IRA beneficiary). If you are looking to create higher annual withdrawals, you would use only a single life expectancy. This does not mean that you should not name a beneficiary on your IRA (you should); it just means that for 72(t) payment purposes, you will use a single life expectancy calculation. When you are annuitizing your IRA before 59½, you cannot change the life expectancy once you elect it, so electing single life at this point affords the highest possible payments to meet your income needs.

By electing single life for calculating 72(t)s, you'll get more mileage out of your IRA than you would with a joint life expectancy, allowing you to annuitize less of your IRA. This is the fundamental strategy for gaining the most benefit out of annuitizing your IRA—because you want to be able to produce the largest possible 72(t) payment from the smallest amount of IRA money. This will preserve more of your IRA for future 72(t) payments, if needed. Once you have accomplished this goal of gaining the most from the least, you can then split your IRA into two or more IRAs and annuitize only the one from which you need to draw income.

Three Methods–Which Should You Choose?

IRS Notice 2022-6, Revenue Ruling 2002-62, and IRS Notice 89-25 describe three allowable methods for calculating 72(t) payments:

1. Minimum distribution method
2. Amortization method
3. Annuity factor method

A WORD TO THE WISE

Although IRS Notice 2022-6, Revenue Ruling 2002-62, and IRS Notice 89-25 offer a list of acceptable 72(t) distribution methods, this does not mean that these methods are the only acceptable ones. According to numerous IRS rulings, if the payments are "part of a series of substantially equal periodic payments," any method that achieves that would be fine. If you do not use one of the three methods officially "blessed" by the IRS, however, you should request your own IRS ruling. It would be foolish to risk a penalty by not having your method "blessed" too. Unfortunately, though, the IRS fees and legal and tax costs for preparing such a ruling can run into thousands upon thousands of dollars. Plus, the IRS ruling process can take six to nine months and, even then, your request may be denied. That's a problem when you need the money now. Instead, avoid this horrendous potential waste of time and money and use one of the three IRS-approved methods.

The *minimum distribution method* is calculated in the same manner as required minimum distributions (RMDs) when you reach your required beginning date (RBD) (see Chapter 4). This method, however, will generally produce the lowest annual 72(t) payment. Increases in the IRA balance each year will increase the annual payments using the minimum distribution method. But unless the IRA balance appreciates substantially each year, the minimum distribution method will still produce lower payments than the other two methods. The IRA balance could also decline, and under the minimum distribution method that would reduce your 72(t) payments.

If you are looking for consistently higher annual withdrawals, the *amortization method* or the *annuity factor method* are the best options. Both will allow you to beef up annual 72(t) payments by applying an interest rate to the payment schedule. The higher the interest rate, the larger your payments will be. You can't go crazy here, though. IRS Notice 89-25 states that the interest rate must "not exceed a reasonable interest rate on the date payments commence."

But what is a reasonable interest rate? In the latest release, Notice 2022-6, the IRS defined a reasonable interest rate as "any interest rate that is not more than the greater of 5 percent or 120 percent of the federal mid-term rate . . . for either of the two months immediately preceding the month in which the distribution begins."

The requirement under all methods that the payments be made

at least annually does not mean that you must use a calendar year. You can choose any year (a fiscal or calendar year) you wish, but once you make your choice you must stick with that year. For example, if your year for taking 72(t) payments begins on September 21, 2024, you must take your required payments for that year by September 20, 2025. You must continue using a September 20 fiscal year for the duration of your 72(t) payment term.

The Best 72(t) Calculation and Planning Resources

Remember that once you create a 72(t) payment plan you must stick with it to avoid penalties. To help you plan and structure your payment schedule (including making all the calculations that will help you compare methods), I advise using software such as Retirement Distributions Planner by Brentmark Software (www.brentmark .com), which includes the latest annuity table.

72(t)s from Your Company Retirement Plan

The annuitizing exception is also available for withdrawals from company plans, but only if you are no longer working there and the plan allows it. You can begin at any age if the 72(t) payments from your company plan begin after your separation from service.

If you qualify to annuitize from your company plan, your distributions are exempt from the 20 percent mandatory withholding tax requirements that apply to most other distributions from qualified plans.

If you begin annuitizing from your company plan, you can still roll the plan money over to an IRA during the payment term if you continue with your IRA on the same 72(t) payment schedule that originated with your plan, without any modifications. The IRS allowed this in two private letter rulings (PLRs 9103046 and 9221052). The IRS did not allow the reverse, however. In another private letter ruling (PLR 9818055), the IRS would not allow an IRA owner who was taking 72(t) payments from her IRA to roll the IRA back to a company plan without triggering the 10 percent penalty retro-actively. Here, the IRS said that this would be a modification be-cause the 72(t) schedule was terminated after the transfer back to the employer plan. But that was before EGTRRA 2001, which now allows all taxable IRA funds (not only conduit IRAs, which are ex-plained in "Talking the Talk" at the start of this book) to be rolled over to company retirement plans. So, the IRS could change its mind on this. Stay tuned.

Is 72(t) Right for You?

There are four common situations where annuitizing a retirement account before reaching 59½ may be a good move: early retire-ment, estate planning, divorce, and financial hardship.

Early Retirement

This is the most common situation. There are more and more early retirees (or, unfortunately, forced retirees) who either are unable to go back to work or do not want to just yet. Many of them don't know what they want to do. They often leave their company with a large retirement account but have little else to live on while they are on hiatus. If this sounds like you, then a 72(t) schedule fits the bill. If you don't have money available to you beyond your retire-ment savings, you'll need to tap your account. If you are under 59½, a 72(t) schedule can provide you with an income stream to live on without incurring the 10 percent penalty. If you are age 55 or over in the year you retire, you can tap your company retirement plan penalty-free. If you do not qualify for the age-55 exception, then you should roll over the retirement account to an IRA. If you are no longer working for your company, you could begin the 72(t) schedule from your company plan. But that is usually not the best option given the increased flexibility of an IRA. After you roll it over, you can split your IRA into two or more IRAs. One IRA will be annuitized while the other(s) will remain intact. The amount of the split depends on the amount of annual income that you'll need during the 72(t) term.

Estate Planning

One estate-planning objective is liquidity. This means having money (other than IRA funds) to pay estate taxes. Buying life insurance is the most cost-effective way to provide this kind of cash. But if all your funds are tied up in your IRA, where will the money come from to pay the insurance premiums? The answer may be 72(t) payments. This is a powerful strategy because you can use IRA withdrawals to cover the premiums without incurring penalties, even though you're under 59½. The life insurance should be set up outside your estate to keep the proceeds estate-tax-free—but you already know that from Chapter 8.

If your IRA is large and represents most of your estate, you can annuitize it and use the money to make gifts as a way of removing some of your IRA from your estate without having to wait until age 59½, when the 10 percent penalty will no longer apply.

The trade-off with each of the estate planning strategies I've cited is that you will be giving up the long-term benefits of the tax deferral.

Divorce

"She cried, and the judge wiped her tears with my checkbook," commented much-married millionaire Tommy Manville (1894-1967) on the subject of divorce. Since these days an IRA often represents the largest single asset in an estate, it is no surprise that these accounts are being thrust into the divorce arena more frequently. If cash is needed to fund a property settlement or to pay ongoing maintenance (alimony), the IRA may be the only place to find it. If you are under 59½, then a 72(t) payment schedule may be the answer. The only problem is, again, that the payments under even the best 72(t) method may not be enough to cover the actual expense, especially for young IRA owners.

An IRA can be transferred tax- and penalty-free to a former spouse, pursuant to a divorce or separate maintenance decree, by transferring the IRA assets to the former spouse's IRA. But that means the IRA owner loses all or part of the IRA. By using the 72(t) exception instead, the IRA owner keeps his or her IRA and can tap it penalty-free (not tax-free, though, as in the transfer to the former spouse) and use the 72(t) payments to make ongoing support or alimony payments without forking over the IRA to the former spouse.

If the IRA owner is bound by a divorce agreement to transfer a part of the IRA from which he or she is currently taking 72(t) payments for the former spouse, then the IRS will allow the 72(t) payments to be reduced based on the amount remaining in the IRA.

For example, if you are taking 72(t) payments from your IRA and the divorce agreement says you must give 55 percent of that IRA to your ex-spouse, you can reduce your 72(t) payment schedule so it is based on having only 45 percent left of your IRA. This will not be considered a modification and your ex-spouse will not have to continue taking 72(t) payments on the 55 percent of your IRA balance that he or she receives. Several IRS PLRs have allowed this treatment.

Another divorce scenario that might call for 72(t) payments is when most of one spouse's non-IRA property is transferred to the former spouse. In return for transferring the non-IRA property, the spouse keeps his or her large IRA. Since this may now be his or her only source of funds to live on, a 72(t) payment schedule could be set up to provide current income.

Financial Hardship

Before you begin a 72(t) schedule to raise cash to resolve money problems, first see if one of the other exceptions to the 10 percent penalty applies. For example, a common financial hardship stems from medical bills. But an exception for medical expenses already exists, and you do not have to itemize on your taxes to qualify for this exception. Similarly, you are also exempt from the 10 percent penalty if you need to withdraw from your IRA to pay for education, you qualify as a first-time homeowner, or you need to pay health insurance premiums while you are unemployed. The SE-CURE 2.0 Act has created a new financial emergencies exception to the 10 percent early distribution penalty from both IRAs and company plans, but it is very limited. The most that can be withdrawn is $1,000 in a year. Beyond this limited exception, there is no exemption from the 10 percent penalty for indeterminate "financial hardship"—only those specified under one of the other exceptions qualify. The 72(t) schedule then should only be used as a last resort if no other funds are available and no other exceptions apply.

Who Should Be Using 72(t)?

Many early retirees look at 72(t) as an easy way to get to their retirement cash without paying the 10 percent toll. Before you take the 72(t) plunge, ask yourself the following questions:

Can You Afford to Deplete Your Retirement Savings Now?

With all the exceptions it offers, Congress has actually made it too easy to tap retirement funds early. The *R* in IRA is for retirement. Although your IRA or other retirement account has built up nicely over the years, the buildup is *not* for spending now. So, any decision to dip into your nest egg early should be carefully and seriously evaluated. Annuitizing your IRA early should be done only as a last resort, and the money used only for necessities, not for a vacation, that new $1,000 iPhone, or any other purchase that you could do without and still survive. (Well, maybe not the new iPhone!)

If you tap into your savings now, what will be left for you when you retire? Keep in mind that it's very hard to just withdraw a little. That's like being on a diet and cheating just a bit. You know how that goes. You (and I) figure that since you've already had the fried chicken, you may as well have the French fries, and then dessert quickly follows. Pretty soon you're combing the local convenience stores for the newest Ben & Jerry's ice cream flavors—and then you're too tired and full to hit the gym.

Tapping your retirement account early is just as tempting. Even though under Section 72(t) you will only be withdrawing a small amount penalty-free, the fact that you are already breaking into it (just like going off your diet a little) may lead you to start withdrawing more and paying the penalty, rationalizing along the way that there's still plenty of money left in the account and why shouldn't you enjoy it now? But soon your hard-won *retirement* savings account becomes a costly piggy bank funding all kinds of things. That temptation may lead you to eventually wipe out your retirement savings before you have even reached age 59½.

How Much Do You Have in Your Retirement Account?

The more you have in an IRA or other retirement account, the higher your 72(t) payments will be, and even after you complete the 72(t) term you will have plenty left for retirement. There are many people, especially professionals and executives, who have large retirement accounts and few other assets to live on. For this group and others with a healthy retirement account, the 72(t) option works well.

The real question is usually: How little do you have in your IRA? That is often the problem. If there is not much to annuitize, then your 72(t) payments will be too small to make a difference, unless you don't really need much.

Are You Too Young or Too Old?

Did you ever think that being 45 years old would be too young for anything? Well, it's probably too young for 72(t). If you begin annuitizing too early, you'll be stuck with a long-term payment schedule. The payments will be small and not likely to be enough to meet your needs. That's because you have two factors working against you.

First is your life expectancy. The younger you are, the longer your life expectancy is for 72(t) calculation purposes and the smaller your annual payments will be. No, you cannot file for a living-on-the-edge exception to lower your life expectancy and withdraw larger amounts under 72(t).

The second problem with starting a 72(t) schedule too early is that the younger you are, the less money you are likely to have accumulated in your IRA. If you are in your forties and need some cash, the last thing you should be considering is a long-term plan to deplete your retirement savings. You might be better off with a home equity loan. Or, if you need the funds for a onetime expense and have no other place to withdraw from except your IRA, then you could withdraw what you need for that one time and pay the 10 percent penalty. This way, you take the hit and don't have to bother with maintaining a 72(t) schedule.

For those of you between 54½ and 59½ years old, you will have to maintain the 72(t) for five years. If you can wait it out without withdrawing from your IRA until you reach 59½, you are probably better off doing so because then you will be able to take out as much as you like with no penalty. You won't have to stick to any schedule at all. In fact, between 59½ and 73, you will not have an IRA penalty. The 10 percent penalty applies only before age 59½.

If you are close to 59½, it may even pay to forget the 72(t) schedule, withdraw what you need from your IRA, and pay the 10 percent penalty on the amount you withdraw. For example, let's say you are 58 and need $50,000 for a onetime expense, but have no source to tap other than your IRA. Unfortunately, your IRA balance is not large enough to produce a $50,000 annual payment under any of the various 72(t) payment methods. You can withdraw the $50,000 from your IRA, pay the tax and a $5,000 penalty, and be done with it. The following year, you'll turn 59½ years old and after that you can withdraw any amount you like penalty-free, without being stuck with a payment schedule (that likely does not produce enough annually anyway).

If you borrowed from a bank, or worse, used your credit card, the interest cost over even a few years would far exceed the $5,000 IRS penalty.

Are You Ready for a Commitment?

I'm not talking about marriage here, but something that lasts longer than many marriages: a 72(t) payment schedule. At a minimum, you will be locked into a 5-year schedule. Depending on your age, that schedule could extend over many more years. For example, a 40-year-old must continue the 72(t) schedule for almost 20 years. Are you ready to commit for that long? Even on the short side, for those age 54½ or over, it's still a 5-year plan. The younger you are, the longer your schedule will be and the more you should give the 72(t) option some serious thought before saying "I do."

What Other (Non-IRA) Sources of Funds Are Available?

IRA withdrawals are expensive even without the 10 percent penalty. You must pay ordinary income tax on your IRA or retirement plan distributions, and no capital gains rates or other preferential tax treatments apply on IRA withdrawals.

A sale of stock that was held more than one year might be taxed at only 15 percent (or even zero percent if you're within lower bracket). Withdrawing money from a savings account is not taxable at all. Borrowing is also tax-free, but carries an interest cost, although that cost may be offset if the interest is tax-deductible as either home mortgage interest or investment interest expense, whereas the interest on a loan from your 401(k) plan is considered personal nondeductible interest. I may sound like a broken record, but this is important: Only use your IRA money as a last resort. Retirement money is not only the most expensive money to use, it is also the hardest money to replace since it only accumulates over many years of disciplined saving. You'll also be losing out on the benefit of the long-term tax-deferred buildup.

Have You *Really* Retired?

Have you really retired before reaching 59½? If so, you had better have a ton of cash put away because you will need it. You might well spend more years in retirement than you did working—so, before you consider annuitizing your IRA, factor in the possibility of taking another job either out of necessity or sheer boredom.

If you are pretty sure about early retirement and most of your wealth is tied up in an IRA or qualified retirement plan, then annuitizing your IRA would be a good idea for two reasons. First, it's the only money you have; second, you are using the money for its intended purpose: your retirement (albeit a bit early). If you can afford it, good for you! (I'm jealous.) Once you complete your 72(t) term, you can keep withdrawing at any pace you like.

But if there is some chance you'll go back to work, you may be better off not beginning a long-term 72(t) schedule. See if you can use other non-IRA funds until you are sure that retiring at age 35 is really right for you. (Where do you sign up for that, anyway? Oh right, you can join the FIRE movement ["financial independence, retire early"]. I'll get right on that!) But, seriously, after what this country and our workers have been through recently, many of us will have to put those dreams on hold for a while. We need to plan for the long term and unexpected "black swan" events along the way. Keep saving all you can.

Do You Have a Company Plan?

If you have a retirement plan from a company and you parted ways between the ages of 55 and 59½, you can withdraw from your company plan with no penalty. It does not matter why you are no longer working—whether you quit, got fired, retired, or were downsized. As long as you were what the tax law calls "separated from service" at age 55 or older, you can withdraw from your company plan with no 10 percent penalty.

The age-55 exception is available only on withdrawals from company plans—401(k)s, qualified plans, etc.—and not from IRAs. If this applies to you (for example, if you are 56 years old and left your company after your 55th birthday), then you do not need to annuitize your IRA. Do not roll your plan money over to your IRA until you reach 59½. Until then, you can withdraw as much as you wish penalty-free from your company plan. You'll still pay income tax, of course, but no 10 percent penalty.

In addition to the age-55 exception, an age-50 exception is available for distributions from governmental plans by state, local, and federal public-safety workers such as police, firefighters, emergency medical service workers, certain customs officials, Border Protection officers, air traffic controllers, nuclear materials couriers, U.S. Capitol Police, Supreme Court Police, and diplomatic security special agents of the Department of State. The exception applies if you have separated from service in the year that you turned age 50 or older. SECURE 2.0 Act of 2022 extends the age-50 public safety exception to private-sector firefighters and corrections officers who are employees of state and local governments. It also modifies the exception to apply upon the earlier of age 50 or 25 years of service.

The age-50/25-years exception, like the age-55 exception, can eliminate the need for setting up early-payment plans—72(t) payment schedules—in order to avoid the 10 percent penalty.

Snapshot of the 72(t) Rules

The 72(t) payments:

- Must continue for at least five years or until age 59½, whichever period is longer.
- Must be distributed at least annually (calendar or fiscal year).
- Must be substantially equal; the payment formula cannot be changed; the payments cannot be stopped during the payment term, unless you become disabled or die (except that the IRS allows a onetime switch to the RMD method).
- Generally cannot make any deposits to, or other distributions from, the 72(t) account.
- Can be computed using either a single or joint life, but once you select single or joint life, you must stick with that choice throughout the 72(t) term.
- Will be larger using a single life expectancy as opposed to a joint life expectancy.
- Cannot begin from a company plan until after you leave your company.
- Can begin at any age from an IRA.
- Are applicable only to the IRA being annuitized (IRAs can be split so that one IRA can be annuitized while others can remain intact for future use).

"My IRA Has Fallen and It Can't Get Up!"

What if the stock market heads south and the value of your IRA or 401(k) is in free fall? Are you entitled to any tax benefits on losses? Unfortunately, due to the Tax Cuts and Jobs Act, which eliminated most of the miscellaneous itemized deductions, Uncle Sam offers little help in this regard.

72(t) Payments and IRA Losses

If you are withdrawing a series of substantially equal periodic payments—which, as you now know, are called 72(t) payments—a market decline may create tax problems for you. If the value of the IRA from which you are withdrawing your 72(t) payments has declined substantially, there may not be enough funds in the IRA to satisfy your required 72(t) payment—or your payment may be eating up a much larger portion of your IRA than you had planned. And if you do not satisfy your required 72(t) payment, you will have modified the payment schedule, thus triggering the 10 percent penalty retroactively.

But take heart. Happily, all is not lost, in this case at least. The IRS has come through with some relief for you, however limited. IRS Notice 2022-6 allows you a onetime-only switchover from the method you are currently using to determine your 72(t) payments (either the amortization or annuity factor) to the minimum-distribution method. Under this method, 72(t) payments for future years are based on your updated retirement account balance. If your balance increases, your payments increase. If it declines, your 72(t) payments decline—but in either case you don't trigger the dreaded 10 percent retroactive penalty.

Relief for Decimated Retirement Accounts

May this provision never apply to you. If you are on a 72(t) schedule and have been literally wiped out—that is, your account balance equals zero—the IRS has a heart. Obviously if there is nothing left, you cannot continue your 72(t) payments. The IRS will not consider this a modification and will not assess the 10 percent penalty. They are kindly limiting your losses to 100 percent. To do otherwise would be pretty darned evil.

> ### TIP!
>
> If your IRA has bottomed out because of a plunging stock market, consider converting to a Roth IRA if you qualify (see Chapter 7). For example, if you have an IRA that has lost 40 percent of its value, you will only pay tax on its current value by converting now. That's like a 40-percent-off sale! And when the market rebounds and grows over the long haul, which has historically been the case, all that increase in value will go untaxed in the Roth!

Company Stock

If your 401(k) or other company retirement plan contains highly appreciated company stock, you can withdraw the stock instead of rolling it over and only pay tax on the original cost to the plan. So, if the cost of the stock in your plan was $10 and now it is worth $50, your stock has appreciated by $40. This appreciation is called *net unrealized appreciation (NUA)* and is explained in detail in Chapter 3. But here's the *Reader's Digest* version: NUA is not taxed until the stock is sold, and even then, it is only taxed at capital gains rates, regardless of how long the stock was held in the plan. But what happens if the stock declines in value? Is there such a thing as *net unrealized depreciation (NUD)*? By golly, Jethro, yes there is! Here's a real-life example of, first, NUA at work, then NUD:

Assume that the cost of the stock in your plan was $10 and the value at the time you distribute the shares from the plan to your taxable broker account (not a rollover) is $50. The NUA is $40. When you transfer the shares out of the plan, you'll pay tax on only the $10 cost. The NUA is not taxed until the shares are sold. The $40 NUA will be taxed at long-term capital gains rates when the shares are sold.

Now let's say instead that you sell the shares 10 months after they were transferred to you from the plan, at which time they are worth $55. The $40 of NUA is taxed at the capital gains rate and the $5 of further appreciation is taxed at ordinary income tax rates. If the stock had been held for more than one year from the date of the distribution from the plan, then the $5 would have been taxed at capital gains rates as well.

OK, same facts as before, except now let's say the stock has dropped in value from $55 to $30 when you sell your shares. Are you locked into paying tax on the $40 NUA? No. That value does not exist anymore. To determine the amount that will be taxed when the stock is sold for $30, you begin with your basis in the stock, which is the original $10 cost you already paid tax on. You'll now pay tax on $20. If the shares dropped to $4 when you sold, you would have a long-term capital loss of $6 (the $10 basis less the $4 selling price).

Alternate Valuation and IRAs

Here is one way to get the government to really share your pain when the market drops. If you're killed by a plunging decline in the value of your estate—and I mean literally—then your heirs may benefit from any subsequent declines. This benefit is called *alternate valuation*, and your estate may get to pay estate tax on a lower value (generally measured six months after you're gone) because of it.

Alternate valuation can only be used to reduce estate tax—and only if elected on all estate assets. It cannot be elected, say, only on your IRA.

Hardship Withdrawals

Contrary to myth (often a stand-in word for *wishful thinking*), there is no exemption from the 10 percent early withdrawal penalty for financial hardship due to a plunging stock market. (See Chapter 4 for all legit exemptions, including the very limited one—only $1,000 annually—for financial emergencies.) If you tap your IRA before you're 59½ and no exception applies, you pay the penalty. The End.

There is, however, a financial hardship provision in many 401(k) plans. But it only permits participants to withdraw earlier than the plan otherwise allows. The withdrawal itself is still taxable and still subject to the 10 percent early withdrawal penalty (assuming no other exceptions apply).

"I Forgot to Take My RMD!"

Can you get out of the 25 percent penalty, or are you completely screwed? The answer is yes! (Yes, you can get out of it. Scared you, didn't I?)

For years, the penalty for a missed RMD was 50 percent of the amount not taken. SECURE 2.0 changed things beginning in 2023. The penalty was reduced to 25 percent and can be further reduced to 10 percent if the missed RMD is withdrawn during a correction window. For most people, the correction must be made by the end of the second calendar year following the year for which the RMD was missed. The RMD would need to be taken and the 10 percent penalty paid during this window.

Let's say that Bruce celebrates his 74th birthday on September 23, 2024. He has an RMD from his IRA for 2024 that he must take by December 31, 2024. If he fails to take this RMD, he will owe a 25 percent penalty on the amount not taken. However, this penalty will be reduced to 10 percent if he takes the 2024 RMD and pays the penalty by December 31, 2026. It also is not unheard of for the IRS to completely waive the RMD penalty for those who make an honest mistake—and even the IRS can consider forgetting an RMD to be an honest mistake (unless you've read this book—in which case, make sure the IRS doesn't find out). Just don't let things slide and do nothing when you realize you missed an RMD, hoping the IRS won't catch you. People often ask me, "How will the IRS find out?"

And my answer, usually accompanied by a shrug, is, "Beats me; ask the guy in the cell next to you!"

How do you miss an RMD? Sometimes the problem is a miscalculation, or a beneficiary not being aware that they must take RMDs even though they are not yet 73. Taking your RMD out of another person's IRA triggers the penalty as well—another mistake people often make because they misunderstand the rule that says you can withdraw your RMD from any one of your IRAs. One taxpayer (and he's not alone) assumed this meant he could pull from his or his wife's IRA and so he took both of their RMDs from his wife's IRA. The IRS still required him to take the back RMD he'd missed taking from his own. So, he ended up having to withdraw more and pay more tax, but at least the damage wasn't compounded by a 25 percent penalty.

If you miss an RMD, don't worry about amending your return. Didn't anyone ever tell you that you can't change the past? Any withdrawal you make will be deemed a withdrawal within whatever year you actually take out the money.

Caution: Don't Ignore a Missed RMD

Be sure to report the back distributions you missed on your tax return (Form 1040). You'll owe tax on them. Attach Form 5329 ("Additional Taxes on Qualified Plans [Including IRAs] and Other Tax-Favored Accounts") to your return, along with an explanation of why you did not take the RMD. The best explanation, as in most things, is the truth. If you were not aware of RMDs, say it. If you hired a tax preparer and he or she did not advise you of a required distribution, then say that. These are acceptable reasons for which the IRS has, in the past, waived the RMD penalty. Yes, the IRS can waive the missed RMD penalty, but first you must correct the problem. If you do miss an RMD, don't wait. The IRS may grant you this "get-out-of-jail-free" card, but you must file and ask.

Before SECURE 2.0, because Form 5329 is considered a standalone tax return, the statute of limitations did not start to run until that form was filed. This meant the IRS could potentially go back many years to assess a penalty for missed RMDs. Now, the IRS will be limited to a three-year look-back period. Effective December 29, 2022, SECURE 2.0 established a three-year statute of limitations for missed RMDs. That limitations period starts with the tax-filing deadline (not including extensions) for the year for which the RMD is missed. (For those who do not file, the deadline would be the deadline for their return, had they filed.)

For example, in 2023, Steven forgot to take an RMD from his IRA. The statute of limitations on this missed RMD will start on the due date for filing his 2023 tax return. After three years, the IRS can no longer assess the penalty on the missed RMD.

In addition to the missed RMD penalty, Form 5329 is also used to report the 10 percent early distribution penalty (including exceptions to it) and the 6 percent excess contributions penalty. The same advice above goes for filing the form for these penalties. Don't ignore the problem. File the form so the penalties don't continue to build. The ostrich approach won't fix it, I promise.

Automatic Waivers of a Missed RMD Penalty

If the missed RMD was due to reasonable error and proper steps are taken to fix the mistake—including taking the missed RMD and filing Form 5329 with an explanation of the reason for the error—the IRS will normally waive the penalty. However, the IRS-proposed regulations retain the discretionary waiver and address two situations where the IRS will grant an automatic waiver without even having to file Form 5329.

Two Automatic RMD Penalty Waiver Situations:

1. Missed Year-of-Death RMD

The first situation is new and applies when a beneficiary fails to take a year-of-death RMD by the end of the calendar year in which the IRA owner's (or plan participant's) death occurs. In that case, if the year-of-death RMD is taken by the beneficiary's tax-filing deadline, including extensions, an automatic waiver applies. This waiver will be especially helpful in cases when an owner or participant dies near the end of the year before taking their annual RMD.

Example 1:
Michael, age 75, has a traditional IRA with his wife, Holly, as beneficiary. Michael's annual RMD is normally paid on December 15. Michael dies on December 10, 2023. Although Holly is technically responsible for taking his 2023 RMD, she does not become aware of that obligation until early 2024. Before the proposed regulations, Holly would have faced an RMD penalty for not taking the 2023 RMD by December 31, 2023. Now, Holly would be eligible for an automatic waiver if she takes the 2023 RMD by her 2023 tax-filing deadline (April 15, 2024, or October 15, 2024, if she goes on extension).

2. Missed stretch IRA RMD by an EDB, when the IRA owner dies before the RBD
The second automatic waiver can be used by an eligible designated beneficiary (EDB) of an IRA owner (or plan participant) who dies before his or her RMD required beginning date. The automatic waiver applies if the EDB is subject to the stretch by default. If the EDB misses one or more annual RMDs, the RMD penalty for any missed RMD is automatically waived if the EDB elects the 10-year rule by the end of the year nine of the 10-year period. Once the EBD chooses the 10-year rule, he or she must empty the account by the 10th calendar year following the year of death of the IRA owner or plan participant.

Example 2:
Kate died in 2023 at age 65 (before her required beginning date), leaving her IRA to her friend Allie, age 60 (who qualifies as an EDB, and gets the stretch IRA). The IRA document allows EDBs to choose between the 10-year payment and the stretch, and it provides that if no election is made the EDB defaults to the stretch. Because Allie, an EDB, forgot to make an election, the IRA defaulted to the stretch. Then she failed to take her annual RMD for 2024 and 2025. If Allie elects the 10-year rule by December 31, 2032, she will receive an automatic waiver of the RMD penalty for her failure to take the 2024 and 2025 annual RMDs.

Planning Point for EDBs: The 10-Year Rule vs. Stretch IRA

An EDB can elect the 10-year rule, but only when death occurs before the RBD (refer to Chapter 6 for details on the 10-year rule and EDBs). Under the IRS-proposed regulations, when death occurs before the RBD, there are no annual RMDs for years one through nine. The entire balance must be withdrawn by the end of the 10-year term, but there is withdrawal flexibility within the 10 years, allowing the beneficiary to take more tax-efficient withdrawals during that period.

But remember that once the 10-year rule is elected, the stretch IRA is lost.

"I Overcontributed to My IRA . . . Now What?"

Excess IRA Contributions: Too Much of a Good Thing

While it's smart to fund your IRA for retirement, there are limits. You can put in too much. A contribution that is not permitted in an IRA is called an excess contribution. While the bad news is that excess contributions happen easily and often, the good news is that there are many options to fix the problem.

What Is an Excess IRA Contribution?

Some excess contributions are easy to understand; others may be a bit trickier to grasp. For example, if you contribute more than the annual limit to an IRA for the year, that will be considered an excess contribution. This one is pretty clear. Just keep in mind that the contribution limit is *whichever is less* between the amount of earned income or the annual limit (in 2024 this was $7,000).

Another common cause of excess Roth IRA contributions is contributing in a year when income is too high. Many individuals and advisors are not aware of the income limits for Roth IRA contribution eligibility. Income fluctuations or unexpected income in a year can leave you particularly vulnerable. This doesn't pose a problem for traditional IRAs, which don't include income limits on contribution eligibility.

Ineligible rollovers can also result in an excess contribution. How could this happen? Well, if you mistakenly roll over after the 60-day rollover period has already expired or violate the once-per-year rollover rule, you will end up with an excess contribution, instead of a rollover, in your IRA.

For example, let's say Kyle does a 60-day rollover of a distribution from one traditional IRA to another. The next day he rolls over a distribution from his Roth IRA to another Roth. Kyle has violated the once-per-year rollover rule. As a result, the funds that were deposited to the Roth IRA are not considered a rollover, and Kyle now has an excess contribution in his Roth IRA.

Older individuals can be at a higher risk for excess contributions due to rollover mistakes. This is because of the rule that says that the required minimum distribution (RMD) for the year cannot be rolled over. In fact, the RMD for the IRA must be taken before any of the funds in the IRA are eligible for rollover. If you mistakenly roll over an RMD, you will end up with an excess contribution. For this purpose, conversions to Roth IRAs are considered rollovers. So, if you include your RMD in a conversion, you will wind up with an excess contribution in your Roth IRA.

For example, take Carla, age 75, who has not taken her $9,000 RMD for the year. Instead, she converts her entire IRA balance to a Roth IRA. Now Carla's RMD of $9,000 is considered an excess contribution in the Roth IRA. Unfortunately, she can't fix the problem just by taking the $9,000 distribution from the Roth account. It is not that easy! She will have to follow certain procedures to correct the excess contribution.

What's the Fix?

Fixing an excess contribution depends upon several different factors. The first is timing, which, as in much of life, is everything. The options you have available will depend a great deal on *when* you're fixing the excess contribution.

The second factor that matters is *what* you want to achieve. Do you want to move the funds to a different type of IRA by recharacterizing? Do you want to withdraw the excess? Remember, you are limited by what the rules allow.

October 15 Deadline

When it comes to timing for excess contribution correction, the key deadline to remember is October 15 of the year following the year for which the excess contribution is made. There are two very different sets of options for correcting excess contributions: one that applies to corrections made before the deadline and another that applies after the deadline.

A 6 percent penalty applies to excess contributions. This penalty is not a one-and-done thing but instead will apply every year that an excess contribution remains in the IRA (subject to a six-year statute of limitations, discussed below). *The only way to avoid the 6 percent penalty when an excess contribution occurs is to correct it by the October 15 deadline.* This is why when it comes to correcting excess contributions sooner is always better.

Fixes *Before* the Deadline

If an excess contribution is discovered before the deadline, you will have two avenues for remedying the error before the 6 percent penalty kicks in: You can withdraw the contribution or recharacterize it. With either choice, the net income attributable (NIA) to the excess contribution must accompany the contribution. The IRS determines earnings in the total account and then determines the portion attributable to the excess contribution. The NIA is calculated using a special IRS-approved formula. Many times, the IRA custodian will do the calculation, but a worksheet with the formula can also be found in IRS Publication 590-A.

If a contribution is withdrawn, only the NIA is taxable for the year in which the contribution was made. The amount of the contribution, although withdrawn, is not taxable. For example, let's

say Dawn, age 42, made a $6,500 Roth IRA contribution. She discovered that her income was too high for her to be eligible to make that contribution but corrected the excess contribution before the October 15 deadline by withdrawing it along with the NIA of $400. While the excess contribution amount of $6,500 is not taxable, the earnings of $400 are taxable for the year in which Dawn made the contribution. There is no way to avoid this. Fortunately for Dawn, the SECURE 2.0 Act eliminated the 10 percent early distribution penalty on NIA removed as part of a correction of an excess contribution.

If a contribution is recharacterized, it will move from one type of IRA to another in a reportable, nontaxable transfer. The contribution will be treated as though it had originally been made to the IRA to which it is recharacterized.

Let's take our previous example. Instead of correcting her excess contribution by withdrawal, Dawn might decide to recharacterize it to a traditional IRA. That would allow her to do a "back-door" Roth IRA by then converting the traditional IRA contribution. Unlike Roth IRA contributions, Roth conversions have no income limits. If Dawn decides to recharacterize, she would instruct her IRA custodian to transfer the contribution amount and the NIA from her Roth IRA to a traditional IRA. This transfer would be tax-free. Assuming Dawn had no other IRAs, SEP, or SIMPLE accounts, she could then convert the traditional IRA contribution to fund her Roth IRA. Not a bad outcome!

After the Deadline

If you discover the excess IRA contribution after the deadline, you have different options for fixing the mistake. Unfortunately, there is no escaping the 6 percent penalty that must be paid for each year the excess has remained in the IRA. *This penalty will apply for each year the excess contribution is not removed by December 31, and the IRS will not waive it.*

But there is some good news for retirement savers who make mistakes and end up with excess contributions. SECURE 2.0 estab-

lished a six-year statute of limitations on excess IRA contributions. The statute of limitations starts running with the tax-filing deadline (not including extensions) for the year for which the excess occurs. Prior to SECURE 2.0, the statute of limitations was not considered to start until Form 5329 was filed. That meant the IRS could have potentially assessed penalties on excess contributions at any time. Now, the IRS will be limited to the most recent six years.

For example, Rosalita made a Roth IRA contribution for 2023. Unfortunately, she was ineligible because her income was too high. The statute of limitations on this excess contribution started to run on her 2023 tax return due date. After six years, on April 15, 2030, the IRS will no longer be able to assess the penalty on the 2023 excess contribution, and Rosalita will have dodged the 6 percent bullet. But was it a risk worth taking? Nope.

Keep in mind that the excess contribution penalty of 6 percent applies for *each year* that the excess contribution remains in the IRA. That means the cost of an excess contribution from years ago could compound year after year. Rosalita could have ended up paying a hefty $2,520 had the IRS noticed the excess before six years had passed. But at least the new SECURE 2.0 prevents the IRS from looking back even further!

Let's say Richard made a $7,000 IRA contribution for 2022. Because he was retired and no longer had any taxable compensation, the IRS considers this amount an excess contribution. Not realizing this, Richard failed to make a correction, leaving the funds in his IRA. If the IRS decides ten years later, in May 2032, to assess the 6 percent penalty on this excess contribution, they will only be able to assess it for years 2026, 2027, 2028, 2029, 2030, and 2031.

There is a creative exception to the six-year statute of limitations for certain excess contributions. SECURE 2.0 specifically says that no statute of limitations applies in the case of an excess contribution that is "attributable to acquiring property for less than the fair market value." This language allows the IRS and the Tax Court to continue to use the rules for excess contributions to shut down abusive Roth IRA schemes indefinitely, as they have in the past. Such was the approach the IRS took, and the Tax Court approved,

in the 2011 *Paschall* and *Swanson* cases. In these abusive IRA cases, the Tax Court ruled that because Form 5329 was never filed, the statute of limitations never started to run. The IRS was permitted to go back many years to assess penalties based on excess contributions to Roth IRAs. SECURE 2.0 does not change this indefinite look-back ability in bargain sale situations.

So, what should you do if you discover after the October 15 deadline that you have made an excess contribution? Once the deadline has passed, you can fix an excess contribution by withdrawing it or carrying it forward. In the case of withdrawal, you need only remove the contribution amount. For some reason (understood only by the IRS), removing any net income attributable is not required for a withdrawal correction made after the deadline. However, the money withdrawn could result in the contribution becoming taxable on the way out of a traditional IRA, which could mean double taxation—a serious tax hit.

Given that fact, carrying the contribution forward (instead of withdrawing it) may be the way to go. In this case, you do not touch the IRA. Instead, you report the excess contribution on your tax return as a contribution in the next year or several years. The custodian does not need to be notified and does not change any previous reporting. You will be responsible for the 6 percent penalty for each year the excess contribution amounts remain in the IRA.

Consider the following scenario: Hannah, age 48, made a $6,500 contribution to her traditional IRA in January 2023. She forgot about this contribution and made another $6,500 contribution later in the year. She did not discover her error until December 2024, well after the October 15 correction deadline had passed. If she is eligible to make a traditional IRA contribution for 2024, Hannah may consider carrying forward the contribution instead of withdrawing it. She would claim the $6,500 as a contribution on her tax return for 2024. She would have to pay the 6 percent excess contribution penalty for 2023 because the excess was not corrected before the end of the year, but she won't face potential double taxation and she will have grown her nest egg that much bigger.

"I Did a Bad, Bad Thing!"

When IRA market investments are exposed to unprecedented wild volatility—where stocks take a beating one day and then show growth the next—many IRA holders ask about alternative investments for their besieged IRAs. There are alternatives, but you need to be careful. If not handled properly, these transactions could be deemed "prohibited" by the IRS. What happens then? Tax law grants the IRS the power to make your IRA go the way of the dinosaur. The entire balance in your IRA could be stripped of its tax-deferred status and treated as if you'd withdrawn the whole account. In that event, the withdrawal will be subject to income tax and could be further subject to the 10 percent penalty if you're under age 59½ as of the date of your total withdrawal (which is deemed to be the first of the year). You can keep whatever is left after taxes, but your IRA tax shelter will have been lost forever.

Alternative Investments

The list of assets in which IRAs are not allowed to invest is very short. Prohibited investments include life insurance, collectibles, coins (except certain coins minted by the U.S. Treasury), and S-corporation stock. All other types of investments are allowed.

While there is no standard definition of alternative IRA investments, they typically include real estate (covered below), non-publicly traded stock, and limited partnerships. Further, the internet is flooded with ads touting the virtues of even more alternative investments, such as precious metals, private equity, hedge funds, and cryptocurrency—*and these are just the tip of the iceberg.*

These alternative investments may be appealing to those seeking diversification, a greater return on investment, or shelter from volatile markets. Often overlooked, however, is the fact that just because an alternative investment is allowed does not necessarily mean it's a good idea.

Custodial agreements for these accounts often specify that you, the IRA owner, are solely responsible for directing your investments. This means you must oversee the selection, management, monitoring, and retention of all investments in the account. You alone bear the consequences of any mistakes.

There are many ways you can run into trouble. This includes not only prohibited investments but also prohibited transactions, unrelated business income, and fair-market-value reporting.

Don't overlook these potential pitfalls. You may have no idea that vacationing at the golf resort where your IRA bought property can result in a prohibited transaction that would liquidate your entire IRA and bring a large tax bill. You may also be unaware that investing your IRA in a local restaurant could mean additional annual tax returns to report unrelated business income in your IRA. In addition, you should understand that the IRS requires annual reporting of the fair market value of all assets in IRAs, including self-directed ones. Fair-market-value reporting is straightforward with IRAs invested in conventional assets like stocks and mutual funds but can pose much bigger challenges for real estate or an LLC, which may require a professional appraisal or valuation.

Alternative investments can be very attractive, especially when the markets are swinging wildly. And there are always plenty of promoters out there extolling their benefits while failing to explain all the potential downsides. Unfortunately, the IRS provides very little information for you to educate yourself. Meanwhile, self-directed IRA custodians take a completely hands-off approach when it comes to guidance. This is a recipe for trouble.

The benefits of these investments come with complicated rules and potential hazards. You should know that not only is the IRS already closely watching alternative IRA investments, but it is also planning to step up future enforcement. Those of you who may be thinking about going down the alternative-investment path need to get the full story before going all-in. While there may be certain advantages to alternate investments, there are also important risks (often undisclosed by promoters) that can jeopardize your hard-earned retirement savings. Proceed with caution!

Prohibited Transactions

IRS Publication 590-A defines a *prohibited transaction* as "any improper use of your account . . . by you or any disqualified person." A *disqualified person* is defined as a fiduciary, you, a member of your family, or any other entity such as a corporation, partnership, trust, or estate that is 50 percent or more controlled by you or your family members. For an IRA plan, you, the IRA owner, are a fiduciary even though you are not the plan custodian. This is because you have discretion and control over the IRA investments. In other words, you can't blame it on the bank. If you misuse your IRA, it's your fault.

Simply put, prohibited IRA transactions are those that would put the government at risk of never receiving the tax due because you got cute and bought an alternative investment with IRA money not reported as a taxable distribution. To be clear, prohibited transactions only occur when funds *within* your IRA are used improperly. You can always withdraw from your IRA, pay the tax (and penalty if you are under age 59½ and no exceptions apply), and spend the money any way you wish, because in that case the government is happy. It got its tax revenue and the money you are spending is no longer IRA money.

But within the IRA account, the Internal Revenue Code specifically prohibits the following transactions:

▪ **Buying, selling, or leasing any property to or from your IRA.** This is considered "self-dealing," and your IRA plan cannot engage in these transactions with you, even if the price is reasonable and fair. Also, as a fiduciary, you have an obligation to invest prudently. Investing in your own business may seem more prudent to you than investing in the stock market, but that is not the way the IRS looks at it. The IRS assumes you'll lose all your IRA money or withdraw it to pay salaries or for other personal use. (Come on. Be honest. They're probably right!)

▪ **Getting a family member to act in your place.** By *family member*, the IRS means your spouse, ancestors (your parents and grandparents), lineal descendants (your children and grandchildren), or a spouse of a lineal descendant. For example, you cannot have your IRA trustee (the financial institution holding your IRA funds) buy a building owned by your spouse and arrange to lease it back to your spouse.

▪ **Borrowing from or lending money to your IRA.** You cannot borrow from your IRA or use or pledge it as collateral for a loan, even if the interest rate and other loan terms are fair. Any amount pledged as security for a loan will be treated as a taxable distribution. You cannot personally guarantee a loan given to your IRA to buy property. That would be deemed the same as your loaning the money to your IRA. You can, however, borrow from the bank, for example, to make an IRA contribution. That's OK, but you cannot personally borrow your IRA money and your IRA cannot borrow from you.

▪ **Receiving compensation for managing your own IRA.** Your IRA cannot pay you for managing it. Looking at some of the investment returns people with IRAs have received, they should probably be required to pay back their IRAs for the losses they caused their accounts. But actually, that's prohibited too.

▪ **Buying property for personal use with IRA funds.** You cannot use your IRA money to buy property that you (or your family) use personally—for example, a home that you use as your personal residence. This is a prohibited transaction, even if you claim (as one wise guy did) that the home was to be a retirement home and since IRA money is retirement money using it to buy a retirement home should be OK. Pro Tip: It isn't, and he lost.

▪ **Purchasing collectibles.** You cannot invest your IRA funds in collectibles such as works of art, rugs, antiques, metals, gems, stamps, coins, or even baseball cards. IRS Code Section 408(m) also includes alcoholic beverages as collectibles. My guess is this includes either a Dom Pérignon '59, or a 20-year-old can of Bud. Too bad. The amount of IRA money used to buy collectibles will be treated as a taxable distribution. However, an exception applies for gold, silver, and platinum coins minted by the Department of the Treasury, as well as state-issued coins.

▪ **Buying life insurance.** You cannot use your IRA to buy a life insurance policy. ("I knew that!" said Chapter 8.)

Real Estate in Your IRA

But what if you don't trust the traditional stock market-based investments anymore, what with all these pandemics, market corrections, and corporate executives looting their companies? You wind up feeling like you're investing in *someone else's* retirement, not *yours.* Isn't there something that you can use your IRA funds to invest in that will achieve better control without violating the prohibited transaction rules? Like real estate, for instance?

By Jove, you answered your own question. You can buy real estate, but that depends on what type of real estate. If you or your family intend to use the real estate personally (for example, to live on it), then the answer is no, because that qualifies as self-dealing. You can purchase investment real estate with your IRA funds, even though I would advise against it. (I'll explain why in a moment.)

However, if you want to diversify (but remember if you own your home, you've already invested in real estate) and you insist on having some of your IRA invested in real estate, the best way to do that is to invest in a real estate mutual fund. Like any other fund investment, it is generally free of the problems I'll detail shortly. Other than that, buying real estate with IRA funds is fraught with problems. In fact, the only reason I am even addressing it is because so many people are looking to change their IRA investments from stocks and funds to real estate because they feel there is better appreciation potential, and also because any gains or appreciation in the value of the real estate would remain tax-deferred in the IRA (tax-free with a Roth). That may be true, but even if you want to go ahead and invest your IRA funds in real estate, it won't be easy.

There are two ways to do it, and both present problems because IRA investments are subject to rules not applicable to other investments. The easiest way would be to invest in a limited partnership (LP) that invests in real estate—commercial or residential (that you do not control or use personally)—or a real estate investment trust (REIT) that you also do not control or use personally.

The other way is to have your IRA buy a property and manage it, which I would never recommend because you need to be so careful not to violate the self-dealing rules. At least with the professionally managed programs (LPs and REITs), that problem is generally eliminated because you are not exercising any management control or influence.

But either option is fraught with landmines given the prohibited-transaction rules. For example, one of the rules says that you cannot loan money to your IRA to buy property or guarantee a loan by your IRA. This means then that to buy real estate (say, a building or some land) with your IRA, you must pay cash, unless the bank gives you a loan based only on the value of the property without requiring your personal guarantee to repay the loan. This can be accomplished if you can obtain a nonrecourse loan, based solely on equity in the property and not on your personal guarantee. Other than a nonrecourse loan, you generally must pay all cash to buy real estate with your IRA money, and you would need to have a ton of cash in your IRA to buy any decent property today. You'll also need a financial institution willing to take that investment in your IRA. It must be a sound investment; otherwise, you and the financial institution have violated your fiduciary obligation to make prudent investments with your IRA money. Most institutions (other than self-directed IRA custodians) will back away from this—unless you are a high roller with lots of other money on deposit with them. While they might bend their own rules for you, if that were the case you could probably afford to buy the property outside of your IRA and you wouldn't need to bother using your IRA money.

In a traditional IRA, any gains would eventually be taxed upon withdrawal at ordinary income tax rates. If you purchased the property with non-IRA money and held it for more than one year, your gain would be taxed more favorably as a capital gain. Also, most non-IRA property receives a step-up in basis at your death. Your heirs will not pay any income tax on appreciation during your life. But if they inherited an IRA with real estate, that appreciation does not receive a step-up in basis and will eventually be subject to income tax at ordinary rates.

There are other problems with real estate in an IRA. What if you need to put more money into the property? Some properties turn into real money pits. You'd better have enough of a reserve in your IRA to pay the annual property taxes and to fund additional, and sometimes substantial, cash requirements for any maintenance or unexpected expenses or improvements. You cannot simply add more money to your IRA to compensate, either. The only money that can be contributed to your IRA is the regular annual contributions and rollovers from other IRAs or company plans. If you need more money than you have available in your IRA to fund any repairs or improvements, it will be tough finding a bank to lend funds to your IRA without a personal guarantee from you. And such a personal guarantee is the same as loaning to your IRA, which is a prohibited transaction.

What I've gone into so far are the financing problems. But there are other trouble spots—RMDs, for example. What do RMDs have to do with real estate in your IRA? Plenty. Even a Roth IRA will eventually have RMDs when a nonspouse beneficiary inherits. How will you be able to calculate RMDs? What's the value of your IRA? Who knows? With real estate, it's anybody's guess. But if you guess wrong and withdraw less than your RMD, it's a 25 percent penalty.

To find the value of your real estate within your IRA, you'll need an independent appraisal—and it had better be a good one, from a reputable real estate appraiser, not your brother-in-law or your local real estate agent because, if challenged, it must hold up to the IRS's own rigid appraisal. You'll need this appraisal done not only every year once you begin RMDs, but sometimes twice a year—once to determine the year-end balance and once when you take the property out of your IRA (unless you have enough in other IRA cash to withdraw).

Not only must you have a good appraisal of your IRA property's value, the IRS wants that information too. The 1099-R form you receive for any IRA distribution includes a box to alert the IRS that you have distributed IRA assets that did not have a readily available fair market value. You will have to provide that value to your IRA custodian (which will probably be your self-directed IRA company, since most traditional IRA custodians like banks, fund companies, and brokerages will not allow you to invest in real estate and most other alternative investments within your IRA), and the cost of getting that appraisal must be paid from IRA funds, further diminishing the account's value each year. This value will be the one used to determine the tax on IRA distributions, like RMDs and Roth conversions.

And how exactly will you manage taking regular withdrawals a little bit at a time based on life expectancy? How do you distribute a part of the real estate every year?

Well, if you are 73 years old in 2024 and your RMD factor is 26.5 years, then you'll have to deed 1/26.5 of the property that year to yourself from your IRA as a distribution and do the same based on the new factor for every RMD in the future, unless you have enough cash to make the distribution. But eventually you'll run out of cash and will have nothing left in the IRA but the real estate. Then you'll have to begin distributing pieces of it or sell it in the IRA and raise the cash for the distributions. But what if that turns out to be the wrong time to sell? This is another unknown that could be a problem.

Even if there are no RMDs (for example, if you are not yet 73, or if the property is owned by your Roth IRA, where distributions are not required), you will still need an annual appraisal because the IRS requires your financial institution (your IRA custodian) to provide an annual value to you and the IRS on Form 5498, "IRA Contribution Information."

Although the idea of tax-deferred appreciation of real estate in your IRA may seem enticing, real estate investments work best outside of your IRA—first, because of the leverage. Most successful real estate investors make their money by leveraging their properties with mortgages, not by paying all cash up front and tying up all their available money. That kind of leverage is rarely available in an IRA because of the loan restrictions under the prohibited-transaction rules. I'm not saying that you cannot get a mortgage on property purchased with your IRA funds. You can, but who would give you

one without a personal guarantee by you or a family member—
which is when the mortgage becomes a prohibited transaction,
causing your IRA to cease and become immediately taxable. So, the
lack of leverage is another reason to avoid buying real estate with
your IRA money.

Another strike against doing this comes in the form of gains and
losses. For most real estate investors, the benefits come in the tax
deductions, such as depreciation and other property-related write-
offs. You cannot claim any of these when you own the property in
your IRA (but you also do not have to report the rental income
earned in the IRA).

Finally, real estate is traditionally a long-term investment and
not as liquid as investing in stocks and bonds. There is never a
guarantee that your real estate will perform better than the stock
market over the long term. You should assess the amount of long-
term risk you are willing to take with real estate. You'll likely
need this cash for retirement and may be forced to sell the property
at the wrong time. That could happen with stocks too, but it is easier to sell off small amounts of stock, as needed, rather than having
to sell an entire building, for example.

Real estate is illiquid; it eats money and is, therefore, not the most
prudent investment for a retirement account that is intended, after
all, to provide you with income for the rest of your life. So, take my
advice here and avoid the temptation. It may look good on paper but
consider the problems and additional expenses it can create . . . not
to mention the potential loss of your IRA if you cross the line and
the IRS considers your investment a prohibited transaction.

And there you have it. Everything you need to know to make the
most of your retirement savings and to keep it from being devoured
by the IRS.

Well, *almost* everything.

Read on for some additional resources that will come in mighty
handy. I know—I use them myself!

RESESOURCES

I not only use all the brains I have, but all I can borrow.
—WOODROW WILSON (1856-1924),
28TH PRESIDENT OF THE UNITED STATES

At the time Woodrow Wilson wrote those words, he had no idea how wisely they would apply to today's complicated universe of IRAs and other retirement savings accounts. The proof of that is in the following sources.

Learn More About Protecting Your IRA from the IRS

Whether you are a do-it-yourselfer or a professional advisor looking to improve service to your clients, you will find the following resources, by the nation's leading experts in retirement distribution planning, extremely valuable. These are not the only resources for accurate IRA information, but they are the ones I use. So, I can recommend them without reservation. To make the listings easier to use, I have divided these resources into two groups—those for consumers and those for professional advisors.

Resources for Consumers and Professional Financial Advisors

Arsenal of Additional Resources

By reading this book, you have laid a strong foundation for your financial success in retirement. As the landscape is constantly changing, continue to combat the latest threats to your retirement savings with our timely updates and arsenal of free intel.

Visit irahelp.com for quick links to all of these content resources!

Use the camera
on your phone
to scan the code to
visit **irahelp.com**

Free Content and Resources
Start with Our Website: irahelp.com

▪ **Sign up for IRA updates:** Receive a monthly email recap of all the latest blog posts, articles, and media appearances with America's IRA Experts.

▪ *The Great Retirement Debate* **podcast:** Tune in to *The Great Retirement Debate*, where financial heavyweights Ed Slott, CPA, and Jeffrey Levine, CPA/PFS, CFP®, go head-to-head discussing critical topics in the retirement landscape. **Although they take opposing sides by a flip of a coin**, their end goal is to provide the good, bad, and necessary information to make an informed decision. Each episode provides an information knockout that will leave you the real winner.

▪ **Follow us on social media:** Be the first to hear breaking news impacting retirement accounts by following us on your favorite social networks.

  ⬦ X: @theslottreport
  ⬦ Facebook: @AmericasIRAExperts

⋄ LinkedIn: Ed Slott and Company

⋄ YouTube: Ed Slott and Company IRAtv

▪ **Read articles on *The Slott Report*:** Follow our team of IRA experts as they address a range of tax-planning, estate-planning, and IRA topics each week.

▪ **Send questions to *The Slott Report* mailbag:** We select and answer new topics each Thursday on *The Slott Report*. Email your questions to our IRA experts at mailbag@irahelp.com.

▪ **Visit our newsroom:** Browse the latest articles by Ed Slott and find information about media appearances with leading national and industry publications and outlets.

▪ **Bookmark IRA FAQs and resources:** Access the latest contribution limits, tax tables, checklists, fact sheets, and IRS publications.

▪ **Join the discussion:** Interact with our community and start or join the conversation on our Discussion Forum.

▪ **Watch on public television:** Ed Slott is one of the top pledge drivers of all time, having raised more than $65 million for public television with his educational specials. Check your local listings to find out when *Ed Slott's Retirement Freedom!* will be airing near you.

▪ **Find an advisor:** Quickly locate members of *Ed Slott's Elite IRA Advisor Group*^{SM} nearest you. These Elite IRA Advisors train with Ed Slott and Company on a continual basis and have completed requisite training, passed background checks, attended required workshops, and completed mandatory exams. Additionally, they are immediately notified of changes to the tax code and updates on retirement planning, as they happen, to keep your retirement strategies up to date!

Premium Content

▪ **IRA shopping center:** Purchase in-depth and user-friendly multimedia resources as educational gifts for all occasions.

▪ **Book a private speaking event:** Ed Slott is available to speak and present educational webinars for your company, civic group, or other organization to provide essential retirement expertise personalized for your audience. Email info@irahelp.com or call (800) 663-1340 to learn more.

Advanced Materials for Financial Professionals

Empty claims of being a "retirement expert" can quickly end in costly mistakes for those unequipped with the latest knowledge and advice—costly for your clients in unnecessary taxes and missed opportunities, and costly for you as a liability for your business!

▪ **Smart subscriptions:** For the latest, most robust, and actionable education available to financial professionals, order a subscription to our monthly newsletters:

- *Ed Slott's IRA Advisor* is the go-to "all things IRA" monthly newsletter and reference tool for financial professionals. Take advantage of tips and techniques from the industry's top IRA experts so you can be the fiduciary that your clients deserve.

- *Heather Schreiber's Social Security Advisor* is the go-to "all things Social Security" monthly newsletter and reference tool for financial professionals. As the primary source of income for most retirees today, being knowledgeable on the latest strategies and insights is a critical aspect of income planning for retirement.

To start your subscriptions today, go to irahelp.com/newsletter for immediate access to our online newsletters, including back issues. You can also email newsletter@irahelp.com or call (877) 337-5688.

▪ **Advisor training opportunities:** Ed Slott and his team of IRA Experts host intensive semiannual training workshops for financial advisors, CPAs, attorneys, and other professionals wanting to learn the most up-to-date IRA expertise and planning strategies. Earn continuing education (CE) credit and take advantage of Q&A opportunities with America's IRA Experts. Completing this course is also a prerequisite for joining *Ed Slott's Elite IRA Advisor Group*^{SM}. Visit irahelp.com/2-day to learn more and register for our next 2-Day IRA Workshop.

Free Resources from the IRS—Yes, They Can Help You!

IRS.gov: Official government website containing free information on IRA plans, tax forms, instructions, and all things tax-related.

Contribution rules for IRAs and retirement plans: https://www.irs.gov/retirement-plans/plan-participant-employee/retirement-topics-contributions.

Early distributions—exceptions to the 10 percent penalty: https://www.irs.gov/retirement-plans/plan-participant-employee/retirement-topics-tax-on-early-distributions.

Rollover information: https://www.irs.gov/retirement-plans/plan-participant-employee/rollovers-of-retirement-plan-and-ira-distributions.

IRS Publication 590-A, Contributions to Individual Retirement Arrangements (IRAs): https://www.irs.gov/pub/irs-pdf/p590a.pdf.

IRS Publication 590-B, Distributions from Individual Retirement Arrangements (IRAs): https://www.irs.gov/pub/irs-pdf/p590b.pdf.

Medicare and Social Security Resources

Medicare.gov: Official government website containing free information on all things related to Medicare, including enrollment costs and how to find doctors, providers, hospitals, plans, and supplies.

SSA.gov (Social Security Administration): Free government website where individuals can access their personal account, receive personalized estimates of future benefits based on their real earnings, see their latest statement, and review their earnings history.

Consumer Resource Websites

AARP.org: The nation's largest nonprofit, nonpartisan organization dedicated to empowering Americans 50 and older to choose how they live as they age. Website includes retirement calculators and a wide range of news articles covering topics from general finances to Medicare.

Investopedia.com: Leading source of financial content, ranging from market news to retirement strategies to investing education. Investopedia helps you understand complex financial concepts, improve your investing skills, and learn how to manage your money.

Morningstar.com: An investment research company offering mutual fund, ETF, and stock analysis, ratings, and data, and portfolio tools. Articles cover topics from RMD traps to Social Security.

Fool.com (The Motley Fool): Provides financial advice for investors through various stock, investing, and personal finance services.

Kiplinger.com: Leader in personal finance news and business forecasting. "Get trusted advice on investing, retirement, taxes, saving, real estate, cars, college, insurance."

WSJ.com: Online coverage of breaking news and current headlines from the U.S. and around the world. Includes columns, expert retirement blogs, and opinions pertaining to the economy, business, retirement, etc. (subscription required).

Forbes.com: Global media company focusing on business, investing, technology, entrepreneurship, leadership, and lifestyle. Money section articles cover topics on trusts, estate planning, and general retirement topics, and include retirement calculators.

Consumer Books to Help You Protect Your Savings

The Bucket Plan:
Protecting and Growing Your Assets for a Worry-Free Retirement

Jason L. Smith

Jason Smith is the founder and CEO of Clarity 2 Prosperity, a financial training, coaching, and IP development organization. I wrote the foreword for this book because I liked the organized approach to financial and income planning. Based on a true story of the planning process a retiring couple underwent to structure their assets for retirement, it shows you each of the steps they took to eliminate key risks and create a practical and sensible financial plan. This story illustrates a simple and comprehensive process for how you can protect and prolong your savings, leaving you free from worry, stress, or uncertainty about your long-term financial security. This is an easy and educational read that makes good sense.

*The 7 Biggest Mistakes Trustees Make
and How to Avoid Them*

Sandeep Varma, RIA©

I have known Sandeep Varma, president of ATS Financial, an independent financial planning firm in San Diego, California, for many years. You'll like the stories in here, which are both scary and very relatable to your own family situation. You'll also benefit greatly from the glossary in the back of the book that explains many financial and tax-planning terms that can sometimes be confusing.

Additional Resources for Professional Advisors

Ed Slott's IRA Advisor: Published monthly by Smart Subscriptions, LLC, $150 per year. To order, call 877-337-5688 or order online at www.irahelp.com.

IRA Reference Manual and IRA Desk Reference: Published by PMC. Order online at www.pmc-corp.com or call 800-233-3207. The *IRA Reference Manual* regularly lists for $245.00 and the *IRA Desk Reference* lists for $69.95. PMC now also offers a cloud-based IRA Digital Reference Manual.

Life and Death Planning for Retirement Benefits by Natalie B. Choate, Esq.; published by Ataxplan Publications, 2019, 8th edition, $99.95 plus shipping. To order, call 978-829-2553 or visit www .ataxplan.com. Also available in electronic edition: visit www .retirementbenefitsplanning.us.

Appleby's IRA Publications: Appleby's IRA Publications includes the popular *IRA Reference Guides* booklet. A compilation of Quick Reference Guides, the booklet summarizes and simplifies explanations of the rules that apply to IRAs and rollovers from employer plans. These resources also provide detailed information and address many of the most frequently asked questions, which allows the user to save time that would otherwise be spent on research. Most are available for immediate download. Orders can be placed at www.IRApublications.com. For a 30 percent discount storewide, enter code: Slott.

Professional Publications and Tax Services I Use

Estate Planning (www.ria.thomson.com/journals)
Trusts & Estates (www.trustsandestates.com)
Financial Advisor **magazine** (www.fa-mag.com)
InvestmentNews (www.investmentnews.com)
Tax Notes by Tax Analysts (www.taxanalysts.com)
Checkpoint by Thompson Reuters (https://tax.thomsonreuters
.com/en/checkpoint)

IRA Information Websites I Use

These sites contain not only a tremendous concentration of retirement distribution information, but additional resources, articles, seminar information, discussion forums, and breaking tax news. From these sites, you can link to IRA resources anywhere.

Ed Slott's IRA Advisor (www.irahelp.com)

Natalie Choate, Esq. (www.ataxplan.com)

Leimberg Information Services, Inc. (www.leimbergservices.com): Leimberg Information Services, Inc. (LISI), is one of the truly great professional resources I use nearly every day. LISI brings together the most brilliant professional advisors and scholars whose perspectives are included in LISI's daily briefings. If you want the most up-to-date tax information, educational webcasts, court cases, IRS rulings, financial statistics, and professional opinions, I cannot recommend Steve Leimberg's information service strongly enough.

Benefitslink.com (www.benefitslink.com): A free daily newsletter that covers compliance, administration, design (especially cost savings), and policy for all kinds of employee benefit plans: 401(k), pension, profit-sharing, and other retirement plans; group health, disability, and other kinds of welfare plans; and executive benefits—whether sponsored by a governmental entity, a church, or any other kind of employer, plus so much more.

DOL.gov (ERISA): Official Department of Labor website that includes blogs, news articles, forms, and statistics on trending business topics.

IRS.gov: Official government website containing free information on IRA plans, tax forms, instructions, and all things related to taxes.

Software Resources I Depend On

▪ I use **Brentmark Software Inc. (www.brentmark.com or 1-800-879-6665)** software products almost exclusively. I find that they have an easy-to-use program for all the IRA and estate-planning calculations I need. That includes minimum distributions, 72(t) payments, and a wide variety of estate-tax calculations and projections that can be used for estate planning. Software programs they offer that are pertinent to this book include:

▪ The **Retirement Plan Analyzer** evaluates various strategies for taking distributions from traditional IRAs, Roth IRAs, Roth 401(k)s, and other qualified retirement plans. One of the most desired features of the Retirement Plan Analyzer is the Roth IRA conversion feature, used for comparing and evaluating conversions to a Roth IRA. The program allows you to compare between a 100 percent conversion or conversions over several years. To order, visit https://www.brentmark.com/product/retirement-plan-analyzer/.

▪ The **Retirement Distributions Planner**, available for desktop or online, calculates RMD schedules, handles up to five beneficiaries, models death of plan owner, spousal rollovers, distributions of IRA assets at the beneficiary level, and three ways to calculate 72(t). To order, visit https://www.brentmark.com/product/retirement -distributions-planner/.

▪ **Estate Planning Tools** is the program I use the most. It has every financial and tax-planning calculation you will ever need. This is mostly used by estate-planning attorneys, bankers, financial planners, CPAs, and other tax advisors. With more than one hundred dynamic planning models in sixteen different areas, Estate Planning Tools contains all the calculations necessary for you and professional financial advisors. To order, visit https://www.brentmark .com/product/estate-planning-tools/.

▪ **inTELOSfp** is a planning and presentation program providing the actual dollar amount results of numerous planning alternatives. Users can immediately see the tax results (the math) on items like Roth conversions, IRA distributions to fund life insurance, and an overall analysis of the tax savings and estate accumulation under various planning scenarios. I use this program because it provides high-impact planning output. To order, visit www.intelosfp.com.

▪ **NumberCruncher: Estate-, Tax-, and Financial-Planning Software.** NumberCruncher is an estate- and financial-planning program created by Stephan R. Leimberg and Robert T. LeClair that is essential for every financial advisor. I use this program for all the estate, income tax, and compound-interest computations in my books, newsletters, and advisor course manuals. But most of all, we use it to help our clients with planning, and so should you. Number-Cruncher includes a financial-planning module in addition to the estate-planning module. It's the only program professional advisors need to instantly put real numbers onto any type of planning situation. It includes every imaginable tax- and financial-planning calculation. It sells for $595 (plus shipping and handling) and can be ordered at https://leimberg.com/Software/NumberCruncher/Overview.

Finding a Financial Advisor Who Knows IRAs

After going through this book, you may find that you are now better versed in IRA-distribution planning than your own financial advisor and would feel more secure working with someone who has specialized knowledge in this area. To make your search easier, I have created **Ed Slott's Elite IRA Advisor Group**^{SM}, celebrating its twentieth year in 2024. It's a prestigious array of professional financial advisors trained by me and my firm who participate in our ongoing, advanced-education programs to stay current on all issues relating to IRA and company retirement-plan-distribution planning. Some of these elite advisors have been in our program for years and have even reached the level of Master Elite IRA Advisor. To find an Elite IRA Advisor in your area, check our website: www.irahelp.com.

APPENDIX

IRS Tax Forms and Publications You Should Have
(and Where to Get 'Em)

Everything here can be accessed *free* (since it's already yours as a taxpayer) from the IRS website, www.irs.gov.

IRS Tax Forms

When downloading these tax forms, always get the instructions for them as well. Often the instructions contain key information not always found in the forms themselves. (The form writers probably felt, "What the hey, close enough for government work!")

■ **Form 706, United States Estate (and Generation-Skipping Transfer) Tax Return.** Obviously, you don't need this for yourself since it deals with your estate and that means you're dead, but you should order it anyway so you can see how the estate-tax system really works. It will help with your estate planning. After your death, your beneficiaries will have to fill this out and calculate any estate tax owed. Your beneficiaries should keep your completed estate tax return as a permanent record of property values on your date of death. They will also use it to see if they are entitled to an IRD (income in respect of a decedent) deduction (see Chapter 8). That's a big tax deduction they should not miss.

▪ **Form 1099-R, Distributions from Pensions, Annuities, Retirement or Profit-Sharing Plans, IRAs, Insurance Contracts, etc.** The 1099-R is the key information form that will clue you in about what type of distribution you have received from your retirement plan (or as a beneficiary of one), the applicable tax treatment, and the tax forms you will be required to file with your tax return. Any distribution from a retirement plan triggers a 1099-R, and your plan or IRA financial institution sends a copy to both you and the IRS. Before even attempting to file your taxes, you should scrutinize the amounts and codes listed on the 1099-R form to see how the amounts will be reported. You also need to be sure it is accurate. Companies do make mistakes on this form!

▪ **Form 4972, Tax on Lump-Sum Distributions.** This form is used to report lump-sum distributions and capital gain treatment, and to figure the income tax on 10-year averaging.

▪ **Form 5329, Additional Taxes on Qualified Plans (Including IRAs) and Other Tax-Favored Accounts.** This form is usually attached to your personal tax return (Form 1040), but it can be filed by itself if you are not required to file an income tax return for the year. Form 5329 is used to report and figure the tax on early (before age 59½) distributions from retirement plans. It is also used to notify the IRS of any exception that may apply to the 10 percent early withdrawal penalty. Form 5329 is the place to report and compute the 6 percent tax on excess contributions and the 25 (or 10) percent RMD tax on any amount of your required distribution not withdrawn. These 6 percent and RMD penalty taxes apply to all IRA owners and beneficiaries even if they are age 59½ or older.

▪ **Form 5498, IRA Contribution Information.** Your IRA financial institution sends this to you and the IRS to report your annual IRA activity and the value of your IRA and Roth IRA accounts each year. The IRA activity reported here is not needed to prepare your tax return, but it does provide official documentation that can support items on your return. It shows your annual IRA and Roth IRA contributions, rollovers, Roth conversions, Roth recharacterizations, and the fair market value of your IRA account as of the end of the tax year. This form is generally issued in May for the prior year.

▪ **Form 8606, Nondeductible IRAs.** This form also is usually attached to your personal tax return, but it too can be filed by itself if you are not required to file an income tax return for the year. Form 8606 is used to report an array of IRA transactions, including nondeductible IRA contributions, distributions from IRAs that include nondeductible contributions, and distributions from Roth IRAs. Roth conversions are also reported here. This is the form where the pro-rata rule is computed for distributions from IRAs that contain nondeductible contributions or after-tax funds rolled into the IRA from a company plan.

IRS Publications

IRS Publication Number	Title
559	Survivors, Executors, and Administrators
560	Retirement Plans for Small Business (SEP, SIMPLE, and Qualified Plans)
571	Tax Sheltered Annuity Plans (403[b] Plans) for Employees of Public Schools and Certain Tax-Exempt Organizations
575	Pension and Annuity Income
590-A	Contributions to Individual Retirement Arrangements (IRAs)
590-B	Distributions from Individual Retirement Arrangements (IRAs)
721	Tax Guide to U.S. Civil Service Retirement Benefits
915	Social Security and Equivalent Railroad Retirement Benefits
939	General Rule for Pensions and Annuities
976	Disaster Relief
3125	An Important Message for Taxpayers with IRAs: The IRS Does Not Approve IRA Investments

ACKNOWLEDGMENTS

Thank you to Jessica DuLong, the talented writer and wordsmith who edited this book. Jessica had to once again translate our explanations of the latest tax law changes so that you can understand and take advantage of all the new planning opportunities available. It seems that each year Congress finds new ways to make these retirement tax rules tougher to navigate, yet you need to know them. Thank you, Jessica, for helping me and the readers get the most out of this book.

Thank you also to John McCarty, my original collaborator and editor, over 20 years ago. John is an experienced writer but had little knowledge of this topic (for example, at the time his latest book was *The Films of Mel Gibson*). Talk about switching gears. There I was, forcing him to learn all these IRA and tax rules and relying on him to turn my writing and ideas into a digestible, useful, educational book that people would actually enjoy reading. But he did it, and he did it in record time. He is now a financial advisor (only kidding, he's retired—I think this book was the last straw). Thanks, John, for being an amazing communicator.

Thanks also to Beverly DeVeny, our long-time and now happily retired IRA expert, who contributed greatly to several prior updates as tax laws have changed over the years.

Thank you to Joy Tutela, my literary agent at the David Black Agency, New York. Joy was instrumental in getting this new edition off and running. Joy has been representing me for many years through several book projects and has always been a loyal advocate. Thank you, Joy, for guiding me through this endeavor.

Thank you to the great people at Penguin Random House: Patrick

Nolan, publisher, and Isabelle Alexander, Emma Dollar, Andy Dudley, Matt Giarratano, Nick Michal, Jennifer Tait, Aurora Slothus, and Colin Webber, who were instrumental in and supportive of this completely revised edition.

Thank you to Alana Kohl, Jill Jagelski Schofield, Courtney Browning, Tara Glennon, and the team from AdvisorPR for providing high-impact communication and marketing strategies to get our brand and messages out to the masses. Your professionalism and expertise are unmatched and continue to be a critical asset to Ed Slott and Company in our mission to educate advisors and consumers alike on the importance of retirement tax planning.

The original edition of this book would not have been possible without Seymour "Sy" Goldberg, Esq., CPA. Sy is the longtime colleague and friend who started it all for me, and many others who wound up specializing in this unforgiving area. He jumped on IRA-distribution planning before most professional advisors knew anything about it, and he has generously shared his expertise ever since. Thank you, Sy, for getting me started in the wonderfully confusing world of IRAs. You are a genius!

Thank you to Sarah A. Brenner, J.D., the director of retirement education at our company. An attorney with decades of experience in the IRA tax rules, Sarah is one of the best in the business. She was invaluable in updating this book, especially for the SECURE 2.0 Act and the latest IRS tax rules. Sarah, your efforts have greatly enhanced this new edition.

Sarah also works with our other IRA technical consultants, Andy Ives, CFP®, AIF®, and Ian Berger, J.D. Together they provide technical support not only for me but also for the members of *Ed Slott's Elite IRA Advisor Group*SM, as well as supplying expert content for our website and running webcasts and other IRA financial advisor training programs. Sarah, Andy, and Ian often find themselves working at all hours when IRS or Congress changes the rules (as they have done plenty recently), springing into action to digest the new tax rules and explain them to the media sources, financial advisors, and consumers who rely on us. This is no easy task, when everyone is looking for immediate information in this fast-paced world, and especially when it seems that lately both tax law changes and IRS updates are released at the last possible minute, usually on Friday afternoon! In addition, Sarah, Andy, and Ian write and edit our signature monthly newsletter for financial advisors, *Ed Slott's IRA Advisor*—and there is never a month off. They have also contributed updated content for this edition. These brilliant, hardworking professionals (IRA geniuses!) stand ever ready to answer questions and help advisors do the best retirement and tax-planning job possible for their clients. They are an incredible team and a valuable resource to our company. I am lucky to have them on board. A heartfelt thank you to all of you.

Heather Schreiber of HLS Retirement Consulting is an expert in all things Social Security and Medicare. While this book focuses on retirement planning, Social Security is a critical part of any retirement plan, and Heather has helped us tremendously when these questions arise, as they do almost daily. She is a fantastic resource, and that's why we partner with Heather on her monthly newsletter, *Heather Schreiber's Social Security Advisor*. It's so valuable to so many. You can check it out at www.irahelp.com/newsletter.

As you've seen from reading any single chapter in this book, these are some tough tax rules. No one person can know it all, and yet, thanks to the brilliant minds I have had access to over the years, everything you need to know is here within these pages. (The key, I've learned, is not knowing it all, but knowing enough people who know some.) I could probably write another whole book about how helpful and generous these people have been with their time and talent, but for now I'll just list them and call them the IRA Guru Club, a collection of highly intelligent folks who know all about the nuances of IRAs and the related tax rules—a unique group for sure. I thank each of them for helping me grapple with the implications of technical tax rules. Many of these IRA experts have written extensively on the topic, and I have included information on how to order some of their publications in the Resources section.

Thank you all very much:

Seymour Goldberg, Esq., CPA

Natalie Choate, Esq.

Robert S. Keebler, CPA, MST

Michelle L. Ward, J.D., LLM,
Keebler & Associates

Shannon Evans, J.D., LLM

Barry C. Picker, CPA/PFS,
CFP®

Michael J. Jones, CPA

Bruce D. Steiner, Esq.

Denise Appleby, APA, CISP,
CRC, CRPS, Appleby
Retirement Consulting

Jeffrey Levine, CPA/PFS, CFP®

Heather Schreiber, RICP®

Christopher R. Hoyt, Esq.,
University of Missouri
(Kansas City)

Gordon F. Weis, CLU, CPC,
ChFC

Stephen J. Krass, Esq.

David A. Foster, CPA, CFP®

Martin M. Shenkman, CPA,
MBA, JD

Guerdon T. Ely, MBA, CFP®

Jeremiah W. Doyle IV, Mellon
Private Asset Management

Steven E. Trytten, Esq.

Gary S. Lesser, J.D.

James Lange, Esq.

Mary Kay Foss, CPA

Peggy Cabaniss, CFP®

Harley Gordon, Esq.

Special thanks to the following for being instrumental in my career and to our company's growth over the years:

Joel A. Goodhart, Accredited
Investment Fiduciary®, CRC,
CLU, RFC

Sandeep and Nisha Varma,
Advanced Trustee Strategies,
Inc.

Dean Barber, Modern Wealth
Management

Heather Schreiber, HLS
Retirement Consulting,
LLC

Brad Pistole, Trinity Insurance &
Financial Services & Safe
Money Radio

Dan Sullivan, The Strategic
Coach

Jason L. Smith, president and
CEO, Clarity 2 Prosperity

Jim Bowman, Advisors
Excel

David McKnight, The Power of
Zero

Neil D. Katz, Esq., managing
partner, Katz Chwat, P.C.

Mark I. Rozell, Esq.

Alan and Joyce Kahn, The AJK
Financial Group

Patrick Kuster, CFP®, AIF, Buckingham Strategic Wealth

Don Graves, RICP®, CLTC®, CSA®, HECM Advisors Group, HousingWealthBook.com

Van Mueller, LUTCF, host of www.vanmueller.com

Joel P. Bruckenstein, CFS, CMFC, CFP®

Bob Veres, Inside Information

Joe Wirbick, CFP®, CEPA, CDFA

Marc A. Silverman, CLU, ChFC

Sidney Kess, CPA, Esq.

Robert Powell, CFP®

As always, I acknowledge the members of *Ed Slott's Elite IRA Advisor Group*^{SM} for their dedication to education and expertise, and for the true long-term value and financial security they provide to their clients. In these challenging times, I am proud to see the many ways that these financial advisors have shared their valuable knowledge in the IRA and retirement tax-planning area to help consumers all over the country who need accurate and reliable information to make important financial decisions. This group of highly informed and educated advisors, now together for more than 20 years, continues to show us how they are making people's financial lives better. Thanks to all of you for your commitment to being the best in the business. If you are a consumer reading this book, look for one of these advisors to help you plan to reach your retirement and financial goals. You can find them on our website www.irahelp.com under "Find an Advisor."

I would like to also acknowledge the following groups and people who have continuously supported my work to provide consumers and advisors with the highest level of advice and education. Thank you to:

Advisor PR

The American College of Financial Services

CPA Academy

AARP

Financial Planning Association (FPA), including FPA chapters across the country

Leimberg Information Services, Inc. (LISI)

MDRT (Million Dollar Round Table)

TOT (Top of the Table)

NAIFA (National Association of Insurance and Financial Advisors)

NAPFA (National Association of Personal Financial Advisors)

AALU (Association for Advanced Life Underwriting)

AICPA (American Institute of Certified Public Accountants)

New York State Society of CPAs

InvestmentNews (Susan Kelly)

Financial Advisor magazine, Evan Simonoff, editor in chief and editorial director

Melanie Waddell, Washington Bureau Chief, Investment Advisory Group

Christine Benz, Director of Personal Finance, Morningstar

Thank you to this long list of companies who have helped me spread the retirement tax-planning message with seminars and presentations across the county:

New York Life

Sammons Financial

Midland National® Life Insurance Company

North American—A Sammons Financial Company

Advisors Excel

Aegis Financial Group, Inc.

Athene USA

Brookstone Capital Management

White Glove

Ameriprise Financial

TruChoice Financial

Avantax Wealth Management

TruStage

Charles Schwab

LPL Financial

Advisor Group

FSC Securities Corp.

Royal Alliance

SagePoint Financial

Woodbury Financial

Northwestern Mutual

Transamerica

Nationwide

Jackson National Life Insurance Company

The Guardian

Park Avenue Securities

First Protective Insurance Company

Insurmark, Inc.

Life Pro Financial Services

Lifetime Financial Growth

Ohio National Financial Services

Fidelity Investments

American Equity

American Portfolios

Securian Financial

Thrivent

Fairway Independent Mortgage Corporation

Wells Fargo

Morgan Stanley

M & O Marketing

Prudential

VALIC

Private Advisor Group

First Heartland® Capital, Inc.

Knights of Columbus

Asset Marketing Systems

Recruiting Services of Arizona

Luttner Financial Group

Sigma Financial Corporation

Parkland Securities

NelsonCorp Wealth Management

Cadaret Grant

Brokers International

Clarity 2 Prosperity

Gradient Financial Group

Brentmark

Tarkenton Financial

Invesco

TruAdvisor Network

American Tax Planning Institute

inTELOSfp

Nothing would ever get done without the help of the home team—the wonderful people I work with every day.

Laurin Levine, the managing partner of our company, has been taking care of virtually every aspect of our business for more than 30 years. Laurin has been instrumental not only in working around the clock to manage our programs, conferences, and events all over the country, but in putting us in front of millions of public television viewers. Laurin is constantly promoting our message (even when she is supposed to be on vacation!) that to protect your retirement savings you must educate yourself on this critical subject. Her passion is contagious. Anyone who has met her knows what I mean. Most of all she is a real friend and fun to work with. Thank you, Laurin, for being a critical part of our shared success.

Thank you to Margot Reilly, our company controller and a great friend. Margot, who also helps with our CPA practice, has been with me for more than 30 years and is always a pleasure to work with. Thank you, Margot, for the great work you do, and for keeping me free from worrying about all the details that you take care of. I'm so glad you are here.

Thank you to our office staff: Glenda Alvarado, Robin Mollin, and Lisa Lighter, who not only run our office but also help with office and program administration, travel arrangements, booking events, and shipping hundreds of boxes of materials all over the country for my speaking engagements and our advisor training programs.

Thank you to Kira Fasanella, our marketing director, who does a wonderful job developing and building our relationships with other businesses. She works with the enterprises that sponsor our programs, bringing companies of value to our workshops, as well as connecting our company with ongoing educational industry events.

I also must thank Matt Smith, our member relations manager, who ably serves the hundreds of members who have earned their spot in *Ed Slott's Elite IRA Advisor Group*[SM]. Matt does a brilliant job of monitoring and managing all the logistics necessary to help our members get the most out of this program, including issuing Elite Alerts that provide up-to-the-minute information about any new tax laws that enable our advisors to best serve their clients.

Matt has also been a big help with producing our podcast *The Great Retirement Debate*, in which I team up with IRA and tax expert Jeffrey Levine, CPA/PFS, CFP®. Thanks also to the team at Buckingham Strategic Wealth, who have devoted their time and technical assistance to the podcast. Jeff and I take opposing sides on each of your most pressing tax, estate, and retirement-planning questions. The goal is to help you make an informed decision, leaving you the real winner of this debate.

Thank you to Ryan Fortese, our director of operations. His company, Fortese Management, does a fantastic job running all our marketing and programs. Ryan has also been instrumental to the success of *Ed Slott's Elite IRA Advisor Group*[SM]. He has been with us for more than 20 years. Thank you, Ryan, for being consistently reliable and dedicated to our missions of educating financial advisors and consumers. While your work is mostly behind the scenes, I wanted everyone to know how important you are to our company. I also want to thank Brandon Bellomy, who works with Ryan in helping us out at our IRA training workshops.

In today's wired world, so much of the work of our company, like most other organizations, relies on technology, streaming, online security, backups, and network maintenance. This is where I want to especially thank Rich Wienclaw, our "computer guy." Rich and his company, manasysinc.com, have been keeping us up and running for years, through power outages, equipment failures, program updates, and the dreaded computer system upgrades. These are such critical aspects for any business, and we are fortunate that he's on the case all the time. Thanks, Rich!

Thank you also to Debbie Slott, who does all our graphics for program and marketing purposes. Thank you for making us look so good.

Thank you to Don Korn, one of the most talented and knowledgeable tax and financial writers I know. He is great at interviewing IRA, tax, and legal experts and turning their language into practical and useful articles for *Ed Slott's IRA Advisor* newsletter— no easy task. Thanks, Don.

Thank you to all the public television stations around the country that have supported our message and helped us make viewers aware of what they must do to protect more of their money from taxes. It's a huge and important mission, and I am proud to be associated with the public television stations that are undertaking it with me. I believe strongly in educating the public, and so does public television, so it's a perfect fit!

Thank you to Bob Marty, a fantastic producer and great supporter of our work who took a chance on me when he introduced me to public television. He has since produced all our shows and helped to turn them into great successes. Thank you, Bob.

And to my family: To my wife, Linda, our daughter Ilana and son-in-law Andrew (special thank you for my grandson, Simon!), and to our daughter Rachel. Thank you for your support and love. Even though we are often spread around the country now, I always look forward to our time together.

And to my parents, Bob and Beverly Slott. Every success I have ever enjoyed had something to do with your encouragement. I was so lucky to have had parents like you.

ABOUT THE AUTHOR

Ed Slott is a nationally recognized IRA distribution expert, professional speaker, television personality, and bestselling author. He is known for his unparalleled ability to turn advanced tax strategies into understandable, actionable, and entertaining advice. He has been named "The Best Source for IRA Advice" by *The Wall Street Journal*, and *USA Today* wrote, "It would be tough to find anyone who knows more about IRAs than CPA Slott."

As president and founder of Ed Slott and Company, LLC, the nation's leading source of accurate, timely IRA expertise and analysis to financial advisors, institutions, consumers, and media, he provides:

1. Advanced training to help financial professionals become knowledgeable, recognized leaders in the retirement marketplace; and

2. Answers to retirement savers' most important questions, with practical, easy-to-understand information on IRA, retirement, tax, and financial planning topics.

Slott is a professor of practice at the American College of Financial Services and regularly gives keynote presentations on IRA and estate-planning strategies at both consumer events and conferences for financial advisors, insurance professionals, CPAs, and attorneys, including virtual events drawing thousands of attendees nationwide.

Among the most popular of his resources are his advanced training programs for financial professionals. He is the creator of *Ed*

Slott's Elite IRA Advisor Group^{SM}, an organization of more than 500 of the nation's top financial professionals who attend his ongoing continuing-education programs to maintain a mastery of advanced retirement account and tax-planning laws. Additionally, his *Instant IRA Success* program is a live, two-day IRA workshop covering up-to-the-minute information with immediately actionable intel, and *IRA Success* is an on-demand, CE-eligible, twelve-course program powered by the American College of Financial Services.

Slott is an accomplished author of many financial books, including most recently *Ed Slott's Retirement Decisions Guide: 2024 Edition* (IRAHelp, 2024) and *Fund Your Future: A Tax-Smart Savings Plan in Your 20s and 30s* (IRAHelp, 2024). He also authors *IRA Advisor*, a monthly newsletter for financial professionals to stay educated on "all things IRA." His popular website, irahelp.com, is a resource for financial professionals and consumers, where *The Slott Report* blog is followed by tens of thousands of readers. And in 2022, he launched a podcast, *The Great Retirement Debate*, in collaboration with Jeffrey Levine, CPA/PFS, CFP®, providing lively commentary on opposing sides of retirement planning strategies.

As the go-to resource for media needing timely insight on breaking news as it relates to retirement and tax-planning laws and strategies, Slott is often quoted in *The New York Times*, *The Wall Street Journal*, *Forbes*, *USA Today*, *Kiplinger*, *Investor's Business Daily*, and numerous additional national magazines and financial publications. He regularly provides a Q&A column to AARP and is also a contributing columnist and media resource to *Financial Advisor* and *InvestmentNews* magazines. He has appeared on many national television and radio programs, including NBC, ABC, CBS, CNBC, CNN, FOX, Fox Business, NPR, Bloomberg, and Morningstar. He is one of the top pledge drivers of all time with his educational specials, including his most recent, *Ed Slott's Retirement Freedom!* (2022).

Slott has been recognized for his significant contributions to the financial industry as an *InvestmentNews* Innovator, Sidney Kess Award Winner for excellence in continuing education by the AICPA®, *ThinkAdvisor* LUMINARIES Award winner, and recipient of the prestigious Excellence in Estate Planning and Outstanding

Service awards presented by the Foundation for Accounting Education. He is a former board member of the Estate Planning Council of New York City and is an Accredited Estate Planner (AEP), distinguished. He is also a past chairman of the New York State Society of CPAs Estate Planning Committee and editor of the IRA planning section of the *CPA Journal*.

Ultimately, through all these efforts combined, Slott has taught millions of Americans (and their financial professionals) how to get the most out of their retirement savings.

To continue protecting your retirement savings and to build upon the education you've established by reading this book, follow Slott online for the latest content and breaking news updates:

Website: irahelp.com
X: @TheSlottReport
LinkedIn: Ed Slott and Company
Facebook: @AmericasIRAExperts
YouTube: Ed Slott and Company IRAtv

HIRE ED TO SPEAK
AT YOUR NEXT EVENT!

**Bring Informative, Entertaining, and Actionable Tax
Education to Your Organization**

Ed Slott is a dynamic speaker who regularly presents on IRA, tax,
and estate-planning topics at both consumer events and industry
conferences. His presentations are filled with action-packed strategies applicable for the attending audience and delivered with high
energy and a touch of humor.

Available in both live and virtual formats, Slott provides the
most up-to-date education available anywhere for:

- Clients, consumers, and civic organizations

- Financial advisors

- Insurance professionals

- CPAs

- Enrolled agents

- Tax attorneys

- Financial institutions, organizations, and membership
  groups

- Similar professionals wanting education on how to take
  financial control, avoid unnecessary taxes, and combat the
  latest threats to retirement savings accounts

Slott has been captivating audiences for more than 20 years, speaking before some of the nation's largest companies, including Fidelity Investments, Nationwide Financial, New York Life, Jackson National, MetLife, Northwestern Mutual, Ameriprise, Charles Schwab, Genworth Financial, and more. Everyone who listens to him speak agrees . . . he truly is outstanding!

What Attendees Are Saying

"Holy moly what a refreshing and amazingly educational experience! Thank you for being such an incredible ambassador for our work. I just wanted to express deep and wide appreciation for the amazing caliber of your presentation. As a former professor, I simply LOVED the charm and humor with which you delivered such critical information. It was the trifecta of pedagogical perfection: you made us grin, you kept us engaged, and we learned game-changing information."

"Ed Slott is by far the ABSOLUTE BEST-recognized expert on tax advice and squeezing every ounce of tax-free advantage out of the tax code. He makes his points clearly and concisely and gets to the heart of the matter with just the right amount of humor along the way."

"I enjoyed Ed Slott. He is knowledgeable and had a great excitement in his voice. He kept me alert and interested."

"Truly outstanding presentation packed with useful information, which was informatively, thoughtfully, and enjoyably delivered. Ed Slott again lives up to his remarkable reputation."

"Ed is extremely knowledgeable and a dynamic speaker!! Great job!!!"

"Incredible! I consider myself an IRA expert but always hope to find something beneficial in IRA webinars. Ed blew it out of the water—I left the webinar with lots of tips and some clarification I didn't know I needed. Fantastic job!!"

"Best presenter ever! I always enjoy Ed."

"Ed is a powerhouse presenter and a complete educator; I was on the edge of my seat for the entire hour! He delivered answers to all my burning questions and proactively answered my follow-up questions . . . ED: Exceptionally-Dedicated!"

"Succinct and exceptionally instructive."

"So much fast-paced yet in-depth information that I never want to miss a minute of the presentations! Energy was outstanding and the program was every bit as well done [virtually] as in-person programs have been."

"Ed Slott! Yes, THE Ed Slott! It doesn't get any better than this for fast-paced, informative webinars! Too bad instructor ratings only go up to 5. He's a 10!"

Slott is available for keynote presentations, live and virtual trainings, and private events. For more information, please contact Laurin Levine, managing partner, at laurin@irahelp.com, or call (800) 663-1340. You can also visit https://www.irahelp.com/speaking/overview to download a speaker kit and learn more about Slott's latest speaking programs.

**Use the camera
on your phone
to scan the code to
visit irahelp.com**

INDEX

Note: Italicized page numbers indicate material in tables or illustrations.

ED SLOTT'S
IRA ADVISOR
$150 PER YEAR!

Tax & Estate Planning For Your Retirement Savings

LEARN MORE...*TO EARN MORE!*

Ed Slott's IRA Advisor 8-page newsletter is the go-to "all things IRA" monthly reference tool for professionals:

- Expand your knowledge to help your clients and increase earning capacity.
- Stay current on the latest tax rulings and need-to-know retirement information.
- Take advantage of tips and techniques from the industry's top experts.
- Utilize easy-to-follow outflow pieces to generate inflow and stir up conversations.
- Be the fiduciary that your clients deserve.

STAY EDUCATED.
You owe it to your clients and to your practice.

AVAILABLE IN PRINT OR ONLINE

To order or learn more: **Call:** 877- 337-5688 **Visit:** irahelp.com/newsletter **E-mail:** newsletter@irahelp.com

Copyright © 2024 by Ed Slott and Company, LLC

HEATHER SCHREIBER'S
$150 PER YEAR!
SOCIAL SECURITY ADVISOR

Social Security Planning for Retirement

LEARN MORE...*TO EARN MORE!*

Heather Schrieber's Social Security Advisor 8-page newsletter is the go-to "all things Social Security" monthly reference tool for professionals:

- Social Security Advisor is designed to be your go-to resource for all things Social Security.
- Social Security rules are anything but simple and the decision on how and when to file is complex, requiring consideration of a multitude of factors.
- In all editions, the "Advisor Mailbag" will highlight questions received from the trenches so that we can collectively learn from what your clients are asking.

STAY EDUCATED.
You owe it to your clients and to your practice.

AVAILABLE IN PRINT OR ONLINE

To order or learn more: **Call:** 877- 337-5688 **Visit:** irahelp.com/newsletter **E-mail:** newsletter@irahelp.com

Copyright © 2024 by Ed Slott and Company, LLC